Comprehensive

STRESS
MANAGEMENT

Comprehensive

S T R E S S
MANAGEMENT

Third Edition

JERROLD S. GREENBERG

University of Maryland

 Wm. C. Brown Publishers

Book Team

Editor *Chris Rogers*
Developmental Editor *Sue Pulvermacher-Alt*
Designer *Laurie J. Entringer*
Art Editor *Janice M. Roerig*
Production Editor *Barbara Rowe Day*
Photo Research Editor *Carrie Burger*
Visuals Processor *Joseph P. O'Connell*

Wm. C. Brown Publishers

President *G. Franklin Lewis*
Vice President, Editor-in-Chief *George Wm. Bergquist*
Vice President, Director of Production *Beverly Kolz*
Vice President, National Sales Manager *Bob McLaughlin*
Director of Marketing *Thomas E. Doran*
Marketing Communications Manager *Edward Bartell*
Marketing Manager *Kathy Law Laube*
Manager of Visuals and Design *Faye M. Schilling*
Production Editorial Manager *Colleen A. Yonda*
Production Editorial Manager *Julie A. Kennedy*
Publishing Services Manager *Karen J. Slaght*

Cover photo by Bryan F. Peterson

The credits section for this book begins on page 427, and is considered an extension of the copyright page.

To my Dad

Lacking sufficient finances, lacking a college education, and lacking health for much of his life, he managed to raise three sons who are all college graduates and who loved him dearly.

Contents

Preface

This book evolved out of two needs. The first pertained to my discussions with students, colleagues, friends, and relatives who, as I listened more carefully, seemed to be crying out for help in dealing with the stress of life. Upon closer scrutiny, I realized that the only cries I was deaf to were my own. I, too, needed help to manage stress. The second need related to the nature of texts on this subject. I thought they were informative or interesting but seldom both. Furthermore, I didn't think stress management was presented as the complex I envision it to be. I thought books on this subject explored parts of stress management but omitted several key components.

This book, then, is written in a more personal, informal manner than most and is organized to consider stress as a function of situations in life that, when perceived as distressing, result in emotional and physiological arousal. There is an abundance of scientific and statistical information in this book, but it hangs onto anecdote, humor, and personal experience to breathe life into this content. In addition, numerous means of assessment are provided so that content takes on personal meaning for each reader.

We all learn from our experiences, and your author is no exception. Consequently, this third edition of *Comprehensive Stress Management* incorporates changes recommended by readers of the first two editions while maintaining those elements valued by those readers. Revisions include the following:

1. A new section in chapter 3 on stress and the immunological system which discusses psychoneuroimmunology

2. A new section in chapter 3 on stress and its relationship to serum cholesterol

3. A new section in chapter 3 on temporomandibular joint (TMJ) problems and their relationship to stress

4. An expanded discussion in chapter 5 detailing the relationship between nutrition and stress

5. A new section in chapter 7 on humor and stress

6. A presentation in chapter 7 of the most current information on Type A behavior pattern, including the controversy surrounding its ability to accurately predict one's proneness to coronary heart disease

7. An expanded discussion in chapter 7 of the literature related to the hardiness concept

8. An expanded discussion in chapter 11 of the literature related to the effectiveness of biofeedback and the controversy pertaining to its usefulness for relaxation training and stress management

9. A presentation and discussion in chapter 11 of relaxation techniques not previously included: body scanning, diaphragmatic breathing, massage and acupressure, and yoga and stretching

10. An almost completely revised presentation in chapter 12 of how to use exercise to manage stress and how to exercise in a healthful manner

11. An expanded discussion in chapter 15 of sex and stress, and an added section on acquired immune deficiency syndrome (AIDS) and its implications for stress and stress management

12. A new section in chapter 18 on caregiving which discusses the stressors associated with caring for elderly relatives

In addition, references have been updated and greatly expanded so as to allow for the presentation of the most current thinking—the state of the art—on the topic, with accompanying documentation. Statistics and figures included in previous editions of *Comprehensive Stress Management* have also been updated, and a greatly expanded bibliography allows you to explore selected topics in greater depth.

Part 1 of this book contains a complete discussion of the stress reaction and its relationship to specific illnesses and diseases. Parts 2, 3, and 4 teach you how to intervene—to step between the stressor and physiological arousal. Consequently, you should be able to limit the harmful effects of the stressors you encounter. In brief, you will learn how to adjust your life situations, perceive events differently, react less emotionally, and use the products of stress to limit their duration. Part 5 discusses the particular stress needs of homemakers, workers outside the home, children and youth, college students, and the elderly. The stress management procedures presented in parts 2, 3, and 4 are applied to each of these specific populations to demonstrate their use in alleviating the harmful effects of stress.

The major theme of this book is that people usually have greater control over their lives and their environments than they realize. Unfortunately, many of us do not exercise this control and become rudderless in a rapidly changing and stressful society. Stress management is learning to recapture control of ourselves, and this book describes how to do that.

Acknowledgments There are many people who have helped bring this project to completion. They can never be adequately thanked, but perhaps a mention here will let them know that their help has been appreciated.

First are my students, who have taught me as much about stress management as I have ever taught them. Not only do I learn from their term papers and other assignments, but the way in which they live their lives teaches me much about managing stress.

Then, there are my colleagues at the University of Maryland. My fellow faculty encourage, stimulate, and provoke me to be as competent and as qualified as I can—if for no other reason than to keep pace with them. In particular, I wish to thank Robert Feldman, the author of chapter 13, whose contribution to this book is obvious, albeit immeasurable.

And, of course, there are those reviewers whose comments exasperated, bewildered, and angered me. They also created more work and revision than I desired. However, they also encouraged and provided important guidance. Because of them, this book is better than it otherwise would have been. These reviewers include: John Brennecke, Mt. San Antonio College; Robert Diller, Cabrillo College; JoAnn M. Eickhoff, University of Nebraska at Omaha; Jane Glover, Sinclair Community College; Susan Herron, Diablo Valley College; Paul W. Horn, Indiana State University; Darrel Lang, Emporia State University; Roseann M. Lyle, Purdue University; Stephen Nagy, University of Alabama; Angela Provitera-McGlynn, Mercer County Community College; Stanley Snegroff, Adelphi University.

Lastly, and most importantly, there is my family. They not only respected my need for quiet time to write but also provided much of the inspiration I needed. Karen, Keri, and Todd—I don't tell you often enough how much you contribute to my work and productivity, but you do, and I recognize your support and value it.

PART I

▼

Scientific
Foundations

What Is Stress?

It was a pleasant spring day—about seventy degrees, with the sun shining and a slight breeze. It was the kind of day I would have enjoyed celebrating by playing tennis, jogging, and helping my son learn how to ride his bicycle (an aggravating but necessary task). Instead, I was on the shoulder of a country road in upstate New York with my hands on my knees, vomiting. The story of how I wound up on such a glorious day in such an inglorious position serves as an important lesson.

At the time, I was an assistant professor, imposing my know-it-all attitude upon unsuspecting and innocent college students at the State University of New York at Buffalo. I had become quite successful in each of three areas the university established as criteria for promotion and tenure: teaching, research and other publications, and university and community service. The student evaluations from my last class session, for example, were quite flattering. I had published approximately fifteen articles in professional journals and was contracted to write my first book. So much for teaching and the proverbial "publish or perish" syndrome. It is the community service criteria about which I need to elaborate.

To meet the community service standards of acceptance for promotion and tenure, I made myself available as a guest speaker to community groups. I soon found that I was able to motivate groups of people through speeches or workshops on numerous topics, both directly and tangentially related to my area of expertise—health education. I spoke to the local Kiwanis Club on the topic "Drug Education Techniques" and to the Green Acres Cooperative Nursery School parents and teachers on "Drug Education for Young Children." I was asked to present the senior class speech at Medaille College on "Sex Education" and wound up conducting workshops for local public school districts on such concerns as "Why Health Education," "Values and Teaching," "Group Process," and "Peer Training Programs for Cigarette-Smoking Education." Things started jelling and I expanded my local presentations to state and national workshops, and to presenting papers at various state and national meetings.

My life changed rapidly and repeatedly. I came to Buffalo as an assistant professor and was promoted twice, leaving as a full professor with tenure and administrative responsibility for the graduate program in health education. When I left Buffalo, I had published over forty articles in professional journals, and my second book was soon to come off the presses. During my tenure at SUNY/Buffalo, I appeared on radio and television programs and was the subject of numerous newspaper articles. I came to Buffalo and there bought my first house, fathered my two children, and won my first tennis tournament. In short, I became a success.

So why the vomiting? Well, I was experiencing too much change in too short a period of time. I wondered if I was as good as others thought I was or if I was just lucky. I worried about embarrassing myself in front of other people and became extremely anxious when due to speak in front of a large group—so anxious that on a nice spring day, about seventy degrees, with the sun shining and a slight breeze, as I was on my way to address a group of teachers, school administrators, and parents in Wheatfield, New York, I became sick to my stomach. I pulled the car off the road, jumped out, vomited, jumped back in, proceeded to Wheatfield, and presented a one-hour speech which to this day is still not remembered by anyone who was there.

What I didn't know then, but know now, is that I was experiencing stress—too much stress. I also didn't know what to do. Everything seemed to be going very well; there seemed to be no reason to become anxious or ill. Well, I think I understand it all now and want to explain it to you. I want to help you learn about stress and how to manage it so that your life will be better and you will be healthier.

The Pioneers

I don't know about you, but I found the history courses I was required to take as an undergraduate not as interesting as they might have been. On the other hand, the information included in those classes was important to learn—not for the facts per se, but for the general concepts. For example, although I have long forgotten the specific economic factors preceding the World Wars, I have remembered that wars are often the result of economic realities and not just conflicts of ideology. That is an important concept that I would not have appreciated had I not enrolled in History 101.

Well, this wordy introduction to the history of stress management somewhat assuages my conscience, but won't help you much unless I make this discussion interesting. Accepting this challenge, and with apologies for my failures to meet it, let's wander through the past and meet some of the pioneers in the field of stress.

The first person we meet is Walter Cannon. In the early part of the twentieth century, Walter Cannon was a noted physiologist employed at the Harvard Medical School. It was he who first described the body's reaction to stress.[1] Picture this: You're walking down a dark alley at night, all alone, and you forgot your glasses. Halfway through the alley (at the point of no return) you spot a big, burly figure carrying a club and straddling your path. Other than thinking "Woe is me," what else happens within you? Well, your heart begins to pound and speed up, you seem unable to catch your breath, you begin to perspire, your muscles tense, and a whole array of changes occur within your body. Cannon was the researcher who first identified this stress reaction as the **fight-or-flight response.**

Your body prepares itself, when confronted by a threat, to either stand ground and fight or run away. In the alley, that response is invaluable because you want to be able to mobilize yourself quickly for some kind of action. We'll soon see, though, that in today's society the fight-or-flight response has become a threat itself—a threat to your health.

Curious about the fight-or-flight response, a young endocrinologist studied it in detail. Using rats and exposing them to **stressors**—factors with the potential to cause stress—Hans Selye was able to specify the changes in the body's physiology. Selye concluded that regardless of the source of the stress, the body reacted in the same manner. His rats developed a "substantial enlargement of the cortex of the adrenal glands; shrinkage or atrophy of the thymus, spleen, lymph nodes, and other lymphatic structures; an almost total disappearance of eosinophil cells [a kind of white blood cell]; and bleeding ulcers in the lining of the stomach and duodenum."[2] His research was first published in his classic book *The Stress of Life*.[3] Selye summarized stress reactivity as a three-phase process termed the general adaptation syndrome:

Phase 1: Alarm reaction. The body shows the changes characteristic of the first exposure to a stressor. At the same time, its resistance is diminished and, if the stressor is sufficiently strong (severe burns, extremes of temperature), death may result.

Phase 2: Stage of resistance. Resistance ensues if continued exposure to the stressor is compatible with adaptation. The bodily signs characteristic of the alarm reaction have virtually disappeared and resistance rises above normal.

Phase 3: Stage of exhaustion. Following long-continued exposure to the same stressor, to which the body had become adjusted, eventually adaptation energy is exhausted. The signs of the alarm reaction reappear, but now they are irreversible, and the individual dies.

Hans Selye defined stress as "the nonspecific response of the body to any demand made upon it."[4] That means good things (for example, a job promotion) to which we must adapt (termed **eustress**) and bad things (for example, the death of a loved one) to which we must adapt (termed **distress**); both are experienced the same physiologically.

Selye was really onto something. His research proved so interesting and important that he drew a large number of followers. One of these was A. T. W. Simeons, who related evolution to psychosomatic disease in his classic work, *Man's Presumptuous Brain*.[5] Simeons argued that the human brain (the diencephalon, in particular) had failed to develop at the pace needed to respond to symbolic stressors of twentieth-century life. For example, when our self-esteem is threatened, the brain, Simeons stated, prepares the body with the fight-or-flight response. If the threat to self-esteem stems from fear of embarrassment during public speaking, neither fighting nor running away are appropriate reactions. Consequently, the body has prepared itself physiologically to do something our psychology prohibits. The unused stress products break down the body, and psychosomatic disease may result.

Other researchers have added to the work of Cannon, Selye, Simeons, and others to shed more light on the relationship of stress to body processes. With this understanding has come a better appreciation of which illnesses and diseases are associated with stress, and how to prevent these conditions from developing. For example, Dr. Harold Wolff became curious why only one in one hundred prisoners of war held by the Germans during World War II died before their release, while thirty-three in one hundred held in Japanese camps died before their release. Keeping nutrition and length of time held captive constant, Wolff found that emotional stress, much greater in Japanese prisoner-of-war camps than in German ones, was the cause of much of this difference.[6]

Others also helped clarify the effects of stress: Stewart Wolf demonstrated its effects on digestive function;[7] Lawrence LeShan studied its effects on the development of cancer;[8] George Engel studied stress and ulcerative colitis;[9] Meyer Friedman and Ray Rosenman identified the relationship between stress and coronary heart disease;[10] and Wolf and Wolff studied stress and headaches.[11]

Others have found ways of successfully treating people with stress-related illnesses. For example, Carl Simonton, believing personality to be related to cancer, has added a component to the standard cancer therapy: it consists of visualizing the beneficial effects of the therapy upon the malignancy.[12] For some headache sufferers, Budzynski has successfully employed biofeedback for relief.[13] Herbert Benson, a cardiologist, first became interested in stress when he studied transcendental meditation (TM) with Robert Keith Wallace.[14] Benson then developed a relaxation technique similar to TM and has used it effectively to treat people with high blood pressure.[15,16]

Relaxation techniques have also been studied in some detail. In addition to Benson's **relaxation response,** some of the more noteworthy methods include **autogenic training** and **progressive relaxation.** Around 1900, a physiologist, Oskar Vogt, noted that people were capable of hypnotizing themselves. A German psychiatrist, Johannes Schultz, combined this knowledge with specific exercises to bring about heaviness and warmth in the limbs—that is, a state of relaxation.[17] This autohypnotic relaxation method became known as autogenic training and was developed and studied further by Schultz's student Wolfgang Luthe.[18]

Another effective and well-studied relaxation technique involves the tensing and relaxing of muscles so as to recognize muscle tension and bring about muscular relaxation when desired. This technique, progressive relaxation, was developed by Dr. Edmund Jacobson when he noticed his bedridden patients were still muscularly tense in spite of their restful appearance.[19] Their muscular tenseness (**bracing**), Jacobson reasoned, was a function of nerve impulses sent to the muscles, and it was interfering with their recovery. Progressive relaxation, sometimes termed **neuromuscular relaxation,** involves a structured set of exercises that train people to eliminate unnecessary muscular tension.

Although Benson's relaxation response, a form of meditation, became popular in the 1970s, meditation has been around for a long time. In fact, records of meditation date back two thousand years. Indian yogis and Zen monks were the first meditators to be scientifically studied. The results of these studies demonstrated the slowing-down effect (**hypometabolic state**) of meditation upon many

Muscle Tension

As you begin to read this, FREEZE. Don't move a bit! Now pay attention to your body sensations and position.

Can you drop your shoulders? If so, your muscles were unnecessarily raising them.

Are your forearm muscles able to relax more? If so, you were unnecessarily tensing them.

Is your body seated in a position in which you appear ready to do something active? If so, your muscles are probably unnecessarily contracted.

Can your forehead relax more? If so, you were tensing those muscles for no useful purpose.

Check your stomach, buttocks, thigh, and calf muscles. Are they, too, contracted more than is needed?

Unnecessary muscular contraction is called *bracing*. Many of us are guilty of bracing and suffer tension headaches, neck aches, or bad backs as a result.

Take a moment for yourself now. Place this book aside and concentrate on just letting as many of your muscles relax as possible. Notice how that feels.

When we discuss deep muscle relaxation, and progressive relaxation in particular, you'll learn skills enabling you to bring about this sensation more readily.

---

body processes: heart rate, breathing, and muscle tension to name but a few. For example, Therese Brosse reported Indian yogis able to control their heart rates;[20] Anand and colleagues showed changes in brain waves during meditation;[21] Kasamatsu and Hirai confirmed and expounded upon Anand's findings;[22] and Goleman and Schwartz found meditators more psychologically stable than non-meditators.[23]

Lastly, a whole area of study regarding life changes to which we must adapt and their effect upon health has emerged. Thomas Holmes and Richard Rahe showed that the more significant the changes in one's life, the greater the chance of the onset of illness.[24] Based on these conclusions, researchers are working toward a better understanding of this relationship. For example, Lazarus,[25] DeLongis,[26] and their colleagues have found that everyday hassles are even more detrimental to one's health than major life changes.

Well, this brief overview was painted with a broad brush. Subsequent chapters will refer back to these pioneers and their work, providing you with an even better understanding of the significance of managing stress and tension. When we discuss stress-related illnesses and diseases, for example, you will once again read about Friedman and Rosenman, Simonton, Wolff, and others. When we discuss life-situation stressors, reference will be made to Lazarus and to Holmes and Rahe. When we discuss relaxation techniques, we will elaborate upon the work of Benson, Schultz, Luthe, Jacobson, and others.

For now, I hope you have come away from this brief history of the stress field with the concept that stress may not just be bothersome, but may be downright unhealthy, and that stress may lead to other negative consequences such as poor relationships with loved ones or low academic achievement. However, there are means of lessening these unhealthy and negative effects. Stress management is serious business to which some very fine minds have devoted their time and effort. As you'll find out in this book, this study has paid off and is continuing to do so.

The Stressor

Now let's get down to business. What causes stress? Part of the answer is "a stressor." The other part is "stress reactivity." A stressor is a stimulus with the potential of triggering the fight-or-flight response. The stressors for which our bodies were evolutionarily trained were threats to our safety. The caveman who saw a lion looking for its next meal needed to react quickly. Cavemen who were not fast enough or strong enough to respond to this threat didn't have to worry about the next threat. They became meals for the lions. The fight-or-flight response was necessary, and its rapidity was vital for survival.

Modern men and women also find comfort and safety in the fight-or-flight response. We periodically read of some superhuman feat of strength in response to a stressor, such as a person lifting a heavy car off another person pinned under it. We attribute this strength to an increase in adrenalin, and it is true that adrenalin secretion does increase as part of the fight-or-flight response. However, there are less dramatic examples of the use the fight-or-flight response has for us. When you step off a curb, not noticing an automobile coming down the street, and hear the auto's horn, you quickly jump back onto the curb. Your heart beats fast, your breathing changes, and you perspire. These are all manifestations of your response to a stressor, the threat of being hit by a car. They indicate that your body has been prepared to do something active and to do it immediately (jump back onto the curb).

So far, these examples of stressors have all required immediate action to prevent physical harm. Other stressors you encounter have the potential for eliciting this same fight-or-flight response, even though it would be inappropriate to respond immediately or with some action. These stressors are symbolic ones—for example, the loss of status, threats to self-esteem, work overload, or overcrowding. When the boss overloads you with work, it is dysfunctional to fight with him or her and equally ridiculous to run away and not tackle the work. When you encounter the stressors associated with moving to a new town, fighting with new people you meet or shying away from meeting new people are both inappropriate means of adjustment.

We encounter many different types of stressors. Some are biological (toxins, heat, cold), some psychological (threats to self-esteem, depression), others sociological (unemployment, death of a loved one), and still others philosophical (use of time, purpose in life). In any case, as Selye discovered, regardless of the stressor, the body's reaction will be the same. The pituitary, thyroid, parathyroid, and adrenal glands, as well as the hypothalamus and other parts of the brain, are activated by stressors.

The point is, our bodies have evolved to respond to stressors with an immediate action by altering their physiology for greater speed and strength. When we encounter symbolic stressors, our bodies are altered in the same manner, although we do not use the changed physiology by responding with some action. Therefore, we build up stress products, which include elevated blood pressure and increased muscular contractions, serum cholesterol, and secretions of hydrochloric acid in the stomach. We do not use these stress products but rather "grin and bear" the situation. The results are illness and disease when the stress reaction is chronic, prolonged, or goes unabated.

This need not be the case. We can learn to take control of ourselves and our bodies to prevent the fight-or-flight response from developing when encountering symbolic threats. We can also learn how to use stress products once our physiology has changed to prevent them from resulting in illness, disease, or other negative consequences. Remember, stressors are stimuii with the *potential* of triggering the fight-or-flight response; they need not lead to such a response. With this book and the practice of the skills it describes, they need not lead to such a response in you.

Stress Reactivity

The fight-or-flight response is termed **stress reactivity.** This reaction, described in more detail in the next chapter, includes increased muscle tension; increased heart rate, stroke volume, and output; elevated blood pressure; increased neural excitability; less saliva in the mouth; increased sodium retention; increased perspiration; change in respiratory rate; increased serum glucose; increased release of hydrochloric acid in the stomach; changes in brain waves; and increased urination. This reaction prepares us for swift action when such a response is warranted. It is when we build up stress products that we don't use that this stress reaction becomes unhealthy.

The longer our physiology varies from its baseline measures (**duration**) and the greater the variance from that baseline (**degree**), the more likely we are to experience ill effects from this stress reactivity. Of the two, duration and degree, duration is the most important. For example, if you awaken to realize your alarm clock didn't go off, and you'll be late for work, you would become physiologically aroused from that stressor. If in your haste you accidentally pour too much milk into your cereal, that stressor will result in further physiological arousal. Next, you get into the car only to learn you're out of gas. Ever have a day like that? Although each of those stressors will probably result in less arousal than having to jump back from a car bearing down on you, it is the length of time that these stressors are with you that makes them more harmful.

People who have learned stress management skills will often respond to a greater degree to a stressor but will return to their resting rate sooner than those not trained in stress management. An analogy can be made with joggers, whose heart rate may increase tremendously when they exercise but returns to normal sooner than that of out-of-shape exercisers. Try the exercise in figure 1.1 to demonstrate the effects of a stressor upon your physiology.

While seated in a comfortable position, determine how fast your heart beats at rest using one of the following methods. (Use a watch that has a second hand.)

1. Place the first two fingers (pointer and middle finger) of one hand on the underside of your other wrist, on the thumb side. Feel for your pulse and count the number of pulses for thirty seconds. (See the drawing.)

2. Place the first two fingers of one hand on your lower neck, just above the collarbone; move your fingers toward your shoulder until you find your pulse. Count the pulses for thirty seconds.

3. Place the first two fingers of one hand in front of your ear near your sideburn, moving your fingers until you find your pulse. Count the pulses for thirty seconds. Multiply your thirty-second pulse count by two to determine how many times your heart beats each minute while at rest.

Now close your eyes and think of either someone you really dislike or some situation you experienced that really frightened you. If you are recalling a person, think of how that person looks, smells, and what he or she does to incur your dislike. Really feel the dislike, don't just think about it. If you recall a frightening situation, try to place yourself back in that situation. Sense the fright, be scared, vividly recall the situation in all its detail. Think of the person or situation for one minute and then count your pulse rate for thirty seconds, as you did earlier. Multiply the rate by two and compare your first total with the second.

Most people find that their heart rate increases when experiencing the stressful memory. This increase occurs despite a lack of any physical activity; just thoughts increase heart rate. This fact demonstrates two things: the nature of stressors and the nature of stress reactivity. The stressor is a stimulus with the potential of eliciting a stress reaction (physiological arousal).

Figure 1.1 Stress and stress reactivity

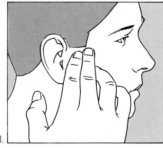

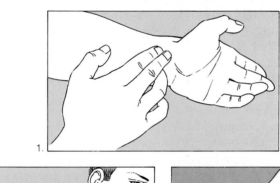

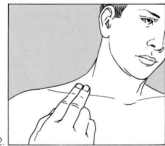

Stress

Now that you know what a stressor is and what stress reactivity is, it is time to define stress itself.

Although Lazarus has offered a definition of stress that encompasses a whole spectrum of factors (stimulus, response, cognitive appraisal of threat, coping styles, psychological defenses, and the social milieu),[27] for our purposes that may be too encompassing. Defining stress becomes a problem even for the experts. Mason aptly described this problem by citing several different ways the term **stress** is used:[28]

1. *The stimulus.* This is our definition of stressor.
2. *The response.* This is our definition of stress reactivity.
3. *The whole spectrum of interacting factors.* This is Lazarus' definition.
4. *The stimulus-response interaction.*

For our purposes, we will operationally define stress as the last-named: *the combination of a stressor and stress reactivity.* Without both of these components there is no stress. A stressor only has the *potential* of eliciting a stress reaction. To illustrate this point, imagine two people fired from their jobs. One views being fired as catastrophic: "How will I support my family? How will I pay my rent? What do I do if I get ill without health insurance in force?" The other views being fired as less severe and says: "It's not good that I was fired, but I never really liked that job anyhow. This will give me the impetus to find a job I'll enjoy. I've been working too hard anyhow. I needed a vacation. Now I'll take one." As you can see, the stressor (being fired) had the potential of eliciting physiological arousal, but only the thought processes employed by the first person would result in such a reaction. The first person encountered a stressor, perceived it as stressful, and wound up with physiological arousal. By definition, that person experienced stress. The second person encountered the same stressor (being fired) but perceived it in such a way as to *prevent* physiological arousal. That person was not stressed. Table 1.1 demonstrates how two different people might respond to the same stressors differently.

Hot Reactors

Are you a hot reactor? Some people tend to react to stressors with an all-out physiological effort that takes a toll on their health. In a sense, their bodies are overreacting to the stressful situation. We call these people **hot reactors.**[29] If you notice you anger easily, you are often anxious or depressed, you urinate frequently, you experience constipation or diarrhea more than usual, or you experience nausea or vomiting, you may be a hot reactor. In that case, you may want to obtain regular medical examinations to identify illnesses when they can be easily cured or contained, and learn and use stress management techniques and strategies such as those in this book. The next chapter will present the body's responses to stress and you should therefore be better able to understand why it is so important to learn to cope with stress. Subsequent chapters will identify specific illnesses, diseases, and other negative consequences that are stress-related and discuss ways to prevent these from developing.

Table 1.1
A Day in the Life of Joe and Roscoe

Stressor	Joe (Chronic Stress Pattern)	Roscoe (Healthy Stress Pattern)
Oversleeps—Awakes at 7:30 Instead of 6:30	Action: Gulps coffee, skips breakfast, cuts himself shaving, tears button off shirt getting dressed. Thoughts: I can't be late again! The boss will be furious! I just know this is going to ruin my whole day. Result: Leaves home anxious, worried, and hungry.	Action: Phones office to let them know he will be late. Eats a good breakfast. Thoughts: No problem. I must have needed the extra sleep. Result: Leaves home calm and relaxed.
Stuck Behind Slow Driver	Action: Flashes lights, honks, grits teeth, curses, bangs on dashboard with fist. Finally passes on blind curve and nearly collides with oncoming car. Thoughts: What an idiot! Slow drivers should be put in jail! No consideration of others!	Action: Uses time to do relaxation exercises and to listen to his favorite radio station. Thoughts: Here's a gift of time—how can I use it?
Staff Meeting	Action: Sits in back, ignores speakers, and surreptitiously tries to work on monthly report. Thoughts: What a waste of time. Who *cares* what's going on in all those other departments? I have more than I can handle keeping up with my own work. Results: Misses important input relating to his department. Is later reprimanded by superior.	Action: Listens carefully, and participates actively. Thoughts: It's really good to hear my co-workers' points of view. I can do my work a lot more effectively if I understand the big picture of what we're all trying to do. Results: His supervisor compliments him on his suggestions.
Noon—Behind on Deskwork	Action: Skips lunch. Has coffee at desk. Spills coffee over important papers. Thoughts: That's the last straw! Now I'll have to have this whole report typed over. I'll have to stay and work late.	Action: Eats light lunch and goes for short walk in park. Thoughts: I'll be in better shape for a good afternoon with a little exercise and some time out of the office.
Evening	Action: Arrives home 9 P.M. Family resentful. Ends up sleeping on couch. Does not fall asleep until long into the morning. Thoughts: What a life! If only I could run away and start over! It's just not worth it. I'll never amount to anything. Results: Wakes up late again, feeling awful. Decides to call in sick.	Action: Arrives home at usual time. Quiet evening with family. To bed by 11 P.M., falls asleep easily. Thoughts: A good day! I felt really effective at work, and it was nice reading to the kids tonight. Results: Wakes up early, feeling good.

Source: "Dealing with Potential Stress," in *Medical Self-Care*, no. 5 (1978):11. Reprinted by permission of the publisher.

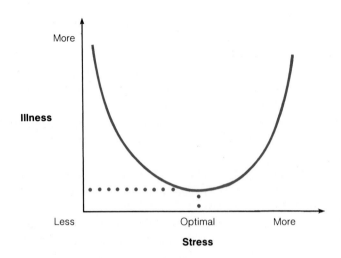

Figure 1.2 The relationship between stress and illness is a complex one. Illness may result from too *little* stress just as it might from too much stress.

Stress Management Goals

Before concluding this chapter, we should note that the goal of stress management is not to eliminate all stress. Life would certainly be dull without both joyful stressors to which we have to adjust and distressors needing a response. Furthermore, stress is often a motivator for peak performance. For example, when you are experiencing stress about an upcoming test, you will be more likely to study more intensely than if you are not concerned. If you are to speak in front of a group of people and are apprehensive, you probably will prepare a better speech. Stress can be useful, stimulating, and welcome. So even if it were possible, we should not want to eliminate all stress from our lives.

Our goal should be to limit the harmful effects of stress while maintaining life's quality and vitality. Some researchers have found that the relationship between stress and illness could be plotted on a U-shaped curve, as shown in figure 1.2. The curve illustrates that with a great deal of stress, a great deal of illness occurred. However, it also indicates that with only a minute amount of stress, a great deal of illness could still occur. These researchers found that there is an optimal amount of stress—not too much and not too little—that is healthy and prophylactic.[30] We will keep that important finding to the fore as we proceed toward taking control of our stress.

Summary

1. Physiologist Walter Cannon first described the stress response. Cannon called this the fight-or-flight response.
2. Endocrinologist Hans Selye was able to specify the changes in the body's physiology that resulted from stress.
3. Selye found rats that he stressed developed substantial enlargement of the adrenal cortex; shrinkage of the thymus, spleen, lymph nodes, and other lymphatic structures; a disappearance of the eosinophil cells; and bleeding ulcers in the lining of the stomach and duodenum.

4. Selye summarized stress reactivity as a three-phase process: alarm reaction, stage of resistance, and stage of exhaustion. He defined stress as the nonspecific response of the body to any demand made upon it.

5. Cardiologist Herbert Benson studied transcendental meditation and developed a similar meditative technique which he successfully employed to help reduce his patients' levels of high blood pressure.

6. A stressor is a stimulus with the potential of triggering the fight-or-flight response. Stressors can be biological, psychological, sociological, or philosophical in origin.

7. The longer one's physiology varies from its baseline measures (duration) and the greater the variance (degree), the more likely one is to experience ill effects from stress reactivity.

8. Stress has been defined differently by different experts. Some define stress as the stimulus, others as the response, and still others as the whole spectrum of interacting factors. This book defines stress as the combination of a stressor and stress reactivity.

Notes

1. Walter B. Cannon, *The Wisdom of the Body* (New York: W. W. Norton, 1932).

2. Kenneth R. Pelletier, *Mind as Healer, Mind as Slayer* (New York: Dell Publishing Co., 1977), 71.

3. Hans Selye, *The Stress of Life* (New York: McGraw-Hill Book Co., 1956).

4. Hans Selye, *Stress without Distress* (New York: J. B. Lippincott, 1974), 14.

5. A. T. W. Simeons, *Man's Presumptuous Brain: An Evolutionary Interpretation of Psychosomatic Disease* (New York: E. P. Dutton, 1961).

6. Harold G. Wolff, *Stress and Disease* (Springfield, Ill.: Charles C. Thomas, 1953).

7. Stewart Wolf, *The Stomach* (Oxford: Oxford University Press, 1965).

8. Lawrence LeShan, "An Emotional Life-History Pattern Associated with Neoplastic Disease," *Annals of the New York Academy of Sciences,* 1966.

9. George L. Engel, "Studies of Ulcerative Colitis—III: The Nature of the Psychologic Processes," *American Journal of Medicine,* August 1955.

10. Meyer Friedman and Ray H. Rosenman, *Type A Behavior and Your Heart* (Greenwich, Conn.: Fawcett, 1974).

11. Stewart Wolf and Harold G. Wolff, *Headaches: Their Nature and Treatment* (Boston: Little, 1953).

12. Carl O. Simonton and Stephanie Matthews-Simonton, "Belief Systems and Management of the Emotional Aspects of Malignancy," *Journal of Transpersonal Psychology* 7(1975):29–48.

13. Thomas Budzynski, Johann Stoyva, and C. Adler, "Feedback-Induced Muscle Relaxation: Application to Tension Headache," *Journal of Behavior Therapy and Experimental Psychiatry* 1(1970):205–11.

14. Robert Keith Wallace, "Physiological Effects of Transcendental Meditation," *Science* 167(1970):1751–54.

15. Herbert Benson, *The Relaxation Response* (New York: Avon Books, 1975).

16. R. K. Peters, Herbert Benson, and John Peters, "Daily Relaxation Response Breaks in a Working Population: II. Effects on Blood Pressure," *American Journal of Public Health* 67(1977):954–59.

17. Johannes Schultz, *Das Autogene Training* (Stuttgart, Germany: Geerg-Thieme Verlag, 1953).

18. Wolfgang Luthe, ed., *Autogenic Training* (New York: Grune & Stratton, 1965).

19. Edmund Jacobson, *Progressive Relaxation,* 2d ed. (Chicago: Chicago Press, 1938).

20. Therese Brosse, "A Psychophysiological Study," *Main Currents in Modern Thought* 4(1946):77–84.

21. B. K. Anand et al., "Studies on Shri Ramananda Yogi during His Stay in an Air-Tight Box," *Indian Journal of Medical Research* 49(1961):82–89.

22. A. Kasamatsu and T. Hirai, "Studies of EEG's of Expert Zen Meditators," *Folia Psychiatrica Neurologica Japonica* 28(1966):315.

23. Daniel J. Goleman and Gary E. Schwartz, "Meditation as an Intervention in Stress Reactivity," *Journal of Consulting and Clinical Psychology* 44(1976):456–66.

24. Thomas H. Holmes and Richard H. Rahe, "The Social Readjustment Rating Scale," *Journal of Psychosomatic Research* 11(1967):213–18.

25. Richard S. Lazarus, "Puzzles in the Study of Daily Hassles," *Journal of Behavioral Medicine* 7(1984):375–89.

26. Anita DeLongis et al., "Relationship of Daily Hassles, Uplifts, and Major Life Events to Health Status," *Health Psychology* 1(1982):119–36.

27. Richard S. Lazarus, *Psychological Stress and the Coping Process* (New York: McGraw-Hill Book Co., 1966).

28. James W. Mason, "A Historical View of the Stress Field," *Journal of Human Stress* 1(1975):22–36.

29. Robert S. Eliot, "Are You a Hot Reactor: How Do You React to Stress?" *Shape,* February 1987, 66–73, 128–31, 138.

30. Clinton G. Weiman, "A Study of Occupational Stressors and the Incidence of Disease/Risk," *Journal of Occupational Medicine* 19(1977):119–22.

Stress Psychophysiology

Whenever I walk through a large shopping mall with my children, Todd and Keri, my shrewdness is put to the test. I kid them by saying I should have had two more children so I could have named them "the four me's": Buy Me, Give Me, Take Me, and Show Me. If it isn't a soft pretzel they want, it's a new baseball bat, or a new doll, or a new doll holding a new baseball bat. Well, as we leave our neighborhood shopping mall, we are bombarded by a cacophony of noise (bings, bongs, rings, buzzes, and crashes) and a rainbow of colors and lights. If you haven't guessed yet, our mall is "blessed" with an arcade. Now, arcade games were probably invented by a malicious child who was punished so often that revenge was foremost in his or her mind. The object of this revenge was parents; the means of revenge was the arcade.

As we walk past the arcade, I start talking about the last soccer game my daughter played or is anticipating. Sometimes I'll discuss a movie they both enjoyed or a vacation we're planning. Do you get the picture? Anything to divert their attention from the arcade and those money-hungry machines. I know my diversion has been successful when I have left the mall without having my arm tugged out of its socket or my pants yanked below my waist. More often than not, I leave the mall with fewer quarters than when I entered.

Computer games are the most popular at these arcades. There are several reasons for this: the sounds and noises are rewarding, and the player can fantasize a trip or battle in space and vent some aggression in a socially acceptable manner. There probably are other reasons as well, and I'm willing to bet one of these is our vision of the future as "computerized." Little do we realize, though, that in a sense, we have had computers for ages. You and I even program computers. Our programs instruct our computers to bing, bong, ring, buzz, and crash and to project rainbows and lights. We have, in other words, our own arcade!

Our computers are our brains, our programs are our minds, and our arcades are our bodies. Enter this arcade with us now and learn how our machines operate, especially when stressed.

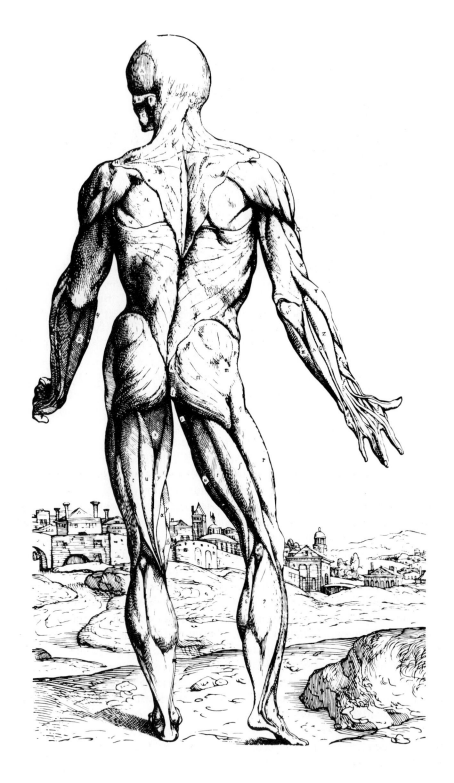

The study of the human body has a long history, as indicated by this illustration from the second book of De humani corporis fabrica libri septem *by Andreas Vesalius, printed in 1543.*

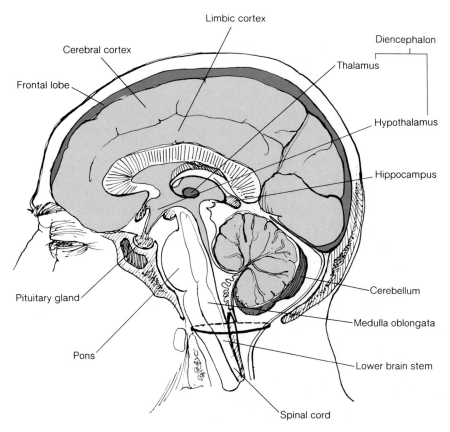

Figure 2.1 The brain

Limbic cortex

Cerebral cortex

Frontal lobe

Diencephalon

Thalamus

Hypothalamus

Hippocampus

Pituitary gland

Pons

Cerebellum

Medulla oblongata

Lower brain stem

Spinal cord

The Brain

When we are talking about stress management, we are really talking about managing psychological or sociological stressors. Although stress can be caused by biological agents (e.g., viruses), the environment (e.g., temperature), and other sources, the focus of this book is on threats to our self-esteem, the loss of a loved one and the resultant loneliness, and other such stressors. These psychological and sociological stressors are perceived by the mind and translated by the brain. The brain, in turn, instructs the rest of the body how to adjust to the stressor.

The brain includes two major components: the **cerebral cortex** (the upper part) and the **subcortex** (the lower part). Figure 2.1 shows the structures of the brain and their locations. The subcortex includes the **cerebellum** (coordinates body movements), the **medulla oblongata** (regulates heartbeat, respiration, and other such basic physiological processes), the **pons** (regulates the sleep cycle), and the **diencephalon.** The diencephalon has many purposes, including the regulation of the emotions. It is made up of the **thalamus** and **hypothalamus,** as well as nerve cells. The thalamus relays sensory impulses from other parts of the nervous system to the cerebral cortex. The hypothalamus, a key structure in stress reactivity, is the primary activator of the **autonomic nervous system,** which controls basic body processes such as hormone balance, temperature, and the constriction and dilation of blood vessels.

The **limbic system,** called the "seat of emotions," is interconnected to the diencephalon and is primarily concerned with emotions and their behavioral expression. The limbic system is thought to produce such emotions as fear, anxiety, and joy in response to physical and psychological signals. As you might expect, since emotions play a big role in the stress response, the limbic system is an important structure when discussing stress psychophysiology.

Now to the cerebral cortex (called the **gray matter**). The cerebral cortex controls higher-order abstract functioning, such as language and judgment. The cerebral cortex can also control more primitive areas of the brain. When the diencephalon recognizes fear, for instance, the cerebral cortex can use judgment to recognize the stimulus as nonthreatening and override the fear.

Lastly, there is the **reticular activating system (RAS).** In the past, cortical and subcortical functions were considered dichotomized. That is, human behavior was thought to be a function of one area of the brain or the other. Now, brain researchers believe there are neurological connections between the cortex and subcortex that feed information back and forth. This network of nerves called the RAS can be considered the connection between mind and body. The "reticular system is a kind of two-way street, carrying messages perceived by the higher awareness centers to the organs and muscles and also relaying stimuli received at the muscular and organic levels up to the cerebral cortex. In this manner, a purely physical stressor can influence the higher thought centers, and a mentally or intellectually perceived stressor can generate neurophysiological responses."[1]

Now that the brain's key structures have been outlined, let's see how a stressor affects the brain, and how the brain functions to prepare the rest of the body to react. When we encounter a stressor, the body part (eyes, nose, muscles, etc.) that first notes the stressor passes a message along nerves to the brain. These messages pass through the reticular activating system either from or to the limbic system and the thalamus. The limbic system is where emotion evolves, and the thalamus serves as the switchboard, determining what to do with the incoming messages. The hypothalamus then comes into play.

When the hypothalamus experiences a stressor, it activates the two major stress reactivity pathways: the **endocrine system** and the autonomic nervous system. To activate the endocrine system, the anterior portion of the hypothalamus releases **corticotropin releasing factor (CRF),** which instructs the pituitary gland at the base of the brain to secrete **adrenocorticotropic hormone (ACTH).** ACTH then activates the adrenal cortex. To activate the autonomic nervous system, a message is sent by the posterior part of the hypothalamus via a nerve pathway to the adrenal medulla. Figure 2.2 diagrams the brain's stress-reactive function.

There are other functions performed by the hypothalamus as well. One of these is the releasing of **thyrotropic hormone releasing factor (TRF)** from its anterior portion, which instructs the pituitary to secrete **thyrotropic hormone (TTH).** TTH then stimulates the thyroid gland to secrete the hormone **thyroxin.** The anterior hypothalamus also stimulates the pituitary gland to secrete **oxytocin** and **vasopressin (ADH).**[2] The functions of these hormones (adrenal medulla and cortex

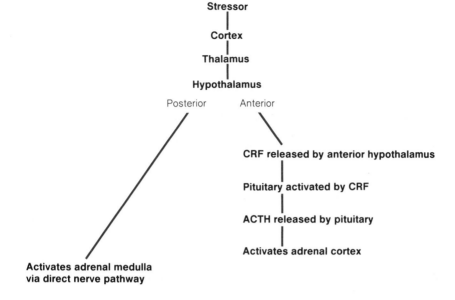

Figure 2.2 The brain and stress

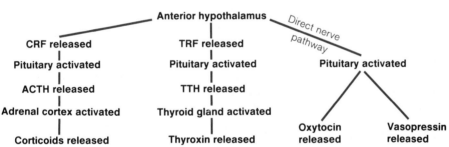

Figure 2.3 Stress and the anterior hypothalamus

secretions, thyroxin, oxytocin, and vasopressin) will soon be discussed. Figure 2.3 is designed to summarize the functions of the anterior hypothalamus.

Now that you have an understanding of the relationship between stress and the brain, you might be interested in some recent research that indicates stress may result in irreversible brain damage.[3] However, several pieces of information are important to know to understand these findings. First, you need to know that the **hippocampus** is the part of the brain that "sounds the alarm" that stress is present. Next you need to know that glucocorticoids are hormones released by the adrenal glands. The presence of these glucocorticoids is detected by receptors on the cells of the hippocampus. Prolonged stress has been found to damage these receptors and the cells of the hippocampus themselves. Since brain cells do not regenerate, their death means we have lost these cells forever. The net effects of this process are not completely understood, but it probably means we do not respond to stress as well since we do not have as many glucocorticoid receptors. Research is being done to better understand this process and its implications.

The Endocrine System

One of the most important parts of the body that is related to stress is the endocrine system. The endocrine system includes all the glands that secrete hormones. These hormones alter the function of other bodily tissues and are carried through the circulatory system to various targets. The endocrine system includes the pituitary, thyroid, parathyroid, and adrenal glands, as well as the pancreas, ovaries, testes, pineal gland, and thymus gland. The locations of these endocrine glands are shown in figure 2.4.

When the anterior hypothalamus releases CRF, and the pituitary then releases ACTH, the outer layer of the adrenal glands, the **adrenal cortex,** secretes **glucocorticoids** and **mineralocorticoids** (see fig. 2.5). The primary glucocorticoid is the hormone **cortisol,** and the primary mineralocorticoid is **aldosterone.**

Cortisol provides the fuel for battle (fight-or-flight). Its primary function is to increase the blood sugar so we have the energy for action. It does this by the conversion of amino acids to glycogen, which occurs in the liver. When glycogen is depleted, the liver can produce glucose from amino acids. This process is termed **gluconeogenesis.** In addition, cortisol mobilizes free fatty acids from fat (adipose) tissue, breaks down protein, and increases arterial blood pressure. All of this is designed to prepare us to fight or run from the stressor. Cortisol also causes other physiological changes. One of the more significant changes is the decrease of lymphocytes released from the thymus gland and lymph nodes. The lymphocytes, in their role of destroying invading substances (e.g., bacteria), are important for the effectiveness of the immunological system. Consequently, an increase in cortisol decreases the effectiveness of the immune response, and we are more likely to become ill.

Aldosterone also prepares us for action. Its major purpose is to increase blood pressure so we can transport food and oxygen to the active parts of our body—limbs as well as organs. The manner in which aldosterone raises blood pressure is to increase blood volume. This is accomplished in two ways: a decrease in urine production and an increase in sodium retention. Both of these mechanisms result in less elimination of body fluids, greater blood volume, and a subsequent increase in blood pressure.

Blood pressure is measured as systolic or diastolic. Systolic blood pressure is the amount of pressure on the arterial walls when blood is pumped from the heart. Diastolic blood pressure is the pressure of blood against the walls of the arteries when the heart is relaxed. An average blood pressure for a young adult is 120/80; the higher number is the systolic reading (120 mm Hg), and the lower is the diastolic reading (80 mm Hg). Aldosterone can raise systolic blood pressure 15–20 mm Hg. Although health scientists are not in total agreement regarding the point at which hypertension (high blood pressure) begins, generally a systolic reading above 140 or diastolic reading above 90 is considered harmful.

In addition to the involvement of the adrenal cortex in stress reactivity, the **adrenal medulla** (the inner portion of the adrenal gland) is activated through a direct nerve connection from the posterior portion of the hypothalamus. The adrenal medulla then secretes the catecholamines **epinephrine** (commonly called

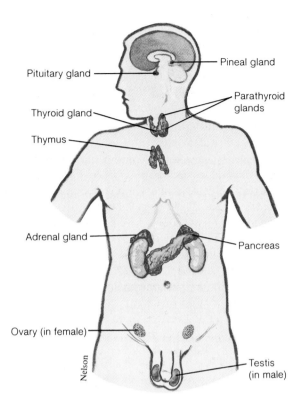

Pituitary gland

Pineal gland

Thyroid gland

Parathyroid glands

Thymus

Adrenal gland

Pancreas

Ovary (in female)

Nelson

Testis (in male)

Figure 2.4 Locations of major endocrine glands

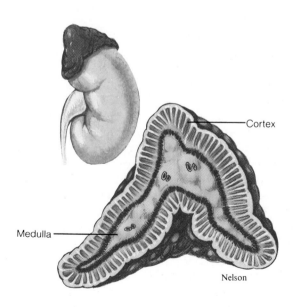

Cortex

Medulla

Nelson

Figure 2.5 An adrenal gland consists of an outer cortex and an inner medulla that represent distinctly different glands.

adrenalin) and **norepinephrine** (commonly called **noradrenalin**). These hormones lead to various changes within the body, including the following:

1. Acceleration of heart rate
2. Increased force at which blood is pumped out of the heart
3. Dilation (widening) of coronary arteries
4. Dilation of bronchial tubes (through which air passes to and from the lungs)
5. Increase in the basal metabolic rate (that is, most body processes speed up)
6. Constriction (narrowing) of the blood vessels in the muscles and skin of the arms and legs
7. Increase in oxygen consumption

▼

Stress Psychophysiology Quiz

Stop for a moment to test your recall of the stress psychophysiology presented so far. See if you can match the numbered items in the column on the left with the lettered items in the column on the right.

_____ 1. Limbic system
_____ 2. Subcortex
_____ 3. Diencephalon
_____ 4. Cerebral cortex
_____ 5. Adrenal medulla
_____ 6. Adrenal cortex
_____ 7. Hypothalamus
_____ 8. Aldosterone
_____ 9. Pituitary
_____ 10. Norepinephrine

a. Thalamus and hypothalamus
b. Upper part of brain
c. Activated by ACTH
d. "Seat of emotions"
e. Cerebellum, medulla oblongata, pons, and diencephalon
f. Secreted by adrenal cortex
g. Activated by nerves from hypothalamus
h. Releases ACTH
i. Gluconeogenesis
j. Releases CRF
k. Vasopressin
l. Secreted by adrenal medulla

Check your answers with the key below. If you didn't answer at least seven correctly, you might be wise to review the beginning of this chapter before proceeding further.

Answer key: 1. d, 2. e, 3. a, 4. b, 5. g, 6. c, 7. j, 8. f, 9. h, 10. l

The **thyroid gland** is also involved in the stress reaction. Activated by TTH from the pituitary, it secretes thyroxin, which performs the following functions:

1. Increases the basal metabolic rate
2. Increases free fatty acids
3. Increases rate of gluconeogenesis
4. Increases gastrointestinal motility (often resulting in diarrhea)
5. Increases the rate and depth of respiration
6. Accelerates the heart rate
7. Increases blood pressure
8. Increases anxiety
9. Decreases feelings of tiredness

To sum up so far, during stress the hypothalamus activates the adrenal and thyroid glands (either through the pituitary or direct nerve innervation), which in turn secrete cortisol, aldosterone, epinephrine, norepinephrine, and thyroxin. These hormones affect numerous body processes to prepare the stressed person to respond in some physically active manner.

The Autonomic Nervous System

Some people have suggested that you've been feeling terrible for several centuries. Well, maybe not you personally, but the collective you (us)—that is, human beings. The argument goes that human beings viewed themselves as having major importance until Copernicus demonstrated that Earth is but one of many planets revolving about the sun rather than being the center of the universe. We could no longer command the "center of attention" (get it?). The next major blow to *Homo sapiens* was Darwin's theory of evolution. To think that we come from apes! Yuk! Although just a theory, Darwin's ideas became widely accepted, and human beings were relegated to just one rung on the ladder of life. Lastly, when such notables as Galen, da Vinci, and others described the structure and function of the human body, it became apparent that much of that function was involuntary—beyond our control. This was another blow to our self-esteem; we had less free will than we previously believed.

Well, hearken brothers and sisters, good news is just ahead. As we shall see, stress research has demonstrated that we are in greater control than we thought. The involuntary functions of the body are controlled by the autonomic (involuntary) nervous system. A general view of the nervous system appears in figure 2.6. Examples of involuntary functions are heart rate, blood pressure, respiratory rate, and body fluid regulation. This control is maintained by the two components of the autonomic nervous system: the sympathetic and the parasympathetic nervous systems (see fig. 2.7). Generally, the **sympathetic nervous system** is in charge of expending energy (e.g., increasing respiratory rate), while the **parasympathetic nervous system** is in charge of conserving energy (e.g., decreasing respiratory rate).

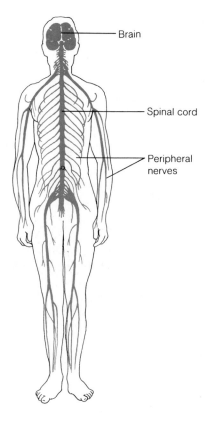

Figure 2.6 The nervous system consists of the brain, spinal cord, and numerous peripheral nerves.

Brain

Spinal cord

Peripheral nerves

When you encounter a stressor, the sympathetic nervous system, activated by the hypothalamus, regulates the body to do the following:

1. Increase heart rate
2. Increase force with which heart contracts
3. Dilate coronary arteries
4. Constrict abdominal arteries
5. Dilate pupils
6. Dilate bronchial tubes
7. Increase strength of skeletal muscles
8. Release glucose from liver
9. Increase mental activity
10. Dilate skin and muscle arterioles
11. Significantly increase basal metabolic rate

Because of these physiological changes, people have been able to perform incredible feats in emergencies. A relatively frail person who pulls a car off of a child pinned beneath it is an example of the power of this fight-or-flight response. The parasympathetic nervous system is generally responsible for returning us to a relaxed state once we are stressed.

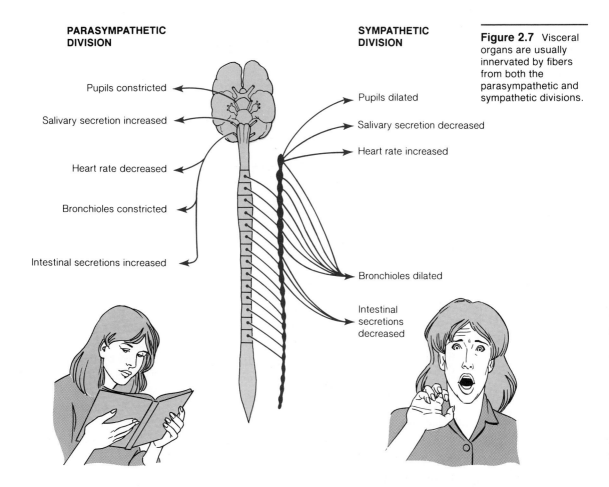

PARASYMPATHETIC DIVISION

Pupils constricted

Salivary secretion increased

Heart rate decreased

Bronchioles constricted

Intestinal secretions increased

SYMPATHETIC DIVISION

Pupils dilated

Salivary secretion decreased

Heart rate increased

Bronchioles dilated

Intestinal secretions decreased

Figure 2.7 Visceral organs are usually innervated by fibers from both the parasympathetic and sympathetic divisions.

Now to my earlier promise of better things to come. It has been suggested that the first major scientific finding that improves, rather than diminishes, the self-esteem of human beings is the discovery that the involuntary functions of the human body are not totally involuntary. The development of biofeedback equipment, which instantaneously measures and reports what is occurring in the body, has allowed research studies of the voluntary control of "involuntary" body processes. So, for instance, people have been taught to control their blood pressure, to regulate their heart and respiratory rates, to emit particular brain waves, and to dilate and constrict blood vessels in various parts of their bodies. In other words, people now know they are able to be more in control of themselves (and their bodies) than they ever believed possible. It is suggested that this knowledge is a major influence on the level of esteem in which people hold themselves.

What some consider to be even more significant is the understanding that we often control our physiology to allow ourselves to become ill. However, once we understand that, we can stop viewing ourselves as helpless and hopeless victims of illnesses and diseases; we can consider ourselves capable of preventing them.

Stress Phrases

The stress reaction, as we have come to realize, results in numerous changes in our physiology. These physiological changes often lead to emotional interpretations, as witnessed by our use of phrases such as *cold feet*. We get cold feet when we are stressed because there is a constriction of blood vessels in the arms and legs. When we are stressed we may feel *uptight*. Of course we do! We have increased muscle tension.

Can you think of other "stress phrases" that have a physiological basis? Write them below.

Phrase	*Physiological basis*
1.	1.
2.	2.
3.	3.
4.	4.
5.	5.

Here is one last word about the sympathetic and parasympathetic nervous systems. We should note that although these two systems are generally counteractive, this is not always the case. Certain things are influenced by the sympathetic system only (e.g., sweat glands and blood glucose) and others are influenced by the parasympathetic system alone (e.g., the ciliary muscles of the eye). Generally, however, the parasympathetic nervous system is responsible for the relaxation response.

The Cardiovascular System

My family and I have recently moved into a new house and have experienced a most frustrating situation. It seems that every few weeks I have to dismantle the faucet to clean out debris. The builder tells me this is to be expected in a new house, but I've had a house built before and never experienced that problem. You can imagine the discussions we have had over this situation! In any case, every few weeks the screen in the faucet gets clogged, and I have to take it out and clean it.

The reason I relate this story is that my problem is analogous to that of your body's fluid system, which includes your heart, blood, and blood vessels (see fig. 2.8). This circulatory system can also become clogged—although this takes a lot of years—but, unfortunately, cannot be cleansed. When your blood vessels get clogged (not at one end—more like rusting throughout) several things may happen: organs awaiting the oxygen and food in the blood may die if not enough of these substances are received; blood vessels may burst due to increased pressure on their walls; or other blood vessels may sprout to provide alternative routes to the waiting organs and cells.

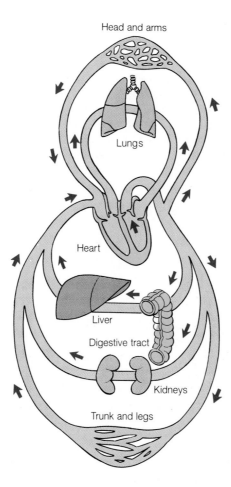

Head and arms

Lungs

Heart

Liver

Digestive tract

Kidneys

Trunk and legs

Figure 2.8 The cardiovascular system functions to transport blood between the body cells and organs that communicate with the external environment.

The effects of stress upon the circulatory system are pronounced. When the hypothalamus reacts to a stressor, it signals the pituitary to release oxytocin and vasopressin. Both of these hormones cause contraction of the smooth muscles resulting in constriction in the walls of the blood vessels. Vasopressin also increases the permeability of the blood vessels to water, resulting in greater blood volume. Coupled with the sodium retention brought about by aldosterone, the constriction of blood vessels and the increased permeability to water result in an increase in blood pressure caused by stress.

In addition, the heart itself (see fig. 2.9) is affected by stress. It increases its force of contraction and pumps out more blood when stressed. Further, serum cholesterol and other free fatty acids increase during stress. This increases the possibility of clogging of the arteries supplying the heart and death of a part of the heart resulting from a lack of blood supply to that part. Lastly, severe stressors can shock the heart to such an extent that sudden death occurs.

Figure 2.9 Internal
structure of the heart

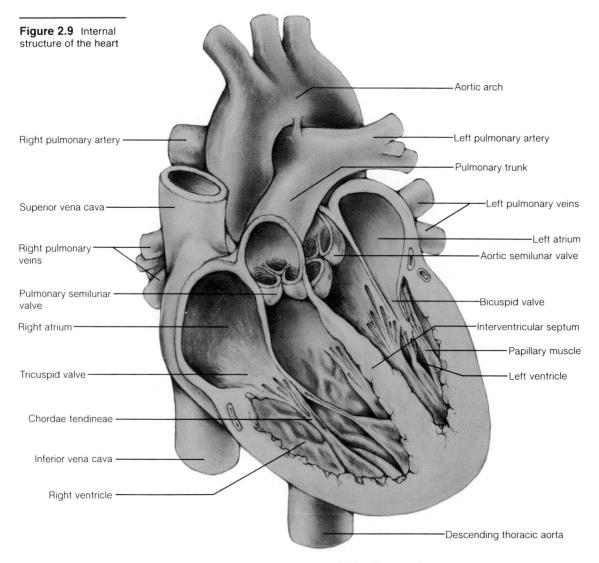

Right pulmonary artery

Superior vena cava

Right pulmonary
veins

Pulmonary semilunar
valve

Right atrium

Tricuspid valve

Chordae tendineae

Inferior vena cava

Right ventricle

Aortic arch

Left pulmonary artery

Pulmonary trunk

Left pulmonary veins

Left atrium

Aortic semilunar valve

Bicuspid valve

Interventricular septum

Papillary muscle

Left ventricle

Descending thoracic aorta

1. Right pulmonary artery
2. Superior vena cava
3. Right pulmonary veins
4. Pulmonary semilunar
   valve
5. Right atrium
6. Tricuspid valve
7. Chordae tendineae
8. Inferior vena cava
9. Right ventricle
10. Aortic arch

11. Left pulmonary artery
12. Pulmonary trunk
13. Left pulmonary veins
14. Left atrium
15. Aortic semilunar valve
16. Bicuspid valve
17. Interventricular septum
18. Papillary muscle
19. Left ventricle
20. Descending thoracic
    aorta

I began this book by describing myself vomiting by the side of a road. You now know that my condition was a function of stress overload. It is obvious, then, that the **gastrointestinal (GI) system** is a component of the stress response.

Some of you may have seen the Woody Allen movie *Everything You Wanted to Know about Sex but Were Afraid to Ask*. In that movie, a scene of the inside of a male's reproductive system includes actors as sperm. You can imagine the fun Woody Allen has with that situation! Well, let's use a similar approach in describing the structure and function of the GI system. The purpose of this system is to accept, break down, and distribute food, and to eliminate waste products resulting from this process.

"Hey Harry, here comes another shipment," said Joe *Saliva* to his brother. The Salivas live in the mouth and, when food enters, they help break it down to small manageable pieces. These pieces are then mailed by pneumatic tube (the *esophagus*) to Phil *Hydrochloric Acid* who lives in *Stomach*ville. Hydrochloric acid (HCl) activates enzymes that break the food down even further so it can pass into the small intestine. Another town, *Liver,* sends Bobby *Bile* to help break down the fatty shipments. Once these shipments (food) are made small they can be placed in local post offices for delivery to various other cities (body parts). The pieces without zip codes are unusable and are discarded by being sent via the large intestine through the anus into space (that is, flushed into another galaxy).

So as to make sure my attempt at levity hasn't been more confusing than motivating, let me summarize: food enters the mouth where it is broken down by chewing and **saliva.** It then passes down the food pipe (the **esophagus**) into the **stomach,** where a number of substances break the food down further. Two of these substances are **hydrochloric acid** and protein-splitting enzymes. The food substances then pass into the **small intestine** where they are broken down further. The usable food then passes through the walls of the small intestine into the bloodstream for passage to various body parts. The unusable food substances (waste) are transported through the small intestine to the **large intestine,** finally making their way out of the body through the **anal opening.** Figure 2.10 depicts the structure of the GI system.

Stress has a most significant effect upon the GI system. Because stress decreases the amount of saliva in the mouth, people are often so nervous before speaking in public that their mouths are too dry to speak. Because stress may result in uncontrollable contractions of the muscles of the esophagus, swallowing may be difficult. Because stress increases the amount of hydrochloric acid in the stomach, ulcers (small fissures in the stomach wall) may develop. Because stress may alter the rhythmic movements (**peristalsis**) of the small and large intestines necessary for the transport of food substances, diarrhea (if peristalsis is too fast) or constipation (if peristalsis is too slow) may result. "Constipation goes with depression and dullness, diarrhea with panic."[4] Even blockage of the bile and pancreatic ducts, as well as pancreatitis (inflammation of the pancreas), have been associated with stress.[5]

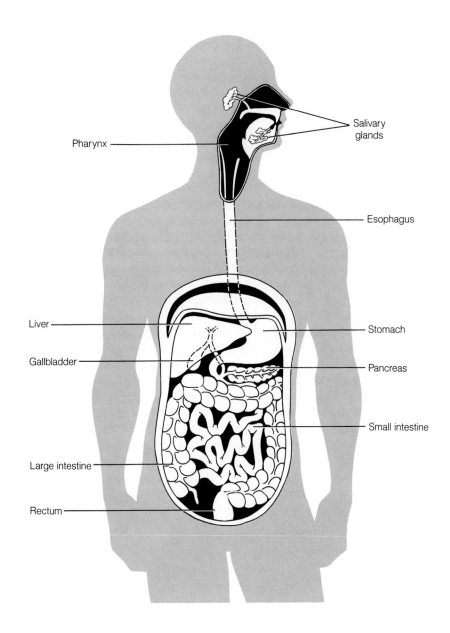

Figure 2.10 Major organs of the GI system

Pharynx

Salivary glands

Esophagus

Liver

Stomach

Gallbladder

Pancreas

Small intestine

Large intestine

Rectum

To hold yourself in a certain posture or position, or to move, you send messages **The Muscles**
to your muscles. These messages result in muscular contraction. The absence of
these messages results in muscular relaxation. Interacting systems in your body
feed back the results of muscular contraction to the brain so you don't contract
a muscle group too much or too little for your purposes. To demonstrate this
point, place an empty gallon paint can on the floor and tell someone it is full of
paint and very heavy. Then ask that person to pick up the "full" can. You will
notice how quickly and how high the can is lifted before the muscles adjust to a
lighter load. What really happened is that the brain perceived a can full of paint
and sent that message to the muscles. Based on past experience, the muscles were
instructed that x amount of contraction was needed to lift the full can. When the
can was lifted, a message (visual and kinesthetic) was sent to the brain ("Hey,
dummy, this can ain't full, it's empty!"), which resulted in an adjustment to make
the amount of muscular contraction more appropriate to the task.

Stress results in muscles contracting—tensing. Some people appear as if they
are always ready to defend themselves or to be aggressive. They seem "at the
ready." This type of muscle tension is called **bracing.**[6] As we shall discuss in the
next chapter, this muscular bracing can lead to numerous states of poor health
such as tension headaches and backaches. How many times have you heard
someone say, "I've got a knot in my shoulders"? When people say they are "uptight," they mean their muscles are bracing and fatiguing.

Many of us never realize our muscles are tensed. We squeeze our pens when
writing letters of complaint. We sit on the edges of our chairs ("on edge") during
a scary movie. We hold our steering wheels more tightly than necessary during
a traffic jam. Or we clench our jaws when angered. Intermittent muscle tension
is not the problem; it is the frequent stressor to which we react with bracing that
is harmful. When a new stressor is introduced while muscle tension is present,
even greater muscle tension is the result.

The examples used above involved **skeletal muscles**—muscles attached to
bones (see fig. 2.11). In addition, we have **smooth muscles** that control the contraction of the internal organs. The stress response results in these muscles being
contracted as well. So, for example, when we experience a stressor, the pituitary
hormones oxytocin and vasopressin result in increased blood pressure due to their
contracting the smooth muscles in the walls of the blood vessels. No wonder that
chronic stress can lead to hypertension. When the smooth muscles in the stomach
walls contract, we might get stomachaches; when the smooth muscles of the intestines contract, we might wind up with diarrhea; and so on throughout the body.

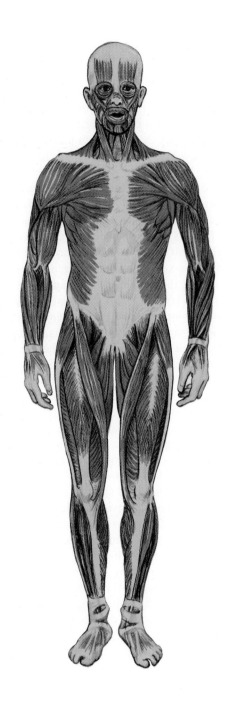

Linda was a doctoral student advisee of mine several years ago. One September, she surprised me by saying, "This year I'm not breaking out." When asked to explain what she meant, she told me that each summer she would leave campus and return home to a relatively unstressful existence. During the summer her skin was very smooth, but when September rolled around and school began, she "broke out" with acne. Linda was telling me several things besides "You guys put too much pressure on us students." She was saying that she manifested her stress in "the window to her body"—her skin—and that she believed she could control that response.

Although there is no definitive relationship between stress and acne, the skin is involved in our stress response. The skin's ability to conduct electrical currents and the skin's temperature are both affected. During stress, perspiration increases. Even though this increased perspiration may be imperceptible, it will increase electrical conductance and can be measured by a galvanometer. This measure is called your **galvanic skin response** (**GSR**) and is a major part of the lie detector test. One of the reasons that the lie detector test is not infallible and is viewed with caution is that people can control their nervousness (and, therefore, their level of skin moisture), thereby affecting their GSR. A good liar may have a lower GSR than a nervous innocent suspect, although a well-trained, experienced lie detector administrator will often (but not always) be able to distinguish between the two.

During stress, the surface temperature of the skin decreases. Since norepinephrine constricts the blood vessels of the skin of the arms and legs, for example, fingers and toes feel colder during stress than otherwise. The skin may also appear pale due to this vasoconstriction. We often hear of people described as appearing "white as a ghost." Now you know why the skin of nervous, anxious, stressed people is described as cold, clammy, and pale.

Now that you have an idea of how your body reacts to stress, you are in a better position to be more specific. In table 2.1, indicate how often each of the physical symptoms happens to you.

If you scored between 40 and 75, the chances of becoming physically ill as a result of stress are minimal. If you scored between 76 and 100, you have a slight chance of becoming physically ill from the stress in your life. If you scored between 101 and 150, it is likely you will become ill from the stress you experience. If you scored over 150, you may very well already be ill from the stress you have experienced. Luckily, you are reading this book and will find out how to better manage the stress you encounter and how to eliminate some stressors in the first place.

The Skin

Symptoms, Stress, and You

What Do Your Scores in Table 2.1 Mean?

Table 2.1

Physiological Reactions to Stress

Circle the number that best represents the frequency of occurrence of the following physical symptoms and add up the total number of points.

	Never	Infrequently (More than Once in Six Months)	Occasionally (More than Once per Month)	Very Often (More than Once per Week)	Constantly
1. Tension headaches	1	2	3	4	5
2. Migraine (vascular) headaches	1	2	3	4	5
3. Stomachaches	1	2	3	4	5
4. Increase in blood pressure	1	2	3	4	5
5. Cold hands	1	2	3	4	5
6. Acidy stomach	1	2	3	4	5
7. Shallow, rapid breathing	1	2	3	4	5
8. Diarrhea	1	2	3	4	5
9. Palpitations	1	2	3	4	5
10. Shaky hands	1	2	3	4	5
11. Burping	1	2	3	4	5
12. Gassiness	1	2	3	4	5
13. Increased urge to urinate	1	2	3	4	5
14. Sweaty feet/hands	1	2	3	4	5
15. Oily skin	1	2	3	4	5
16. Fatigue/exhausted feeling	1	2	3	4	5
17. Panting	1	2	3	4	5
18. Dry mouth	1	2	3	4	5

Source: H. Ebel et al., eds., *Presidential Sports Award Fitness Manual*, 197–98. Copyright © 1983 FitCom Corporation, Havertown, PA.

Summary

1. The brain includes two major components: the cerebral cortex and the subcortex. The subcortex includes the cerebellum, medulla oblongata, pons, and diencephalon. The diencephalon is made up of the thalamus and the hypothalamus.

2. When the hypothalamus experiences a stressor, it releases corticotropin releasing factor which instructs the pituitary to secrete adrenocorticotropic hormone. In addition, the hypothalamus directly activates the adrenal medulla.

Table 2.1
(continued)

	Never	Infrequently (More than Once in Six Months)	Occasionally (More than Once per Month)	Very Often (More than Once per Week)	Constantly
19. Hand tremor	1	2	3	4	5
20. Backache	1	2	3	4	5
21. Neck stiffness	1	2	3	4	5
22. Gum chewing	1	2	3	4	5
23. Grinding teeth	1	2	3	4	5
24. Constipation	1	2	3	4	5
25. Tightness in chest or heart	1	2	3	4	5
26. Dizziness	1	2	3	4	5
27. Nausea/vomiting	1	2	3	4	5
28. Menstrual distress	1	2	3	4	5
29. Skin blemishes	1	2	3	4	5
30. Heart pounding	1	2	3	4	5
31. Colitis	1	2	3	4	5
32. Asthma	1	2	3	4	5
33. Indigestion	1	2	3	4	5
34. High blood pressure	1	2	3	4	5
35. Hyperventilation	1	2	3	4	5
36. Arthritis	1	2	3	4	5
37. Skin rash	1	2	3	4	5
38. Bruxism/jaw pain	1	2	3	4	5
39. Allergy	1	2	3	4	5

Interpretation

40–75	Low physiological symptoms of stress response
76–100	Moderate physiological symptoms of stress response
101–150	High physiological symptoms of stress response
Over 150	Excessive physiological symptoms of stress response

3. Once instructed by the hypothalamus and pituitary, the adrenal cortex secretes glucocorticoids and mineralocorticoids. The primary glucocorticoid is cortisol, and the primary mineralocorticoid is aldosterone. In addition, the hypothalamus instructs the adrenal medulla to secrete the catecholamines epinephrine and norepinephrine.

4. Adrenal hormones cause a number of physiological changes which include accelerated heart rate, dilation of coronary arteries, dilation of bronchial tubes, increased basal metabolic rate, constriction of blood vessels in the limbs, increased oxygen consumption, increased blood sugar, and increased blood pressure.

5. In addition to the adrenal gland response to stress, the thyroid gland releases thyroxin and the pituitary secretes oxytocin and vasopressin. These hormones also help prepare the body for a physical response to the stressor.

6. The autonomic nervous system is made up of the sympathetic nervous system (generally in charge of expending energy—such as during stress) and the parasympathetic nervous system (generally in charge of conserving energy—such as during relaxation).

7. Stress results in secretions of oxytocin and vasopressin which cause contractions of smooth muscles (such as in the walls of the blood vessels). Therefore, blood vessel constriction occurs. Vasopressin secretion also results in a greater blood volume. The combination of these effects leads to increased blood pressure, which can threaten the cardiovascular system.

8. Stress decreases the amount of saliva in the mouth, leaving a feeling of cotton mouth. It may also lead to uncontrollable contractions of the esophagus, making swallowing difficult. Stress also causes greater secretions of hydrochloric acid which can result in ulcers.

9. The contraction of skeletal muscle that results from stress can lead to tension headaches, backaches, and fatigue. The smooth muscle contractions of the walls of blood vessels can lead to hypertension.

10. The skin's ability to conduct electrical currents and the skin's temperature are both affected by stress.

Notes

1. Kenneth R. Pelletier, *Mind as Healer, Mind as Slayer* (New York: Dell Publishing Co., 1977), 51.

2. G. Makara, M. Palkovits, and J. Szentagothal, "The Endocrine Hypothalamus and the Hormonal Response to Stress," in *Selye's Guide to Stress Research,* ed. Hans Selye (New York: Van Nostrand Rinehold, 1980), 280–337.

3. "Of Rats and Men," *Psychology Today,* July 1985, 21.

4. Walter McQuade and Ann Aikman, *Stress* (New York: Bantam Books, 1974), 52.

5. Daniel A. Girdano and George S. Everly, *Controlling Stress and Tension: A Holistic Approach* (Englewood Cliffs, N.J.: Prentice-Hall, 1986), 37.

6. Barbara B. Brown, *Stress and the Art of Biofeedback* (New York: Harper & Row, 1977), 28.

3

Stress and Illness/Disease

If stress were only discomforting—that is, if it led only to increased muscle tension, perspiration, rapid and shallow breathing, or a general psychological state of uneasiness—it would be bad enough. Unfortunately, chronic stress also leads to poor health.

Bill's wife died last year, and he grieved long and hard over her death. He felt it unfair (she was such a kind person) and a sense of helplessness crept over him. Loneliness became a part of his every day, and tears became the companions of his late evening hours. There were those who were not even surprised at Bill's own death just one year after his wife's. They officially called it a heart attack, but Bill's friends, to this day, know he died of a "broken heart."

Psychosomatic Disease

You probably know some Bills yourself—people who have died or become ill from severe stress, with seemingly little physically wrong with them. Maybe you have even been guilty of telling these people, "It's all in your mind," or at least thinking that. Well, in Bill's case it was not "all in his mind"—it was, obviously, partially in his heart. Some illnesses are easily seen as being physical (e.g., a skin rash), while others are assuredly recognized as being mental (e.g., neuroses); yet it is impossible to deny the interaction between the mind and the body and the effects of one upon the other.

Why is it, for example, that when we are infected with a cold-causing virus we do not always come down with the common cold? We shall soon discuss numerous diseases and illnesses to which the mind makes the body susceptible. These conditions are called **psychosomatic** (*psyche* for mind; *soma* for body). Psychosomatic disease is not "all in the mind" but involves both mind and body. In fact, the term **psychophysiological** is now sometimes used in place of psychosomatic. Psychosomatic disease is real, can be diagnosed, and is manifested physically. However, it also has a component in the mind, although it is not easily measured. That common cold may be a function of psychological stress, which decreases the effectiveness of the immunological system and results in the body being more vulnerable to cold viruses. That cold may also be caused by psychological stress using up particular vitamins in the body and leading to decreased effectiveness in combatting cold viruses. Mental stress has caused or aggravated symptoms in 50 to 90 percent of all hospital inpatients in the United States.[1]

Psychosomatic disease may be psychogenic or somatogenic. **Psychogenic** refers to a physical disease caused by emotional stress. Ulcers and asthma are examples of psychogenic psychosomatic diseases. In these cases there is no invasion of disease-causing microorganisms; the mind changes the physiology so that parts of the body break down. **Somatogenic** psychosomatic disease occurs when the mind increases the body's susceptibility to some disease-causing microbes or some natural degenerative process.[2] Examples of diseases suspected of being somatogenic are cancer and rheumatoid arthritis.

Stress and the Immunological System

There is a new field of scientific inquiry which studies the chemical basis of communication between the mind and the body—in particular, the link between the nervous system and the immune system. In 1980, psychologist Robert Adler of the University of Rochester medical school named this scientific field **psychoneuroimmunology.** The focus of researchers in this field is upon both the illness-causing and the healing effects the mind can have upon the body. Robert Ornstein and David Sobel summarized data linking the social world to a decrease in the effectiveness of the immunological system.[3] They cite studies that have found the following: bereaved people have immunological systems functioning below par; rats exposed to stress develop larger cancerous tumors than other rats; West Point cadets who develop mononucleosis came disproportionately from families with fathers who were overachievers; and reoccurrences of oral herpes simplex are associated with stress and the person's emotional reaction to the disease.

Presently, Dr. Candace Pert, a neuroscientist and the former section chief of brain biochemistry at the National Institute of Mental Health, is investigating chemicals which send messages between cells to various parts of the brain and between the brain and other parts of the body. To date, some fifty of these brain message transmitters (called *neuropeptides*) have been found that are produced by the brain itself. The pertinent aspect to our discussion of the mind-body connection is that Pert believes some of these neuropeptides are also produced in small amounts by the macrophages—white blood cells which ingest and destroy bacteria and viruses.[4] In addition, the macrophages are attracted to neuropeptides produced by the brain. That is, if neuropeptides are produced by the brain to fight off an invasion of bacteria, for instance, macrophages will also travel to help combat the invasion. Since relaxation and some forms of visualization result in the production of neuropeptides (for example, beta-endorphins), it may be possible to purposefully cause the brain to produce more of these substances, thereby making the immunological system more effective. The result may be less disease.

Other evidence of the importance of the mind to physical illness also exists. For example, dental students who had depressed moods were also found to have lowered antibody production, and thereby were more susceptible to foreign substances.[5] Women experiencing marital separation had 40 percent fewer natural killer cells (cells which fight viruses and tumors) and 20 percent fewer T cells than married women of similar age and social background.[6] Men's recoveries from heart attacks are also affected by their minds. When men recovering from a heart attack were given an illusion of some control over their health (such as very simple exercises to do) they encountered fewer complications and shorter stays in the cardiac care unit.[7] The suspicion is that feeling in control alleviated the stress experienced from helplessness.

Stress and Serum Cholesterol

The amount of cholesterol roaming about your blood can accumulate on the walls of your blood vessels, blocking the flow of blood to various parts of your body. When it is the heart that is blocked, you may develop coronary heart disease or die of a heart attack caused by an insufficient supply of oxygen to the heart. When it is the brain that is blocked, you may develop a stroke or die from an insufficient supply of oxygen to the brain. Researchers have attempted to determine the causes of increased levels of serum cholesterol so they can help people avoid this condition; they have found stress to be one of the culprits. Friedman, Rosenman, and Carroll conducted one of the early investigations of the relationship between stress and serum cholesterol.[8] They studied accountants during times of the year when they had deadlines to meet—for example, when tax returns had to be prepared—and found average serum cholesterol increased dramatically. Other researchers have verified these results. For example, when medical students were studied just before and just after their final examinations, twenty of twenty-one of them had higher serum cholesterol levels before this stressful event.[9] In another investigation, military pilots at the beginning of their training showed increased serum cholesterol levels, and the levels were highest during examination periods.[10] Clarifying the relationship between stress and serum cholesterol is the study of 7,000 men by Tucker, Cole, and Friedman in which they conclude that "when it comes to differences in serum cholesterol levels, the perceptions people have of their problems play a more significant role than the problems themselves."[11] They go on to recommend that "given this finding and the supporting results of related research,[12] increased efforts to determine the impact of managing perceptions of stress to alter serum cholesterol levels would appear warranted and worthwhile." We will pay particular attention to the role of perception and its effect on levels of stress in chapter 7.

Specific diseases and illnesses will be discussed below, but the important concept here is that a person is an interconnected whole. A separation, even just for discussion or research purposes, of the mind from the body is inappropriate. The mind is ultimately affected by what the body experiences, and the body is ultimately affected by what the mind experiences.

Specific Conditions

Now that you understand the psychosomatic disease concept, we can look at specific diseases and their relationship to stress. As you will discover, stress can lead to both psychogenic and somatogenic psychosomatic diseases.

Hypertension

Hypertension (high blood pressure) is excessive and damaging pressure of the blood against the walls of the arterial blood vessels. Blood pressure is measured with a **sphygmomanometer,** an instrument consisting of an inflatable cuff placed around the upper arm and a stethoscope. The cuff cuts off the blood flow in the brachial artery until it is deflated to the point where the blood pressure forces the blood through. That measure is called the **systolic** blood pressure, and 120 mm Hg is considered average (normal). At the point where the cuff is deflated further and the blood is not impeded at all, another measure is taken. That measure is termed the **diastolic** blood pressure, and 80 mm Hg is considered average. The total blood pressure is given in this formula: systolic/diastolic (120/80). Systolic blood pressure represents the force against the arterial blood vessel walls when the left ventricle contracts and blood is pumped out of the heart. Diastolic blood pressure represents the force against the arterial walls when the heart is relaxed.

High blood pressure is a relative term. Health scientists disagree as to its exact beginning, but generally a systolic pressure greater than 140 mm Hg or a diastolic pressure greater than 90 mm Hg is considered hypertension. Since average blood pressure tends to be higher in the elderly than others, measures slightly above 140/90 are not unusual for this age group. However, that is not to say they are inevitable. Increased blood pressure may be related more to life-style than to age.

There are several causes of hypertension. Excessive sodium (salt) intake may cause hypertension in those genetically susceptible. Since we can't determine who is genetically susceptible, dietary guidelines in the United States suggest no more than a 5,000 mg daily ingestion of salt. The average American diet has been estimated to consist of 10–20g (10,000–20,000 mg) of salt daily. The problem with monitoring salt in our diets is that it is hidden in many processed foods. Those who just eliminate the saltshaker may still be ingesting too much salt.

Hypertension may also be caused by kidney disease, too narrow an opening in the aorta (main blood vessel through which blood exits the heart), Cushing's syndrome (oversecretion of corticol hormones), obesity, and the use of oral contraceptives.[13] However, these conditions cause only an estimated 10 percent of all hypertension. Approximately 90 percent of hypertension is termed **essential hypertension** and has no known cause.

Twenty percent of the United States population of age seventeen and older have been diagnosed as hypertensive. Given that hypertension occurs without signs or symptoms, imagine the number of cases yet undiagnosed! More men than women are hypertensive, and the likelihood of developing hypertension increases with age. Proportionately more blacks than whites are hypertensive, with the lowest incidence in white women and the highest incidence in black females (see fig. 3.1 and table 3.1).

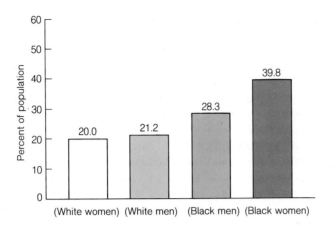

Figure 3.1
Prevalence rates of hypertension for persons 25–74 years of age by race and sex: United States, 1976–1980.

Data from National Center for Health Statistics, "Blood Pressure Levels and Hypertension in Persons Ages 6–74 Years: United States 1976–1980" in *Advanced Data*, October 8, 1982, p. 10.

Table 3.1
Prevalence Rates of Elevated Blood Pressure Levels[a] for Persons 25–74 Years by Race, Age, and Sex: United States, 1976–1980

Race and Age	Both Sexes — Rate per 100 Population	Male — Rate per 100 Population	Female — Rate per 100 Population
All Races[b]	14.5	16.4	12.8
25–34 Years	5.5	8.7	2.6
35–44 Years	9.9	11.8	8.2
45–54 Years	17.8	20.9	14.9
55–64 Years	21.7	23.7	20.0
65–74 Years	26.6	24.9	27.9
White	13.5	15.9	11.4
25–34 Years	5.3	8.4	2.3
35–44 Years	8.5	10.6	6.5
45–54 Years	16.5	21.2	12.1
55–64 Years	20.2	22.3	18.3
65–74 Years	25.5	24.5	26.3
Black	22.8	22.4	23.2
25–34 Years	7.6	11.7	4.3
35–44 Years	19.6	22.3	17.6
45–54 Years	30.7	23.0	37.3
55–64 Years	37.6	39.2	36.4
65–74 Years	36.5	27.5	43.4

Source: Data from National Center for Health Statistics, "Blood Pressure Levels and Hypertension in Persons Ages 6–74 Years: United States 1976–1980," *Advance Data*, 8 October 1982, 10.

Note: All blood pressures are the average of three measurements.

[a]Systolic blood pressure of at least 160 mm Hg and/or diastolic blood pressure of at least 95 mm Hg.

[b]Includes other racial groups in addition to white and black.

Imagine, for a moment, the Alaska pipeline. Through that tube is pumped oil that passes through Alaska. When that pipeline works correctly, oil is provided in sufficient quantity without any breaks in the pipeline. What would happen, though, if so much oil were pumped through that it created too great a pressure against the metal tube? Well, the tube would probably rupture. The same thing happens with blood pressure, blood, and blood vessels. Blood is analogous to oil and blood vessels (in particular, arteries) to the pipeline. If blood creates too great a pressure upon the arterial walls, they will rupture, and the blood intended for some destination beyond the point of rupture will not reach its goal. If the rupture is in the brain, we call that a **cerebral hemorrhage.** If a coronary artery ruptures, and a part of the heart dies from a lack of oxygen usually transported to it via the blood, we call that a **myocardial infarction.** Blood can also be prevented from reaching its destination by blockage of the blood vessels or a narrowing of the vessels by debris (**plaque**) collecting on their inner walls.

Since blood pressure as well as serum cholesterol increase during stress (plaque is made up of cholesterol), the relationship between stress and hypertension has long been suspected. "Emotional stress is generally regarded as a major factor" in the etiology of hypertension.[14] Recognizing this relationship, educational programs for hypertensives have included stress management.[15] Although hypertension can be controlled with medication, the possibility of disturbing side effects from these drugs has led to attempts to control hypertension in other ways. Since obesity, cigarette smoking, and lack of exercise are correlates to hypertension, programs involving weight control, smoking withdrawal, and exercise, as well as decreased ingestion of salt, have all been used to respond to high blood pressure.

Stress management has also been employed to control high blood pressure. Unfortunately, too many health care providers will tell a hypertensive person that he or she needs to "relax" without providing instruction in how to do so. A notable exception is Dr. Herbert Benson. Dr. Benson is a cardiologist who has used meditation to reduce blood pressure in hypertensive patients. His patients are instructed in how to meditate and do so in the clinical setting with instructions to meditate between hospital visits. Described in his book *The Relaxation Response*,[16] Dr. Benson's technique has been quite successful.[17]

Further evidence of the relationship between stress and essential hypertension appears in the massive study of 1,600 hospital patients by Flanders Dunbar in the 1940s.[18] Dunbar found that certain personality traits were characteristic of hypertensive patients; for example, they were easily upset by criticism or imperfection, possessed pent-up anger, and lacked self-confidence. One can readily see the role stress might play in "setting off" these susceptible people.

Stroke

Apoplexy (also termed **stroke**) is a lack of oxygen in the brain resulting from a blockage or rupture of one of the arteries that supply it. Depending on the exact location of the brain tissue dying from this lack of oxygen and the amount of time oxygen was denied, paralysis, speech impairment, motor-function impairment, or death may result. Stroke is related to hypertension, which may also

Scientific Foundations

result in a cerebral hemorrhage (rupture of a major blood vessel supplying the brain). Cardiovascular disorders, of which apoplexy is one, kill more Americans each year than any other disorder. Stroke has been related to high blood pressure, diet, and stress.

Heart attacks kill more Americans than any other single cause of death. That stress is related to coronary heart disease is not surprising when we consider the physiological mechanisms that stress brings into play: accelerated heart rate, increased blood pressure, increased serum cholesterol, and fluid retention resulting in increased blood volume. Further, the stereotypical heart attack victim has been the highly stressed, overworked, overweight businessman with a cigarette dangling from his lips and a martini in his hand.

Coronary Heart Disease

Coronary heart disease has been associated with diets high in saturated fats, a lack of exercise, obesity, heredity, and even maleness and baldness. However, the three major risk factors generally agreed to be most associated with coronary heart disease are *hypercholesterolemia* (high serum cholesterol), hypertension, and cigarette smoking. And yet, two researchers state:

Largely unquestioned, however, has been the repeated finding that these factors are completely absent in more than half of all the new cases of coronary heart disease encountered in clinical practice. Indeed, most patients do not have high blood cholesterol, and only a fraction have high blood pressure. Data from pooled prospective studies in the United States actually show that of men with two or more of these alleged risks, only about 10 percent develop coronary heart disease over a ten-year period, while the remainder do not. . . . Almost twenty years ago we discovered that young coronary patients could be differentiated from healthy control subjects far more readily by the dimensions of occupational stress than by differences in heredity, diet, obesity, tobacco consumption, or exercise. In our study it was found that at the time of their attack 91 percent of 100 patients as compared with only 20 percent of healthy controls had been holding down two or more jobs, working more than sixty hours per week, or experiencing unusual insecurity, discontent, or frustration in relation to employment.[19]

These researchers go on to present data from studies in which various professionals ranked the specialties within their professions by stress level. Next, the prevalence of coronary heart disease by specialty was determined. As can be noted in tables 3.2, 3.3, and 3.4, generally the more stressful the specialty, the more prevalent was coronary heart disease. When we add to this our knowledge that heart attack deaths for American men are most prevalent on Mondays and least prevalent on Fridays, we can consider stress in general, and occupational stress in particular, a major cause of coronary heart disease.

Further evidence of the relationship between stress and coronary heart disease was presented in the studies of Meyer Friedman and Ray Rosenman. These two cardiologists and their work are discussed in more detail in chapter 7. For purposes of this discussion, suffice it to say that Friedman and Rosenman identified a **Type A** behavior pattern disproportionately represented among heart attack patients. These patients were aggressive, competitive, time-urgent, hostile, often found themselves doing things quickly, overly concerned with numbers

Table 3.2
Percentage Prevalence of Coronary Heart Disease in Selected Specialties of Medicine Ranked by Stressfulness

Occupational Field	Stress Rank	Age at Survey				
		40–49	50–59	60–69	40–69 (Avg.)	40–69 (Age Adjusted)
Dermatology	Least	0.9	5.1	7.8	3.2	3.8
Pathology		1.8	5.2	11.7	4.1	5.0
Anesthesiology		2.6	13.7	30.0	8.9	12.2
G.P.	Most	6.0	12.0	23.3	11.9	11.7
Average		2.8	8.6	18.4	7.0	8.1

Source: Henry I. Russek and Linda G. Russek, "Is Emotional Stress an Etiological Factor in Coronary Heart Disease?" *Psychosomatics* 17 (1976): 63–67. © 1967 Academy of Psychosomatic Medicine, Cligott Publishing Co., Greenwich, CT. Reprinted by permission.

Table 3.3
Percentage Prevalence of Coronary Heart Disease in Selected Specialties of Dentistry Ranked by Stressfulness

Occupational Field	Stress Rank	Age at Survey				
		40–49	50–59	60–69	40–69 (Avg.)	40–69 (Age Adjusted)
Periodontia	Least	0.0	4.7	6.1	3.8	2.9
Orthodontia		0.7	7.2	8.8	4.3	4.7
Oral Surgery		1.3	8.5	12.5	6.3	6.1
G.P., Dentistry	Most	1.7	8.8	21.9	9.1	8.4
Average		1.1	7.6	13.8	6.4	6.0

Source: Henry I. Russek and Linda G. Russek, "Is Emotional Stress an Etiological Factor in Coronary Heart Disease?" *Psychosomatics* 17 (1976): 63–67. © 1967 Academy of Psychosomatic Medicine, Cligott Publishing Co., Greenwich, CT. Reprinted by permission.

Table 3.4
Percentage Prevalence of Coronary Heart Disease in Selected Specialties of Law Ranked by Stressfulness

Occupational Field	Stress Rank	Age at Survey				
		40–49	50–59	60–69	40–69 (Avg.)	40–69 (Age Adjusted)
Patent Law, Nontrial	Least	0.7	4.8	7.1	3.7	3.5
Other Specialties		2.5	5.9	12.5	6.9	5.8
Trial Law		3.4	7.2	13.8	8.8	6.9
G.P., Law	Most	6.9	11.3	16.3	11.0	10.4
Average		3.4	7.2	12.8	7.6	6.7

Source: Henry I. Russek and Linda G. Russek, "Is Emotional Stress an Etiological Factor in Coronary Heart Disease?" *Psychosomatics* 17 (1976): 63–67. © 1967 Academy of Psychosomatic Medicine, Cligott Publishing Co., Greenwich, CT. Reprinted by permission.

(quantity rather than quality), and often did more than one thing at a time (for example, read the newspaper over breakfast).[20] A comprehensive review of studies of the Type A behavior pattern has verified the relationship between these stress-related behaviors and coronary heart disease;[21] however, other researchers have found conflicting results. We discuss Type A behavior pattern in greater detail in chapter 7.

The physiological mechanisms that appear to lead from chronic stress down the road to coronary heart disease seem to be related to the increased serum cholesterol, blood pressure, blood volume, and accelerated heart rate associated with stress reactivity. The latter three make the heart work harder, and the former (hypercholesterolemia) leads to clogging of arteries (**atherosclerosis**) and eventual loss of elasticity of the coronary and other arteries (**arteriosclerosis**). Both of these conditions also result in an excessive work load for the heart muscle as well as a decreased supply of oxygen to the heart itself. Not to be disregarded, however, is the interaction between other coronary risk factors and stress. One might expect a person who is overstressed not to have time to exercise, or to overeat as a reward for "hard work," or to smoke cigarettes to relax (actually nicotine is physiologically a stimulant). Consequently, the negative effects of stress upon the heart are often multiplied by the introduction of other heart-damaging behaviors.

Ulcers

Ulcers are fissures or cuts in the wall of the stomach, duodenum, or other part of the intestines. Although the exact cause of ulcers is unknown, it is suspected that the increase of hydrochloric acid in and just outside the stomach is at least partly, if not predominantly, responsible. There is ample evidence for this conclusion. Selye reported that ulcers developed in the stomach and duodenum of rats exposed to stress.[22] When studying grief reactions, Lindemann reported thirty-three out of forty-one ulcer patients "developed their disease in close time relationship to the loss of an important person."[23] Others have noted a sense of utter helplessness among ulcer patients and believe this feeling preceded, rather than resulted from, the development of the ulcers.[24] Even unemployment has been shown to result in ulcers in men laid off from their jobs *and in the wives* of those men.[25]

One theory explaining the effects of stress on the development of ulcers pertains to the mucous coating which lines the stomach. The theory states that during chronic stress, norepinephrine secretion causes capillaries in the stomach lining to constrict. This, in turn, results in a shutting down of mucosal production, and the mucous protective barrier for the stomach wall is lost. Without the protective barrier, hydrochloric acid breaks down the tissue and can even reach blood vessels, resulting in a bleeding ulcer.

Migraine Headaches

Terry was a very busy and productive woman. She had two adorable boys and an equally adorable dentist husband (whom the boys greatly resembled). Since she felt her roles as mother and wife were not fulfilling enough, and because she had a special talent, Terry painted most afternoons and eventually entered a master's degree program in art. She did so well in her graduate work that upon the awarding of her master's degree, she was asked to join the faculty. All of this wasn't enough, so she served on committees for local museums and civic organizations.

It was clear to everyone but Terry herself that she was doing too much. She had been having headaches. Soon, the headaches came more frequently and became more severe. Many a time Terry's neighbors had to watch her children while her husband drilled teeth, and she hibernated in a bedroom darkened by drawn shades, waiting out the migraine. I know because I was one of Terry's neighbors.

Migraine headaches are the result of a constriction and dilation of the carotid arteries of one side of the head. The constriction phase, called the **preattack** or **prodrome,** is often associated with light or noise sensitivity, irritability, and a flushing or pallor of the skin. When the dilation of the arteries occurs, certain chemicals stimulate adjacent nerve endings, causing pain.

The migraine is not just a severe headache. It is a unique type of headache with special characteristics, and it usually involves just one side of the head. There is a prodrome consisting of warning signs, such as flashing lights, differing patterns, or some dark spaces. The prodrome usually occurs one or two hours prior to the headache itself. The actual headache usually involves a throbbing pain that lasts approximately six hours (although this may vary greatly from person to person). An interesting point about migraine attacks is that they usually occur after a pressure-packed situation is over, rather than when the pressure is being experienced. Consequently, attacks often occur on weekends. Many of Terry's weekends were spent waiting out a migraine.

Diet may precipitate migraine headaches for some people. Chocolate, aged cheese, or red wine are implicated culprits. However, predominant thought on the cause of migraine pertains to emotional stress and tension. "Feelings of anxiety, nervous tension, anger, or repressed rage are associated with migraine . . . an attack may be aborted when the individual gives vent to underlying hostility."[26] A typical migraine sufferer is a perfectionist, "ambitious, rigid, orderly, excessively competitive, and unable to delegate responsibility."[27] Sound like someone you know?

Although migraines most often occur between the ages of sixteen and thirty-five and are greatly reduced in frequency by age fifty, migraine sufferers aren't willing to wait years for relief. Medications of various sorts are available for migraine sufferers, most of which contain ergotamine tartrate and are taken during the prodrome to constrict the carotid arteries. Migraine medication, however, may produce side effects: weakness in the legs, muscle pain, numbness, and heart-rate irregularity.

Other relief is available to sufferers of migraine headaches that does not produce disturbing side effects. Since the major problem is the dilation of blood vessels in the head, any method of preventing an increased blood flow to the head would help prevent or treat migraine. Relaxation techniques that are discussed later in this book (biofeedback, meditation, and autogenic training) result in an increased blood flow in the peripheral blood system (arms and legs). This increased flow comes from several areas of which the head is one. As you might imagine, these techniques have been found successful in the prevention and treatment of migraine.[28]

An important point needs to be made here. Migraines are a sign and symptom of a life-style gone awry. Treating signs and symptoms with either medication or meditation without eliminating the underlying cause (one's life-style) reminds me of the following poem:

Twas a dangerous cliff, as they freely confessed,
Though to walk near its crest was so pleasant;
But over its terrible edge there had slipped
A duke, and full many a peasant.
The people said something would have to be done,
But their projects did not at all tally.
Some said, "Put a fence 'round the edge of the cliff'";
Some, "An ambulance down in the valley."
The lament of the crowd was profound and was loud,
As their hearts overflowed with their pity;
But the cry for the ambulance carried the day
As it spread through the neighboring city,
A collection was made to accumulate aid,
And the dwellers in highway and alley
Gave dollars or cents—not to finish a fence—
But an ambulance down in the valley.
The story looks queer as we've written it here,
But things oft occur that are stranger,
More humane, we assert, than to succor the hurt,
Is the plan of removing the danger.
The best possible course is to safeguard the source;
Attend to things rationally.
Yes, build up the fence, and let us dispense
With the ambulance down in the valley.

Courtesy American Chiropractic Association, Arlington, VA.

Rather than care for the migraine after it occurs or during the prodrome, why not prevent it in the first place by changing your life-style? Help in doing that is available in subsequent chapters of this book.

Tension Headaches

Headaches may be caused by muscle tension accompanying stress. This muscle tension may include the forehead, jaw, or neck. I'm often amazed at the numbers of students who come to my classes, especially the early or late evening ones, with tension headaches. Perhaps a whole day of work or school is the instigator, but we all have control over our own muscles. If we only knew how to relax them prior to the onset of a tension headache! Once the headache occurs, it tends to fuel itself. It is difficult to relax when you're in pain.

Treatment for tension headaches may include medication (aspirin or a tranquilizer), heat on tense muscles, or massage. However, just as I'm amazed at the number of students entering my classes with tension headaches, I'm also amazed

(actually I've long since stopped being amazed about the potency of stress management) at the numbers of students who leave my classes without headaches when we've been practicing a relaxation technique. Others have also reported on the effectiveness of relaxation training (in particular, biofeedback) for control and prevention of tension headaches.[29,30] As with migraines, however, an ounce of prevention is worth a pound of cure.

Cancer

Although many people do not realize it, both the prevention and the treatment of cancer are suspected of being related to stress. Cancer is really several diseases, some of which may be caused by ingested **carcinogens** (cancer-causing agents), some by inhaled carcinogens (in the environment or in cigarette smoke), and some by viruses. In any case, cancer is the unbridled multiplication of cells that leads to tumors and, eventually, organ damage.

When a viral cancer occurs, the immunological system is called into play—particularly its lymphocytes.[31] The number of **T-lymphocytes** that normally destroy mutant cells prior to their multiplying and causing damage is reduced during stress. Consequently, some researchers believe that chronic stress results in a chronic inability of the immune response to prevent the multiplication of mutant cells, which some believe are present but normally controlled in most people.

The role of stress in the development of cancer is still being debated, but since cancer is the second leading cause of death in the United States, research in this area has been and is presently being conducted. Support for the role of stress in the development of malignancy has been found in these studies. When experimental mice whose mothers had a cancerous virus were divided into two groups (one stressed and one not), 90 percent of the stressed mice as compared to only 7 percent of the mice not stressed developed cancer.[32] Further, some support has been provided for a cancer-prone personality type. The cancer-prone person has been described as (1) holding resentment with the inability to forgive, (2) using self-pity, (3) lacking the ability to develop and maintain meaningful interpersonal relationships, and (4) having a poor self-image.[33] Cancer patients were also found to have experienced severe emotional disturbances in childhood (parents divorced, death in the family, etc.) resulting in their feeling lonely, anxious, and rejected.[34] Lastly, the classic study by Lawrence LeShan in the 1950s of the psychological characteristics of cancer patients found that these patients differed from healthy controls. The patients more frequently

1. reported a lost relationship prior to the cancer diagnosis,
2. were unable to express hostility in their own defense,
3. felt unworthy and disliked themselves, and
4. had a tense relationship with one or both parents.[35]

Even the treatment of cancer has included the recognition that the mind can affect the body. Cancer patients have been taught to see in their imagination the T-lymphocytes attacking the cancerous cells. These visualization skills and other relaxation techniques are utilized because it seems sensible to conclude that if T-lymphocytes are decreased during the stress response, they will be increased during the relaxation response. The immunological system will then be more potent in controlling the cancerous cells. It should be recognized, however, that this type of treatment for cancer is controversial and experimental. Further, visualization therapy always includes more treatment modalities as well; for example, X-ray, chemical, and surgical methods.

Allergies, Asthma, and Hay Fever

Allergies, of which asthma and hay fever are but two examples, are the body's defense against a foreign, irritating substance called an **antigen.** In response to this antigen, the body produces **antibodies.** Among their other functions, antibodies stimulate the release of chemicals. Histamine, one of these chemicals, causes tissues to swell, mucous secretions to increase, and air passages in the lungs to become constricted. Now you know why the drug of choice for allergy sufferers is an antihistamine.

Some medical scientists, unable to identify any antigen in many asthmatics, have argued that allergies are emotional diseases. Supporting this theory is the result of an experiment in which a woman who was allergic to horses began to wheeze when shown only a picture of a horse; another woman who was allergic to fish had an allergic reaction to a toy fish and empty fishbowl; and others reacted to uncontaminated air when suspecting it contained pollen.[36]

In support of the relationship between emotional factors (in particular, stress) and allergic reactions, recall the decrease in the effectiveness of the immunological system discussed previously. The reduced number of T-lymphocytes that results during stress means decreased effectiveness in controlling antigens, since it is these T cells that destroy the antigens (either by direct contact or by secreting

Figure 3.2 Stress and the immune response

toxins). Further, we know that the cortisol secreted by the adrenal cortex during the stress response decreases the effectiveness of histamine.

Some have concluded, therefore, that either the effects of stress on the immunological system decrease our ability to withstand an antigen (meaning a decreased allergic threshold) or, even in the absence of an antigen, can lead to an allergiclike response (see fig. 3.2). Some allergy sufferers, in particular asthmatics, are being taught relaxation techniques and breathing-control exercises to enable them to control their physiology during allergic reactions. As you will learn in the next chapter, such an approach to stress management is incomplete if it doesn't also include adjustments in the life situation to avoid stressors in the first place or change our perceptions of the stressors we encounter.

Rheumatoid Arthritis

Rheumatoid arthritis afflicts a large number of Americans (three times as many women as men) with inflammation and swelling in various body joints, which may proceed developmentally to be extremely painful and debilitating. The exact cause of this condition is unknown, though it is suspected of being related to the faulty functioning of the immune response.

The normal joint is lined with a synovial membrane, which secretes fluid to lubricate the joint. In rheumatoid arthritis, this synovial membrane multiplies exceedingly fast and creates swelling. This swelling can cause the membrane to enter the joint itself, eventually deteriorate the cartilage covering the ends of the bones, and perhaps even erode the bone itself. The latter stages of this disease process may be the development of scar tissue that immobilizes the joint and makes for knobbiness and deformity. The beginning of rheumatoid arthritis may be an infection of the synovial cells. For some reason, antibodies produced to fight this infection may attack healthy as well as unhealthy cells, leading to multiplication to replace the healthy cells. Then the process described above occurs.

It also appears that some people are hereditarily susceptible to rheumatoid arthritis. Approximately half of the sufferers of this condition have a blood protein called the **rheumatoid factor,** which is rare in nonarthritic people.

Since rheumatoid arthritis involves the body's turning on itself (an **autoimmune response**), it was hypothesized that a self-destructive personality may manifest itself through this disease. Although the evidence to support this hypothesis is not conclusive, several investigators have found personality differences between rheumatoid arthritis sufferers and others. Those afflicted with this disease have been found to be perfectionists who are self-sacrificing, masochistic, self-conscious, shy, and inhibited. Female rheumatoid patients were found to be nervous, moody, and depressed, with a history of being rejected by their mothers and having strict fathers.[37] It has been suggested that people with the rheumatoid factor who experience chronic stress become susceptible to rheumatoid arthritis. Their immunological system malfunctions, and their genetic predisposition to rheumatoid arthritis results in their developing the condition. We know, for instance, that stress can precipitate arthritic attacks. Since the standard treatment of cortisone brings with it the possible side effects of brittle bones, fat deposits, loss of muscular strength, ulcers, and psychosis, it would be very significant if stress management techniques were found to be effective in reducing the amount of cortisone needed.

Backache

Millions of people suffer backache and erroneously bemoan their posture or jobs. Certainly backache may result from lifting a heavy object incorrectly or from structural problems.[38] The vast majority of backache problems, however, are the result of muscular weakness or muscular bracing. One of the experts on backache, Dr. Henry Feffer, suggests exercise as the best preventive measure.[39]

As with tension headaches, bracing causes muscle to lose its elasticity and fatigue easily. Bracing may lead to muscle spasms and back pain. This constant muscular contraction is found in people who are competitive, angry, and apprehensive. Backaches have been found more frequently in people who have experienced a good deal of stress.[40]

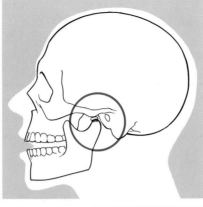

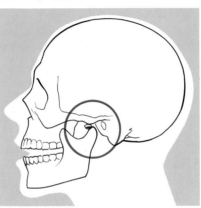

Figure 3.3 The disc separating the bones of the temporomandibular joint may pop loose, causing discomfort. Grinding the teeth as a result of stress can also lead to muscular pain and/or misalignment of the upper and lower jawbones.

The temporomandibular joint, which connects the upper and lower jaw, is a complex structure requiring the coordination of five muscles and several ligaments. When something interferes with the smooth operation of this joint, **temporomandibular (TMJ) syndrome** may develop (fig. 3.3). TMJ syndrome sufferers may have facial pain, clicking or popping sounds when they open or close their mouths, migraine headaches, earaches, ringing in the ears, dizziness, or sensitive teeth. It is most often women between the ages of twenty and forty who develop TMJ syndrome, although estimates vary widely as to how many in the population experience this condition (from 28 percent to 86 percent—obviously it is difficult to diagnose).[41] TMJ syndrome has many causes. It can develop as a result of malocclusion of the teeth, a blow to the head, gum chewing, nail biting, or jaw jutting. However, the most common cause is clenching or grinding of the teeth (termed *bruxism*) due to stress.[42] Treatment often consists of wearing an acrylic mouthpiece (an orthodontic splint)—either twenty-four hours a day or limited to sleep time—and/or the dentist adjusting the bite by selectively grinding the teeth, using crowns and bridges, or by orthodontia. In addition, stress reduction techniques such as biofeedback are taught to TMJ sufferers to relax the jaw and to limit teeth grinding (especially when done during the waking hours).[43]

The TMJ Syndrome

▼

Stressing and Unstressing

Two newspaper articles highlight the mind-body potential for causing illness and for alleviating it. The first one concerns "whistleblower stress"—the stress experienced by government employees who report wrongdoings and misuse of funds to people of authority. It seems that these whistleblowers are subsequently subjected to harassment and strain. They often become suicidal or manifest other signs of mental or physical disease.[44]

The second article describes the research of psychologist Paul Ekman, who has found that facial expressions elicit specific bodily responses. Facial expression of anger leads to an increased heart rate and skin temperature. Expression of fear, however, results in increased heart rate but a decrease in skin temperature. These changes occurred even when the person did not feel these emotions but only acted them out facially.[45]

Could treatment for whistleblowers someday include acting class? Will the rest of us also learn how to mimic emotion facially to make our bodies healthier?

It seems clear from the research literature that illness and disease may be stress-related. Such conditions as hypertension, stroke, heart disease, ulcers, migraines, tension headaches, cancer, allergies, asthma, hay fever, rheumatoid arthritis, backache, TMJ syndrome and others may develop because the body has changed its physiology because of what the mind has experienced. Recognizing the vast physiological changes associated with the stress response, it should not be surprising that poor health can result from stress. Likewise, that poor health is itself stressful and further aggravates the condition is only common sense. The conclusion that can be drawn from all of this is that managing stress can help prevent disease and illness and also serve as a valuable adjunct to therapy once they have developed. The wonders of the mind-body relationship are only beginning to be realized. The fruits from this knowledge are only beginning to be harvested. There are, though, some insights that you can use immediately to improve the quality of your life. These are presented in the next section of this book.

Summary

1. Psychosomatic disease involves the mind and the body; it is a real disease and not "just in the mind."
2. Psychogenic psychosomatic disease refers to a physical disease caused by emotional stress. There is no invasion of disease-causing microorganisms; the mind changes the physiology so that parts of the body break down.
3. Somatogenic psychosomatic disease occurs when the mind increases the body's susceptibility to some disease-causing microbes or some natural degenerative process.
4. Stress-related diseases include hypertension, stroke, coronary heart disease, ulcers, migraine headaches, tension headaches, cancer, allergies, asthma, hay fever, rheumatoid arthritis, backache, and TMJ syndrome.

5. Since stress increases blood pressure and serum cholesterol, it is no surprise that studies have found it associated with hypertension, stroke, and coronary heart disease.

6. Stress decreases the effectiveness of the immunological system by decreasing the number of T-lymphocytes. A less effective immunological system is suspected of resulting in allergic reactions, asthma attacks, and even cancer.

7. Stress results in increased muscle tension and bracing. It is this phenomenon that is thought to be the cause of tension headaches, backaches, and neck and shoulder pain.

Notes

1. John D. Curtis and Richard A. Detert, *How To Relax: A Holistic Approach to Stress Management* (Palo Alto: Mayfield Publishing Co., 1981), 134.

2. Daniel A. Girdano and George S. Everly, *Controlling Stress and Tension: A Holistic Approach* (Englewood Cliffs, N.J.: Prentice-Hall, 1979), 11–12.

3. Robert Ornstein and David Sobel, *The Healing Brain: A New Perspective on the Brain and Health* (New York: Simon and Schuster, 1987).

4. Sally Squires, "The Power of Positive Imagery: Visions to Boost Immunity," *American Health,* July 1987, 56–61.

5. Arthur A. Stone et al., "Evidence that Secretory IgA Antibody is Associated with Daily Mood," *Journal of Personality and Social Psychology* 52(1987):988–93.

6. "Women's Health: More Sniffles in Splitsville," *American Health,* July/August 1986, 96, 98.

7. "Putting the Heart in Cardiac Care," *Psychology Today,* April 1986, 18.

8. Meyer Friedman, Ray Rosenman, and V. Carroll, "Changes in the Serum Cholesterol and Blood Clotting Time in Men Subjected to Cycle Variation of Occupational Stress," *Circulation* 17(1958):852–64.

9. F. Dreyfuss and J. Czaczkes, "Blood Cholesterol and Uric Acid of Healthy Medical Students under Stress of an Examination," *Archives of Internal Medicine* 103(1959):708–11.

10. N. Clark, E. Arnold, and E. Foulds, "Serum Urate and Cholesterol Levels in Air Force Academy Cadets," *Aviation and Space Environmental Medicine* 46(1975):1044–48.

11. Larry A. Tucker, Galen E. Cole, and Glenn M. Friedman, "Stress and Serum Cholesterol: A Study of 7,000 Adult Males," *Health Values* 11(1987):34–39.

12. L. van Doornen and K. Orlebeke, "Stress, Personality and Serum Cholesterol Level," *Journal of Human Stress* 8(1982):24–29.

13. *Hypertension Update* (Chicago: Abbott Laboratories, 1976), 5.

14. Kenneth Lamott, *Escape from Stress: How to Stop Killing Yourself* (New York: G. P. Putnam, 1974), 40.

15. Lawrence W. Green, David M. Levine, and Sigrid Deeds, "Clinical Trials of Health Education for Hypertensive Outpatients: Design and Baseline Data," *Preventive Medicine* 4(1975):417–25.

16. Herbert Benson, *The Relaxation Response* (New York: William Morrow, 1975).

17. Ruanne K. Peters, Herbert Benson, and John M. Peters, "Daily Relaxation Response Breaks in a Working Population: II. Effects on Blood Pressure," *American Journal of Public Health* 67(1977):954–59.

18. Flanders Dunbar, *Psychosomatic Diagnosis* (New York: Harper, 1943).

19. Henry I. Russek and Linda G. Russek, "Is Emotional Stress an Etiological Factor in Coronary Heart Disease?" *Psychosomatics* 17(1976):63.

20. Meyer Friedman and Ray H. Rosenman, *Type A Behavior and Your Heart* (Greenwich, Conn.: Fawcett, 1974).

21. Jack Sparacino, "The Type A Behavior Pattern: A Critical Assessment," *Journal of Human Stress* 5(1979):37–51.

22. Hans Selye, *The Stress of Life* (New York: McGraw-Hill Book Co., 1956).

23. Erich Lindemann, "Symptomatology and Management of Acute Grief," in *Stress and Coping: An Anthology,* ed. Alan Monet and Richard S. Lazarus (New York: Columbia University Press, 1977), 342.

24. Walter McQuade and Ann Aikman, *Stress* (New York: Bantam Books, 1974), 56.

25. B. Fier, "Recession Is Causing Dire Illness," *Moneysworth,* 23 June 1975.

26. Kenneth R. Pelletier, *Mind as Healer, Mind as Slayer* (New York: Dell Publishing Co., 1977), 171.

27. Ibid., 171–72.

28. J. D. Sargent, E. E. Green, and E. D. Walters, "Preliminary Report on the Use of Autogenic Feedback Techniques in the Treatment of Migraine and Tension Headaches," *Psychosomatic Medicine* 35(1973):129–35.

29. Thomas H. Budzynski, Johann Stoyva, and C. Adler, "Feedback-Induced Muscle Relaxation: Application to Tension Headache," *Journal of Behavior Therapy and Experimental Psychiatry* 1(1970):205–11.

30. Thomas H. Budzynski et al., "EMG Biofeedback and Tension Headache: A Controlled Outcome Study," *Psychosomatic Medicine* 35(1973): 484–96.

31. Steven F. Maier and Mark Laudenslager, "Stress and Health: Exploring the Links," *Psychology Today,* August 1985, 44–49.

32. V. Riley, "Mouse Mammary Tumors: Alternation of Incidence as Apparent Function of Stress," *Science* 189(1975):465–67.

33. Carl O. Simonton and Stephanie Simonton, "Belief Systems and Management of the Emotional Aspects of Malignancy," *Journal of Transpersonal Psychology* 7(1975):29–48.

34. Pelletier, *Mind as Healer,* 134.

35. Lawrence LeShan and R. E. Worthington, "Some Recurrent Life-History Patterns Observed in Patients with Malignant Disease," *Journal of Nervous and Mental Disorders* 124(1956):460–65.

36. McQuade and Aikman, *Stress,* 69.

37. R. H. Moos and George F. Solomon, "Psychologic Comparisons between Women with Rheumatoid Arthritis and Their Nonarthritic Sisters," *Psychosomatic Medicine* 2(1965):150.

38. Esther Wanning and Michael Castleman, "Healing Your Aching Back," *Medical Self-Care,* Fall 1984, 26–29.

39. "How To Prevent Back Trouble," *U.S. News & World Report,* 14 April 1975, 45–48.

40. T. S. Holmes and Thomas H. Holmes, "Short-term Intrusions into the Life-Style Routine," *Journal of Psychosomatic Research* 14(1970): 121–32.

41. Robin Marantz Henig, "The Jaw Out of Joint," *Washington Post, Health,* 9 February 1988, 16.

42. Gini Hartzmark, "Teeth," *Ms.,* May 1985, 106–8.

43. Mary Tasner, "TMJ," *Medical Self-Care,* November–December 1986, 47–50.

44. Jack Anderson, "Whistleblower Stress," *Washington Post,* 24 March 1985, C7.

45. Sally Squires, "When You're Smiling, the Whole Immune System Smiles with You," *Washington Post,* 9 January 1985, 16.

PART II

▼

General
Applications:
Life-Situation
and Perception
Interventions

4

Intervention

A young boy asked his older brother where babies came from. The older brother told him that babies came from the stork. Seeking verification of this shocking revelation, the young boy asked his father where babies came from. The father said that babies came from the stork. Not wanting to be impolite but still not completely satisfied, the boy approached the wise old sage of the family, his grandfather, and asked him where babies came from. The grandfather, following the party line, told him that babies came from the stork. The next day in school the young boy related his conversations with his brother, father, and grandfather to the teacher and his classmates, concluding that there hadn't been normal sexual relations in his family for at least three generations.

So as to prevent any miscommunication regarding stress management, part 1 of this book has provided you with information about the nature of stress, examples of stressors, the manner in which the body reacts to stressors, and illnesses and diseases associated with stress. You are, therefore, more prepared to see stress management as a complex of activities rather than something accomplished simply by following some guru. There are no simple "storklike" answers to coping with stress. There is, however, a comprehensive stress management system that you can employ to control stress and tension. This chapter presents a model of stress and its relationship to illness, and stress management techniques are seen as interventions within this model. **Interventions,** then, are activities to block a stressor from resulting in negative consequences such as psychological discomfort, anxiety, illness, or disease. You'll soon see that comprehensive stress management is sensible, logical, and possible, and that you can manage your own stress.

A Model of Stress

Stress begins with a life situation that knocks you (gently or abruptly) out of balance. You are nudged or shoved into disequilibrium and need to right yourself. This life situation could be a change in temperature, a threat from another person, the death of a loved one, or some other change in your life to which you need to adapt.

However, we all know that the same situation presented to different people may result in different reactions. That is because different people will interpret the situation differently. This is termed their **cognitive appraisal** and, as we will see later, can be controlled.

Some people may view the death of a loved one, for example, as terrible and dwell on that loss. Others may also view the death of a loved one as terrible but think about the nice times experienced with the one who has died. A life situation to which you must adapt is therefore a necessary but not sufficient component of stress. What is also necessary is your perception of that life situation as stressful.

So far, then, we have a life situation that is perceived (or cognitively appraised) as distressing. This is represented in figure 4.1. What occurs next is an emotional reaction to the distressing life event. Such feelings as fear, anger, or insecurity, or feelings of being rushed, overwhelmed, frustrated, or helpless may be results of perceiving a life situation as stressful.

Life situation

Perceived as stressful

Figure 4.1
Perception of a life
situation

These feelings lead to physiological arousal. As described in detail in chapter 2, stress reactivity includes increases in serum cholesterol, respiratory and heart rates, muscle tension, blood pressure, and blood glucose, along with decreases in the effectiveness of the immunological system, strength of the cardiac muscle, digestion, and histamine effectiveness. If physiological arousal is chronic, prolonged, or goes unabated, illness or disease may result. In addition to illness or disease (be it physical or psychological), stress can lead to poor performance in school or on the job, poor interpersonal relationships, or other such negative effects. The stress model is now complete and appears in figure 4.2.

Let's follow a person down this road to the consequences of prolonged stress to demonstrate the functioning of this model. Suppose you work for the automobile industry and are relatively well-adjusted. Your job is pleasing and you've been employed at the same location for eight years. You have become comfortable interacting with your fellow workers, and you know when the coffee breaks occur, the best routes to travel to and from work, and to whom to be especially nice. Unfortunately, the economy takes a turn for the worse. Credit becomes tight and interest rates rise. People stop buying cars, and your company decides to lay off several hundred employees. Your pink slip appears in the envelope with your paycheck. Thus, a life situation has presented itself to which you need to adapt.

You consider this situation earth-shattering! How will you pay the rent, buy food, pay medical bills? How will you occupy your time? What will people think of you? Can you get another job? How should you begin to look for one? Questions, questions, concerns, concerns. You have now progressed to the second component of the model: you perceive being fired as distressing. Recognize, though, that not everyone will perceive this same event as distressing. Some of your fellow employees may be saying:

1. It's not good being fired, but I really do need a rest. I've been working too hard lately.
2. I'm going to use this opportunity to spend more time with my children.
3. I think I'll take advantage of this situation by going back to school. I always wanted the time to be able to do that.

These people have set up a roadblock between the life situation and their perceptions of that situation. They have changed their cognitive appraisal of being fired. They are not perceiving the event as a major catastrophe and, therefore, it will not become one.

Figure 4.2 Stress model

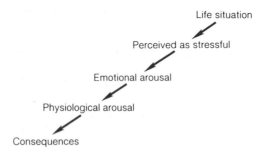

Life situation

Perceived as stressful

Emotional arousal

Physiological arousal

Consequences

You, however, have perceived being fired as traumatic and subsequently are aroused emotionally. You feel *fear* about the future. You become *unsure* of your self-worth. You are *angry* at the boss for choosing you as one of those fired. You're *frustrated* at the whole situation and *confused* about what to do next. These feelings result in physiological arousal. You wind up with more blood fats roaming within your blood vessels. You perspire more, breathe differently, brace your muscles, secrete more hydrochloric acid in your stomach, have less lymphocytes in your blood to combat infectious agents, and so forth. If you don't use these built-up stress products in some way, and if this situation and your reaction to it remain the same, you may contract a stress-related illness.

Setting Up Roadblocks

Once the progression from a life situation through perception, emotion, physiological arousal, and vulnerability to disease and other consequences is understood, it is then possible to intervene short of these consequences. Intervention entails setting up roadblocks at various points on the stress theory model. Since this model includes sequential phases with each phase dependent upon the full development of the previous phase, any interruption of this sequence will short-circuit the process. For example, even though a life situation requiring adaptation presents itself to you, a roadblock between that life situation and the next phase (perceiving it as stressful) could be set up. This roadblock might consist of pre-scribed medications (sedatives, tranquilizers, depressants), illicit drugs (marijuana, cocaine), or an insistence on your part that you just will not allow yourself to view this situation as disturbing. Regarding the last option, you might decide to focus upon the positive aspect of the situation (there is something good about *every* situation, even if that "good" is that things can't get any worse). A roadblock between the perception phase and the emotion phase can also be established. Relaxation techniques are also excellent ways to keep emotional reactions from leading to prolonged physiological arousal. Once physiological arousal occurs, a roadblock between it and poor health must consist of some form of physical activity that uses the built-up stress products. Remember that at the point of physiological arousal your body has prepared itself with the fight-or-flight response. A physical activity (for example, jogging) will use the body's preparedness rather than allow the state of arousal to lead to poor health.

The Fourteen-Day Stress Diet

Day one: Have an argument with your spouse or lover or both. This seemingly simple and common stress situation was selected to start you on the program gradually without causing serious side effects, such as alcoholism or an urge to fly to Bolivia.

Day two: Go an entire night without sleep. Since the diet inhibits sleep as a rule, you will never make up the lost night's sleep and future stress periods will be greatly intensified.

Day three: Spend the day with a friend who recently gave up smoking. An entire day around someone who will not stop telling you how good he/she feels after forty-eight hours without tobacco will be extremely stressful. You will also note that your appetite has almost completely disappeared by now.

Day four: Have several cavities filled by a dentist nicknamed "Jackhammer." The anticipation alone will melt away that ugly fat.

Day five: Have your sixteen-year-old daughter ask you to explain the difference between morning sickness and flu.

Days six and seven: Force yourself to consume the "Three C's"—coffee, cola, and chocolate—and nothing else. The accumulation of caffeine will do wonders to your stress levels during the second week.

Day eight: Run out of gas at 3:00 A.M. in the "bad" part of town. (If you have a CB radio in your car, leave it at home.) By now you should be sporting that fashionable gaunt look, particularly around the neck and face.

Day nine: Go see your son or daughter in a fourth-grade production of *War and Peace.*

Day ten: Let your boss find a half-empty Scotch bottle in your desk. Or, if you don't work, let your spouse find the same bottle under your pillow. Fear of the unemployment line, whether corporate or domestic, makes for good dieting.

Day eleven: Bet your entire paycheck on the lottery. If you lose, and you should, worrying about how to pay the mortgage will be wonderful for your waistline. And if you win, worry about the IRS.

Day twelve: Eat oysters in a month without an *r* in it or order a cheeseburger in a Chinese restaurant. By now you will have lost most of your weight and you should start to regain a passing acquaintance with food.

Day thirteen: If you can still drive in a straight line, commute to work during rush hour while two of the three lanes of the highway are closed for repair.

Day fourteen: Visit your physician and listen to him describe the way your body has deteriorated over the past two weeks.

At this point you should begin your Stress Diet Maintenance Plan, which includes one low-level crisis each day and two major anxiety attacks each week. Do not, under any circumstances, begin the two-week Stress Diet again for at least three years. If you should become ill during the fourteen days and try to blame the Stress Diet, be advised that the developer of this plan has the best lawyers available and has arranged his affairs so that he cannot be sued successfully. The stress from any such attempt will simply help your diet.

Comprehensive Stress Management

Some *incomplete* stress management programs teach participants only one, or just a few, stress management skills. Consequently, they are prepared to set up a roadblock at only one location on the stress theory model. Some programs teach people meditation, yoga, or time management. To understand the reason these programs are incomplete, you must first be introduced to the sievelike aspect of the stress theory model.

At each level on the model it is only possible to filter out a portion of the stress experience. Consequently, a roadblock (intervention technique) employed at only one place on the road will not stop *all* the "bad guys" from getting through. Each roadblock will stop some "bad guys," but no *one* roadblock will stop all it encounters. Each roadblock, then, is like a sieve that sifts and filters out some stress but allows some to pass through to the next phase of the stress theory model. It follows, then, that programs teaching only one or just a few stress management skills are helping their participants to some extent but not to the greatest degree possible.

Complete, comprehensive stress management includes intervention at *all* phases of the stress theory model and *several* means of intervening at *each* of these locations. As you can see from the table of contents of this book, chapter 5 through chapter 13 do just that. Each of those chapters focuses upon one phase of the stress theory model and describes several ways to sift out some of the stress experienced at that phase. Your goal, however, will not be to eliminate all of your stress. Remember from our earlier discussion that there is an optimum amount of stress. It is impossible, and undesirable, to eliminate all stress. Complete stress management does not subscribe to that goal but conveys the nature of eustress to its participants.

Eustress and the Model

So far we have focused upon the negative consequences of stress: illness, disease, poor performance, and impaired interpersonal relationships. However, we can use the same stress model to better understand the positive consequences of stress.

An example of eustress will make this point more clear. When I teach stress management, the class is conducted informally but includes most of the topics discussed in this book. A glance at the table of contents will show the array and number of topics studied. It would be easy for these topics to be lost and for their interconnectedness to be overlooked. My dilemma was how to keep the class interesting and yet encourage students to study the content so as to realize how, for example, time management and biofeedback (two seemingly unrelated subjects) were cousins in the same stress management family.

I decided on a final examination as the vehicle by which students would be required to deal with the array of topics studied as a meaningful whole. The test, then, served as an eustressor—it led to stress for the students who sought to do well on the exam and resulted in more learning than would have otherwise been accomplished. The stress was beneficial and useful (more learning occurred) and was, therefore, positive—eustress.

Using the stress model to explain the positive consequences in this example, the test is the life situation. Next, my students interpret the test as a threat and perceive it as stressful. That perception results in such emotions as fear, self-doubt, and worry, which lead to physiological arousal. However, because of this stress my students study longer and, consequently, learn more. The positive outcome is that they know more about stress and how to manage it than they would have if they hadn't experienced this situation, and they do better on the test than they might have otherwise. So you see, the stress model can be used to explain both the negative and the positive consequences of stress.

I'll bet you have experienced stress that, when it was over, made you consider yourself better for the experience. Either it was a positive life event that required significant adjustment (a move to a grass shack in Hawaii) or a more threatening event that led you to make important changes in your life (a brush with death that made you reorganize your priorities). In any case, you were stressed "for the better." That is eustress. The following are some other examples of eustressors:

1. Having to make a presentation before a group of people and preparing better because of the stress
2. Asking someone out on a date and rehearsing a better way of doing it because of the stress
3. Having someone you love tell you the things he or she dislikes about you and using that information to make you a better you

Taking Control

If there is only one concept by which you remember this book, I would wish it to be that *you are in much greater control over yourself than you ever realized.* Managing stress is really just exercising that control rather than giving it up to others or to your environment. Let me give you an example of the kind of control you have over yourself. Recall an occasion when you became angry with someone. As vividly as you can, remember what preceded your anger. What happened earlier that day? What was the weather like? What were you anticipating? What was your previous relationship with that person? What did that person do that made you angry? Also recall your angry response in all its detail. That is, how did you feel, what did you want to do, what did you actually do, and how did it all work out?

So often we hear others say, "So-and-so made me angry!" No one can make you angry. Rather, you *allow* yourself to be angered by what so-and-so has said or done. When you describe your behavior as dependent upon another's, you have given up control of that behavior *to* that other person. To demonstrate this point for yourself, manipulate the variables in the situation you just recalled. Instead of a rainy day, imagine it to have been warm and sunny. Instead of a person with whom you have had a bad relationship doing or saying the thing about which you became angry, imagine it to have been the person you love most. Further, imagine that you received word of getting straight A's in school, or a promotion, or a salary raise, or some other nice event just prior to the situation about which you became angered. Now to summarize, you've awakened to a nice, warm, sunny day. When you arrived at work you were told you were promoted and given a substantial increase in salary. Soon afterward, a person whom you so dearly love does or says X (X = the event about which you became angered). Responding to the situation as it is now described in the same manner in which you responded to the original situation probably seems incongruous. The point is that the actual event does not necessarily have anger as its consequence. The anger was brought to that situation by you—not by the event or the other person. On some days, the same event would not have resulted in your becoming angry. You may have been having a great day and telling yourself it was so great that nothing was going to ruin it. And, what's more, nothing did! You are in charge of your behavior. You may not be able to get other people to change what they say or do, but certainly you can change how you react to what they say or do. **You are in charge of you.**

In the space provided, rewrite each of the statements to indicate that *you* are really in control. The first statement serves as an example.

1. You make me upset.

   When you do that I allow myself to become upset.

2. It was my insecurity that forced me to do that.

   _____

3. I was so frightened, I was helpless.

   _____

4. It's just a rotten habit that I can't break.

   _____

5. I'm just destined to be a failure.

   _____

6. If I were articulate, I'd be better at my job.

   _____

7. I was successful because I work well under pressure.

   _____

8. I'm the way I am because of my upbringing and parents.

   _____

Generalizing this concept of control to stress management, it is *your* decision whether or not to increase your blood pressure, your heart rate, or your muscle tension. It is *your* decision whether or not to become frightened or anxious, or to vomit at the sides of roads. It is *your* decision whether or not you will regularly practice relaxation techniques (for example, meditation). The practice of these techniques is a good example of taking control and assuming responsibility for (owning) your own behavior. Students and participants in workshops I conduct often tell me they would like to meditate but don't have the time. Hogwash. I don't care if you have ten screaming, unruly teenage werewolves at home and don't think you can find the place, the time, or a quiet-enough environment to meditate. I've heard it all before. The *time* you already have. You have just chosen to use it for something else. The *quiet* you can get. I recall meditating in a car

in the garage of the apartment house in which my parents lived, because their two-bedroom apartment with four adults, two children, and several neighbor children creating dissonance (one screeching violin strings and the other hammering the keys of an irreparably out-of-tune piano) was not conducive to relaxation.

The *place* is also available, since you can meditate anywhere. I've meditated on airplanes, under a tree on a golf course in the Bahamas, and once in the front seat of a car my wife was driving at sixty miles per hour on a highway in Florida.

In any case, you are in charge of what you do or do not do to manage your stress. Further, you are responsible for that decision and must accept its consequences. The intervention skills presented in this book can help you to control the stress and tension you experience. Whether they do that depends upon whether you learn these skills, practice them, and incorporate them into your daily routine.

It would be dysfunctional to employ stress management techniques in a stressful way—and yet, that is not uncommon. Trying very hard to control stress will, in and of itself, create stress. Since you have not bothered to use comprehensive stress management for the many years of your life, don't rush into it now. Read slowly and carefully. Try the skills; use those that work for you and discard the others. If you are under medical care, check the appropriateness of these techniques and skills with your physician. You may need less medication, or certain procedures may be contraindicated for one with your condition. Enjoy managing stress rather than making it just one more thing to do. Use comprehensive stress management to free up, rather than clutter up, your day.

Making a Commitment

While you are advised not to rush into this stress management system, a beginning should be made immediately. This beginning may only consist of a commitment to read this book so as to learn more about stress and its control. That first step is significant, however, since subsequent steps depend upon it. Since stress reactivity that is chronic, prolonged, or goes unabated may result in your becoming ill, the longer you wait to begin controlling your stress, the less healthy you can expect to be. If you're healthy now, you want to maintain that status. If you're presently ill and that illness is exacerbated by stress, you can move toward health by managing that stress. Are you willing to begin? How much are you willing to do? Behaviorists know that behavior that is reinforced will be repeated, whereas behavior that is punished tends to be eliminated. Determine your commitment to managing your stress by completing a contract with yourself; you can use the contract presented here. Notice that it contains a reward for accomplishing what you contract to do, and a punishment for not living up to the contract.

▼

Contract of Commitment

I, _____ , am concerned about the effects of stress upon my health and have decided to learn how to better manage the stress I encounter. Therefore, I commit myself to completely reading this book, practicing the skills presented, and incorporating at least two of these skills into my daily routine.

If I have met this commitment by _____
(two months from now)

I will reward myself by _____
(buying something you would not ordinarily buy, or

_____ .
doing something you would not ordinarily do)

If I have not met this commitment by the date above, I will punish myself by

_____ .
(depriving yourself of something you really enjoy)

_____   _____
(Signature)   (Date)

Now don't make this contract too stressful. Try to be realistic. Here are some examples of rewards you might use:

buying tickets to the theatre
buying a new coat
restringing your tennis racket with gut
lying in the sun the whole day
eating dinner with your fingers
asking someone you love to pamper you

Here are some possible punishments:

not watching television for one week
not eating ice cream for three weeks
not playing bridge for one month
eating alone for four days

Well, there's no time like the present; a stitch in time saves nine; he who hesitates is lost; the early bird . . . **the sooner the better.**

Summary

1. Interventions are activities designed to block a stressor from resulting in negative consequences such as illness or disease. Stress management consists of the use of these interventions.
2. Stress begins with a life situation that knocks you out of balance. However, for the stress response to develop, this situation has to be perceived and cognitively appraised as distressing.
3. When life situations are perceived and cognitively appraised as distressing, emotional reactions such as fear, anger, or insecurity develop. These emotional reactions then lead to physiological arousal.
4. Physiological arousal that is chronic, prolonged, or goes unabated can lead to negative consequences such as illness or disease, poor performance, or impaired interpersonal relationships.
5. Stress management involves "setting up roadblocks" on the road leading from life situations through perception, emotional arousal, and physiological arousal, and ending at negative consequences.
6. Incomplete stress management programs teach only one, or just a few, stress management skills. Comprehensive programs teach means of intervening at each level of the stress model.
7. Stress that leads to positive consequences is called eustress. Eustress involves change which still requires adaptation but which is growth producing and welcome. A test can be an example of an eustressor when concern for a good grade results in your studying and learning more.
8. You are in much greater control of you than you ever realized. Managing stress is really just exercising that control, rather than giving it up to others or to your environment.

Life-Situation Interventions—Intrapersonal

One task of this chapter can best be presented in contrast to the story of the conscientious science teacher who always conducted demonstrations so students would better understand science. One day, to the students' surprise, the teacher's pocket made a gulping sound. After 2½ gulps, one freckle-faced, red-haired student asked what was in the pocket, and did it always make that disgusting sound? The teacher reached into the pocket and, in the midst of the next "gulp," presented a frog. Placing the frog on the desk, the teacher yelled, "Jump!" and, magically it seemed, the frog jumped. Instructing the students to observe carefully, another yell of "Jump!" resulted in the same reaction—the frog jumped. The students were almost in shock after what next occurred. Reaching into the other pocket, the teacher pulled out a scissor and, before anyone could say a word, proceeded to cut off the frog's legs. "Now, carefully observe the frog's reaction this time," the teacher instructed just prior to his next yell of "Jump!" Lo and behold, this time the frog did not jump! Since the students still had the sound of scissor-against-frog-leg in mind, they were unable to draw a conclusion from the experiment. Upset but undaunted, the teacher concluded by stating: "You see, when you cut off a frog's legs, it loses its hearing."

We will make better sense of scientific findings than this science teacher. In this chapter we will relate the various aspects of stress management at the life-situation phase to each other in a cohesive, sensible manner. The topics presented all relate to intrapersonal matters; that is, what is between you and you rather than between you and others. Our conclusion will be more sensible than the science teacher's and more useful to your own life. Rather than bits and pieces of ways to control stress and tension, a management system for adjusting your life is described—a system that will be meaningful and relevant for you and will make you healthier and happier.

Eliminating Unnecessary Stressors

The higher on the stress theory model you can siphon off stressors, the more likely it is that you will be able to manage the stress in your life. You would think if you eliminated all stressors from your life, and could, you would never experience stress and, therefore, never become ill from it. Since that goal is both impossible

Stressor	Reactions		Means of coping	Means of coping better
	Physical	Psychological		
1. Routine				
a.				
b.				
2. Unique				
a.				
b.				

Relaxation techniques tried	Effectiveness of technique
1.	
2.	
3.	

Ailments

Physical   Psychological

Figure 5.1 The stress diary

and undesirable, your attempt at stress management at the top level of the model (life situation) should be to eliminate as many distressors as is feasible. To accomplish this end, this chapter presents you with introspective activities for identifying unnecessary stressors in your life and eliminating them.

In my course "Controlling Stress and Tension," students keep a diary for three weeks. Why don't you keep a diary as well? A sample page appears in figure 5.1. This diary must include seven components for each day:

1. Stressors for that day
    a. Routine stressors (experienced often)
    b. Unique stressors (seldom encountered)
2. Reactions to *each* stressor encountered
    a. Physical reactions (e.g., perspiration, increased pulse rate, muscle tension)
    b. Psychological reactions (e.g., fear, anxiety, confusion)
3. Means of coping with *each* stressor

4. Better means of coping that might have been attempted
5. Relaxation techniques tried that day
6. Effectiveness of these relaxation techniques
7. Ailments during that day
    a. Physical (e.g., headache, stomach discomfort, backache)
    b. Psychological (e.g., anxiety attack, feelings of insecurity, sense of being rushed)

In addition to reporting how tedious it becomes to keep a diary for three weeks, students say they value this learning experience highly among others with which they have ever been presented. To understand this reaction requires an explanation of how we use the diary once the three-week period is concluded. The contents of the diary are considered data from which generalizations (or patterns) about each student and each student's life can be gleaned. Rather than focusing upon one occurrence or even one day, we try to identify consistent features that will provide insight into how each student interacts with the stress of his or her life. To accomplish this end, we ask the following questions:

1. What stressors do you frequently experience?
2. Do you need or want to continue experiencing these stressors?
3. If you do not, which routine stressors can you eliminate? How?
4. How does your body typically react to stressors?
5. How does your psyche typically react to stressors?
6. Can your body's or mind's reactions to stress teach you ways to identify stress early in its progression so as to make it less harmful?
7. Are there any coping techniques that you use more than others?
8. Do these techniques work for you or against you?
9. Are there any coping techniques that you believe would be helpful but don't use often enough?
10. How can you get yourself to use these infrequently used coping techniques more often?
11. Are any particular relaxation techniques more effective for you than others?
12. Are you experiencing difficulty in employing a relaxation technique? No time? No place? No quiet?
13. How can you better organize your life to obtain periods of relaxation?
14. Are there any physical ailments that you usually experience either preceding or following stressful events?
15. Are there any psychological ailments that you usually experience either preceding or following stressful events?
16. Are there ways to prevent either physiological or psychological ailments developing from your stress?
17. Summarize what you will *do* as a result of recording and analyzing this diary. Be as specific as you can; for example, rather than state that you will relax more, describe the time of day, place, and method of relaxation.

After three weeks ask and answer the previous seventeen questions. You will probably gain much insight into your stress experience and be able to adjust your life to experience fewer stressors. What you will be doing is taking charge of your life to prevent stressors from leading to poor health by eliminating unnecessary stressors before they even begin their journey down the stress road. The more stressors you can eliminate in this fashion, the less likely it is that stress will cause illness or disease for you. The importance of eliminating unnecessary stressors will become even more evident in the section that follows.

Nutrition and Stress

The relationship between nutrition and stress remains unclear. This is definitely one stress-related area fertile for research. However, we do know that certain food substances can produce a stresslike response, that other substances provided by foods can be depleted by stress, and that certain stress-related illnesses can be exacerbated by dietary habits. Before ways to eliminate nutrition stressors are recommended, a discussion of nutrition per se seems in order.

To be nutritionally healthy you need to eat a balanced diet. A balanced diet is one which contains a variety of foods which will, therefore, provide you with a variety of nutrients (proteins, carbohydrates, fats, minerals, vitamins, and water). To assure you get the appropriate variety of foods, you should eat foods from the following four food groups daily, in the amounts cited in parentheses: milk and milk products (two servings); meat, fish, and poultry (two servings); fruits and vegetables (four servings); and grains (four servings). Being malnourished means you either eat too little of the recommended foods, too much, or ingest some nutrients in inappropriate amounts.

In addition to being malnourished, ingesting too much or too little of particular nutrients can lead to illnesses that in and of themselves can cause a great deal of stress. The relationship of nutrition to heart disease and cancer will be discussed as examples here because of the prevalence of those conditions in our society. However, there are many other illnesses that are also related to nutrition.

Coronary heart disease results when the arteries supplying the heart with oxygen are clogged so that blood cannot pass through; the heart, therefore, does not get the needed oxygen. As a result, parts of the heart may die and, if those parts are in certain places in the heart or are extensive throughout the heart, the victim may die. In chapter 3 we noted a caution regarding ignoring the effects of stress on coronary heart disease. However, it is generally agreed that diets high in saturated fats (derived from red meats, whole milk, butter) will increase the amount of cholesterol in the blood. The cholesterol then accumulates on the walls of the arteries and coronary heart disease develops. As a result, diets should be restricted in saturated fats. One way to do this is to substitute monosaturated fats (for example, peanut and olive oils) or polyunsaturated fats (for example, liquid vegetable oils such as corn, soybean, or safflower oils) for saturated fats.

Cancer has also been found to be associated with diet. The data indicate that people are more prone to developing certain cancers if their diets are low in fiber (for example, bread, cereals, flours, fruits, vegetables, nuts, and popcorn) or high in saturated fats. To prevent certain cancers, the American Cancer Society recommends diets low in fats (to prevent breast, colon, and prostate cancers); diets high in fiber (to prevent colon cancer); high in vitamins A and C (to prevent larynx, esophagus, stomach, and lung cancers); sufficient amounts of cruciferous vegetables such as broccoli, cauliflower, or brussels sprouts (to prevent digestive tract cancers); and limits on the use of alcohol (to prevent mouth, larynx, throat, esophagus, and liver cancers).[1] In addition, obesity increases the risk of uterine, cervical, and breast cancers in women. It seems that with more body fat, women produce more estrogen and thereby increase their chances of contracting one of these forms of cancer.[2]

Although it is desirable to control your body weight, an overemphasis on dieting can itself be unhealthy. Sometimes, for example, obesity can be in the mind of the beholder. That is, we are bombarded with media images of the ideal body type as being thin with all the curves in just the right places. Consequently, when our bodies do not measure up to this ideal (at least mine doesn't), we become distressed and vow to diet that extra weight off. The popularity and abundance of diet books attest to the desire of Americans to lose weight. Unfortunately, some of these diets are themselves unhealthy and therefore can lead to even more stress. An evaluation of some of the more popular of these diets appears in table 5.1. In addition, for some people, this obsession with being thin takes the form of excessive weight loss (a condition called *anorexia nervosa*) or binge eating and purposely vomiting afterward (a condition called *bulimia*).[3] The great majority of anorexics and bulimics are women, although there are a number of men who suffer from these conditions as well. Since anorexia nervosa and bulimia can eventually lead to severe illness and/or death, if you know someone with one of these conditions, you ought to encourage them to seek professional help as soon as possible. If you find you are obsessive about your own weight and you really needn't be (see table 5.2), you might want to consult with a counselor at your campus health center or with your personal physician.

Furthermore, certain food *substances* have particular relationships with stress. For example, a group of food substances can actually produce a stresslike response. These substances are called **psuedostressors** or **sympathomimetics.** That is, they mimic sympathetic nervous system stimulation. Colas, coffee, tea, and chocolate that contain caffeine are examples of sympathomimetic agents. Tea also contains theobromine and theophylline which are sympathomimetics. These substances increase metabolism, make one highly alert, and result in the release of stress hormones, which elevate the heart rate and blood pressure. In addition to creating a pseudostress response, sympathomimetics make the nervous system more reactive, and thereby more likely to have a stressor elicit a stress response. Nicotine (found in tobacco) is also a sympathomimetic agent.

Another way nutrition is related to stress is by the effect of stress on *vitamins*. The production of cortisol (the stress hormone produced by the adrenal cortex) requires the use of vitamins.[4] Consequently, chronic stress can deplete the vitamins we take into our bodies. In particular, the B complex vitamins (thiamine, riboflavin, niacin, pantothenic acid, and pyridoxine hydrochloride) and vitamin C seem to be the most affected. A deficiency in these vitamins can result in anxiety, depression, insomnia, muscular weakness, and stomach upset. Not only may stress deplete these vitamins, but since these vitamins are used to produce adrenal

Table 5.1
Summary and Evaluation of Widely Publicized Diets

Diet	Special Claims	Allowable Foods	Evaluation
Gimmick Diets			
Pritikin Program	Low-fat and exercise combine to produce weight loss.	Whole grains, vegetables, legumes, fruit; snack on raw vegetables all day and 1 portion from dairy, grain, and fruit groups	High fiber content causes gas and diarrhea; protein is insufficient; difficult to follow; contains one-quarter normal fat intake; fairly well-rounded; devoid of cholesterol, salt, and artificial sweeteners.
Save Your Life Diet	Fiber in foods leads to weight loss, which increases by rapid transport of food through the digestive tract.	Vegetable group emphasized, and 1 cup of bran added to six foods; meats and eggs deemphasized	Side effects may include gassiness, frequent defecation, and soft, bulky stools. Too much fiber binds to some trace minerals and may cause them to pass through the system without being absorbed.
Nibbling Diet	Eating smaller portions will result in fewer calories than eating three meals per day and snacking.	Low carbohydrate, high protein, and nutritious snacking	With careful calorie counting, weight loss is likely to occur, but difficult to get a balanced diet, and not easy to follow for long periods of time.
Cellulite Diet	Promises removal of the "fat gone wrong" (so-called fat, water, and toxic wastes).	High in fruits and vegetables, low fat and carbohydrate intake; involves kneading the skin, massage under heat lamps to melt the fat away	No medical condition known as cellulite exists. The fat being described as cellulite cannot be eliminated by a combination of diet and massage.
Cooper's Fabulous Fructose Diet	"Fructose" (sugar from fruit) is used to help lose weight, maintain constant blood-sugar level, keep up energy, and satisfy the sweet tooth.	High protein intake and 1.0 to 1.5 oz fructose supplement	Weight loss may occur from caloric deficit, not from use of a fructose supplement. Fructose does not help you consume fewer calories and contains the same number of calories as sucrose (4 per gram).
Lecithin, Vinegar, Kelp, and B_6 Diet	Grapefruit and lecithin burn off fat by regulating metabolic rate.	One teaspoon of vinegar with each meal of normal foods	No one claim (grapefruit or vinegar) can be supported.
The Body Clock Diet	When you eat is nearly twice as important as the number of calories you consume. Lose by eating "breakfast like a king, lunch like a prince, and dinner like a pauper."	Any type of food can be consumed or any diet adapted to the body clock diet.	There is no convincing evidence that eating the big meals early in the day will cause significant weight loss without very close calorie counting. The somewhat hidden implication that calories don't count is inaccurate.

Table 5.1
(continued)

Diet	Special Claims	Allowable Foods	Evaluation
High-Protein Diets Women Doctor's Diet for Women New You Diet Doctor's Quick Weight Loss Diet Complete Scarsdale Medical Diet Miracle Diet for Fast Weight Loss	"Specific dynamic action" (SDA) is the basis for some high-protein diets: extra calories burned through the process of digesting protein.	Lean meats and poultry, fish, seafood, eggs, and low-fat cheese; no calorie counting	SDA has no basis. Protein calories are no more or less important than carbohydrate calories. Diets are boring; hard to follow; lacking in vitamins, minerals, and fiber; and can increase blood serum cholesterol levels; dangerous for pregnant women and a poor choice for anyone who wants weight loss to be permanent after a change in eating habits. **Ketosis**—a condition in which there is an excess of **ketones** (metabolized fatty acids) secreted by the liver—can be dangerous to some people.
High-Fat Diets Dr. Atkin's Super-Energy Diet Calories Don't Count Diet	In the absence of carbohydrates, stored fat is mobilized and burned for energy. Fat-mobilizing hormone (FMH) is said to be activated to fuel your body with the fat stores.	Unlimited fatty foods (bacon, meat, mayonnaise, rich cream sauces, and the like); no calorie counting and avoidance of fruits, vegetables, sugars, starches, bread, and potatoes	Carbohydrates are needed to oxidize fat completely. If in short supply, fat cannot be used completely and fatigue occurs. Ketone bodies build up in the blood and are excreted in the urine. The existence of a fat-mobilizing hormone has never been substantiated. The diet neglects the four food groups, is dangerous for pregnant women, and is high in cholesterol. Most weight loss is water, which is temporary.
Low-Carbohydrate Diets Diet of a Desperate Housewife The Drinking Man's Diet No Breakfast Diet Dr. Yudkin's Lose Weight, Feel Great Diet The Brand New Carbohydrate Diet	Claims are similar to those for high-protein diets: a state of ketosis provides a condition conducive to fat loss.	Protein in unlimited amounts with few or no carbohydrates permitted	Most weight loss is water, and temporary fatigue results from insufficient carbohydrate intake. Ketosis is potentially dangerous over prolonged periods of time. These diets fail to provide adequate foods from the basic four food groups and are difficult to follow.

Table 5.1
(continued)

Diet	Special Claims	Allowable Foods	Evaluation
One-Food Diets			
Grapefruit, egg, poultry, melon, banana, steak, beer, fruit, juice, yogurt, rice, and the like	Dieters must concentrate on the food they choose, use a multiple vitamin, and drink plenty of fluid.	Only the one food is permissible.	Impossible to obtain the proper nourishment, even with a vitamin supplement, boring, and nearly impossible to follow. Fails to change eating habits, short-term approach. Potentially very dangerous because it is impossible to obtain proper nutrition from the four food groups.
Pill Diets			
Appetite suppressants: anorexiants (amphetamines, Dexedrine, digitalis	Appetite is depressed; metabolism is increased.	Medication is designed to restrict total caloric intake. Often used in conjunction with specific diets.	Anorexiants curb appetite and increase metabolic rate. Nervousness, depression, and dependence (physical and mental) are some of the possible side effects.
Metabolic medication: thyroid hormone	Increases metabolic rate and energy output to burn more calories. Promotes breakup of lipids.	Used in conjunction with numerous diets.	No evidence is available to support the breakup of lipids. Additional calories are burned as metabolic rate increases. Thyroid hormone induces a state of hyperthyroidism and is dangerous to people with heart disease. It also disrupts the entire endocrine system.
Diuretics: thiazides	Excess body fluid is lost.	Used in conjunction with numerous diets. Additional potassium is needed to replace that lost through fluid.	Does not increase caloric expenditure. Fluid loss is unrelated to fat and permanent weight loss. Can cause dehydration, nausea, weakness, and drowsiness.
Cathartics (laxatives)	Speeds food through the intestine so nutrients are not absorbed.	Used in conjunction with numerous diets.	May result in bowel difficulty, dehydration, and poor nutrition. Not an effective method of weight loss.
Nonprescription drugs: sugar candy	Curbs appetite when taken before meals.	Used in conjunction with numerous diets.	Only mildly effective. Claims of advertisements are not met.
Benzocaine and methylcellulose	Deadens taste buds to kill hunger and provides a feeling of fullness in stomach.	Used in conjunction with numerous diets.	The amount that can be legally sold is not enough to be effective.

Table 5.1
(continued)

Diet	Special Claims	Allowable Foods	Evaluation
Starvation and Fasting Diets			
The Zip Diet Lockjaw Zen Macrobiotic Diet Liquid Protein Diet	Diets eliminate practically everything but liquids. Jaws wired shut (lockjaw diet) to aid willpower. With no calories from chewable foods, weight loss will occur rapidly.	Liquids and some foods	Extremely dangerous; lacking in vitamins, minerals, roughage. Anemia is likely. The liquid protein diet may have caused over sixty deaths. Weight loss is dramatic at first, then slows considerably, even though you are consuming practically no calories. Quality of weight loss is poor. Too much loss of lean muscle mass, along with fat loss, keeps you flabby.
Vegetarian Diets			
Vegetarian	Reduction in animal fats and cholesterol and less likelihood of excess body fat and heart disease.	Only foods of plant origin, including seeds, grains, nuts, fruits, and vegetables	Studies in the United States indicate that vegetarians have heart attacks ten years later in life than meat eaters. An excellent, healthy way to lose weight and keep it off. The diet is safe, providing sufficient protein, iron, calcium, and vitamin B_{12} can be consumed (an iron and B_{12} supplement may be needed). Have your physician confirm that you do not have a peptic ulcer or other inflammation of the digestive tract. On the negative side, the new habits of cooking, purchasing, and eating are not easy to follow at first.
Lactovegetarian		Foods of plant origin, plus foods made of milk (yogurt, cheese, and cream)	
Lacto-ovovegetarian		All plant foods, plus dairy products and eggs	
Very-Low-Calorie Formula Diets			
Cambridge Diet Plan Herbalife Meritene Slim Fast People's Natural Weight-Loss Plan	Rapid weight loss due to only 330 calories daily from liquid, containing all necessary vitamins, minerals, carbohydrates, and proteins.	None—one meal per day supplement after the first two weeks for some plans; evening meal balanced diet plus formula diet for breakfast and lunch for others	This type of diet is potentially dangerous to those with heart problems, diabetes, or gout, and to pregnant or nursing mothers. FDA reports weakness, dizziness, dehydration, low blood pressure, and cardiac irregularities in some. Some danger of serious illness and death for some people.

Source: George B. Dintiman and Jerrold S. Greenberg. *Health through Discovery*, 3d ed. (New York: Random House, 1986), 179–82

Table 5.2

Metropolitan Life Insurance Height-Weight Tables

	Men[a]					Women[b]		
Height		Small	Medium	Large	Height		Small	Medium	Large
Feet	Inches	Frame	Frame	Frame	Feet	Inches	Frame	Frame	Frame
5	2	128–134	131–141	138–150	4	10	102–111	109–121	118–131
5	3	130–136	133–143	140–153	4	11	103–113	111–123	120–134
5	4	132–138	135–145	142–156	5	0	104–115	113–126	122–137
5	5	134–140	137–148	144–160	5	1	106–118	115–129	125–140
5	6	136–142	139–151	146–164	5	2	108–121	118–132	128–143
5	7	138–145	142–154	149–168	5	3	111–124	121–135	131–147
5	8	140–148	145–157	152–172	5	4	114–127	124–138	134–151
5	9	142–151	148–160	155–176	5	5	117–130	127–141	137–155
5	10	144–154	151–163	158–180	5	6	120–133	130–144	140–159
5	11	146–157	154–166	161–184	5	7	123–136	133–147	143–163
6	0	149–160	157–170	164–188	5	8	126–139	136–150	146–167
6	1	152–164	160–174	168–192	5	9	129–142	139–153	149–170
6	2	155–168	164–178	172–197	5	10	132–145	142–156	152–173
6	3	158–172	167–182	176–202	5	11	135–148	145–159	155–176
6	4	162–176	171–187	181–207	6	0	138–151	148–162	158–179

Source: Basic data from *1979 Build Study,* Society of Actuaries and Association of Life Insurance Medical Directors of America, 1980. Courtesy *Statistical Bulletin,* Metropolitan Life Insurance Company.

[a]Weights at ages 25–59 based on lowest mortality. Weight in pounds according to frame (in indoor clothing weighing 5 lbs., shoes with 1″ heels).

[b]Weights at ages 25–59 based on lowest mortality. Weight in pounds according to frame (in indoor clothing weighing 3 lbs., shoes with 1″ heels).

hormones, their depletion makes one less able to respond satisfactorily to stress. Thereby, a vicious cycle develops. Vitamin B can be obtained by eating cereals, green leafy vegetables, liver, or fish. Vitamin C is contained in citrus fruits, tomatoes, cabbage, and potatoes.

In addition, stress can interfere with calcium absorption in the intestine and can increase calcium excretion, as well as increase the excretion of potassium, zinc, copper, and magnesium.[5] This is of particular concern to women who are trying to prevent the development of osteoporosis (a condition in which the bones become weak and brittle and the woman is at increased risk of fractures) since osteoporosis is a result of a decalcification of the bones. Although postmenopausal women are most prone to osteoporosis (decalcification is related to decreased levels of estrogens), it appears that long-term life-style habits (diet and exercise, in particular) affect one's susceptibility to this condition. Eating a diet sufficient in calcium, exercising regularly, and managing stress—all begun at a young age—are the best ways to prevent and/or postpone the development of osteoporosis.

Sugar is another stress culprit. To break down sugar, the body must use some of its B complex vitamins. We now know what that means. This results in the symptoms described previously and a diminished ability to produce adrenal hormones in response to stressors. *Processed flour* also requires the body to use B complex vitamins (as well as other nutrients) and, unless enriched with vitamins and minerals, can have the same effect as sugar.

Sugar ingestion has other stress implications. Ingestion of a large amount of sugar in a short period of time or missing meals and then ingesting sugar over a period of time can result in a condition called **hypoglycemia** in susceptible individuals. Hypoglycemia is low blood sugar that is preceded by elevated levels of blood sugar. This condition may be accompanied by symptoms of anxiety, headache, dizziness, trembling, and irritability. Subsequent stressors are likely to provoke an unusually intense stress response.

Furthermore, the stress response and accompanying cortisol production cause an elevation in the level of blood glucose. To respond to the blood glucose, the beta cells of the islets of Langerhans produce insulin. Stress that is chronic can burn out these beta cells. Since these cells are not replaceable, the body's ability to produce insulin is compromised. The result might be the development of diabetes in those individuals genetically susceptible.

Another food substance that has a relationship to stress is *salt*. Some people are genetically susceptible to sodium and will develop high blood pressure when they ingest too much of it. The federal government recommends no more than 5,000 milligrams of salt (sodium chloride), which translates to 2,000 milligrams of sodium, daily. On a short-term basis, sodium ingestion can raise blood pressure by retaining body fluids. As we learned in chapter 3, when a person whose blood pressure is elevated encounters stress, his or her blood pressure may be further elevated to a dangerous level.

Now that you have an appreciation for the relationship of nutrition to stress, it is time to study ways of using this information to manage stress better. Here are some ways you can reduce stressors in your diet:

1. Eat a balanced diet that includes foods from each of the four food groups.
2. Limit the amount of saturated fats in your diet and increase the amount of fiber.
3. Add cruciferous vegetables (such as broccoli, cauliflower, and brussels sprouts) to your diet and limit the amount of alcohol you ingest.
4. Be more realistic about your weight. That is, lose weight if you need to, but don't expect to measure up to the ideal projected by the media. Remember, obsession about weight can lead to anorexia nervosa and/or bulimia.
5. Limit your intake of cola, coffee, tea, and chocolate or other products containing caffeine. Also, do not smoke cigarettes or use other tobacco products (snuff, chewing tobacco).
6. During particularly stressful times you might want to consider supplementing your diet with vitamins. In particular, focus on vitamin C and the B complex vitamins. However, many experts believe that eating a balanced diet that includes a wide variety of foods will assure a sufficient amount of vitamins.
7. Limit foods containing sugar. If ingesting sugar, do not take in large amounts in a short period of time, and do not skip meals.

8. Limit intake of processed flour. However, some experts believe that if the flour is enriched with vitamins and minerals, it need not be avoided.
9. Limit your intake of sodium.

Part of eliminating unnecessary stressors includes eliminating those food substances that either make us more prone to stress or create a stresslike response. Here's another area of our lives we need to take charge of.

Anyone who has roomed with a noisy person, worked in a noisy office, or tried **Noise and Stress** to study with a party going on in the next room can attest to the effect of noise on one's level of stress. Noise can raise blood pressure, increase heart rate, and lead to muscle tension. Noise has been found to be related to job dissatisfaction and to result in irritation and anxiety.[6] One expert describes noise as the most troublesome of all stressors in our environment.[7]

Most disturbing is that noise which constantly changes in pitch, intensity, or frequency. We may become used to more common and stable noise and almost ignore it. People who live near airports, for example, seem to not even hear the planes after a while. However, just because you become accustomed to the noise or able to tune it out doesn't mean you are not being affected by it.

Noise is measured in decibels. At 85 decibels, stress responses usually develop, and prolonged exposure to sounds above 90 decibels can result in hearing damage. Of course, depending on one's level of concentration and the task being performed, even low levels of noise can be bothersome. Figure 5.2 lists decibel ratings for some common sounds.

To reduce noise levels you can:

1. use cotton or ear plugs if your job requires constant exposure to loud noises;
2. sit as far away as possible from the band at loud rock, symphony, or band concerts;
3. learn to enjoy listening to music at home at a moderate volume;
4. put drapes over windows to reduce street noise;
5. choose acoustical tile for ceilings and walls when building a house or adding a room;
6. use carpeting or select an apartment with carpeting in all rooms adjacent to other units;
7. keep noise-making appliances away from bedrooms, den, and living room; and
8. select home sites or apartments away from truck routes, airports, businesses, and industrial areas.

In spite of its potential for stress, noise can at times be soothing. In fact, on many stress management audiotapes, you will find noise to help you relax. This is called "white noise" and its purpose is to drown out other sounds that may

Figure 5.2 Common sounds and their decibel rating

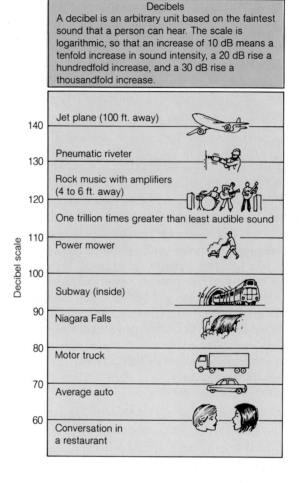

Decibels
A decibel is an arbitrary unit based on the faintest sound that a person can hear. The scale is logarithmic, so that an increase of 10 dB means a tenfold increase in sound intensity, a 20 dB rise a hundredfold increase, and a 30 dB rise a thousandfold increase.

Decibel scale

140 — Jet plane (100 ft. away)

130 — Pneumatic riveter

120 — Rock music with amplifiers (4 to 6 ft. away)

One trillion times greater than least audible sound

110 — Power mower

100

90 — Subway (inside)

Niagara Falls

80 — Motor truck

70 — Average auto

60 — Conversation in a restaurant

interfere with relaxation. Sounds such as the surf rolling onto the shore, birds chirping, or the wind rustling through the leaves can all serve as comforting sounds. In addition, some sounds are used to focus upon to bring about relaxation. For example, some forms of meditation use a word (called a **mantra**) for focusing and other methods of relaxation employ chanting.

So you can see that *noise* can be stressful but that certain *sounds* can be relaxing. You can take greater control of your life by limiting disturbing noises and seeking out relaxing sounds. Walk through the woods, recline on a beach. Noise or relaxing sound—it's up to you.

The information in this section will have more meaning for you if you follow these instructions. If you are presently a college student, determine which events below you have experienced within the last year. This first life-events scale was developed by G. E. Anderson.

Mean value	Event
(50)	Entered college
(77)	Married
(38)	Had either a lot more or a lot less trouble with your boss
(43)	Held a job while attending school
(87)	Experienced the death of a spouse
(34)	Experienced a major change in sleeping habits (sleeping a lot more or a lot less, or a change in part of the day when asleep)
(77)	Experienced the death of a close family member
(30)	Experienced a major change in eating habits (a lot more or a lot less food intake, or very different meal hours or surroundings)
(41)	Made a change in or choice of a major field of study
(45)	Had a revision of your personal habits (friends, dress, manners, associations, etc.)
(68)	Experienced the death of a close friend
(22)	Have been found guilty of minor violations of the law (traffic tickets, jaywalking, etc.)
(40)	Have had an outstanding personal achievement
(68)	Experienced pregnancy or fathered a child
(56)	Had a major change in the health or behavior of a family member
(58)	Had sexual difficulties
(42)	Had trouble with in-laws
(26)	Had a major change in the number of family get-togethers (a lot more or a lot less)
(53)	Had a major change in financial state (a lot worse off or a lot better off than usual)
(50)	Gained a new family member (through birth, adoption, older person moving in, etc.)
(42)	Changed your residence or living conditions
(50)	Had a major conflict in or change in values
(36)	Had a major change in church activities (a lot more or a lot less than usual)

(58)	Had a marital reconciliation with your mate
(62)	Were fired from work
(76)	Were divorced
(50)	Changed to a different line of work
(50)	Had a major change in the number of arguments with spouse (either a lot more or a lot less than usual)
(47)	Had a major change in responsibilities at work (promotion, demotion, lateral transfer)
(41)	Had your spouse begin or cease work outside the home
(74)	Had a marital separation from your mate
(57)	Had a major change in usual type and/or amount of recreation
(52)	Took a mortgage or loan *less* than $10,000 (such as purchase of a car, TV, school loan, etc.)
(65)	Had a major personal injury or illness
(46)	Had a major change in the use of alcohol (a lot more or a lot less)
(48)	Had a major change in social activities
(38)	Had a major change in the amount of participation in school activities
(49)	Had a major change in the amount of independence and responsibility (for example, for budgeting time)
(33)	Took a trip or a vacation
(54)	Were engaged to be married
(50)	Changed to a new school
(41)	Changed dating habits
(44)	Had trouble with school administration (instructors, advisors, class scheduling, etc.)
(60)	Broke or had broken a marital engagement or a steady relationship
(57)	Had a major change in self-concept or self-awareness

If you are older than the typical college student, determine which of the following events you have experienced within the past year.

Mean value	Event
(100)	Death of spouse
(73)	Divorce
(65)	Marital separation
(63)	Jail term
(63)	Death of close family member
(53)	Personal injury or illness
(50)	Marriage

(47)	Fired at work
(45)	Marital reconciliation
(45)	Retirement
(44)	Change in health of family member
(40)	Pregnancy
(39)	Sex difficulties
(39)	Gain of new family member
(39)	Business readjustment
(38)	Change in financial state
(37)	Death of close friend
(36)	Change to different line of work
(35)	Change in number of arguments with spouse
(31)	Mortgage or loan for major purchase (home, etc.)
(30)	Foreclosure of mortgage or loan
(29)	Change in responsibilities at work
(29)	Son or daughter leaving home
(29)	Trouble with in-laws
(28)	Outstanding personal achievement
(26)	Wife begin or stop work
(25)	Change in living conditions
(24)	Revision of personal habits
(23)	Trouble with boss
(20)	Change in work hours or conditions
(20)	Change in residence
(19)	Change in recreation
(19)	Change in church activities
(18)	Change in social activities
(17)	Mortgage or loan for lesser purchase (car, TV, etc.)
(16)	Change in sleeping habits
(15)	Change in number of family get-togethers
(15)	Change in eating habits
(13)	Vacation
(12)	Christmas
(11)	Minor violations of the law

To obtain your score, multiply the number of times an event occurred by its mean value. Then total all of the scores.

Your score is termed your *life-change units (LCU)*. This is a measure of the amount of significant changes in your life to which you have had to adjust. In other words, your LCU is a measure of the stressors you have encountered this past year. The original research in this field was conducted by Holmes and Rahe who developed the second scale, the Social Readjustment Rating Scale. They argued that if stress resulted in illness and disease, then people experiencing a great deal of stress should report more illness than people reporting only a little stress. Their theory was supported when they found that people who scored 150–199 LCU in one year showed a 37 percent chance of those stressors leading to illness or disease the following year; those scoring 200–299, a 51 percent chance; and those scoring over 300, a 79 percent chance. The first scale appearing in this section is an adaptation of the Holmes and Rahe scale made relevant to the lives of college students.

Many other researchers have since supported the findings of Holmes and Rahe.[8-11] However, not all studies measuring life-change units have been so supportive of this theory. The inconsistency of these research findings should not be surprising. If you'll recall the stress theory model, all that these life-events scales measure is the top phase (life situation). We know, though, that changes in life situations alone are not enough to cause illness and disease. These changes must be perceived as distressing and result in emotional and, subsequently, physiological arousal that is chronic, prolonged, or unabated. We also now know that it is possible to establish roadblocks (intervention techniques) to inhibit the development of illness or disease from stressors we experience. Researchers have found one such roadblock to be **social support.**[12] People who experienced a great deal of life change but had family or friends with whom to discuss their problems contracted no more illness than people who experienced less life change. However, people who experienced a great deal of life change but *did not* have family or friends with whom to discuss their problems contracted much more illness than the others. Social support is discussed in more detail in chapter 6. Suffice it to say that life change does not, in and of itself, lead to poor health.

What should you do if your score on the life-events scale concerns you? First, let's look at how people typically react to a stressful period of time. We often hear people say, "I've been under a lot of stress lately. I need a vacation." If you have too many life-change units, why add more? Vacation is worth 13 points! Rather than add to your stress, you'd be better advised to make your life more routine to reduce your need to adapt to changes. Rather than taking a vacation, maintain your daily routine (perhaps eliminating some events, but *not* substituting others). I'm often asked how such pleasant events as a vacation and Christmas can be stressors. Remember that stress occurs when we are knocked out of balance. We are in equilibrium when suddenly something occurs requiring us to use energy to adapt. Just think about all you must do prior to taking a vacation.

Once you have arrived at the vacation spot, you need to adjust further. You have established a daily routine (your equilibrium) that does not include going to sleep at 3:00 A.M., lying on a beach doing nothing, eating such delicacies as fried this and greasy that, or having to interact with the people accompanying you for such a large part of your day. The sum of all the adjustment required prior to, during, and returning from a vacation is the reason that a vacation can be a stressor.

It's the daily hassles that might be more threatening to your health than major life events.

Another interesting revelation can be inferred from the Holmes and Rahe scale. If you have a marital separation, you accumulate 65 stressor points. That event requires you to adjust from being married and the routines you have established within your particular marriage to being single again. The functions your spouse performed now need your attention. The time you spent together now needs to be used for another purpose. You need to adjust to aloneness, or loneliness, or both. You need to spend time meeting new people. It is evident that this separation requires a great deal of adaptation energy and can be quite stressful. Let's assume that you have spent six months adjusting to your marital separation and have finally adapted to your new routines and way of living. Lo and behold, the old flame flickers once again, and you and your spouse decide to try a reconciliation. Notice, though, that marital reconciliation is worth 45 stressor points. Once again, you are requiring yourself (mind and body) to adapt to being married just after you have finally adapted to being single. Your daily routines need changing, your associations and affiliations may need to be readjusted, and you must develop your marital relationship more effectively than before.

The moral of this story is to be sure of your need for marital separation (and other breaks in your relationships with loved ones) prior to the separation, and once you have made that decision, do not easily revert to that old relationship. Of course, there are intervening variables associated with these decisions. For some people, the separation can be so stressful and the adaptation so difficult that the stress associated with reconciliation would be less than the stress of continuing the separation. Others may be willing to tolerate the threat to their health in order to reestablish their marriage (or other relationship). You can probably think of other considerations that enter into this decision. However, recognize that the more your life situation requires adaptation, the more likely you are to become ill. Some stressors you may not be able to eliminate (for example, the death of a spouse or close friend), but others you can control. You can, therefore, decide that they will no longer be a part of your life; to do so would be to improve your health.

Hassles and Chronic Stress

Carrying the life change-stress relationship further, Lazarus[13] and his colleagues hypothesized that everyday **hassles** would be even more detrimental to health than major life events. They defined hassles as daily interactions with the environment that were essentially negative and, because of their chronic nature, could take a significant toll on our health. Losing a wallet, smoking too much, and troublesome neighbors are examples of these hassles. Furthermore, Lazarus[14] proposed that the absence of **uplifts**—positive events that make us feel good— would also be related to ill health.

Although the absence of uplifts has not been found to be related to ill health, the presence of hassles has. Hassles have been shown to be predictive of psychological distress,[15] the dynamics of stress and aging,[16] and related to poorer mental and physical health.[17,18] In general, Lazarus' theory has been shown to be correct in asserting that hassles are related to subsequent illness and disease to a greater degree than are major life events.[19]

The scale used to measure hassles is too lengthy to reproduce here, but you can analyze your hassles by studying your diary or by making up a list of everyday interactions with your environment that you find bothersome. Do you have trouble relaxing? Do you have problems with fellow workers? Do you lack money for basic necessities? Once you have identified these hassles, try to eliminate as many of them as you can while recognizing that many others will either take a long time to change or are unchangeable (you will have to learn to live with these).

Success Analysis

A friend of mine has written a book that I recommend to you. The title of this book reflects both her personality and her reality. It's entitled *Success: You Can Make It Happen*.[20] What's more, you too can make it happen. Success need not be left to chance. As the gambling casinos around the world give themselves an edge to ensure a profit, you can give yourself an edge to ensure being successful. Giving yourself success (don't miss the importance of this phrasing) will result in your thinking better of yourself. Stated more pedantically, success will lead to improved self-esteem. The converse, of course, is that lack of success (failure) will lead to diminished self-esteem resulting in a very significant stressor.

At this point, you need some information about yourself to infer personal meaning from our discussion. Complete your success chart (table 5.3) by dividing your life into three equal time periods beginning at age five. If you are fifty years old, your three time periods will be five to twenty, twenty-one to thirty-five, and thirty-six to fifty; if you are twenty years old, they'll be five to ten, eleven to fifteen, and sixteen to twenty. Next, think of three successes of yours during each of those periods of your life *and* the reasons why you consider these successes.

Table 5.3
Your Success Chart

Age	Success Experience	Reasons It Was a Success
	1. 2. 3.	
	1. 2. 3.	
	1. 2. 3.	
Most Successful Experience		**Reason**
Least Successful Experience		**Reason**

From Swell, Lila, *Success: You Can Make It Happen.* © 1976 by Lila Swell. Reprinted by permission of Lila Swell.

Place these successes and reasons within your success chart. Lastly, write in what you consider to be the most successful experience of your life and the least successful one, along with the reasons you consider them such. The last part of this data-gathering procedure requires you to list, on a separate sheet of paper, ten strengths of yours—ten of your most positive characteristics and talents. Please do this before reading further.

Success is multifaceted and, like beauty, is in the eyes of the beholder. What you view as successful, others might not. Some consider themselves successful when they achieve independence, and their success charts reflect this viewpoint with successes such as owning their first car, getting their first job, or moving into their own apartment. Their reasons for regarding these as successes might be "Didn't have to rely on others" or "Now I had money to do my own thing."

Others view success as competing and winning. Their success charts might include successes such as playing on a championship team, winning a trophy, or competing with other students and winning a scholarship to college. The reasons given might be "The competition was intense" or "A lot of people tried to do this, but only I succeeded." Still others define success in other ways:

1. Being chosen (or elected) by others
2. Pleasing others (parents, teachers, friends)
3. Being helpful

4. Achieving academically
5. Achieving in sports activities
6. Being the best
7. Achievement in spite of great obstacles and difficulty (if too easy, the achievement is not viewed as a success)
8. Learning a skill
9. Recognition from others
10. Being happy

How do you define success? Scan your success chart and list at least four patterns that emerge. Make sure that your patterns are just that—patterns. They must appear several times within the chart. You should conclude with a sentence that begins: Success to me is . . .

Now that you know your own view of success, how can you achieve it? The best way is to use the strengths you listed previously. Try to maximize those strengths and minimize any weaknesses you have in order to "fix the deck" and increase your chances of being successful. Prescribe life experiences for yourself that use those strengths; shy away from experiences that rely on talents, skills, or characteristics that you lack. For example, if you perceive success as achieving independence, don't seek success occupationally by working on an assembly line. If you don't have the "gift of gab," you should not become a salesperson. You might try to be successful as an author if you view success as recognition from others and have a talent for writing. If you also have *helping others* as a component of your success definition, the books you write should present information that can be used to help others. Now you know why I wrote this book!

With the data you have acquired regarding your definition of success and your list of strengths, you are now able to *give yourself* success. You are now in control of one more possible stressor. You are now better able to maintain your health and improve the quality of your life. *But* you will do this only if you use this information to make your life situation consistent with what you have learned.

Summary

1. Good nutrition may help in managing stress. Foods should be eaten from a variety of sources. Eating the recommended amounts of foods from the four food groups is one way of assuring that you eat a balanced diet.
2. Maintaining nutritional health by practices such as limiting the amount of saturated fats and alcohol you ingest and increasing the amount of fiber and cruciferous vegetables eaten may also reduce stressors in your diet.
3. Food substances that produce a stresslike response are called pseudostressors or sympathomimetics since they mimic sympathetic nervous system stimulation. Foods containing caffeine are examples of these substances.

4. Stress may deplete the B complex and C vitamins; in the case of chronic stress, the diet may require supplementation with vitamins and minerals. Ingestion of sugar or processed flour may make this situation even worse since both of these use up valuable nutrients when the body metabolizes them.

5. To manage stress better, limit intake of caffeine, sugar, and foods containing processed flour that has not been enriched. During stressful times, consider vitamin supplementation.

6. Noise can be either distressing or relaxing. Noises louder than 85 decibels usually elicit a stress response, and prolonged exposure to sounds above 90 decibels can result in hearing damage. White noise is used to drown out disturbing noises while one is trying to relax.

7. Thomas Holmes and Richard Rahe found that the more significant changes a person had in his or her life, the greater the chance that he or she would contract some physical or psychological illness. Since they conceptualized stress as adapting to change, Holmes and Rahe viewed more change as equivalent to more stress and, consequently, more illness and disease.

8. Richard Lazarus found that the daily hassles a person experiences are more harmful to his or her health than are the significant life changes that concerned Holmes and Rahe. Lazarus believes these daily events are so damaging to health because of how frequently they occur, as compared to the major life events that Holmes and Rahe researched, which were usually encountered only rarely.

Notes

1. American Cancer Society, *Cancer Facts & Figures—1987* (New York: American Cancer Society, 1987), 18.

2. Marjie Patlak, "Eating to Avoid Cancer Gets More Complicated," *Washington Post, Health,* 2 April 1986, 16–17.

3. George B. Dintiman and Jerrold S. Greenberg, *Health Through Discovery,* 3d ed. (New York: Random House, 1986), 171.

4. Roger J. Allen, *Human Stress: Its Nature and Control* (Minneapolis: Burgess, 1983), 75.

5. "Nutrients and Stress," *Medical Self-Care,* Summer 1985, 18.

6. Jeanne Stellman and Mary Sue Henifen, *Office Work Can Be Dangerous to Your Health* (New York: Pantheon, 1983), 118.

7. Sheldon Cohen, "Sound Effects on Behavior," *Psychology Today,* October 1981, 38–49.

8. V. Lundberg, T. Theorell, and E. Lind, "Life Changes and Myocardial Infarction: Individual Differences in Life-Change Scaling," *Journal of Psychosomatic Research* 19(1975):27–32.

9. R. T. Rubin, E. Gunderson, and R. J. Arthur, "Prior Life Change and Illness Onset in an Attack Carrier's Crew," *Archives of Environmental Health* 19(1969):753–57.

10. T. Theorell and R. Rahe, "Life-Change Events, Ballistocardiography and Coronary Death," *Journal of Human Stress* 1(1975):18–24.

11. M. Masuda et al., "Life Events and Prisoners," *Archives of General Psychiatry* 35(1978):197–203.

12. S. Gore, "The Effects of Social Support in Moderating the Health Consequences of Unemployment," *Journal of Health and Social Behavior* 19(1978):157–65.

13. A. D. Kanner, Richard S. Lazarus et al., "Comparison of Two Modes of Stress Management: Daily Hassles and Uplifts versus Major Life Events," *Journal of Behavioral Medicine* 4(1981):1–39.

14. Richard S. Lazarus, "Puzzles in the Study of Daily Hassles," *Journal of Behavioral Medicine* 7(1984):375–89.

15. C. K. Holahan, C. J. Holahan, and S. S. Belk, "Adjustment in Aging: The Roles of Life Stress, Hassles, and Self-efficacy," *Health Psychology* 3(1984):315–28.

16. Richard S. Lazarus and A. DeLongis, "Psychological Stress and Coping in Aging," *American Psychologist* 38(1983):245–54.

17. Kanner and Lazarus, "Comparison of Two Modes of Stress Management," 1–39.

18. J. J. Zarski, "Hassles and Health: A Replication," *Health Psychology* 3(1984):243–51.

19. Nancy Burks and Barclay Martin, "Everyday Problems and Life Change Events: Ongoing versus Acute Sources of Stress," *Journal of Human Stress* 11(1985):27–35.

20. Lila Swell, *Success: You Can Make It Happen* (New York: Simon & Schuster, 1976).

6

Life-Situation Interventions—Interpersonal

Chapter 5 described life-situation interventions that can be successfully employed when no one else is directly involved. This chapter presents life-situation interventions that are useful when the situation involves other people as well as yourself. The topics we will consider include assertiveness; resolving conflicts; communicating effectively with others; and managing time wisely and coordinating it with coworkers, family, and friends. We will also consider how to develop a network of supporters to serve as a buffer between stress and its negative consequences.

Since other people are involved, you might want to consider teaching these stress management techniques to the people you interact with often. In that way, when a situation presents itself that calls for one of the stress management strategies discussed in this chapter and you forget to use it, the other person might remember. The result can only be more effective interactions for you, and that can only mean less stress.

Ring! Gladys picks up the telephone to hear the dulcet sounds of her friend Sue. "Gladys, I have an appointment for lunch. Can you watch Billy from noon until three?"

"Sure, Sue. Take your time and enjoy yourself. I'll expect you at noon." But in Gladys's mind another conversation is being recorded: "I don't believe that Sue! She's always asking me to watch her kid. What am I, a babysitter? I was looking forward to scheduling a tennis match with Joan today. Well, there goes that idea."

Asserting Yourself

This scenario is not atypical and not exclusive to women. Men and women who find it difficult to say no when asked by the boss if they can handle one other chore or responsibility, and youth who can't say no to friends when teased into trying a mood-altering substance (alcohol or other drugs), have the same problem as Gladys does. Training programs have been mushrooming throughout the country and world to help people say no when they should, yes when they want to, and, in general, behave in a self-actualizing manner. These training programs teach assertive behavior. Several definitions are necessary at this point:

1. *Assertive behavior:* Expressing yourself and satisfying your own needs. Feeling good about this and not hurting others in the process.
2. *Nonassertive behavior:* Denying your own wishes to satisfy someone else's. Sacrificing your own needs to meet someone else's needs.
3. *Aggressive behavior:* Seeking to dominate or to get your own way at the expense of others.

To determine your general pattern of behavior, indicate how characteristic or descriptive each of the following statements is of you by using the code that follows. This scale was developed by Rathus.

+3 = very characteristic of me, extremely descriptive
+2 = rather characteristic of me, quite descriptive
+1 = somewhat characteristic of me, slightly descriptive
−1 = somewhat uncharacteristic of me, slightly nondescriptive
−2 = rather uncharacteristic of me, quite nondescriptive
−3 = very uncharacteristic of me, extremely nondescriptive

_____ 1. Most people seem to be more aggressive and assertive than I am.
_____ 2. I have hesitated to make or accept dates because of "shyness."
_____ 3. When the food served at a restaurant is not done to my satisfaction, I complain about it to the waiter or waitress.
_____ 4. I am careful to avoid hurting other people's feelings, even when I feel that I have been injured.
_____ 5. If a salesperson has gone to considerable trouble to show me merchandise that is not quite suitable, I have a difficult time in saying no.
_____ 6. When I am asked to do something, I insist upon knowing why.
_____ 7. There are times when I look for a good, vigorous argument.
_____ 8. I strive to get ahead as well as most people in my position.
_____ 9. To be honest, people often take advantage of me.
_____ 10. I enjoy starting conversations with new acquaintances and strangers.
_____ 11. I often don't know what to say to attractive persons of the opposite sex.
_____ 12. I will hesitate to make phone calls to business establishments and institutions.
_____ 13. I would rather apply for a job or for admission to a college by writing letters than by going through with personal interviews.
_____ 14. I find it embarrassing to return merchandise.
_____ 15. If a close and respected relative were annoying me, I would smother my feelings rather than express my annoyance.
_____ 16. I have avoided asking questions for fear of sounding stupid.
_____ 17. During an argument I am sometimes afraid that I will get so upset that I will shake all over.
_____ 18. If a famed and respected lecturer makes a statement that I think is incorrect, I will have the audience hear my point of view as well.

_____ 19. I avoid arguing over prices with clerks and salespeople.
_____ 20. When I have done something important or worthwhile, I manage to let others know about it.
_____ 21. I am open and frank about my feelings.
_____ 22. If someone has been spreading false and bad stories about me, I see him (her) as soon as possible to "have a talk" about it.
_____ 23. I often have a hard time saying no.
_____ 24. I tend to bottle up my emotions rather than make a scene.
_____ 25. I complain about poor service in a restaurant and elsewhere.
_____ 26. When I am given a compliment, I sometimes just don't know what to say.
_____ 27. If a couple near me in a theatre or at a lecture were conversing rather loudly, I would ask them to be quiet or to take their conversation elsewhere.
_____ 28. Anyone attempting to push ahead of me in a line is in for a good battle.
_____ 29. I am quick to express an opinion.
_____ 30. There are times when I just can't say anything.

To score this scale, first change (reverse) the signs (+ or −) for your scores on items 1, 2, 4, 5, 9, 11, 12, 13, 14, 15, 16, 17, 19, 23, 24, 26, and 30. Now total the plus (+) items, total the minus (−) items, and subtract the minus total from the plus total to obtain your score. This score can range from −90 through 0 to +90. The higher the score (closer to +90) the more assertively you usually behave. The lower the score (closer to −90) the more nonassertive is your typical behavior. This particular scale does not measure aggressiveness.

In the phone conversation just described, Gladys acted **nonassertively.** She gave up her need for scheduling recreation time and did not express her feelings of being used and taken advantage of by Sue. If she had been **aggressive,** Gladys might have said, "How dare you ask me to watch that brat of yours? I have more important things to do. You're selfish and self-centered. You never even asked if you could watch my children." Acting aggressively, Gladys would have denied Sue's right to ask a favor of her. Gladys would have gone about fulfilling her needs, but she would have done so in a manner that was unfair to Sue. Sue has the right to ask, and Gladys should not deny her that right. However, Gladys owns her own behavior. She has the right to say no. In a more assertive response to Sue's request, Gladys might have replied, "I can appreciate your need for someone to watch Billy, but I've been so busy lately that I promised myself today I wouldn't take on any such commitments. I really need some recreation time, so I'm going to play tennis with Joan. Perhaps Mary is free to watch Billy. Do you have her phone number?" It would also be appropriate during this response, or sometime soon after, for Gladys to express to Sue her feelings of being used. If these feelings are expressed, they can be dealt with, and Sue will have the information she needs to change her behavior. However, if Gladys never lets Sue know how she feels, Sue will continue to make the same request, and Gladys's feelings will persist, diminishing the quality of their relationship. Soon we will discuss how Gladys can express these feelings assertively—both verbally and nonverbally.

The relationship of assertive behavior to stress lies in satisfaction of needs. If you generally act assertively, you are usually achieving your needs while maintaining effective interpersonal relationships. If you generally act nonassertively, you are not satisfying your needs, and those unsatisfied needs will become stressors. If you generally behave aggressively, your needs are met but at the expense of your relationships with others. Poor interpersonal relationships will become stressors. You can see that to siphon off stressors at the life-situation level, you need to learn, practice, and adopt assertive behavior as your general pattern of satisfying needs.

Assertion theory is based upon the premise that every person has certain basic rights. Unfortunately, we are often taught that acting consistently with these rights is socially or morally unacceptable. We are taught some traditional assumptions as children—which stay with us as adults—that interfere with basing our behavior on these basic rights. These assumptions violate our rights, and we need to dispense with them. Table 6.1 lists some basic human rights along with the assumptions we have been taught, and often use, to deny these rights. Which of these assumptions do you use? Which do you want to give up? How will you behave differently if you dispense with the traditional assumptions you possess?

Nonverbal Assertiveness

Unwilling to deny your basic human rights, you may choose to become more assertive. Behaving assertively is more difficult for some than others, but the hints in this section should allow everyone to begin moving in the assertive direction. Assertiveness is not only a matter of *what* you say, but also a function of *how* you say it. Even if you make an assertive verbal response, you will not be believed if your body's response is nonassertive. Those who express themselves assertively

1. stand straight, steady, and directly face the people to whom they are speaking while maintaining eye contact;
2. speak in a clear, steady voice, loud enough for the people to whom they are speaking to hear them; and
3. speak fluently, without hesitation, and with assurance and confidence.

In contrast, nonassertive body language includes

1. lack of eye contact; looking down or away;
2. swaying and shifting of weight from one foot to the other; and
3. whining and hesitancy when speaking.

Aggressive behavior can also be recognized without even hearing the words; it includes

1. leaning forward with glaring eyes;
2. pointing a finger at the person to whom you are speaking;
3. shouting;
4. clenching the fists; and
5. putting hands on hips and wagging the head.

Table 6.1
Basic Human Rights and Related Assumptions Violating These Rights

Mistaken Traditional Assumptions	Your Legitimate Rights
1. It is selfish to put your needs before others' needs.	You have a right to put yourself first, sometimes.
2. It is shameful to make mistakes. You should have an appropriate response for every occasion.	You have a right to make mistakes.
3. If you can't convince others that your feelings are reasonable, then they must be wrong, or maybe you are going crazy.	You have a right to be the final judge of your feelings and accept them as legitimate.
4. You should respect the views of others, especially if they are in a position of authority. Keep your differences of opinion to yourself. Listen and learn.	You have a right to have your own opinions and convictions.
5. You should always try to be logical and consistent.	You have a right to change your mind or decide on a different course of action.
6. You should be flexible and adjust. Others have good reasons for their actions and it's not polite to question them.	You have a right to protest unfair treatment or criticism.
7. You should never interrupt people. Asking questions reveals your stupidity to others.	You have a right to interrupt in order to ask for clarification.
8. Things could get even worse; don't rock the boat.	You have a right to negotiate for change.
9. You shouldn't take up others' valuable time with your problems.	You have a right to ask for help or emotional support.
10. People don't want to hear that you feel bad, so keep it to yourself.	You have a right to feel and express pain.
11. When someone takes the time to give you advice, you should take it very seriously. They are often right.	You have a right to ignore the advice of others.
12. Knowing that you did something well is its own reward. People don't like show-offs. Successful people are secretly disliked and envied. Be modest when complimented.	You have a right to receive formal recognition for your work and achievements.
13. You should always try to accommodate others. If you don't, they won't be there when you need them.	You have a right to say no.
14. Don't be antisocial. People are going to think you don't like them if you say you'd rather be alone instead of with them.	You have a right to be alone, even if others would prefer your company.
15. You should always have a good reason for what you feel and do.	You have a right not to have to justify yourself to others.
16. When someone is in trouble, you should help them.	You have a right not to take responsibility for someone else's problem.
17. You should be sensitive to the needs and wishes of others, even when they are unable to tell you what they want.	You have a right not to have to anticipate others' needs and wishes.
18. It's always a good policy to stay on people's good side.	You have a right not to always worry about the goodwill of others.
19. It's not nice to put people off. If questioned, give an answer.	You have a right to choose not to respond to a situation.

Source: Martha Davis, Matthew McKay, and Elizabeth Robbins Eshelman, *The Relaxation and Stress Reduction Workbook.* © 1980 New Harbinger Publications, Richmond, California. Reprinted by permission.

If you want to act assertively, then, you must pay attention to your body language. Practice and adopt assertive nonverbal behavior while concentrating on eliminating signs of nonassertive and aggressive behavior.

Verbal Assertiveness

Now to *what* you say. A formula I have found effective in helping people verbally express themselves assertively is the **DESC form.** The verbal response is divided into four components:

1. *Describe:* Paint a verbal picture of the other person's behavior or the situation to which you are reacting. "When you . . ."; "When . . ."

2. *Express:* Relate your feelings regarding the other person's behavior or the situation you have just described. Use "I" statements here: "I feel . . ."

3. *Specify:* Be specific by identifying several ways you would like the other person's behavior or the situation to change. Rather than saying, "You should . . . ," again use "I" statements: "I would prefer . . . ," "I would like . . . ," "I want . . ."

4. *Consequence:* Select the consequences you have decided to apply to the behavior or situation. What will you do if the other person's behavior or the situation changes to your satisfaction? "If you do _____ , I will . . ." What will be the consequences if nothing changes, or if the changes do not meet with your needs? "If you don't _____ , I will . . ."

To demonstrate the DESC form of organizing assertive responses, let's assume Jim and Kathy are dating. Jim wants Kathy to date him exclusively. Kathy believes she's too young to eliminate other men from her love life. Jim's assertive response to this situation might take this form:

(Describe) When you go out with other men, (Express) I feel very jealous and have doubts about the extent of your love for me. (Specify) I would prefer that we only date each other. (Consequence) If you only date me, I'll make a sincere effort to offer you a variety of experiences so that you do not feel you've missed anything. We'll go to nice restaurants, attend plays, go to concerts, and whatever else you'd like that I can afford and that is reasonable. If you do not agree to date me exclusively, I will not date you at all. The pain would just be more than I'm willing to tolerate.

A woman in my class whose boss required she work Monday through Friday and *Saturdays* organized the following DESC form assertive response:

(Describe) When I am expected to work six days a week, (Express) I feel tired and abused. (Specify) I would prefer working only Monday through Friday. (Consequence) If I can work only those five days I will be conscientious about doing all my work well and on time. If need be, I'll work through some lunch hours, stay later when necessary, or even be willing to take some work home. However, if I'm required to work on Saturdays, I will resign and look for another job. That is how strongly I feel about my right to have a total weekend for myself.

Organize your own assertive response! Think of a situation that has been of concern to you for which an assertive response would be helpful. For example, one of my students recalled having invited a friend to dinner. While dinner was cooking, the friend received a call from a man she was longing to see. Before the telephone conversation was too old, he asked her out for dinner that night, and she accepted. Upon hanging up, this "friend" apologized to my student as she left to have dinner with her male acquaintance. Another student was anticipating her son's return from college with his girlfriend for a Christmas vacation. She knew he would want to sleep in the same room as his girlfriend, since they shared a room while away at school. Believing that these sleeping arrangements would violate her rights, she chose to prepare an assertive response to convey to her son. She prepared a response, stated it to her son and his girlfriend, and reported that things worked out marvelously.

Is there a situation in your life crying out for assertive behavior? Can you give up the assumptions preventing you from claiming your basic human rights in this situation? Write what you would say if you responded assertively.

_____

_____

_____

How does that feel to you? Will you do it? If so, remember to have your body language be assertive as well.

If you are effective in resolving conflict, your interpersonal relationships will be improved. The result of this improvement will be a decrease in the number of stressors you experience. Less conflict of shorter duration resolved to your satisfaction will mean a less-stressed and healthier you. **Conflict Resolution**

Before we proceed with suggestions for effectively resolving conflict, you might be interested in an identification of your typical modus operandi; that is, how you usually deal with conflict situations. To make this determination, circle the answer that best describes how you would react to each of the following situations.

1. If a salesgirl refuses to give me a refund on a purchase because I've lost the sales slip
   a. I tell her, "I'm sorry—I should have been more careful," and leave without the refund.
   b. I tell her, "You're the only store in town that handles this brand of merchandise. I demand a refund, or I'll never shop here again."
   c. I say, "Look, if I can't have a refund, can I exchange it for something else?"

2. If I had irritated a teacher by questioning his theoretical position and he retaliated by giving me a *D* on an excellent paper
   a. I wouldn't say anything; I would realize why it happened and be quieter in my next class.
   b. I would tell him he was dead wrong and that he couldn't get away with being so unfair.
   c. I would try to talk to him and see what could be done about it.
3. If I worked as a TV repairman and my boss ordered me to double-charge customers, I would
   a. go along with him; it's his business.
   b. tell him he's a crook and that I won't go along with his dishonesty.
   c. tell him he can overcharge on *his* calls, but I'm charging honestly on mine.
4. If I gave up my seat on the bus to an older woman with packages, but some teenager beat her to it
   a. I would try to find the woman another seat.
   b. I would argue with the teenager until he moved.
   c. I would ignore it.
5. If I had been waiting in line at the supermarket for twenty minutes and then some woman rushed in front of me saying, "Thank you—I'm in such a hurry!"
   a. I would smile and let her in.
   b. I would say, "Look, what do you think you're doing? Wait your turn!"
   c. I would let her in *if* she had a good reason for being in such a hurry.
6. If a friend was to meet me on a street corner at 7:00 one night and at 8:00 P.M. he still wasn't there, I would
   a. wait another thirty minutes.
   b. be furious at his thoughtlessness and leave.
   c. try to telephone him, thinking, "Boy, he'd better have a good excuse!"
7. If my wife (or husband) volunteered me for committee work with someone she (or he) *knew* I disliked, I would
   a. work on the committee.
   b. tell her (or him) she (or he) had no business volunteering my time, call and tell the committee chairperson the same.
   c. tell her (or him) I want her (or him) to be more thoughtful in the future, and then make a plausible excuse she (or he) can give the committee chairperson.
8. If my four-year-old son "refused" to obey an order I gave him, I would
   a. let him do what he wanted.
   b. say, "You do it—and you do it now!"
   c. say, "Maybe you'll want to do it later on."

To score your responses for each item *except number 4,* give yourself 1 point for an *a* answer, 5 points for a *b* answer, and 3 points for a *c* answer. For item 4, give yourself 3 points for an *a,* 5 points for a *b,* and 1 point for a *c.* Add up your points. The total should fall between 8 and 40.

Your score should give you a hint regarding your usual manner of dealing with conflict. The closer you are to a score of 8, the more submissive (nonassertive) you are when involved in a conflict; the closer you are to a score of 40, the more aggressively you respond. A score near the midpoint (24) indicates you generally compromise as a means of dealing with conflict.

Resolving conflict can be relatively simple. What confounds the situation, however, are usually a lack of listening, an attempt at winning, an inability to demonstrate an understanding of the person with whom you are in conflict, and a rigidity that prevents you from considering alternative solutions. Consider the following example from *Sex Education: Theory and Practice* (Bruess and Greenberg).

Paul: Well, Barbara, as you know, Thanksgiving vacation is soon, and I'd like you to come home with me and spend it with my family.

Barbara: Now you ask! I've already told my folks to expect us for Thanksgiving dinner!

Paul: You've got some nerve! You didn't even ask me if I wanted to go to your house for Thanksgiving.

Barbara: Ask you? You've been hitting the books so much lately that I've hardly seen you long enough to say hello, much less ask you to Thanksgiving dinner.

Paul: What would you rather I do, fail my courses? You're pretty selfish, aren't you?

Barbara: I've had it! Either we're going to my house for Thanksgiving or you can say goodbye right now.

Paul: In that case, GOODBYE!

In this situation, both Paul and Barbara are trying to win. That is, each is trying to get the other to spend Thanksgiving vacation at the family home. However, neither Paul nor Barbara can win! You see, there are several choices presented by them, either overt or implied:

1. Spend the vacation at Paul's house
2. Spend the vacation at Barbara's house
3. Break up their relationship

If they decide to spend the vacation at Paul's, Barbara will be required to cancel her plans with her family and put up with the hassle that would entail. Further, she will feel that her wishes are not very important in the relationship. The bottom line is that she will resent being at Paul's for Thanksgiving.

On the other hand, if they spend the vacation at Barbara's house, Paul will resent having to be *there*. He might feel that since he asked first, they should be at his house. Further, he objects to Barbara's assuming she can make plans that include him without even bothering to consult him.

It becomes evident, then, that regardless of whose house they visit for the vacation, one or the other will be resentful. This resentment will probably result in the Thanksgiving vacation being uncomfortable and unenjoyable for all concerned. In other words, no matter who wins, both really lose. They both wind up with a miserable vacation. The third possibility, dissolving the relationship, is also obviously a no-win solution as well.

How might the issue of where to spend Thanksgiving vacation be better decided? Consider the following communication.

Paul: Well, Barbara, as you know, Thanksgiving vacation is soon, and I'd like you to come home with me and spend it with my family.

Barbara: Now you ask! I've already told my folks to expect us for Thanksgiving dinner!

Paul: You thought we would go to your house for Thanksgiving vacation?

Barbara: Yes, and my parents have made preparations already.

Paul: Your parents would be upset if we cancelled Thanksgiving dinner with them?

Barbara: You bet! And I wouldn't want to be the one to have to tell them either!

Paul: You think that your parents would really hassle you if you didn't spend Thanksgiving with them?

Barbara: Yes.

Paul: Would you also feel some embarrassment in having to change plans that your parents thought were definite?

Barbara: Yes, I guess I would.

Paul: It sounds like you were really looking forward to our being together at your house and with your family this vacation.

Barbara: Yes, I really was.

Paul: I'm glad that you included me in your Thanksgiving plans, but I really was looking forward to spending this vacation together with you and with *my* family. I haven't seen my family for a while and, further, I know that they would really like you. And I'm a little bothered that you didn't consult me before making plans for the vacation.

Barbara: Gee, I guess you have some rights, too. I'm sorry.

Paul: Well, let's see if there are some alternatives that we haven't considered.

Barbara: Maybe we could spend half the vacation at my house and half at yours.

Paul: Or perhaps we could invite your family to my house.

Barbara: How about staying here and not spending Thanksgiving with either of our families?

Paul: It seems like we have several possibilities. We could divide the vacation in half at each of our houses, but that would mean that we waste a good part of the vacation in travel.

Barbara: It's not very realistic, either, to expect that my whole family could cancel their plans to go to your house.

Paul: At the same time, if we stayed here, both sets of parents and family would be disappointed. That would be cutting off our noses to spite our faces.

Barbara: Would it make sense to agree to spend Thanksgiving vacation at one of our houses and the next vacation at the other's?

Paul: That seems sensible, and since you've already made plans, let's spend Thanksgiving at your house.

Barbara: Okay. Remember, though, the next vacation will be at your house.

In this example, Paul followed a simple procedure to resolve interpersonal conflict. The steps of this communication process consist of the following:

1. Active listening (reflecting back to the other person his or her *words* and *feelings*)
2. Identifying your position (stating your *thoughts* and *feelings* about the situation)
3. Exploring alternative solutions (brainstorming other possibilities)

He began by employing a technique known as **active listening,** or **reflective listening.** This technique requires the listener to paraphrase the words of the speaker so the speaker knows that his or her meaning has been received. Further, it requires the listener to go beyond the words of the speaker to paraphrase the *feelings* left unspoken. Note that Paul understood Barbara would be embarrassed to have to cancel Thanksgiving vacation with her family, even though she never explicitly stated that she would. By reflecting the speaker's *words* and *thoughts,* the listener creates an awareness on the speaker's part that the listener cares enough to really understand his or her views. Once the speaker appreciates this fact, he or she is more receptive to hearing and understanding the listener's viewpoint than previously. The net result will be both people understanding each other's point of view better; they will also be less insistent that their way is the only way.

The next step is to explore alternative solutions by "brainstorming." That is, list all possible solutions prior to evaluating their appropriateness. Once all possible solutions are listed, evaluate each proposed solution until both people agree upon one. With this technique it initially appears that no one wins. However, in fact, everyone wins. In the previous example, Paul will accompany Barbara to her house for Thanksgiving without being resentful. He will know that she now understands his need to be involved in their planning, and that the next vacation is going to be spent with his family. Consequently, he will be better able to enjoy being with Barbara and her family. The vacation will be fun, and everyone will win.

I can tell you that many people to whom I have taught this technique have dealt with their conflicts more successfully. Remember, though, that the purpose of this technique is *not* to convince someone that your point of view is correct. It is not a technique to manipulate anyone. The intention is to end up at an *alternative* solution that makes both you and the other person happy. If you are not willing to end up at some other solution than the one you had in mind, do not use this method of resolving conflict. If you are not willing to give up your power over the other person (e.g., parent over child or boss over employee), then don't use this technique.

A student of mine asked, "What happens if I use the steps you outlined and my daughter says, 'There you go with that psychology crap again.' What do I do then?" I told her to tell her daughter, "You're right. This is something I learned at school to help resolve conflict. I love you so much and place such a high value on our relationship that I felt I would try this technique. I hope we can both use it so when we disagree, we come to a solution both of us are happy with. Would you like me to teach it to you?" How can anyone object to the use of a system designed to help them arrive at a solution satisfactory to them both and maintain their relationship? I'll bet there are some conflicts that you can anticipate. Why not try achieving a positive resolution of those conflicts rather than generally giving in or being so stubborn that, although you get your way, you're not happy? Why not try a system that lets both you and the other person win? Try it; you'll like it.

Communication

In addition to learning to be more assertive and to resolve conflicts well, other communication skills will help you get along better with friends, family, and co-workers with the result being less stress.

Nonverbal Communication

Notice the body posture of your classmates. During an interesting lecture or activity, most of them will probably be leaning or looking toward the lecturer or the center of the group, indicating that they are involved in what is going on. During a boring class, they will probably be leaning away from the lecturer or group. We call this physical behavior body language. Communicating by the body posture often says as much as the spoken word. When people feel uncomfortable about expressing their thoughts or feelings verbally, body language is sometimes the only form of communication they participate in.

We all recognize the importance of communicating nonverbally, since we smile when we say hello, scratch our heads when perplexed, and hug a friend to show affection. We also have an array of body terms to describe our nonverbal behavior: "Keep a stiff upper lip," "I can't stomach him," "She has no backbone," "I'm tongue-tied," "He caught her eye," "I have two left feet," and "That was spine-tingling." We show appreciation and affection, revulsion, and indifference with expressions and gestures. We tell people we are interested in them by merely making eye contact and, like the male peacock displaying his feathers, we display our sexuality by the way we dress, walk, and even by how we stand.[1]

Verbal Communication

Unfortunately, the nonverbal expression of feelings and thoughts is easy to misinterpret. Consequently, depending on nonverbal communication alone to express yourself is to risk being misunderstood. Furthermore, if another person is depending on nonverbal communication to express feelings to you, it is up to you to ask—verbally—whether you are getting the right message. Without such a *reality check,* the other person, while totally failing to connect, might assume that he or she is communicating effectively. For example, imagine that a man and woman on their first date begin hugging, kissing, and caressing each other after a movie. The woman's breathing speeds up and the man, taking this as a sign of sexual arousal and interest, presses onward. When the woman suddenly pushes free and complains that the man is too impatient, he is confused. The problem here is one of interpretation rather than incompatibility. The rapid breathing that the man took as a sign of arousal was really a sign of nervousness. If these people had been more effective verbal communicators, they would have been able to clarify the situation in the beginning. Instead they reached a silent impasse, with him confused and her resentful. Check out your impressions of someone's nonverbal communication, and improve your communication by making your nonverbal and verbal messages as consistent as you can.

Planning Time to Talk

One common barrier to communication is the television set. We are often so busy watching it that we don't take the time to talk with those around us. To improve your communication with others, you may need to plan time for discussions. In setting up such times it is wise to do the following:

1. Make sure you allow sufficient time to have a meaningful discussion.
2. Disconnect the phone and don't allow other people to barge in on you.
3. Accept all feelings and the right for the verbal expression of these feelings. For example, it is just as appropriate to say, "I feel angry when . . ." as it is to say, "I feel terrific when . . ."
4. Take a risk and really describe your thoughts and feelings. Don't expect the other person to guess what they are.
5. Approach your discussions with both of you understanding that the goal is to improve your relationship.

Listening

This hint seems obvious and yet, as was demonstrated when we discussed conflict resolution, is often ignored. The listening and paraphrasing (active or reflective listening) is effective in regular conversation as well as during conflict. All of us can do a better job at listening. Try to pay more attention to this aspect of your communications.

Beginning with Agreement

You would be surprised at how much better you can communicate with someone with whom you disagree if you start your message with a point on which you do agree. Of course, this requires you to listen carefully so you can identify something with which you can agree. For example, if you are disagreeing about who should do the dishes, you might begin by saying, "I agree that it is important the dishes be cleaned." If you look and listen intently, you can always find a point of agreement.

"And", Not "But"

The word "but" is like an eraser; it erases everything that precedes it. When someone says, "Yes, your needs are important but . . ." they are saying, "Your needs may be important but let's forget about them because I'm about to tell you what's *really* important." In other words, the importance of your needs are being erased and now we can focus on the real issue. Listen to how people use the word "but" and you will get a real insight into how people communicate. Listen to how *you* use "but"!

Substituting the word "and" for "but" is so simple and yet so significant. "And" leaves what preceded it on the table and *adds* something to it. "Your needs are important and . . ." means that we will not discount (erase) your needs; we will just consider them in addition to considering what will be presented next. Use more "ands" and less "buts."

"I" Statements

Too often we try to get other people to behave or believe as we do. Others naturally resent that, just as we resent it when others try to get us to behave or believe as they do. Part of this problem relates to the words we use when communicating. Remember the DESC form example of the student who was expected to work on Saturdays? If not, reread it now and notice that the wording of her assertive response includes many "I" statements. For example, she doesn't say, "When *you* expect me to work on Saturdays . . ." She says, "When *I* am expected to work on Saturdays . . ." In this manner she doesn't place the focus on the boss's behavior but rather on the situation. Consequently, the boss need not get defensive, and they can better discuss and resolve the situation. When we say "you," we are making the other person feel that he or she is being criticized and needs to defend himself or herself. When we say "I" we are focusing on our feelings, beliefs, and interpretations. Feeling less defensive, the other person is more likely to listen to us, and the result is more effective communication.

Avoid "Why" Questions

As with statements that include "you" instead of "I," questions that begin with "why" make the other person defensive. "Why did you leave so early?" makes the other person have to justify leaving early. In addition, "why" questions are often veiled criticisms. "Why don't you spend more time with me?" may be asked to get an answer but, more often than not, is a statement ("You don't spend enough time with me!") rather than a question. Avoid "why" questions.

Time Management

One of the tasks we are often unsuccessful at is managing our time well. There really is no reason for this, since there are effective time management techniques. These techniques can help you with your most precious possession—your time. Time spent is time gone forever. In spite of what we often profess, we cannot save time. Time moves continually and it is used—one way or another. If we waste time, there is no bank where we can withdraw time we previously saved to replace the time wasted. To come to terms with our mortality (see chapter 18) is to realize that our time is limited. Given this realization and the probability that you would like to better organize your time (I've never met anyone who didn't profess that need), some techniques which can help are presented next.

Assessing How You Spend Time

As a first step in managing time better, you might want to analyze how you spend your time now. To do this, divide your day into fifteen-minute segments. Then, record what you are doing every fifteen minutes (see table 6.2). Afterward, review this time diary and total the time spent on each activity throughout the day (see table 6.3). For example, you might find you spent three hours watching television, one hour exercising, one hour studying, and two hours shopping. Next, evaluate that use of time. You might decide you spent too much time watching television and too little time studying. Based upon this evaluation, decide on an adjustment, but make it specific. For example, I will watch only one hour of television and will study two hours. A good way to actually make this change is to draw up a contract with yourself that includes a reward for being successful. The specifics of developing such a contract appear in chapter 13.

Setting Goals

The most important thing you can do to manage time is to set goals: daily, weekly, monthly, yearly, and long-range. If you don't have a clear sense of where you are headed, you will not be able to plan how to get there. Your use of time should be organized to maximize the chances of achieving your goals.

Prioritizing

Once you have your goals defined, you need to prioritize them and your activities. Not all of your goals will be equally important. Focus on those goals of major importance to you, and work on the other goals secondarily. Likewise, focus on activities most important to the achievement of your highest goals and on other activities afterward. To help with this, develop **A,B,C lists.**

On the A list are those activities which must get done; they are so important that not to do them would be very undesirable. For example, if your term paper is due next week and today is the only day this week you can get to the library to do the research required for that paper, going to the library goes on your A list today.

On the B list are those activities you'd like to do today and need to be done. However, if they don't get done today, it wouldn't be too terrible. For example, if you haven't spoken to a close friend and have been meaning to telephone, you might put that on your B list. Your intent is to call today, but if you don't get around to it, you can always call tomorrow or the next day.

On the C list are those activities you'd like to do if you get all the A and B lists' activities done. If the C list activities *never* get done, that would be just fine. For example, if a department store has a sale and you'd like to go browse, put that on your C list. If you do all of the A's and B's then you can go browse; if not, no big loss.

Table 6.2
Daily Record of Activity

Time (A.M.)	Activity	Time (A.M.)	Activity
12:00		6:00	
12:15		6:15	
12:30		6:30	
12:45		6:45	
1:00		7:00	
1:15		7:15	
1:30		7:30	
1:45		7:45	
2:00		8:00	
2:15		8:15	
2:30		8:30	
2:45		8:45	
3:00		9:00	
3:15		9:15	
3:30		9:30	
3:45		9:45	
4:00		10:00	
4:15		10:15	
4:30		10:30	
4:45		10:45	
5:00		11:00	
5:15		11:15	
5:30		11:30	
5:45		11:45	

Table 6.2
(continued)

Time (P.M.)	Activity	Time (P.M.)	Activity
12:00		6:00	
12:15		6:15	
12:30		6:30	
12:45		6:45	
1:00		7:00	
1:15		7:15	
1:30		7:30	
1:45		7:45	
2:00		8:00	
2:15		8:15	
2:30		8:30	
2:45		8:45	
3:00		9:00	
3:15		9:15	
3:30		9:30	
3:45		9:45	
4:00		10:00	
4:15		10:15	
4:30		10:30	
4:45		10:45	
5:00		11:00	
5:15		11:15	
5:30		11:30	
5:45		11:45	

Table 6.3
Summary of Activities (Sample)

Activity	Total Time Spent on Activity
Talking on the telephone	2 hours
Socializing	2 hours
Studying	1 hour
Watching television	3 hours
Exercising	1 hour
Shopping	2 hours
Housework	2 hours
In class	5 hours
Sleeping	6 hours

In addition, you should make a list of things *not to do*. For example, if you tend to waste your time watching television, you might want to include that on your not-to-do list. In that way you'll have a reminder not to watch television today. Other time wasters should be placed on this list as well.

Scheduling
Once you've prioritized your activities, you can then schedule them into your day. When will you go to the library? When will you grocery shop? Don't forget to schedule some relaxation and recreation as well.

Maximizing Your Rewards
In scheduling your activities, remember what some time management experts say: We get 80 percent of our rewards on only 20 percent of our activities and, conversely, get only 20 percent of our rewards on 80 percent of the time we spend. What that tells us is that we need to make sure we identify and engage in the 20 percent of the activities that give us 80 percent of our rewards *before* we move to the other activities. Maximize your rewards by organizing your time.

Saying No
I have a friend who says, "You mean that I don't have to do everything I want to do?" What he means is that there are so many activities he would love to engage in that he overloads himself and winds up not enjoying them as much and feeling overburdened. Because of guilt, concern for what others might think of us, or a real desire to engage in that activity, we have a hard time saying "no." The A,B,C lists and the scheduled activities will help identify how much time remains for other activities and make saying no easier.

Delegating
When possible, get others to do those things that need to be done, but do not need your personal attention. Conversely, avoid taking on chores which others try to delegate to you. A word of caution: this advice does not mean that you use other

people to do work you should be doing, or that you not help out others when they ask. What I am suggesting is that you be more *discriminating* regarding delegation of activities. Another way of stating this is not to hesitate to seek help when you are short on time and overloaded. Help others only when they really need it and you have the time available.

Evaluating Tasks Once
Many of us will open our mail, read through it, and set it aside to act on later. For example, I often receive a questionnaire from some graduate student doing a study on stress. My tendency is to put the questionnaire aside and fill it out later. However, that is a waste of time. If I pick it up later, I have to once again familiarize myself with the task. As much as possible, look things over only once. That means when you first pick it up be prepared to complete working on it *then*.

Using the Circular File
Another way of handling questionnaires is to file them—in the garbage can. How many times do you receive junk mail that is obvious from its envelope? You know, the kind addressed to "Resident"? In spite of knowing what is enclosed in that envelope and that when we read its contents we will just throw it all out anyhow, we still take the time to open it and read the junk inside. We would be better off bypassing the opening and reading part and going directly to the throwing out.

Limiting Interruptions
Throughout the day we will be interrupted from what we have planned to do. Recognizing this fact, we should actually schedule in times for interruptions. That is, don't make your schedule so tight that interruptions would throw you into a tizzy. On the other hand, try to keep these interruptions to a minimum. There are several ways you can accomplish that. You cannot accept phone calls between certain hours. Ask your roommate or secretary to take messages and call back later. Do the same with visitors. Anyone who visits should be asked to return at a more convenient time, or you should schedule a visit with them for later. If you are serious about making better use of your time, you will need to adopt some of these means of limiting interruptions. Adhere to your schedule as much as you can.

Investing Time
The bottom line of time management is that you need to invest time *initially* in order to benefit by the good use of your time subsequently. Those who attend my classes or workshops often say, "I don't have the time to organize myself the way you suggest. That would put me further in the hole." This is an interesting paradox. Those who feel they don't have time to plan the better use of their time probably need to take the time more than those who feel they do have the time. Confusing enough? Well, let me state it this way: If you are so pressed for time that you believe you don't even have sufficient time to get yourself organized, that in itself tells you that you are in need of applying time management skills. The investment in time devoted to organizing yourself will pay dividends by allowing you to achieve more of what is really important to you.

Social Support Networking

As mentioned earlier, one of the protective factors suspected of preventing stress-related illness or disease is social support. Social support is belonging, being accepted, being loved, or being needed "all for oneself and not for what one can do."[2] In different words, it is having people you can really talk to and to whom you feel close and with whom you share your joys, problems, apprehensions, and love. Social support can be provided by family members, friends, lovers, or anyone else who provides what is described above. The mediating effect of social support lies in the hypothesis that "significant others help an individual mobilize his psychological resources and master his emotional burdens; they share his tasks, and they provide him with extra supplies of money, materials, tools, skills, and cognitive guidance to improve his handling of the situation."[3] They help one deal with and feel better about stressors.

Social support has been found to be related to several indices of health and illness. Pregnant women with good social support, regardless of life-change units, were found to have only one-third the complications of pregnant women with poor social support.[4] Women who were experiencing major life stress but had intimate relationships were found to develop less depression than women experiencing life stress but lacking such relationships.[5] Unemployed men with high social support experienced lower levels of serum cholesterol, symptoms of illness, and emotional responses than did unemployed men with low support systems.[6]

To determine your social support, complete the following scale developed by Dean. For each statement, place one of the following letters in the blank space provided.

A = strongly agree
B = agree
C = uncertain
D = disagree
E = strongly disagree

_____ 1. Sometimes I feel all alone in the world.
_____ 2. I worry about the future facing today's children.
_____ 3. I don't get invited out by friends as often as I'd really like.
_____ 4. The end often justifies the means.
_____ 5. Most people today seldom feel lonely.
_____ 6. Sometimes I have the feeling other people are using me.
_____ 7. People's ideas change so much that I wonder if we'll ever have anything to depend on.
_____ 8. Real friends are as easy as ever to find.
_____ 9. It is frightening to be responsible for the development of a little child.
_____ 10. Everything is relative, and there just aren't any definite rules to live by.
_____ 11. One can always find friends, if one is friendly.
_____ 12. I often wonder what the meaning of life really is.
_____ 13. There is little or nothing I can do toward preventing a major "shooting" war.
_____ 14. The world in which we live is basically a friendly place.

_____ 15. There are so many decisions that have to be made today that sometimes I could just blow up.

_____ 16. The only thing one can be sure of today is that one can be sure of nothing.

_____ 17. There are few dependable ties between people anymore.

_____ 18. There is little chance for promotion on the job unless a person gets a break.

_____ 19. With so many religions abroad, one doesn't really know which to believe.

_____ 20. We're so regimented today that there's not much room for choice even in personal matters.

_____ 21. We are just cogs in the machinery of life.

_____ 22. People are just naturally friendly and helpful.

_____ 23. The future looks very dismal.

_____ 24. I don't get to visit friends as often as I'd like.

This scale measures several factors of alienation, one of which is social isolation. High social isolation scores indicate low social support, and vice versa. The nine items making up the social isolation subscale and the scoring for those items follow:

Item	Scoring
1	A = 4, B = 3, C = 2, D = 1, E = 0
3	A = 4, B = 3, C = 2, D = 1, E = 0
5	A = 0, B = 1, C = 2, D = 3, E = 4
8	A = 0, B = 1, C = 2, D = 3, E = 4
11	A = 0, B = 1, C = 2, D = 3, E = 4
14	A = 0, B = 1, C = 2, D = 3, E = 4
17	A = 4, B = 3, C = 2, D = 1, E = 0
22	A = 0, B = 1, C = 2, D = 3, E = 4
24	A = 4, B = 3, C = 2, D = 1, E = 0

Your total score should range between 0 and 36. The higher your score, the more socially isolated you believe yourself to be. Therefore, the higher your score, the less effective you believe your social support system to be. Do you need to improve your relationship with significant others?

The development of a social support system is complex and would require a whole book to describe. Certainly, the conflict-resolution technique and the assertiveness skills discussed in this chapter contribute to improved relationships. However, one of the keys to developing social support networks is being open and caring with others. It's often easier and less threatening to stay aloof and detached from others. Fear prevents getting close to others. We fear that if we show love for another person, we will be rejected by that person. We fear that we will

be embarrassed. We fear that we will be ridiculed. We even fear that we will find within ourselves an inability to be intimate, caring, and loving. To develop social support systems, however, requires an overcoming of these fears. I vividly recall listening to a colleague of mine, whom I had known casually for several years, give a speech upon the occasion of being awarded a professional honor. His speech was very uplifting and quite emotional. At its conclusion, my colleague was greeted with a standing ovation and hordes of well-wishers. As I was waiting to get close enough to congratulate him on the speech and the honor bestowed upon him, I noticed most women hugged him after their congratulations, whereas *all* the men shook his hand. At that time, I felt very close to my colleague. I wanted very much to grab him and hug his guts out, but fear entered my mind. What would other colleagues of mine think? What if Bob reached out with his hand, thereby rejecting my hug? Do I dare? Will I be embarrassed? Well, I rejected that fear, and when I got close enough, I hugged my colleague and told him how much I had enjoyed his speech and how deserving I believed he was of his honor. Do you know what? He hugged me harder than I hugged him! He turned out to be the "hugger," and I the "huggee"! That small incident remains with me always. If I had not taken a chance, I would have always regretted not hugging Bob. The chance taken resulted in our being closer than before. I now realize that these fleeting moments have great meaning in our lives, and that they present us with opportunities that are removed only too quickly. If we don't take advantage of them when they are presented to us, we probably will never have another chance.

Why don't you take a chance? Tell someone that you love him or her. Get involved with those around you. Show people you care about them. By doing so, you will be improving your social support network. You can expect this love, involvement, and care to rebound to you, allowing you to be more effective in managing the stress of your life.

Summary

1. Assertiveness is expressing yourself and satisfying your own needs while not hurting others in the process. People who cannot have their needs satisfied or who perceive their basic human rights are often violated will be stressed by that situation. The use of the DESC form can help organize a verbal assertive response, while standing straight and speaking clearly, fluently, and without hesitation can convey assertiveness nonverbally.

2. Conflicts resolved to only one person's satisfaction are not effectively resolved. A three-step approach to resolve conflict is effective in satisfying both people. This approach entails active listening, identifying the points of view, and exploring alternative solutions.

3. To improve communication, check out your impressions of someone's nonverbal messages, plan time to have discussions, listen better, begin disagreeing by stating a point of agreement, substitute the word "and" for the word "but," use "I" statements, and avoid "why" questions.

4. Time management skills involve setting goals and prioritizing them, making schedules, saying "no" when that is appropriate, delegating tasks, reviewing materials only once, limiting interruptions, and assessing how time is now spent.

5. Social support is belonging, being accepted, being loved, or being needed all for oneself and not for what one can do. It is having people to whom you feel close and with whom you share your joys, problems, apprehensions, and love. Social support can help protect you from the negative consequences of stress.

Notes

1. Jerrold S. Greenberg et al., *Sexuality: Insights and Issues,* 2d ed. (Dubuque, Iowa: William C. Brown, 1989).

2. G. E. Moss, *Illness, Immunity and Social Interaction* (New York: John Wiley & Sons, 1973), 237.

3. G. Caplan, *Support Systems and Community Mental Health* (New York: Behavioral Publications, 1974), 6.

4. K. Nuckolls, J. Cassel, and B. Kaplan, "Psychosocial Assets, Life Crises, and the Prognosis of Pregnancy," *American Journal of Epidemiology* 95(1972):431–41.

5. G. W. Brown, M. Bhroclain, and T. Harris, "Social Class and Psychiatric Disturbance among Women in an Urban Population," *Sociology* 9(1975):225–54.

6. S. Gore, "The Effects of Social Support in Moderating the Health Consequences of Unemployment," *Journal of Health and Social Behavior* 19(1978):157–65.

Perception Interventions

There's a story going around the sex education circuit that is used to introduce the topic of guilt about sexual behavior. It seems an elephant and an ant, in a moment of unbridled passion, spent the night making love. The next morning the ant learned that the elephant had a terminal disease and would soon die. Amazed and piqued, the ant said, "One night of passion and I spend the rest of my life digging a grave."

The ant viewed that situation as frustrating, unfair, and distressing. That needn't have been the case. The ant might have chosen to focus upon the enjoyable evening spent crawling all over the elephant's wrinkled skin (or however ants make love to elephants). Instead, the ant remembered the displeasing aspects of the situation. In short, that is what this chapter is about: perceiving life changes and other stressors as less distressing by attending to their positive aspects and de-emphasizing their negative ones.

Selective Awareness

We all are free to choose what to think, although most of us don't exercise this control of our thoughts but allow them to ride the high seas rudderless. To complicate matters, we have been taught to be critical rather than supportive—focusing on the bad rather than the good. If you doubt the validity of this observation, consider the following:

1. When people are complimented, they often feel embarrassed. A woman being told how nice her dress is might say, "Oh, it's really quite old." The translation might be "You don't have taste enough to recognize an old *schmatta* (rag)" when the woman is really flattered but too embarrassed (due to lack of experience in being complimented) to know how to react appropriately.

   Or consider this exchange: You may say, "Joe, that was a very nice thing you did." Joe answers, "Oh, it was nothing." (Said with eyes looking down.) Joe is really saying, "I'm too uncomfortable being told something nice. It doesn't happen very often. I'd know how to respond to criticism, but have difficulty when I'm complimented."

2. When term papers are submitted to professors, too often they come back with comments only directed at improving the paper. Noticeably absent are notes underlining the good parts of the paper.

3. If you took two exams and received your grades back today, one a 43% and the other a 93%, which would you remember throughout that day—the one you passed or the one you failed?

Other examples of our inexperience in focusing on the positive can be offered, but I think the point is made. Now, what to do about it? The first step is to realize that in any situation there are both good and bad, positive and negative elements. Before I realized this, I couldn't bear to wait at airports for a plane. I defined that situation as a waste of my valuable time, unnecessary, and frustrating. Now I view the time I wait at airports as an opportunity to study people. I've learned a lot about parenting by observing a wide range of parenting styles in airport terminals. I've gotten ideas about how to coordinate my clothes by noticing well-dressed men at ticket counters. And I've become familiar with the types of literature people are interested in by noting their purchases at the gift shops located in most airports. What enjoyable and interesting places airports can be! Mind you, given the choice, I wouldn't opt for spending time at airports. The point is that I'm often not given a choice. If I want to travel by airplane (my initial choice), I must accept waiting in terminals. However, even though I may not be able to choose whether to wait at airports or not, I can choose how I perceive that situation. To put it physiologically, I can choose to raise my blood pressure, serum cholesterol, heart rate, and muscle tension, or I can choose not to alter these body processes. That choice is mine. Even if the situation is so bad that it couldn't possibly get any worse, I could choose to focus upon the fact that things have to get better.

Some typically distressing situations are listed below. Being selectively aware of a positive aspect of each situation, write in the space provided your positive definition of that situation.

1. Waiting in a long line to register for classes _____

_____

_____

2. Being stuck in bumper-to-bumper traffic _____

_____

_____

3. Having to make a presentation before a group of people _____

_____

_____

4. Being rejected from something because you're too old _____

_____

_____

Selective awareness can help you recognize that even if your life now seems to be heading downhill, it soon will reach the bottom and start upward again.

5. Having a relationship break up _____

_____

_____

Right now there are situations in your life that are causing you a great deal of stress. You may not like where you live, or whom you're living with, or the work you're doing. You may not feel you have enough time to yourself or for leisure-time activities. You may not like the way you look. You may be in poor health. You may be alone. Some of these stressors you may be able to change; some you will not be able to change. You now know, however, that you can become selectively aware of their positive components while de-emphasizing (though not denying) their disturbing features. On a separate sheet of paper why not list these stressors, and list the positive aspects of each upon which you will choose to focus?

Why not go even further? Each time you do something that works out well, keep the memory of that with you. Tell others how proud of yourself you are. Pat yourself on the back. Take time just before bedtime (or some other convenient time of day) to recall all the good things about that day. Don't be like some of your friends who can't sleep because they still feel embarrassed about something they did that day or worried about something over which they have no control. In the words of a best-seller of several years ago, "Be your own best friend." Revel in your good points and the glory of your day.

Life can be a celebration if you take the time to celebrate. It is the curse of the **Stop to Smell** Great Somebody that we work long and hard to achieve some goal, bask in the **the Roses** glow of satisfaction only fleetingly, and proceed to work long and hard toward the next goal. I have been the advisor of many doctoral students. Many of these students have no idea that the four or five years of graduate school they endure will lead to a sense of accomplishment that will dissipate after only several months. For these students not to enjoy this graduate school experience, and to wonder at its conclusion where the time all went, is sad. From my perspective, and I suspect from theirs, graduate students who make the most of this experience but do not complete their degrees are far better off than those who get degrees but have not *experienced* the experience.

It is even sadder to see a person near the end of his or her life who achieved a lot but never enjoyed the achieving. In spite of acquiring money, property, fame, or doctoral degrees, he or she remains disheartened by missing out on what life is all about—living, experiencing, smelling the roses while trying not to get caught on the thorns.

What prevents us from being aware of life as we live it is often the routine of daily experience. When we experience something over and over again in the same manner, we become habituated to it. We are desensitized to that experience and interact with it out of habit, paying little attention to what we're doing. You and I do that very, very often. By way of example, I'll bet that when you travel to school or work, you take the same route each time. As a matter of fact, you probably chose this route because it was the fastest one. There may be other routes that are more scenic or interesting, but you chose quickness as your number one priority. There may be other routes that would bring you in contact with more cars and the opportunity to see more people, but you chose quickness as your number one priority. There may be other routes that would traverse rural, sub-urban, urban, and business areas, thereby allowing for more variety, but you chose quickness as your number one priority.

Aside from missing out on scenery, other cars and people, and varied areas through which to travel, the sameness of whatever route we've chosen also de-sensitizes us to the experience. To create yet another barrier to experiencing the travel, we turn on our car radios. We travel to work or school, and before we know it, we're there. The time just flew. We lost that time and that experience by not being aware of it and consciously smelling the roses en route. Think for a moment:

Do you experience "the getting there" or only "the having gotten there"?

Have you ever consciously felt the *texture* of the steering wheel you hold so often?

Do you ever listen to the *sounds* of your car and the neighborhoods you travel through?

If you travel by public transportation, have you made an effort to talk with people?

Have you gotten off the bus or train a stop before or after your usual one to walk through different streets?

There are other ways to experience life more fully, too. When I was in graduate school, I used to imagine that I was blind by shutting my eyes. This allowed me to concentrate upon my other senses; as a result I smelled smells I hadn't before and heard sounds to which I had previously been deaf. What's more, when I opened my eyes, I allowed myself to be bombarded with a psychedelic array of visual stimulation. For example, I would stare at the colors of the jackets of books in my bookcase. Have you ever done that? What a magnificent sight that can be! I also used to stare at my record album covers and the sizes, shapes, and colors of foods in my refrigerator. Again, the idea is to make yourself consciously aware of your experience, as you are going through it, by adopting less routine and habitual behavior. Try these routine-breaking exercises:

If you have a drawer of silverware neatly compartmentalized (knives here, forks there), take out the divider or tray and place the silverware in the drawer in random fashion. In this way, when you want a spoon you will have to experience the obtaining of one.

If your shoes are in your closet in pairs, or neatly paired in a shoe bag or shoe rack, rearrange them in random fashion. When you need a pair of shoes, you will then have to experience the search for them. You can do the same with your socks if you usually keep them organized in pairs.

Perspective and Selective Awareness

Whenever I think of the importance of perception in general, and selective awareness in particular, I recall one day several years ago that seemed to be heading downhill in a hurry. Before noon I had received a telephone call notifying me that some consulting work I was attempting to organize wasn't coming together, a letter stating that a grant proposal I had submitted would not be funded, and a manuscript I had submitted was rejected. As you might imagine, I was down in the dumps. I was feeling very sorry for myself, forgetting all the consultations I had successfully completed, research studies I'd had funded, and manuscripts I'd written and had published. Now I can say (the fog was too thick at the time) that I chose to be selectively aware of the defeats of that day rather than focus upon past and anticipated future successes.

Well, a proper perspective was soon achieved with just two phone calls. First, I received a call from a colleague at a university where I had previously taught. He told me about two former deans under whom we had worked. It seems that the married daughter of one of them awoke in the middle of the night and, not being able to sleep, arose from bed to get something in another room. Her husband, who was still sleeping when she arose, heard noises in the house, reached for his gun, and thinking her a burglar, shot his wife in the head. As I write this she is still in a coma. My heart went out to Harry when I heard about his daughter's ordeal (and, consequently, his).

The second story my colleague told me during that phone call described the recent accident another dean of ours had while pruning a tree. To get the top of the tree pruned, he extended a ladder and proceeded to climb it. When he found part of the tree out of his reach, he leaned and stretched toward that part, tipping the ladder, falling, and landing on a tree stump. Since he was still in the hospital,

I called him to offer whatever feeble support I could. When I reached him, he described the accident and his severe injuries (to this day he experiences pain daily) and the physical therapy he would need. But he said two things that I'll always remember. He said it took twenty minutes for the ambulance to arrive, during which time he was afraid to move since he had landed on his back and feared a spinal injury. When he was placed on the stretcher, though, he wiggled his toes and fingers, and the knowledge that he was able to do that made him cry. The other thing he said was how great the hospital staff treated him, how competent the ambulance drivers were, and how lucky he was to be alive and able to move. I called him with the intention of cheering him up, and it turned out that he cheered me up. Warren was almost killed, fearful of paralysis, and in a great deal of pain as he spoke with me, but he chose to discuss how lucky he was. WOW!!

After those telephone calls, my consulting, grant proposal, and manuscript did not seem very important. I had my health, a lovely family, and a job I really enjoyed. The rest of my day would, I decided, be appreciated. I would focus on the positive.

I'm reminded of the college student who wrote her parents describing the accident she had falling out of the sixth-floor window of her dormitory. She described how she was writing with her left hand since her right side was paralyzed. She had met a hospital orderly, however, with whom she fell in love, and they had decided to elope and marry just as soon as she recovered. Although he wasn't very educated, was of a different race and religion, and was addicted to heroin, she wrote that he had promised to make a good husband. Well, the letter continued in this way until the closing sentence in which the daughter stated that everything she had written so far was untrue. There was no accident, no paralysis, and no hospital orderly to marry; however, she continued, "I did fail my chemistry course and wanted you to be able to view this in its proper perspective."

Humor and Stress

The definition of an optimist: A seventy-year-old man has an affair with a young, vivacious, curvaceous, twenty-year-old woman. Before too long, she finds out she's pregnant and irately calls her lover. "You old fool! You made me pregnant!" The elderly man answers, "Who's calling, please?"

Humor is used throughout this book. It captures your interest and thereby helps you to learn more about stress than you might otherwise. In addition, humor has been shown to be an effective means of coping with stress.[1] It can defuse stressful situations and/or feelings. Research investigations have verified this conclusion. For example, Martin and Lefcourt found that humor prevented negative life events from resulting in mood disturbances.[2] In a study of 334 undergraduates enrolled in introductory psychology classes, Labott and Martin also found that coping with humor acted as a buffer between negative life events and mood disturbances.[3]

Humor can take several forms. It can use surprise, exaggeration, absurdity, incongruity (like two or more incompatible ideas or feelings), word play (puns, double entendres), or the tragic twist (juxtaposition of the tragic and comic poles of a given phenomenon followed by reconciliation in a humorous synthesis).[4] Regardless of the type of humor, its effects on health have been studied for many years. Summarizing a review of the effects of humor on health, Robinson states, ". . . there has been much support for the emotionally therapeutic value of humor as an adaptive, coping behavior, as a catharsis for and relief of tension, as a defense against depression, as a sign of emotional maturity, and as a survival mechanism. . . . there is some evidence that humor is good for you."[5]

Humor results in both physiological and psychological changes. Laughter increases muscular activity, respiratory activity, oxygen exchange, heart rate, and the production of catecholamines and endorphins. These effects are soon followed by a relaxation state in which respiration, heart rate, blood pressure, and muscle tension rebound to below normal levels.[6] Psychological effects include the relief of anxiety, stress, and tension; an outlet for hostility and anger; an escape from reality; and a means of tolerating crises, tragedy, chronic illnesses and/or disabilities.[7]

On the other hand, humor can be used inappropriately and actually cause distress. Sands states this potential of humor well: ". . . anyone who has seen the hurt and puzzled expression on another's face in response to an ironic remark, or remembers how he or she may have felt as an object of a joke, has witnessed humor's power to cause distress."[8] Unfortunately, Sands continues, humor's effects are not always predictable. Consequently, it is recommended that humor be used carefully when helping someone else cope with stress so as not to exacerbate the situation. However, once consideration is given to the potential negative effects of humor and they are judged to be minimal, don't hesitate to use this approach when you think it would be helpful. Regarding humor-coping for yourself, look for the humorous aspects of a stressful situation or a stress-producing person and you will be better able to manage the stress involved.

Far from humorous are people who always seem busy, are always rushing somewhere, and never seem to slow down. We usually envision these people as business executives with perspiration-stained armpits, cigarettes dangling from their lips, and shirtsleeves rolled up, working overtime at desks piled high with papers. However, as will soon be noted, others also fit into the hurry, rush syndrome. Unfortunately, this stereotype often fits ourselves or our loved ones as well. I say "unfortunately" because a large body of research relates this behavior to the early onset of coronary heart disease.

Type A Behavior Pattern

Before proceeding further, read each item below and check whether the behavior described is like or unlike yours. This scale is based upon one in *Type A Behavior and Your Heart* by Friedman and Rosenman.

Like me	Unlike me	
_____	_____	1. I explosively accentuate key words during ordinary speech.
_____	_____	2. I utter the last few words of a sentence more rapidly than the opening words.
_____	_____	3. I always move, walk, and eat rapidly.
_____	_____	4. I feel an impatience with the rate at which most events take place.
_____	_____	5. I hurry the speech of others by saying "Uh huh" or "Yes, yes," or by finishing their sentences for them.
_____	_____	6. I become enraged when a car ahead of me runs at a pace I consider too slow.
_____	_____	7. I find it anguishing to wait in line.
_____	_____	8. I find it intolerable to watch others perform tasks I know I can do faster.
_____	_____	9. I find myself hurrying my reading or attempting to obtain condensations or summaries of truly interesting and worthwhile literature.
_____	_____	10. I frequently strive to think about or do two or more things simultaneously.

Like me	*Unlike me*	
_____	_____	11. I find it always difficult to refrain from talking about or bringing the theme of any conversation around to those subjects which especially interest me.
_____	_____	12. I always feel vaguely guilty when I relax or do nothing for several hours to several days.
_____	_____	13. I no longer observe the more important, interesting, or lovely objects I encounter.
_____	_____	14. I don't have any time to spare to become the things worth *being* because I am so preoccupied with getting the things worth *having*.
_____	_____	15. I attempt to schedule more and more in less and less time.
_____	_____	16. I am always rushed.
_____	_____	17. When meeting another aggressive, competitive person I feel a need to challenge that person.
_____	_____	18. In conversations, I frequently clench my fist, or bang on the table, or pound one fist into the palm of another for emphasis.
_____	_____	19. I habitually clench my jaw, grind my teeth, or jerk back the corners of my mouth exposing my teeth.
_____	_____	20. I believe that whatever success I enjoy is due in good part to my ability to get things done faster than others.
_____	_____	21. I find myself increasingly committed to translating and evaluating not only my own but also the activities of others in terms of "numbers."

If you've found that a majority of these statements do describe you, you probably possess some degree of **Type A behavior patterns.** Type A behavior is "a particular complex of personality traits, including excessive competitive drive, aggressiveness, impatience, and a harrying sense of time urgency" as well as a "free-floating but well-rationalized form of hostility, and almost always a deep-seated insecurity." This behavior pattern has been found to be associated with the development of coronary heart disease. But that's getting the cart before the horse. The manner in which this association was discovered is interesting in and of itself.

Two cardiologists called in an upholsterer to reupholster the seats in their waiting room. The upholsterer inquired about the type of practice these physicians had, since he noticed that only the front edges of the chair seats were worn out. These cardiologists later realized that people who came to them with heart disease seemed to be "on edge"; they literally sat on the edges of their seats as though preparing for some action. Meyer Friedman and Ray Rosenman, the two cardiologists, defined and named the Type A behavior pattern. They later compared patients with coronary heart disease to healthy controls (people similar in all respects except they did not have coronary heart disease) and found a significantly greater degree of Type A behavior in the patients than in the controls. These retrospective studies[9,10] (comparisons *after* the development of the disease) were followed by prospective studies that monitored subjects without a history of coronary heart disease, tested them for the Type A behavior pattern, and then determined (after more than ten years) whether more Type A's developed coronary heart disease than Type B's.[11,12] Type B's possess an opposite behavior pattern. People possessing the **Type B behavior pattern** exhibit no free-floating hostility or sense of time urgency and aren't excessively competitive. As you might expect, significantly more Type A's than Type B's subsequently developed coronary heart disease.

Type A's tend to smoke cigarettes more and have higher levels of serum cholesterol[13,14] (both risk factors associated with coronary heart disease), but when these factors are held constant, Type A's still experience more coronary heart disease than Type B's. Various reviews[15,16] of the great body of research on the Type A behavior pattern and coronary heart disease have concluded that "individuals classified as Type A more frequently suffer from coronary disease and obstruction of the coronary vessels."[17] In addition, some researchers have found that Type A's who have a heart attack are more likely to have a second attack than Type B's who have a heart attack; they also have more severe heart attacks than Type B's.[18] However, for some as yet unexplained reason, Type A's are more likely to survive a heart attack than are Type B's.[19]

Type A behavior can be exhibited by females just as well as males, and it is just as unhealthy for women as it is for men. Type A women who were subjects in the Framingham Heart Study (where much of our knowledge about heart disease originates) were four times as likely to develop heart disease than their Type B counterparts.[20] In his more recent book, *Treating Type A Behavior and Your Heart,* Meyer Friedman reports that Type A business and professional workers were "found to be suffering from coronary heart disease approximately seven times more frequently than Type B women remaining in their homes as housewives."[21]

However, as with most human behavior, Type A is more complex than simply a set of behaviors leading to a specific disease. Two excellent reviews of research on Type A behavior pattern provide evidence of the problems associated with obtaining a definitive understanding of this concept.[22,23] For example, when Type A behavior is measured by an interview, different results may be obtained than when measured by a paper and pencil test.[24,25] In addition, several large studies have not found any relationship between Type A behavior pattern and mortality[26] or duration of stay in coronary care units.[27]

The person who never seems to have enough time, who is excessively competitive and aggressive, and who often exhibits hostility is said to possess a Type A behavior pattern.

Relative to the constellation of behaviors associated with Type A, it appears that hostility and anger may be the key. Barefoot, Dahlstrom, and Williams tested 255 medical school students on hostility and followed them over the next twenty-five years.[28] Independent of such coronary risk factors as age, smoking status, and family history of hypertension, hostility scores predicted incidence of coronary heart disease and all causes of mortality. Similar results were found in a ten-year follow-up study by Shekelle; that is, hostility scores were related to myocardial infarction or death due to coronary heart disease.[29] Furthermore, studies regarding anger have found that people who hold anger in are more prone to coronary heart disease than are those who express their anger or who at least discuss it.[30] As more studies are being conducted, a further clarification of the role of Type A behavior pattern on our health will develop. For now at least, it seems prudent to attempt to modify our Type A behavior.

Type A Behavior Modification

Well, what can you do about your Type A behavior? First you must realize that Type A behavior is, like all other behavior, learned. From parents who rush us to clean up or get ready for bed, teachers who expect us to complete our work in the time allotted, and bosses who require us to get a lot done, Type A behavior finds reinforcements throughout our society. In fact, recently it was found that

General Applications: Life-Situation and Perception Interventions

Type A fathers tend to produce Type A sons.[31] Behavior that is rewarded tends to be repeated. The key, then, is to reward Type B behavior while ignoring or punishing Type A behavior. For example, if you rush through a traffic light as it begins to turn red in an attempt to prevent delay, that behavior should be punished. You might decide to drive clear around the block for such a Type A demonstration. On the other hand, when you make it through a week without doing business over lunch or have a week in which you engage in some form of relaxation daily, buying yourself a new article of clothing, tennis racket, or something else rewarding would be in order.

One way to begin a Type A behavior modification program is to set weekly, realistic, and attainable goals and to identify rewards to be applied when these goals are achieved. Similarly, list behaviors you wish to eliminate and punishments you are prepared to apply if these behaviors are not eliminated on schedule. Chapter 13 also presents some useful suggestions that can help you adopt new behavior patterns.

Some additional suggestions for decreasing Type A behavior have been offered by Friedman and Rosenman:

1. Recognize that life is always an unfinishedness. It's unrealistic to believe you will finish everything needing to be done without something else needing to be done presenting itself.
2. Listen quietly to the conversation of other people, refraining from interrupting them or in any other way attempting to speed them up.
3. Concentrate on one thing at a time.
4. Don't interfere with others doing a job that you think you can do faster.
5. When confronted with a task, ask yourself—
   a. Will this matter have importance five years from now?
   b. Must I do this right now?
   Your answers will place tasks in proper perspective.
6. Before speaking ask yourself—
   a. Do I really have anything important to say?
   b. Does anyone want to hear it?
   c. Is this the time to say it?
   If the answer to any of these is no, remain quiet.
7. Tell yourself daily that no activity ever failed because someone executed it too slowly, too well.
8. Refrain from making appointments or scheduling your activities when unnecessary Try to maintain as flexible a schedule as possible.
9. Remember that your time is precious and must be protected. When possible, pay someone else to do bothersome chores and save your time.
10. Purposely frequent restaurants, theatres, and other such places where you know there will be some waiting required. Perceive such occasions as an opportunity to get to know your companion better or, if alone, as a chance to get some "downtime" away from the books, phone, or people seeking your time.

11. Practice eliminating polyphasic behavior (doing two or more things at the same time) by reading books that demand your entire attention and patience. A several volume novel that is complex would work well. [Proust's *The Remembrance of Things Past* has been recommended by Friedman and Rosenman.]
12. Plan relaxing breaks from activities you know will result in tension by nature of the time or effort required to do them. Plan these breaks to occur *prior* to the feelings of tension and pressure.
13. Engage in daily practice of a recognized relaxation technique [see the chapters in part 3].
14. Smile at as many people as you can so as to decrease free-floating hostility.
15. Thank people for nice things they've done.
16. Remind yourself daily that no matter how many things you've acquired, unless they've improved your mind or spirit, they are relatively worthless.
17. Consider most of your opinions as only provisionally correct, while maintaining an open mind to new ideas.
18. Seek some "aloneness" regularly.
19. Consolidate your relationships with some friends and acquaintances to make them more intimate and rewarding.
20. Spend time periodically remembering your past and the well from which you sprang.

Self-esteem

What you think of yourself affects how you behave. This concept will be explained shortly, but first read each of the statements below and check whether the qualities described are like or unlike yours. These statements are based upon the Coopersmith Inventory.*

Like me	Unlike me	
_____	_____	1. I'm a lot of fun to be with.
_____	_____	2. I always do the right thing.
_____	_____	3. I get upset easily at home.
_____	_____	4. I'm proud of my schoolwork.
_____	_____	5. I never worry about anything.
_____	_____	6. I'm easy to like.
_____	_____	7. I like everyone I know.
_____	_____	8. There are many times I'd like to leave home.
_____	_____	9. I like to be called on in class.
_____	_____	10. No one pays much attention to me at home.
_____	_____	11. I'm pretty sure of myself.
_____	_____	12. I'm not doing as well at school as I'd like to.

*Reproduced by special permission of the publisher. Consulting Psychologists Press, Inc., Palo Alto, CA from *The Self-Esteem Inventory, School Form* by Stanley Coopersmith, Ph.D. Copyright 1975. Further reproduction is prohibited without the publisher's consent.

You have just completed sample questions from a scale used to measure self-esteem that discloses in how much esteem you hold yourself (how highly you regard yourself, your sense of self-worth). Let's score these sample items and then discuss the implications of self-esteem for stress management. Place the number 1 to the left of items 1, 4, 6, 9, and 11 that you checked "like me." Place the number 1 to the left of items 2, 3, 5, 7, 8, 10, and 12 that you checked "unlike me."

Some people deliberately lie on these types of inventories because they think it's clever, or because they are embarrassed to respond honestly to items that evidence their low regard for themselves. Other people do not provide accurate responses because they rush through the inventory without giving each item the attention and thought necessary. In any case, this inventory contains a *lie scale* to identify the inaccurate responders. A lie scale includes items that can only be answered one way if answered accurately. A look at the items making up the lie scale will quickly elucidate the point. Items 2, 5, and 7 can only be answered one way. No one always does the right thing, never worries, or likes everyone. Add up the points you scored on the lie scale by adding the 1's you placed alongside these three items. If you didn't score at least 2, the rest of your scores are suspect; they may not be valid. Eliminating the three lie-scale items, add up the remaining 1's for your total self-esteem score.

This general self-esteem score, however, doesn't provide the kind of information needed to improve your self-esteem and thereby decrease the stress you experience. You may feel good about one part of yourself (e.g., your physical appearance) but be embarrassed about another part (e.g., your intelligence). Your general self-esteem score, however, averages these scores, and you lose this important information. To respond to this concern, the measure consists of three subscales that are specific to various components of self-esteem. The subscales and the items included within them follow:

Social self	Items 1, 6, 11
Family self	Items 3, 8, 10
School/work self	Items 4, 9, 12

To determine in how much esteem you hold yourself in social settings and interactions, add up the 1's by those three items. Do likewise to see how much regard you hold for yourself in your family interactions and in school or work settings. The closer to three you score, the higher your self-esteem for that particular subscale. Remember, however, that these scores are only a rough approximation; the entire Coopersmith Inventory would have to be taken and scored for an accurate reading.

Before we discuss the relationship between self-esteem and stress, one other component should be added to your knowledge of how you feel about yourself. That component relates to your feelings and thoughts about your physical self—

your physical self-esteem. In the blanks below, place the number on the scale that best represents your view of each body part listed.

1 = very satisfied
2 = OK
3 = not very satisfied
4 = very dissatisfied

____	1. hair	____	13. chest
____	2. face	____	14. eyes
____	3. neck	____	15. toes
____	4. shoulders	____	16. back
____	5. hips	____	17. mouth
____	6. legs	____	18. chin
____	7. fingers	____	19. thighs
____	8. abdomen	____	20. arms
____	9. nose	____	21. knees
____	10. ears	____	22. genitals
____	11. buttocks	____	23. elbows
____	12. hands	____	24. calves

Now for how all of this information can be used. If you don't think well of yourself, you will not trust your opinions or your decisions. You will therefore be more apt to be influenced by others. Not "marching to the beat of your own drum" may result in your conforming to the behaviors of those with whom you frequently interact. As a matter of fact, we know that poor self-esteem is related to drug abuse, irresponsible sexual behavior, and other "unhealthy" activities. People with high self-esteem engage in these activities to a significantly lesser extent.

We've previously discussed assertiveness, success, and social support as components of stress management. Self-esteem is related to each of these. How can you assert yourself and demand your basic rights if you don't deem yourself worthy of these rights? If you hold yourself in low regard, how can you use nonverbal assertive behavior? To stand straight and steady, to speak clearly and fluently, to maintain eye contact, and to speak with assurance require a good degree of self-confidence.

Self-esteem is learned. How people react to us; what we come to believe are acceptable societal standards of beauty, competence, and intelligence; and how our performances are judged by parents, teachers, friends, and bosses affect how we feel about ourselves. It is common sense, then, to expect our successes to improve our self-esteem and our failures to diminish it. Use the success-analysis activity in chapter 5 to help you identify how you can feel more successful and thereby improve your sense of self-worth. You can learn how to "stack the deck" in your life so the odds of success exceed the odds of failure.

Lastly, how can you expect to make friends and establish intimate relationships if you don't think enough of yourself to believe others would want to be your friend or care about you? Since you now know of the buffering effect of social support, you can imagine how poor self-esteem, resulting in a poor social support network, would be related to the development of stress-related illness and disease.

The very essence of stress management requires confidence in yourself and in your decisions to control your life effectively.

Because self-esteem is so important, the means of improving it deserve your serious attention. There are no magic pills to take or laser beams you can be zapped with to improve your sense of self-worth. It has developed over a long period of time, and it will take a while for you to change it. With time, attention, effort, and energy, you can enhance your sense of self or at least feel better about those parts of you that cannot be changed.

The first thing to do is to identify that part of yourself about which you want to feel better. If it's a part of your physical self, your scores (the 3's and 4's) on the body-part scale will direct you to those specific parts that need work. Perhaps an exercise program can improve that part, or you need to begin a weight-control program, pay more attention to how you dress, or use makeup more effectively. After this kind of introspection, one of my students decided to have electrolysis done to remove some hair above her lips. Another student began exercises to tighten the muscles in the buttocks. What can you do to improve a part of your physical self, or to feel better about parts that cannot be improved?

To identify other components of your self-esteem you might want to improve, look for your *lowest* subscale score. This is the part of yourself you hold in lowest regard. Next, ask yourself what you can do to perform better at work or school, in your family role, or in social settings. Perhaps you need to spend more time with your family. Maybe you need to ask your boss if you can attend a training program being offered nearby. Asking the campus librarian to help you use the library better might do the trick. Seeking honest feedback from friends about your strengths and weaknesses could help, as well as being more open with them about your inner thoughts, feelings, passions, and frustrations.

Whatever you decide to do—

Do it now!

Stick with it!

You really can feel better about yourself.

Before discussing this topic, circle the answers below that best describe your beliefs.

Locus of Control

1. a. Grades are a function of the amount of work students do.
   b. Grades depend on the kindness of the instructor.
2. a. Promotions are earned by hard work.
   b. Promotions are a result of being in the right place at the right time.
3. a. Meeting someone to love is a matter of luck.
   b. Meeting someone to love depends on going out often so as to meet many people.
4. a. Living a long life is a function of heredity.
   b. Living a long life is a function of adopting healthy habits.

5. a. Being overweight is determined by the number of fat cells you were born with or developed early in life.
   b. Being overweight depends on what and how much food you eat.
6. a. People who exercise regularly set up their schedules to do so.
   b. Some people just don't have the time for regular exercise.
7. a. Winning at poker depends on betting correctly.
   b. Winning at poker is a matter of being lucky.
8. a. Staying married depends upon working at the marriage.
   b. Marital breakup is a matter of being unlucky in choosing the wrong marriage partner.
9. a. Citizens can have some influence on their governments.
   b. There is nothing an individual can do to affect governmental function.
10. a. Being skilled at sports depends on being born well coordinated.
    b. Those skilled at sports work hard at learning those skills.
11. a. People with close friends are lucky to have met someone to be intimate with.
    b. Developing close friendships takes hard work.
12. a. Your future depends on whom you meet and on chance.
    b. Your future is up to you.
13. a. Most people are so sure of their opinions that their minds cannot be changed.
    b. A logical argument can convince most people.
14. a. People decide the direction of their lives.
    b. For the most part, we have little control of our futures.
15. a. People who don't like you just don't understand you.
    b. You can be liked by anyone you choose to like you.
16. a. You can make your life a happy one.
    b. Happiness is a matter of fate.
17. a. You evaluate feedback and make decisions based upon it.
    b. You tend to be easily influenced by others.
18. a. If voters studied nominees' records, they could elect honest politicians.
    b. Politics and politicians are corrupt by nature.
19. a. Parents, teachers, and bosses have a great deal to say about one's happiness and self-satisfaction.
    b. Whether you are happy depends upon you.
20. a. Air pollution can be controlled if citizens would get angry about it.
    b. Air pollution is an inevitable result of technological progress.

You have just completed a scale measuring locus of control. Locus of control is the perception of the amount of personal control you believe you have over events that affect your life. People with an **external locus of control** believe they have little control of such events, whereas people with an **internal locus of control** believe they have a good deal of control of these events. To determine your locus of control, give yourself one point for each of the following responses:

Item	Response	Item	Response
1	a	11	b
2	a	12	b
3	b	13	b
4	b	14	a
5	b	15	b
6	a	16	a
7	a	17	a
8	a	18	a
9	a	19	b
10	b	20	a

Scores above 10 indicate internality and scores below 11 indicate externality. Of course there are degrees of each, and most people will find themselves scoring near 10.

Studies indicate that "externals" are less likely to take action to control their lives, since they believe such action to be fruitless. It was found, for example, that both hospital patients and prison inmates who were external had less information about the institution and asked fewer questions than "internal" patients and inmates.[32,33] In addition, the internal patients knew more about their medical condition. Other studies have found obesity to be related to externality.[34,35] It seems that the obese are less in control of themselves and more controlled by external cues (e.g., the sight and smell of food) than are internals. The internals will eat when they feel hungry, not just because food is present. Cigarette smokers have also been found to possess external loci of control.[36] They are controlled by the cigarette and don't perceive themselves as either able to stop smoking or able to affect their health if they do. ("The air I breathe is so polluted anyhow.") If you had to guess which gambling games externals and internals prefer, what would you guess? Well, if you guessed that externals preferred games of chance rather than skill, you were correct. Externals preferred roulette and bingo; internals preferred poker and blackjack.[37]

If you've learned anything so far from this book, I suspect it is that we are all in more control of our lives than we believe. On the other hand, it is absurd to believe we are in total control of events that affect us. A colleague of mine,

John Burt, coined the term **cocreator perception deficiency (CCPD)** to describe this important concept. He believes that we are all cocreators of our destiny; that some things we control, but others are beyond our control; and that too many people are deficient in this perception. That is, too many people believe they are either completely in control, or that any significant control is beyond their reach. Neither is the case.

As with self-esteem, locus-of-control orientation develops over a long period of time and cannot be expected to change overnight. However, once the concept is understood, some miraculous possibilities present themselves. After a class on locus of control, one of the women came up to me and said, "You're right. I can become more in control of myself." She resolved right then and there never to smoke another cigarette (she smoked a pack a day). As she threw her half-smoked pack into the trash container on her way out, I knew she would successfully quit smoking. The last I heard, she hadn't smoked a cigarette since that day.

Most of us, though, need to take little steps to reacquire control of our lives and our actions. Certainly we can exercise control over what we ingest, with whom we interact, how we spend our leisure time, and how we react to people.

One important point needs to be made explicit here. *Along with control comes responsibility.* Externals blame both their successes and their failures on things outside themselves. "Oh, I did such a good job because I work well under pressure." It's the pressure, not the person. "Oh, I didn't do too well because I didn't have enough time." It's the lack of time, not the person. Internals might say, "I did so well because of how I decided to adjust to the pressure and time constraints" or "I did poorly because I didn't work hard enough!" Internals accept responsibility for their successes and their failures.

I'm reminded of an activity in which I sometimes ask groups of people to participate. I form several teams, with team members standing at arm's length behind each other. The activity requires everyone to raise their arms shoulder height, elbows straight, palms down, fingers together, and feet adjacent to one another. The first person on any team who either lowers the arms or bends the elbows disqualifies his or her entire team. The team that holds out longest is the winner. You've never seen a funnier sight! Initially, people believe the activity to be ridiculous but decide I'm such a nice fellow they'll humor me. Shortly, however, people try to convince members of other teams to drop their arms— "Your arms are *so* heavy. They hurt *so* badly. Why not drop them and relieve *all* that pain?" At the same time, they encourage their own team members to "hang in there." I've seen grown men and women endure such discomfort in this activity that, at first, I was shocked. However, discussions with the participants after this contest soon led me to believe that most of us understand and accept the responsibility accompanying freedom. Each participant was *free* to drop his or her arms at any time but instead endured physical pain because of a sense of responsibility to the rest of the team. Similarly, when we accept greater control of our lives, we also accept the consequences following the exercise of that control. We must be responsible for our behavior when we are free to choose how we behave.

Beside each item below, indicate whether that item is true or false for you.

____ 1. I do not tire quickly.
____ 2. I am troubled by attacks of nausea.
____ 3. I believe I am no more nervous than most others.
____ 4. I have very few headaches.
____ 5. I work under a great deal of tension.
____ 6. I cannot keep my mind on one thing.
____ 7. I worry over money and business.
____ 8. I frequently notice my hand shakes when I try to do something.
____ 9. I blush no more often than others.
____ 10. I have diarrhea once a month or more.
____ 11. I worry quite a bit over possible misfortunes.
____ 12. I practically never blush.
____ 13. I am often afraid that I am going to blush.
____ 14. I have nightmares every few nights.
____ 15. My hands and feet are usually warm enough.
____ 16. I sweat very easily even on cool days.
____ 17. Sometimes when embarrassed, I break out in a sweat, which annoys me greatly.
____ 18. I hardly ever notice my heart pounding, and I am seldom short of breath.
____ 19. I feel hungry almost all the time.
____ 20. I am very seldom troubled by constipation.
____ 21. I have a great deal of stomach trouble.
____ 22. I have had periods in which I lost sleep over worry.
____ 23. My sleep is fitful and disturbed.
____ 24. I dream frequently about things that are best kept to myself.
____ 25. I am easily embarrassed.
____ 26. I am more sensitive than most other people.
____ 27. I frequently find myself worrying about something.
____ 28. I wish I could be as happy as others seem to be.
____ 29. I am usually calm and not easily upset.
____ 30. I cry easily.
____ 31. I feel anxiety about something or someone almost all the time.
____ 32. I am happy most of the time.
____ 33. It makes me nervous to have to wait.
____ 34. I have periods of such great restlessness that I cannot sit long in a chair.
____ 35. Sometimes I become so excited that I find it hard to get to sleep.
____ 36. I have sometimes felt that difficulties were piling up so high that I could not overcome them.
____ 37. I must admit that I have at times been worried beyond reason over something that really did not matter.

_____ 38. I have very few fears compared to my friends.
_____ 39. I have been afraid of things or people that I know could not hurt me.
_____ 40. I certainly feel useless at times.
_____ 41. I find it hard to keep my mind on a task or job.
_____ 42. I am usually self-conscious.
_____ 43. I am inclined to take things hard.
_____ 44. I am a high-strung person.
_____ 45. Life is a strain for me much of the time.
_____ 46. At times I think I am no good at all.
_____ 47. I am certainly lacking in self-confidence.
_____ 48. I sometimes feel that I am about to go to pieces.
_____ 49. I shrink from facing a crisis or difficulty.
_____ 50. I am entirely self-confident.

You have just completed a scale (the Taylor Manifest Anxiety Scale) that measures the degree to which you manifest anxiety. To score this scale, give yourself one point for each of the following responses:

1. False	14. True	27. True	39. True
2. True	15. False	28. True	40. True
3. False	16. True	29. False	41. True
4. False	17. True	30. True	42. True
5. True	18. False	31. True	43. True
6. True	19. True	32. False	44. True
7. True	20. False	33. True	45. True
8. True	21. True	34. True	46. True
9. False	22. True	35. True	47. True
10. True	23. True	36. True	48. True
11. True	24. True	37. True	49. True
12. False	25. True	38. False	50. False
13. True	26. True		

The average score on this instrument is approximately 19. If you scored below that, you feel less anxious than the average person, and if above that, you feel more anxious than the average person.

Well, now that you know your anxiety score, what is this thing called anxiety? This is a difficult question to answer and one debated by experts. For our purposes, we will define **anxiety** operationally as an unrealistic fear resulting in physiological arousal and accompanied by the behavioral signs of escape or avoidance. For you to be anxious, you must have each of the three components of our definition: you must feel fear; your heart rate, respiratory rate, blood pressure, and other physiological processes must be aroused; and you must seek to escape the stimulus making you anxious once it presents itself, or seek to avoid it in the first place. What's more, the fear you feel must be unrealistic. Those who fear heights, who find their hearts pounding when in a high place, and who immediately seek to come down are anxious. Those who fear crowds, adjust their lives to avoid crowds (have someone else shop for them, never attend a concert, and so forth), and perspire and feel faint when caught in a crowd are anxious.

Anxiety that does not diminish the quality of your life is probably not worth being concerned with. For example, if you become anxious around snakes, avoiding the snake house when visiting the zoo or arranging never to see a snake again will probably not significantly decrease the satisfaction you derive from living. It's probably not worth the time or effort to eliminate your anxiety regarding snakes. However, if we substitute fear of flying in airplanes for fear of snakes, and add that your loved ones are scattered all over the world, your anxiety means you will not be able to see your loved ones as often as you'd like. In this instance, you'd better learn how to manage this anxiety.

So far, we've been considering **state anxiety:** anxiety either temporary in nature or specific to a particular stimulus. However, a general sense of anxiety, **trait anxiety,** which is what the Taylor Manifest Anxiety Scale measures, is a condition deserving of serious attention. You should make a conscious effort to manage your trait anxiety if you scored over 35 on this scale, since your score indicates that your anxiety is evidencing itself in disturbing physical and/or psychological symptoms.[38]

Trait and State Anxiety

Unfortunately, too many people fail to cope successfully with dysfunctional anxiety and only make matters worse. You may do drugs, drink alcohol, or in some other manner alter your state of consciousness to avoid dealing with the anxiety-provoking stimulus. Obviously, these are only temporary solutions and are accompanied by unhealthy consequences. You not only keep your anxiety, but you now have a drug habit to boot. During that period of time when I was overstressed and vomiting on the sides of roads, I developed anxiety regarding speaking before large groups of people. I would decline invitations to run workshops or present speeches, would feel faint and perspire profusely when I did dare to accept such invitations, and was extremely fearful that I would either make a fool of myself or be laughed off the stage. Since my professional goals were thwarted by my anxiety, I decided I needed to do something quickly. I saw my physician, who, with the best of intent, advised me there was nothing to be fearful of and prescribed Valium (a tranquilizer) for those occasions when I could anticipate anxiety. Desperate, I had the prescription filled and a week or so later took two Valium prior to a television talk show on which I was interviewed for thirty minutes. After the show, I decided I would no longer rely upon external means to control my internal fears. I embarked upon a program to manage my anxiety employing the following techniques.

Coping Techniques

Environmental Planning

As stated previously, sometimes it is appropriate to adjust your life and environment to avoid the anxiety-provoking stimulus. For those anxious in crowds, living in a small town will probably be preferable to living in a large city. For those fearful of airplane crashes, living in the flight pattern or too near an airport may not be the wisest of decisions.

I employed environmental planning with subsequent television and radio shows by arriving earlier than expected and being shown around the studio. In this way, the environment became somewhat familiar to me, and therefore I experienced it as less threatening. To this day, I arrive early for public speaking appearances.

Relabeling

Remembering the selective awareness concept, you can relabel any negative experience as a positive one. All that is required is to focus upon the positive aspects rather than the negative ones. If you have test anxiety, rather than considering the test as a possibility of failure, you could consider it an opportunity to find out or to show others how much you know. Rather than conceptualizing an airplane ride as risking your life, you can relabel it as an opportunity to ride on a sea of clouds or see your hometown from a totally new and interesting perspective.

I relabeled public speaking appearances as opportunities to relate some ideas I thought to be valid and important, to help other people improve their lives, and to test the worth of my professional activities. Previously, I viewed these occasions as chances to be ridiculed, scorned, or rejected.

Self-talk

This technique requires some objectivity. You must ask yourself what the real risk is in the anxiety-provoking situation. Usually the real danger is not very significant even if the worst result should occur, and the odds of that worst result occurring are usually meager. If you study well, the odds of failing a test, for example, are usually slim; and if you do fail, so what? It's not good to fail tests, but you still will have your health. There will be other tests. Remember the story of my two former deans! If you're anxious about asking people out on dates, self-talk will help you realize of what you are really afraid: losing self-respect and feeling rejection. It will also help you understand that you probably won't be turned down for that date, but if you are, "there are plenty of fish in the sea." Even when your worst fears are realized, it's not really *that* bad.

I used self-talk to realize that people are generally polite. They won't boo or throw rotten tomatoes. If they thought me absurd, they'd probably fake listening so as not to appear rude. The worst that could realistically happen was that I wouldn't be asked back. That would mean I'd have more time for other activities. That's not all that bad.

Thought Stopping

As simple as it sounds, when you experience negative thoughts, you can shut them off. To employ thought stopping, you should learn one of the deep muscle relaxation techniques presented in part 3. Then, whenever you have anxious thoughts you want to eliminate, tell yourself that you will not allow these thoughts to continue, and employ the relaxation technique. The pleasant sensations of relaxation will serve to reinforce the stopping of anxious thoughts, as well as prevent these thoughts from resulting in potentially harmful physiological consequences.

I began practicing meditation to better manage my anxiety and found it to be most helpful. Any of the other deep muscle relaxation techniques might serve just as well.

Systematic Desensitization

Developed by Joseph Wolpe, **systematic desensitization** involves imagining or experiencing an anxiety-provoking scene while practicing a response incompatible with anxiety (such as relaxation).[39] Widely used by psychotherapists, this technique was found to be nearly as effective when people used it by themselves.[40]

As part of this technique for managing anxiety, you must develop a **fear hierarchy.** The fear hierarchy is a sequence of small steps (at least ten) that lead up to the anxiety-provoking event. For example, if you fear flying in airplanes, your fear hierarchy could be as follows:

1. Deciding where to travel
2. Telephoning the airport for a reservation
3. Packing a suitcase for the trip
4. Traveling to the airport
5. Checking your luggage in at the airport
6. Being assigned a seat at the gate
7. Sitting in the waiting area prior to boarding
8. Boarding the plane
9. Being seated as the plane taxis down the runway
10. Watching and feeling the plane leave the ground
11. Flying above the clouds

You can employ the desensitization procedure in a relatively safe environment by imagining yourself at an airport (**armchair desensitization**), or use it at an actual airport (*in vivo* **desensitization**). The procedure (either armchair or *in vivo*) can be summarized as follows:

1. Learn deep muscle relaxation.
2. Develop a fear hierarchy: list a slightly feared stimulus, then a more fearsome one, and so on (include ten to twenty steps on the fear hierarchy).

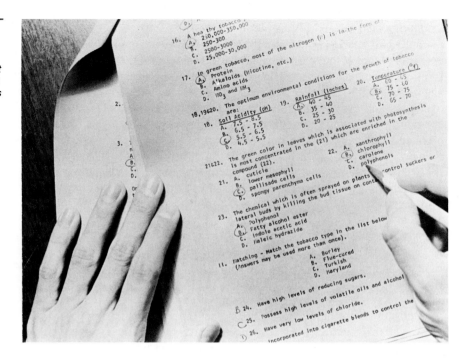

3. Relax yourself and imagine the first item on the fear hierarchy for one to five seconds. Gradually increase the time to thirty seconds in subsequent sessions.

4. After imagining the stimulus for thirty seconds, immediately switch your focus to the feeling of relaxation for thirty seconds.

5. Move down the fear hierarchy similarly. If the stimulus provokes anxiety, shut out the scene and concentrate on the feeling of relaxation.

6. If you have difficulty moving from one point on the fear hierarchy to another, add some intermediate steps. For example, on the airplane-flight fear hierarchy, you may have made too big a leap between step 8 (boarding the plane) and step 9 (the plane speeding down the runway). You may need three steps between those: (1) placing your coat in the rack above your seat, (2) sitting down and fastening your seat belt, and (3) listening to the motors start.

The ABCDE Technique

Psychologist Albert Ellis theorizes that anxiety is a function of irrational beliefs. Ellis argues that we believe the following:

1. We must be thoroughly competent, adequate, and achieving.

2. We must be loved or get approval from all others almost all the time.

3. If things don't go as we wish, it is horrible and catastrophic.[41]

Ellis continues, but I think the point is made. We become afraid to fail or do something different, and develop unrealistic fears because of beliefs that, if we examined them, would prove to be irrational. Consequently, Ellis suggests we do just that—examine them. Ellis's method, the **ABCDE technique,** consists of the following steps:

A. Activating agent (identify stressor)
B. Belief system (identify rational and irrational beliefs)
C. Consequences (mental, physical, and behavioral)
D. Dispute irrational beliefs
E. Effect (changed consequences)[42]

The self-talk technique described earlier in the chapter is helpful in changing old thoughts (irrational beliefs) into new thoughts. For example, the fear of speaking in front of class might translate to "People will laugh at me and think I'm stupid." However, with self-talk—"I know many students who spoke in front of many classes and they survived"—we might interpret speaking in front of the class as a challenge rather than a threat.

Furthermore, such questions as the following can help identify irrational beliefs:

1. What facts are there (if any) to support this belief?
2. Is it a rational or irrational belief?

Why not complete the Managing Anxiety Formula presented here to apply the information you've learned in this section and to better control your anxiety?

Managing Anxiety Formula

1. I experience anxiety when _____
   _____
   _____

2. Self-talk that I could use to manage this anxiety includes:
   a. _____
   b. _____
   c. _____
   d. _____
   e. _____

3. Environmental planning I could do to manage this anxiety includes:
   a. _____
   b. _____
   c. _____
   d. _____
   e. _____

4. If using desensitization to manage this anxiety, I would employ the following fear hierarchy:

a. _____

b. _____

c. _____

d. _____

e. _____

f. _____

g. _____

h. _____

i. _____

j. _____

5. How successful do you think using one or a combination of the above anxiety managing techniques would be? _____ %

Hardiness

Some recent research has been directed at discovering what prevents stress from leading to illness for some people but not for others. Kobasa has found three factors that differentiate the afflicted from the nonafflicted: *commitment, control,* and *challenge.*[43] Commitment is "the tendency to involve oneself in whatever one is doing, control involves the tendency to believe that and act as if one can influence the course of events, and challenge involves the related expectations that it is normal for life to change, and that changes will stimulate personal growth."[44] A key here seems to be viewing change as a challenge rather than a threat. People who have the "three C's" are termed **hardy** and seem to be able to withstand the onslaught of stressors. They don't become ill as often from stressors. A number of studies have been conducted since the hardiness concept was developed which have verified the buffering effects of commitment, control, and challenge on one's health.[45-47]

In addition to the prevention of illness that hardiness appears to provide,[48] and its relationship to lower levels of blood pressure and triglycerides,[49] hardiness also affects nonmedical factors. For example, hardiness has been found to be related to less psychological distress,[50] increased happiness and adjustment,[51] and even to marital happiness.[52]

That is not to say that all researchers agree that hardiness buffers against illness. As with many complex constructs, hardiness and its effects are sometimes elusive. For example, Funk concluded from his research that hardiness was not a separate entity at all but instead was really maladjustment.[53] Others have found that some, but not all three, of the hardiness factors have buffering effects.[54,55] In any case, the hardiness concept is being studied further. Attempts are being made to find out if people can actually be taught to become hardy and, if so, whether they will then become less ill.

1. Selective awareness is deciding on whether to focus on the good or on the bad in a situation or person. Focusing on the good is less stressful.

2. Experiencing life as fully as possible requires conscious effort, since we become habituated to things which are repeated. Varying our experiences (such as taking different routes to school or work) can help in this process.

3. Type A behavior pattern is a particular complex of personality traits including excessive competitive drive, aggressiveness, impatience, a sense of time urgency, and a free-floating but well-rationalized form of hostility almost always accompanied by a deep-seated sense of insecurity. People exhibiting Type A behavior patterns are more prone to coronary heart disease than Type B's. Type B's are less apt to contract heart disease and exhibit just the opposite behavior pattern from Type A's. Hostility and holding in anger seem to be the major variables associated with ill health resulting from Type A behavior.

4. Self-esteem refers to how high a regard you hold for yourself. Those with low self-esteem experience stress from not thinking well of themselves, not trusting their opinions, and acting nonassertively. Self-esteem is learned and can be changed.

5. Locus of control is the perception of the amount of control you believe you have over events that affect your life. An external locus of control refers to a perception of very little control (control is outside yourself) and an internal locus of control refers to a perception of a great deal of control.

6. Anxiety is an unrealistic fear resulting in physiological arousal and accompanied by behavioral signs of escape or avoidance. State anxiety is either temporary in nature or specific to a particular stimulus; trait anxiety is a generalized sense of anxiousness.

7. Anxiety can be managed by environmental planning, relabeling, self-talk, thought stopping, or systematic desensitization.

8. Albert Ellis developed the ABCDE technique for managing anxiety. It consists of examining irrational beliefs which make us anxious, changing those beliefs, and envisioning more positive consequences of our actions.

9. Hardiness consists of three factors: commitment, control, and challenge. Commitment is the tendency to involve oneself in what one is doing, control is the belief that one can influence the course of events, and challenge involves the expectations that change is both normal and will lead to personal growth. Studies have found hardiness associated with less illness, lower levels of blood pressure and triglycerides, less psychological distress, increased happiness and adjustment, and marital happiness.

Notes

1. N. F. Dixon, "Humor: A Cognitive Alternative to Stress?" in *Stress and Anxiety,* ed. I. Sarason and Charles Spielberger (New York: Hemisphere, 1980), 281–89.

2. R. A. Martin and H. M. Lefcourt, "Sense of Humor as a Moderator of the Relationship between Stressors and Mood," *Journal of Personal and Social Psychology* 45(1973):1313–24.

3. Susan M. Labott and Randall B. Martin, "The Stress-moderating Effects of Weeping and Humor," *Journal of Human Stress* 13(1987):159–64.

4. Waleed Anthony Salameh, "Humor in Psychotherapy: Past Outlooks, Present Status, and Future Frontiers," in *Handbook of Humor Research,* Paul E. Mcghee and Jeffrey H. Goldstein (New York: Springer-Verlag, 1983), 75–108.

5. Vera M. Robinson, "Humor and Health," in *Handbook of Humor Research,* Paul E. Mcghee and Jeffrey H. Goldstein (New York: Springer-Verlag, 1983), 111.

6. D. D. Bushnell and T. J. Scheff, "The Cathartic Effects of Laughter on Audiences," in *The Study of Humor,* ed. H. Mindesc and J. Turek (Los Angeles: Antioch University, 1979).

7. Vera M. Robinson, "Humor in Nursing," in *Behavioral Concepts and Nursing Intervention,* 2d ed., ed. C. Carlson and B. Blackwell (Philadelphia: Lippincott, 1978).

8. Steven Sands, "The Use of Humor in Psychotherapy," *Psychoanalytic Review* 71(1984):458.

9. Meyer Friedman and Ray H. Rosenman, "Association of Specific Overt Behavior Pattern with Blood and Cardiovascular Findings: Blood Clotting Time, Incidence of Arcus Senilis, and Clinical Coronary Artery Disease," *Journal of the American Medical Association* 169(1959):1286–96.

10. Meyer Friedman, A. E. Brown, and Ray H. Rosenman, "Voice Analysis Test for Detection of Behavior Pattern: Responses of Normal Men and Coronary Patients," *Journal of the American Medical Association* 208(1969):828–36.

11. Ray H. Rosenman, Meyer Friedman, and Reuban Strauss, "A Predictive Study of Coronary Heart Disease: The Western Collaborative Group Study," *Journal of the American Medical Association* 189(1964):15–22.

12. Ray H. Rosenman, Richard Brand, and C. David Jenkins, "Coronary Heart Disease in the Western Collaborative Group Study: Final Follow-up Experience of 8½ Years," *Journal of the American Medical Association* 223 (1975):872–77.

13. R. B. Shekelle, J. A. Schoenberger, and J. Stamler, "Correlates of the JAS Type A Behavior Pattern Score," *Journal of Chronic Diseases* 29 (1976):381–94.

14. R. D. Caplan, S. Cobb, and J. R. P. French, "Relationships of Cessation of Smoking with Job Stress, Personality, and Social Support," *Journal of Applied Psychology* 60 (1975):211–19.

15. C. D. Jenkins, "Recent Evidence Supporting Psychologic and Social Risk Factors for Coronary Disease," *New England Journal of Medicine* 294 (1976):987–94, 1033–38.

16. K. F. Rowland and B. A. Sokol, "A Review of Research Examining the Coronary-Prone Behavior Pattern," *Journal of Human Stress* 3 (1977):26–33.

17. Jack Sparacino, "The Type A Behavior Pattern: A Critical Assessment," *Journal of Human Stress* 5 (1979):37–51.

18. Ronald J. Burke, "Beliefs and Fears Underlying Type A Behavior: What Makes Sammy Run So Fast and Aggressively?" *Journal of Human Stress* 10(1984):174–82.

19. David R. Ragland and Richard J. Brand, "Type A Behavior and Mortality from Coronary Heart Disease," *New England Journal of Medicine* 318(1988):65–69.

20. Suzanne G. Haynes, M. Feinleib, and W. B. Kannel, "The Relationship of Psychosocial Factors to Coronary Heart Disease in the Framingham Study. III. Eight Year Incidence of Coronary Heart Disease," *American Journal of Epidemiology* 3(1980):37–58.

21. Meyer Friedman and Diane Ulmer, *Treating Type A Behavior and Your Heart* (New York: Alfred A. Knopf, 1984), 84–85.

22. Karen A. Matthews, "Psychological Perspective on Type A Behavior Pattern," *Psychological Bulletin* 91(1982):293–323.

23. Karen A. Matthews and Suzanne G. Haynes, "Reviews and Commentary: Type A Behavior Pattern and Coronary Disease Risk. Update and Critical Evaluation," *American Journal of Epidemiology* 123(1986):923–60.

24. J. R. Anderson and I. Waldon, "Behavioral and Content Components of the Structured Interview Assessment of the Type A Behavior Pattern in Women," *Journal of Behavioral Medicine* 6(1983):123–34.

25. Haynes, Feinleib, and Kannel, "The Relationship of Psychosocial Factors to Coronary Heart Disease," 37–58.

26. R. B. Shekelle et al., "The MRFIT Behavior Pattern Study. II. Type A Behavior and Incidence of Coronary Heart Disease," *American Journal of Epidemiology* 122(1985):559–70.

27. R. B. Case et al., "Type A Behavior and Survival after Acute Myocardial Infarction," *New England Journal of Medicine* 312(1985):737–41.

28. J. C. Barefoot, W. G. Dahlstrom, and W. B. Williams, "Hostility, CHD Incidence, and Total Mortality: A 25-Year Follow-up Study of 255 Physicians," *Psychosomatic Medicine* 45(1983):59–64.

29. R. B. Shekelle et al., "Hostility, Risk of Coronary Heart Disease and Mortality," *Psychosomatic Medicine* 45(1983):109–14.

30. Haynes, Feinleib, and Kannel, "The Relationship of Psychosocial Factors to Coronary Heart Disease."

31. Marilyn Elias, "Type A's: Like Father, Like Son," *USA Today,* 7 August 1985, D1.

32. M. Seeman and J. W. Evans, "Alienation and Learning in a Hospital Setting," *American Sociological Reviews* 27 (1962):772–83.

33. M. Seeman, "Alienation and Social Learning in a Reformatory," *American Journal of Sociology* 69 (1963):270–84.

34. G. Tom and M. Rucker, "Fat, Full and Happy: Effects of Food Deprivation, External Cues, and Obesity on Preference Ratings, Consumption, and Buying Intentions," *Journal of Personality and Social Psychology* 32 (1975):761–66.

35. J. Rodin and J. Slochower, "Externality in the Obese: Effects of Environmental Responsiveness on Weight," *Journal of Personality and Social Psychology* 33(1976):338-44[5]

36. B. C. Straits and L. Sechrest, "Further Support of Some Findings about Characteristics of Smokers and Non-Smokers," *Journal of Consulting Psychology* 27(1963):282.

37. K. Deaux, *The Behavior of Women and Men* (Monterey, Calif.: Brooks/ Cole, 1976).

38. Roger J. Allen and David Hyde, *Investigations in Stress Control* (Minneapolis: Burgess Publishing Co., 1980), 103.

39. Joseph Wolpe, *The Practice of Behavior Therapy,* 2d ed. (New York: Pergamon, 1973).

40. Ronald B. Adler, *Confidence in Communication: A Guide to Assertive and Social Skills* (New York: Holt, Rinehart & Winston, 1977).

41. Albert Ellis and Robert Harper, *A New Guide to Rational Living* (Englewood Cliffs, N.J.: Prentice-Hall, 1979).

42. Albert Ellis and Robert Harper, *A Guide to Rational Living* (N. Hollywood: Melvin Powers, Wilshire Book Company, 1975).

43. Suzanne C. Kobasa, "Stressful Life Events, Personality, and Health: An Inquiry into Hardiness," *Journal of Personality and Social Psychology* 37(1979):1–11.

44. Salvatore R. Maddi, "Personality as a Resource in Stress Resistance: The Hardy Type" (Paper presented in the symposium on "Personality Moderators of Stressful Life Events" at the annual meeting of the American Psychological Association, Montreal, September 1980).

45. Suzanne C. Kobasa et al., "Effectiveness of Hardiness, Exercise, and Social Support as Resources against Illness," *Journal of Psychosomatic Research* 29(1985):525–33.

46. Suzanne C. Kobasa, Salvatore R. Maddi, and Marc A. Zola, "Type A and Hardiness," *Journal of Behavioral Medicine* 6(1983):41–51.

47. Suzanne C. Kobasa, Salvatore R. Maddi, and Mark C. Puccetti, "Personality and Exercise as Buffers in the Stress-Illness Relationship," *Journal of Behavioral Medicine* 5(1982):391–404.

48. Jay G. Hull, Ronald R. Van-Treuren, and Suzanne Virnelli, "Hardiness and Health: A Critique and Alternative Approach," *Journal of Personality and Social Psychology* 53(1987):518–30.

49. John H. Howard, David A. Cunningham, and Peter A. Rechnitzer, "Personality (Hardiness) as a Moderator of Job Stress and Coronary Risk in Type A Individuals: A Longitudinal Study," *Journal of Behavioral Medicine* 9(1986):229–44.

50. Kenneth M. Nowak, "Type A, Hardiness, and Psychological Distress," *Journal of Behavioral Medicine* 9(1986):537–48.

51. Kevin McNeil et al., "Measurement of Psychological Hardiness in Older Adults," *Canadian Journal on Aging* 5(1986):43–48.

52. Julian Barling, "Interrole Conflict and Marital Functioning amongst Employed Fathers," *Journal of Occupational Behaviour* 7(1986):1–8.

53. Steven C. Funk and Kent B. Houston, "A Critical Analysis of the Hardiness Scale's Validity and Utility," *Journal of Personality and Social Psychology* 53(1987):572–78.

54. Susan E. Pollock, "Human Response to Chronic Illness: Physiologic and Psychosocial Adaptation," *Nursing Research* 35(1986):90–95.

55. Lori A. Schmied and Kathleen A. Lawler, "Hardiness, Type A Behavior, and the Stress-Illness Relation in Working Women," *Journal of Personality and Social Psychology* 51(1985):1218–23.

PART III

▼

General
Applications:
Relaxation
Techniques

Before beginning part 3, some instructions are necessary. Part 3 describes relaxation techniques: meditation, autogenic training, progressive relaxation, biofeedback, yoga, and others. A description of each technique, its historical development, how to do it, and its benefits are presented. Remember, these relaxation techniques are but one part of a comprehensive stress management program. Relaxation techniques relate to the level of emotional arousal on the stress model presented in chapter 4 and serve as interventions between stress and illness and disease.

Since you will learn how to do each technique, two additional comments need to be made. First, relaxation techniques result in changes in physiological processes. We've already seen that the relaxation response is a hypometabolic state of lowered blood pressure, heart rate, muscle tension, and serum cholesterol, with other physiological parameters being affected. Those of you using medication that is designed to affect, or incidentally affects, a physiological parameter might be affecting that parameter too much if you engage in relaxation techniques. For example, a person with high blood pressure who is taking medication to lower the blood pressure might lower it too much if relaxation training is added to the medication. It is because of these changes in physiological processes that people who are thinking of beginning relaxation training and are under medical care or taking medication are advised to get the permission of the medical specialist supervising their care *prior* to practicing relaxation skills. In particular, those with heart conditions, epilepsy, hypertension, diabetes, and psychological problems should obtain medical permission to begin relaxation training.

Medical Caution

Secondly, the opportunity to try several different relaxation techniques is designed to help you find one that you prefer and will use regularly. To structure your evaluation of these techniques so you can decide which one is best for you, use the rating scale that appears at the conclusion of chapters 8–10. Unfortunately, there is no good research base to allow you to be diagnosed and a particular relaxation technique prescribed for you. Studies have been conducted to determine, for instance, whether people with certain personality characteristics benefit more from meditation than do people without those characteristics.* Those studies have not been able to differentiate in the manner intended; we still have no system to recommend particular relaxation techniques for particular people. Consequently, you will have to use trial and error to decide which relaxation technique you prefer. The rating scale should help, though.

Relaxation Technique Trials

*Sheila A. Ramsey, "Perceptual Style as a Predictor of Successful Meditation Training" (Master's thesis, University of Maryland, 1981).

The Relaxation Technique Rating Scale

To use the rating scale, it is best to practice each technique for at least one week (the longer, the better). Since your inner environment may change from day to day (e.g., you may eat different foods at different times of the day) and your outer environment is never constant (temperature, outside noises, and quality of the air vary), a one-day trial of one relaxation technique compared to a one-day trial of another will not allow for a valid comparison. Also, practice the technique as recommended—correct posture, frequency, time of day, type of environment—and make your practice consistent with other suggestions. After a sufficient trial period, answer each of the questions on the relaxation technique rating scale, then sum up the point values you gave each answer. The lower the total point value, the more that relaxation technique fits you.

▽
8

Meditation

You may know that some meditators wear muslin robes, burn incense, shave their hair, and believe in the Buddhist religion. You should also know that these things are *not required* in order to benefit from meditative practice. Although wine may be a part of a Catholic religious service, all those who drink wine do not embrace Catholicism. Similarly, all those who meditate need not adopt a particular religion.

Meditation is simply a mental exercise that affects body processes. Just as physical exercise has certain psychological benefits, meditation has certain physical benefits. The purpose of meditation is to gain control over your attention so that you can choose what to focus upon rather than being subject to the unpredictable ebb and flow of environmental circumstances.

What Is Meditation?

Meditation has its tradition grounded in Eastern cultures (e.g., those of India and Tibet) but has been popularized recently for Western cultures. The major exporter of meditation to the Western world has been the Maharishi Mahesh Yogi. The Maharishi developed a large, worldwide, and highly effective organization to teach **transcendental meditation** (**TM**) to a population of people experiencing more and more stress and recognizing the need for more and more of an escape. The simplicity of this technique, coupled with the effectiveness of its marketing by TM organizations, quickly led to its popularity. In a short time, in spite of an initial fee of $125.00 (significantly higher now), large numbers of people learned and began regular practice of TM (10,000 persons were joining the program each month during the early 1970s in the United States).

The Maharishi's background is interesting in itself. Mahest Prasod Varma (his name at birth) was born in 1918 and earned a degree in physics in 1942 from Allahabad University in India. Before he began practicing his profession, however, he met and eventually studied under a religious leader, Swami Brahmananda Saraswati. Thirteen years of religious study later, he was assigned the task of finding a simple form of meditation that everyone could readily learn. It took two years of isolated life in a Himalayan cave to develop TM, which he later spread about via mass communication, advertising, and the Students International Meditation Society.

Types of Meditation

Transcendental meditation is but one form of meditative practice. Chakra yoga, Rinzai Zen, Mudra yoga, Sufism, Zen meditation, and Soto Zen are examples of other meditative systems. In Soto Zen meditation, common external objects (for example, flowers or a peaceful landscape) are focused upon. Tibetan Buddhists use a **mandala**—a geometrical figure with other geometric forms on it that has spiritual or philosophical importance—to meditate upon. The use of imagined sounds (thunder or beating drum) termed **nadam,** or of silently repeated words termed **mantra,** have also been used. Rinzai Zen meditation uses **koans** (unanswerable, illogical riddles), Zazen focuses on subjective states of consciousness, Hindu meditation employs **pranayama** ("Prana" means life force and refers to breathing), and Zen practitioners have been known to focus on **anapanasati** (counting breaths from one to ten repetitively).[1]

Regardless of the type of meditation, however, one of two approaches is used: focusing of attention or opening up of attention. Opening up your attention requires a nonjudgmental attitude: you allow all external and internal stimuli to enter your awareness without trying to use these stimuli in any particular manner. As with a blotter (the inner self) and ink (the external and internal stimuli), everything is just absorbed. When the meditative method requires the focusing of attention, the object focused upon is something either repetitive (e.g., a word or phrase repeated in your mind) or something unchanging (e.g., a spot on the wall).

To understand the two basic methods of meditation, place an object in the center of your room. Try to get an object at least as high as your waist. Come on now. Your tendency will be to keep reading here, to rush to get this chapter read rather than get the most out of it. Remember that people with the Type A behavior pattern, those most prone to coronary heart disease, rush through tasks rather than doing them well. Slow down. Set this book down for a while, get that object, and participate with us.

Now, look at that object for about five seconds. Most likely, you saw and focused upon the object while excluding the other stimuli in your field of vision. Behind the object (in your field of vision) might have been a wall, a window, a table, or maybe a poster. In spite of the presence of these other visual stimuli, you can put them in the background, ignore them, and focus your attention on one object. The object of focus is called the *figure,* and the objects in the background of our field of vision are called the *ground.* When you see and listen to a lecturer, you probably focus upon that person and his or her voice. You choose to place objects other than the lecturer in the background as well as sounds other than the lecturer's voice. You may even be doing that now. As you read this book, you may be hearing your inner voice recite the words while placing in the background other sounds (the heating or cooling system, people and cars outside, birds chirping, or airplanes flying overhead).

Meditation of the focusing-of-attention kind is similar to focusing on the figure while excluding the ground. Meditation of the opening-up-of-attention kind blends the figure and ground together so they are one and the same. Figure 8.1 demonstrates this blend.

Figure 8.1 What do you see? Some people see an elderly woman, while others see a young one. It is a matter of what you choose to focus on. If you cannot see both women, ask someone who sees the one you cannot to trace her for you. Meditation involves choosing to focus on something repetitive or unchanging.

From *Puck*, 6 November 1915.

Benefits of Meditation

Because it is so popular and can be learned quickly and easily, meditation has been one of the most researched of the relaxation techniques. The research findings evidence the physiological and psychological effects of meditation. These findings are presented below. However, the shortcomings of generalizing results about relaxation techniques should be recognized. For example, even though we state findings about meditation, there are many different types of meditation. Findings with different types may differ. Sometimes the level of motivation of the research subjects can affect the results obtained. The experience of the meditators has also been found to affect results (those with at least six months' experience differ from novice meditators). In spite of these limitations, though, there are some things we can say about the effects of meditation.

Physiological Effects

The physiological effects of meditation were discovered by early research on Indian yogis and Zen masters. In 1946 Therese Brosse found that Indian yogis could control their heart rates.[2] Another study of Indian yogis found that they could slow respiration (four to six breaths per minute), decrease by 70 percent their ability to conduct an electrical current (galvanic skin response), emit predominantly alpha brain waves, and slow their heart rate to twenty-four beats less than normal.[3] Other studies of yogis and Zen meditators have reported similar results.[4,5]

More recent studies have verified these earlier findings of the physiological effects of meditation.[6] Allison compared the respiration rate of a subject meditating with that subject's respiration rate while watching television and while reading a book. Respiration rate decreased most while meditating (from twelve and one-half breaths per minute to seven).[7] The decrease in respiration rate as a result of meditation is a consistent finding across research studies.[8,9]

Several researchers have found a decrease in muscle tension associated with meditation. In one study by Zaichkowsky and another by Fee, the decrease in muscle tension in meditators was significantly greater than that experienced by a control group of nonmeditators.[10,11]

The decrease in heart rate found by early studies on Indian yogis has also been verified in more recent studies. When experienced (five years) and short-term (fourteen months) meditators were compared with novice (seven days) meditators and people taught a different relaxation technique, it was found that the most significant decreases in heart rate occurred in the experienced and short-term meditators.[12] Even when meditators and nonmeditators were physiologically stimulated by viewing a film on laboratory accidents, the meditators' heart rates returned to normal sooner than the nonmeditators' heart rates.[13]

Galvanic skin response—the ability of skin to conduct an electrical current—differs between meditators and nonmeditators. The lower the conductance, the less stress. These skin electrical conductance findings lead researchers to conclude that meditators are better able to cope with stress and have more stable autonomic nervous systems.[14]

Much of the research discussed so far was given impetus by the work of Robert Keith Wallace. Wallace was one of the first modern researchers to study the effects of meditation scientifically. In his initial study and in his subsequent work with Herbert Benson, Wallace showed that meditation resulted in decreased oxygen consumption, heart rate, and alpha brain-wave emissions. He also demonstrated that meditation increased skin resistance, decreased blood lactate (thought to be associated with lessened anxiety) and carbon dioxide production, and increased the peripheral blood flow to arms and legs.[15,16]

There is ample evidence, therefore, that meditation results in specific physiological changes that differ from those produced by other relaxation techniques (reading, watching television, sleeping). These changes are termed the **relaxation response (trophotropic response),** and are thought to have beneficial effects upon one's health.

Psychological Effects

By this point you realize that the mind cannot be separated from the body. Consequently, you've probably guessed that the physiological effects of meditation have psychological implications. You are right. Numerous studies have found evidence that the psychological health of meditators is better than that of nonmeditators.

For example, meditators have been found to be less anxious.[17] Even more significant than this, however, is the finding that anxiety can be decreased by teaching people to meditate. Schoolchildren decreased their test anxiety after eighteen weeks of meditation training.[18] Several other studies have shown that people's trait and state anxiety levels decreased after they practiced meditation for varying periods of time.[19–21]

In addition to its effect of decreasing anxiety, researchers have found that meditation is related to an internal locus of control, greater self-actualization, more positive feelings after encountering a stressor, improvement in sleep behavior, decreased cigarette smoking, headache relief, and a general state of positive mental health. In a comprehensive review of psychological effects of meditation, Shapiro and Giber cited studies that found meditation decreased drug abuse, reduced fears and phobias, showed potential for stress management, and was associated with positive subjective experiences.[22]

When you combine these psychological benefits with the physiological ones previously cited, meditation certainly seems worth the time and effort that regular practice requires. No wonder the transcendental meditation organization was able to sell such large numbers of people (at $125.00 a shot) on their technique. Wouldn't you pay that much for the benefits cited above? I would. In fact, I did. When I experienced the stress-overload situation I described at the beginning of this book, I enrolled in the TM program. My subjective evaluation, as limited as that is, leads me to recommend meditation to friends experiencing stress-related problems or wanting to prevent such problems.

I will now teach *you* how to meditate (for much less than $125.00). In that way you might be able to decrease your oxygen consumption and blood lactate level, change other physiological parameters, and be less anxious and more self-actualized. Are you ready?

How to Meditate   Meditation is best learned in a relatively quiet, comfortable environment. However, once you become experienced, you will be able to meditate almost anywhere. As I've already mentioned, I've meditated in the passenger seat of a moving automobile in Florida, on an airplane in flight to California, in my office at the University of Maryland, and under a tree on a golf course in the Bahamas. Of course, the quiet, serene setting of the golf course was the more preferred, but the others sufficed.

Once you have located a quiet place to learn meditation, find a comfortable chair. Since sleep is a different physiological state than meditation, you will not get the benefits of meditation if you fall asleep. To help prevent yourself from falling asleep, use a straight-backed chair. This type of chair encourages you to align your spine and requires only a minimum of muscular contraction to keep you erect (though not stiff). If you can find a chair that will support your upper back and head, all the better.

Be seated in this chair with your buttocks pushed against its back, feet slightly forward of your knees, and your hands resting either on the arms of the chair or in your lap.

Let your muscles relax as best you can. Don't try to relax. Trying is work, not relaxation. Just assume a passive attitude in which you focus upon your breathing. Allow whatever happens, to happen. If you feel relaxed, fine; if not, accept that too.

Next, close your eyes and repeat in your mind the word *one* every time you inhale and the word *two* every time you exhale. Do not consciously alter or control your breathing; breathe regularly. Continue to do this for twenty minutes. It is recommended that you meditate twice a day for approximately twenty minutes each time.

Lastly, when you stop meditating, give your body a chance to become readjusted to normal routines. Open your eyes gradually, first focusing on one object in the room, then focusing upon several objects. Take several deep breaths. Then stretch while seated and, when you feel ready, stand and stretch. If you rush to leave the meditation session, you are apt to feel tired or to lose the sense of relaxation. Since your blood pressure and heart rate are decreased while meditating, rising from the chair too quickly might make you dizzy and is not recommended.

Although you shouldn't experience any problems, if you feel uncomfortable or dizzy, or if you experience hallucinations or disturbing images, just open your eyes and stop meditating. These situations are rare but occasionally do occur.

Here are several more recommendations:

1. Immediately upon rising and right before dinner tend to be good times to meditate. Do not meditate directly after a meal. After eating, the blood is pooled in the stomach area, participating in the digestive process. Since part of the relaxation response is an increased blood flow to the arms and legs, pooled blood in the abdomen is not conducive to relaxation. It is for this reason that you should meditate *before* breakfast and *before* dinner.

2. The object of meditation is to bring about a hypometabolic state. Since caffeine is a stimulant and is included in coffee, tea, cola, and some other soft drinks, and since you do not want to be stimulated but rather to relax, you should not eat these substances before meditating. Likewise, you should avoid smoking cigarettes (which contain the stimulant nicotine) or using other stimulant drugs.

3. I'm often asked "What do I do with my head?" Well, do whatever you want to do with it. Some people prefer to keep it directly above the neck, others rest it against a high-backed chair, and still others let their chins drop onto their chests. If you choose the latter, you may experience some discomfort in your neck or shoulder muscles for several meditation sessions. This is because these muscles may not be flexible enough; for the same reason, some of you can't touch your toes without bending your knees. With stretching, these muscles will acquire greater flexibility and will not result in any discomfort when the head hangs forward.

4. Another question I'm often asked is "How do I know if twenty minutes are up?" The answer is so simple I'm usually embarrassed to give it: Look at your watch. If twenty minutes are up, stop meditating; if not, continue. Although you don't want to be interrupting your meditation every couple of minutes to look at your watch, once or twice when you think the time has expired will not affect your experience. An interesting observation I have noted is that, after a while, you acquire a built-in alarm and will know when twenty minutes have gone by.

5. Whatever you do, do not set an alarm clock to go off after twenty minutes. Since your body will be in a hypometabolic state, a loud sound will startle you too much. Similarly, disconnect the telephone or take the receiver off the hook so it doesn't ring. If the phone goes off, you'll go off.

6. You will not be able to focus on your breathing to the exclusion of other thoughts for very long. You will find yourself thinking of problems, anticipated experiences, and other sundry matters. This is normal. However, when you do realize you are thinking and not focusing on your breathing, gently—without feeling as though you've done something wrong—go back to repeating the word *one* on each inhalation and the word *two* on each exhalation.

7. I'm flabbergasted by people who decide to meditate for twenty minutes and then try to rush through it. They breathe quickly, fidget around a lot, and too often open their eyes to look at their watches in the hope that the twenty minutes have passed. During their meditations, they're planning their days and working out their problems. They'd be better off solving their problems and meditating later. Once you commit yourself to time to meditate, relax and benefit from it. Twenty minutes are twenty minutes! You can't speed it up! Relax and enjoy it. Your problems will be there to greet you later. Don't worry, they're not going anywhere. You won't lose them. The only thing you'll do, perhaps, is to perceive them as less distressing after meditating than before.

*Coping sometimes
requires ingenuity and
a good deal of energy.*

Making Time for Meditation

Meditation can be quite pleasing and can help you better manage the stress in your life—but you have to *do* it. I have known men and women who have told me they see the benefits of meditating but can't get the time or the place to meditate. Either the kids are bothering them or their roommates are inconsiderate. They say they don't have the forty minutes a day to spare. I unsympathetically tell them that if they don't have the time, they really need to meditate; and if they can't find a quiet place in which to spend twenty minutes, they are the ones who need to meditate the most. The time is always available, although some of us choose to use our time for activities holding a higher priority for us. If you really value your health, you'll find the time to do healthy things. The place is available too. As I've already said, I have left my wife, two children, and my parents in my parents' apartment and sat in my car in the indoor parking garage meditating. My health and well-being were that important to me. How important are your health and well-being to you?

If you want a more structured approach to meditation to help you get started, read *Meditation*[23] by Jonathan Smith. That book outlines a several-week program taking the reader through various meditative exercises.

Practice meditation as suggested and regularly. After at least a one-week trial period, answer each of the questions below using the following scale.

1 = very true
2 = somewhat true
3 = I'm not sure
4 = somewhat untrue
5 = very untrue

_____ 1. It felt good.
_____ 2. It was easy to fit into my schedule.
_____ 3. It made me feel relaxed.
_____ 4. I handled my daily chores better than I usually do.
_____ 5. It was an easy technique to learn.
_____ 6. I was able to close out my surroundings while practicing this technique.
_____ 7. I did not feel tired after practicing this relaxation technique.
_____ 8. My fingers and toes felt warmer directly after trying this relaxation technique.
_____ 9. Any stress symptoms I had (headache, tense muscles, anxiety) before doing this relaxation technique disappeared by the time I was done.
_____ 10. Each time I concluded this technique, my pulse rate was much lower than when I began.

Now sum up the values you responded with for a total score. Save this score and compare it with scores for other relaxation techniques you try. The lower the score, the more appropriate a particular relaxation skill is for you.

Summary

1. Meditation is a simple mental exercise designed to gain control over your attention so you can choose what to focus upon.
2. Meditation involves either focusing upon something repetitive (such as a word repeated in your mind) or something unchanging (such as a spot on the wall).
3. There are different types of meditation. Some types use external objects to focus upon, others employ a geometric figure called a mandala, and others use silently repeated words or sounds.
4. Meditation has been used in the treatment of muscle tension, anxiety, drug abuse, and hypertension. It lowers blood pressure, heart and respiratory rates, and the skin's electrical conductance, and increases the blood flow to the arms and legs.
5. Meditation has been found to have several beneficial psychological effects. It can help alleviate anxiety and is related to an internal locus of control, greater self-actualization, improvement in sleep, decreased cigarette smoking, headache relief, and a general state of positive mental health.

6. To learn to meditate, you need a quiet place. Sit in a straight-backed chair and in your mind repeat the word "one" when you inhale and the word "two" when you exhale with your eyes closed. This word should be repeated each time you exhale, and this should continue for twenty minutes.

7. For meditation to be effective, you need to practice it regularly. It is recommended that you avoid consciously altering your breathing, forcing yourself to relax, or coming out of a meditative state too abruptly. Since digestion inhibits peripheral blood flow, it is best to meditate before eating in the morning and evening.

8. Meditation's effectiveness is hindered by the administration of stimulants. Stimulants such as nicotine in cigarettes or caffeine in coffee, tea, or some soft drinks will interfere with the trophotropic (relaxation) response.

Notes

1. For a more detailed description of types of meditation see C. Naranjo and R. E. Ornstein, *On the Psychology of Meditation* (New York: Viking, 1971).

2. Therese Brosse, "A Psychophysiological Study of Yoga," *Main Currents in Modern Thought* 4(1946):77–84.

3. B. K. Bagchi and M. A. Wengor, "Electrophysiological Correlates of Some Yogi Exercises," in *Electroencephalography, Clinical Neurophysiology and Epilepsy,* vol. 3 of the First International Congress of Neurological Sciences, ed. L. van Bagaert and J. Radermecker (London: Pergamon, 1959).

4. B. K. Anand, G. S. Chhina, and B. Singh, "Some Aspects of Electroencephalographic Studies in Yogis," *Electroencephalography and Clinical Neurophysiology* 13(1961):452–56.

5. A. Kasamatsu and T. Hirai, "Studies of EEG's of Expert Zen Meditators," *Folia Psychiatrica Neurologica Japonica* 28(1966):315.

6. For a different point of view see David S. Holmes, "Meditation and Somatic Arousal Reduction: A Review of the Experimental Evidence," *American Psychologist* 39(1984):1–10.

7. J. Allison, "Respiratory Changes during Transcendental Meditation," *Lancet,* no. 7651(1970):833–34.

8. B. D. Elson, P. Hauri, and D. Cunis, "Physiological Changes in Yogi Meditation," *Psychophysiology* 14(1977):52–57.

9. J. Malec and C. N. Sipprelle, "Physiological and Subjective Effects of Zen Meditation and Demand Characteristics," *Journal of Consulting and Clinical Psychology* 45(1977):339–40.

10. L. D. Zaichkowsky and R. Kamen, "Biofeedback and Meditation: Effects on Muscle Tension and Locus of Control," *Perceptual and Motor Skills* 46(1978):955–58.

11. Richard A. Fee and Daniel A. Girdano, "The Relative Effectiveness of Three Techniques to Induce the Trophotropic Response," *Biofeedback and Self-Regulation* 3(1978):145–57.

12. N. R. Cauthen and C. A. Prymak, "Meditation versus Relaxation: An Examination of the Physiological Effects with Transcendental Meditation," *Journal of Consulting and Clinical Psychology* 45(1977):496–97.

13. Daniel Goleman and Gary E. Schwartz, "Meditation as an Intervention in Stress Reactivity," *Journal of Consulting and Clinical Psychology* 44(1976):456–66.

14. David W. Orme-Johnson, "Autonomic Stability and Transcendental Meditation," *Psychosomatic Medicine* 35(1973):341–49.

15. Robert Keith Wallace, "Physiological Effects of Transcendental Meditation," *Science* 167(1970):1751–54.

16. Robert Keith Wallace and Herbert Benson, "The Physiology of Meditation," *Scientific American* 226(1972):84–90.

17. L. A. Hjelle, "Transcendental Meditation and Psychological Health," *Perceptual and Motor Skills* 39(1974):623–28.

18. W. Linden, "Practicing of Meditation by School Children and Their Levels of Field Independence-Dependence, Test Anxiety, and Reading Achievement," *Journal of Consulting and Clinical Psychology* 41(1973):139–43.

19. P. Ferguson and J. Gowan, "TM—Some Preliminary Findings," *Journal of Humanistic Psychology* 16(1977):51–60.

20. D. Thomas and K. A. Abbas, "Comparison of Transcendental Meditation and Progressive Relaxation in Reducing Anxiety," *British Medical Journal* no. 6154(1978):1749.

21. M. C. Dillbeck, "The Effect of the Transcendental Meditation Technique on Anxiety Levels," *Journal of Clinical Psychology* 33(1977):1076–78.

22. D. H. Shapiro and D. Giber, "Meditation and Psychotherapeutic Effects," *Archives of General Psychiatry* 35(1978):294–302.

23. Jonathan C. Smith, *Meditation: A Senseless Guide to a Timeless Discipline* (Champaign, Ill.: Research Press, 1986).

9

Autogenic Training

You're at a magic show and, before you realize what you've done, you've volunteered to be hypnotized on stage. The hypnotist asks you to follow the pendulumlike movement of his chained watch as he slowly and softly mutters, "You're getting tired. Your eyelids are becoming heavy and are difficult to keep open. Your body feels weighted down—very full and heavy. You are relaxed; totally relaxed. You will now listen to my voice and obey its instructions." After several more sentences you are willing to crow like a rooster, look at your watch on cue, or even stand up when a certain word is spoken. How is it that people can be made to do embarrassing things and be laughed at by other people? Well, whatever the reason, hypnosis can be a powerful tool if used appropriately. People who have had difficulty giving up cigarettes or other drugs, or flying on airplanes, or losing weight have been helped by hypnosis.

An interesting aspect of hypnosis is that we can hypnotize ourselves. Autohypnosis is the basis of the relaxation technique to which this chapter is devoted—autogenic training.

What Is Autogenic Training?

Around 1900, Oskar Vogt (a brain physiologist) noted that some patients were able to place themselves in a hypnotic state. Vogt called this condition **autohypnosis.** These patients reported less fatigue, less tension, and fewer psychosomatic disorders (e.g., headaches) than other patients. The German psychiatrist Johannes Schultz had used hypnosis with his patients. In 1932, he developed **autogenic training** (meaning self-generating) using the observations of Vogt as its basis.[1] Schultz had found that patients he hypnotized developed two physical sensations: general body warmth and heaviness in the limbs and torso. Schultz's autogenic training consisted of a series of exercises designed to bring about these two physical sensations and, thereby, an autohypnotic state. The generalized warmth was a function of the dilation of blood vessels, resulting in increased blood flow. The sensation of heaviness was caused by muscles relaxing. Since both vasodilation and muscle relaxation are components of the relaxation response, autogenic training exercises have been employed as a relaxation technique designed to help people better manage the stresses in their lives.

Schultz described autogenic training as a technique to treat neurotic patients and those with psychosomatic illness.[2] However, its use quickly expanded to healthy people who wanted to regulate their own psychological and physiological processes. Part of the reason that autogenic training became a well-known relaxation technique was its description in several sources by Schultz's student Wolfgang Luthe.[3-5] The details of how to do autogenic training as described by Schultz and Luthe appear in a later section of this chapter. For now, we will only mention the need for a passive attitude toward autogenic training exercises. That is, trying to relax gets in the way of relaxing. You just have to do the exercises and let what happens happen.

We should also note that although autogenic training and meditation both lead to the relaxation response, they get there by different means. Meditation uses the mind to relax the body. Autogenic training uses the bodily sensations of heaviness and warmth to first relax the body and then expand this relaxed state to the mind by the use of imagery. This distinction will become more clear to you after the description of autogenic training exercises and your practice of them.

Those that I have taught meditation and autogenic training report interesting and contradictory reactions. Some prefer meditation, because it requires very little learning, can be done almost anywhere, and allows the mind to be relatively unoccupied. Meditation only requires the mind to focus upon something repetitive like a mantra or something unchanging like a spot on the wall. Others find meditation boring and prefer autogenic training's switches of focus from one part of the body to another and its use of imagery to relax the mind. Whichever works for you is the relaxation technique you should employ. Use the relaxation technique rating scale appearing at the end of this chapter to help you evaluate the benefits you derive from your practice of autogenic training.

To summarize, autogenic training is a relaxation technique that uses exercises to bring about the sensations of body warmth and heaviness in the limbs and torso and then uses relaxing images to expand physical relaxation to the mind.

Benefits of Autogenic Training

Autogenic means self-generating. That means you do the procedure to yourself. It also refers to the self-healing nature of autogenics. As you will now see, autogenic training has been shown to have physiological as well as psychological benefits. It is partially for this reason that autogenics is the relaxation method of choice in Europe.[6]

Physiological Effects

The physiological effects of autogenic training are similar to those of other relaxation techniques that elicit the trophotropic response. The heart rate, respiratory rate, muscle tension, and serum cholesterol level all decrease. Alpha brain waves and blood flow to the arms and legs increase. The increased peripheral blood flow has led to success with autogenics in treating Raynaud's disease sufferers, who have a deficient supply of blood flowing to their extremities.[7,8] In addition, migraine headache sufferers and insomniacs have benefitted from autogenic training, as have those with high blood pressure.[9-11] Lastly, an increase in alpha brain waves, a sign of mental relaxation, occurred as a result of autogenics.[12]

Other studies, less well documented but no less rational, show that autogenics also helps with bronchial asthma, constipation, writer's cramp, indigestion, ulcers, hemorrhoids, tuberculosis, diabetes, and lower back pain.[13] Autogenics has also been studied regarding its potential to help cure cancer[14] and to treat tension headaches.[15] In addition, diabetics engaging in autogenic training have been known to regain islet of Langerhans functioning, meaning they need less insulin (note: without an adjustment in the dosage of insulin they are prescribed, they may be overdosed).

Psychological Effects

In one dramatic demonstration of the psychological effects of autogenics, a subject was able to withstand for a minute and a half the pain of a third-degree burn brought about by a lighted cigarette placed on the back of the hand.[16] I don't suggest you attempt such a feat; still, it makes us marvel once again about the influence our minds exert over our bodies. In any case, autogenics can aid those with chronic illnesses that result in pain (e.g., arthritis) to tolerate that pain better.

In addition, autogenic training has been found to reduce anxiety and depression, decrease tiredness, and help people increase their resistance to stress.[17-19] For example, a woman who couldn't wear dentures without gagging was taught to control the gagging by learning autogenics.[20] Another woman who couldn't drive an automobile because of a previous accident and the associated anxiety was helped with autogenics.[21] Even pregnant women were found to experience less pain and less anxiety during childbirth when employing autogenics.[22] Men having a problem with motion sickness also experienced less of a reaction after employing autogenics than did a control group of similar men.[23]

How to Do Autogenic Training

Before describing autogenic training exercises, we should note that people with psychological problems who employ autogenics to alleviate these problems do so in clinical situations with trained clinicians (e.g., a clinical psychologist or psychiatrist). When used in this manner, it may take anywhere from two months to one year before a person becomes proficient.[24]

Although the six initial stages of autogenic training and the second phase (autogenic meditation) are described below, the autogenic training practice that you will experience is a modified version of the standard procedures. Since the purpose of autogenics described here is relaxation rather than therapy, this modified version (easier to learn and found effective for reaching the relaxation response) will suffice.

Prerequisites

Schultz and Luthe cite several factors essential to successful autogenic training:[25]

1. High motivation and cooperation on the part of the subject
2. A reasonable degree of subject self-direction and self-control
3. Maintenance of particular body posture conducive to success

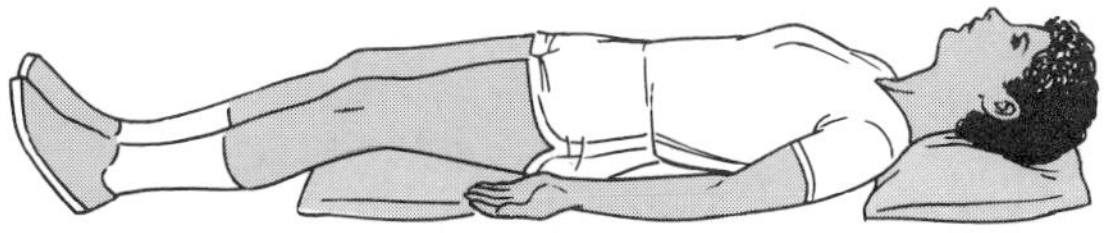

Figure 9.1 The reclining position

4. Reduction of external stimuli to a minimum, and mental focusing on endopsychic processes to the exclusion of the external environment

5. Presence of a monotonous input into the various sensory receptors

6. Concentrated deployment of attention on the somatic processes in order to effect an inward focusing of consciousness

7. Given these conditions, the occurrence of an overpowering, reflexive psychic reorganization

8. The occurrence of disassociative and autonomous mental processes, leading to an alteration of ego functioning and dissolution of ego boundaries

Body Position

There are three basic positions for doing autogenics: one reclining and two seated. In the reclining position (see fig. 9.1), you lie on your back, feet slightly apart, toes leaning away from the body. Cushion any part of the body that feels uncomfortable. Use blankets or pillows for cushioning, but be careful not to misalign the body (e.g., by using pillows under the head that make the chin almost touch the chest). Your arms should lie alongside your body but not touch it, with a slight bend at the elbows and the palms facing upward.

The seated positions (see figs. 9.2 and 9.3) have two advantages: you can do them almost anywhere, and they are less apt to result in sleep. On the other hand, they don't allow as much total muscle relaxation as the reclined position. The best chair to use is a straight-backed one that will provide support for your head and align it with your torso. Your buttocks should be against the back of the chair, and the seat of the chair should be long enough to support your thighs. Your arms, hands, and fingers may relax on the arms of the chair or be supported in your lap.

The second seated position uses a stool or a low-backed chair upon which you sit without support for your back. Sit at the forward part of the chair with your arms supported on your thighs, hands and fingers dangling loosely. The head hangs loosely with the chin near the chest. Your feet should be placed at shoulder width, slightly forward of your knees.

Whichever position you choose, make sure your body is relaxed and that it is supported by as little muscular contraction as possible.

Figure 9.2 The first seated position

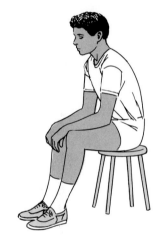

Figure 9.3 The second seated position

Six Initial Stages of Autogenic Training

Here are the six initial stages of autogenic training that precede the use of imagery:

1. Focus on sensations of heaviness throughout the arms and legs (beginning with the dominant arm or leg)
2. Focus on sensations of warmth throughout the arms and legs (beginning with the dominant arm or leg)
3. Focus on sensations of warmth and heaviness in the area of the heart
4. Focus on breathing
5. Focus on sensations of warmth in the abdomen
6. Focus on sensations of coolness in the forehead

These stages are sequential; you need to master the skills of each stage before practicing the next. Sample instructions for each of these stages appear below:

Stage 1: Heaviness

My right arm is heavy . . .

My left arm is heavy . . .

Both of my arms are very heavy.

My right leg is heavy . . .

My left leg is heavy . . .

Both of my legs are very heavy.

My arms and legs are very heavy.

Stage 2: Warmth

My right arm is warm . . .

My left arm is warm . . .

Both my arms are very warm.

My right leg is warm . . .

My left leg is warm . . .

Both of my legs are very warm.

My arms and legs are very warm.

Stage 3: Heart

My heartbeat is calm and regular (repeat four or five times).

Stage 4: Respiration

My breathing is calm and relaxed . . .

It breathes me (repeat four or five times).

Stage 5: Solar plexus

My solar plexus is warm (repeat four or five times).

Stage 6: Forehead

My forehead is cool (repeat four or five times).

With experience in autogenics, it should take you only a few minutes to feel heaviness and warmth in your limbs, a relaxed and calm heart and respiratory rate, warmth in your abdomen, and coolness in your forehead. Remember, though, that it usually takes several months or more of regular practice to get to that point. Regular practice means ten to forty minutes, one to six times per day.[26] However, don't be too anxious to master autogenics, since trying too hard will interfere with learning the skills. Proceed at your own pace, moving to the next stage only after you have mastered the previous stage.

Imagery

Part of autogenic training employs images of relaxing scenes to translate body relaxation into mind relaxation. Some people visualize a sunny day spent on a sailboat on a quiet lake. Others find birds flying gently through the air, or the ocean surf reaching the shore, or a cozy, carpeted room warmed by a fire relaxing. You will use visualization later in this chapter as part of your practice of autogenic training. Rather than using a scene that *I* find relaxing (which may not be relaxing for you), identify an image you can use to relax yourself. The questions below will help you do that.

1. What is the temperature at the scene? _____

2. Who is there? _____

3. What colors are present in your scene? _____
   _____

4. What sounds are present in your scene? _____
   _____

5. What movement is occurring? _____
   _____

6. How are you feeling? _____
   _____

Sometimes called **autogenic meditation,** visualization of relaxing images begins by rotating your eyeballs inward and upward as if you are attempting to look at your own forehead. This procedure alone has been shown to result in increased alpha brain-wave activity.[27] The next step involves practicing visualizing one color in your whole field of vision—any color you choose. Next, visualize colors making pictures. When that is accomplished, practice visualizing one object against a dark background. This object should be seen clearly, be immobile, and be viewed for a long duration (practice sessions may run from forty to sixty minutes).

The next phase of autogenic meditation instructs you to visualize abstract ideas (such as freedom). This phase usually runs from two to six weeks. After this training period, you may then practice focusing upon feeling states while visualizing yourself in various situations. For example, you may focus upon your feelings as you imagine yourself floating on a cloud.

The next phase involves the visualization of other people, first neutral people (e.g., a storekeeper you know), then family or friends. It is hoped that such visualization will result in insight into relationships you have with these people. In particular, relationships with people with whom you are in conflict are thought to be improved by autogenic meditation insights.

Although you would do best to develop your own image of relaxation (different people find different things relaxing), an example of relaxing imagery appears on page 175. In any relaxing imagery, there should be a very vivid scene.

Use as many of your senses as you can to make the image as real as possible. You should smell the smells, hear the sounds, see the colors, feel the sensations, and even taste the tastes present. Images can be of clouds, valleys, a willow tree, a field of wildflowers, a cool forest, a log cabin, a clear stream, a sloping hill[28] or just about any other scene that would relax you. I have chosen a sunny beach as the image to use as an example.

You are driving to the beach with your car window rolled down and no radio on in your car. The wind is blowing through your hair, and the sun is beating down on your thighs through the car window. You can see people walking with beach chairs and blankets; clad in bathing suits and carrying food in picnic baskets and coolers. You park your car, and as you are walking to the beach, you hear the surf rolling onto the shore and can smell the salt in the air. You find a quiet spot of beach away from other people and spread your blanket out there. Being tired from the drive, you are relieved to allow your muscles to relax as you lie on the blanket with your feet extending beyond, onto the sand.

As you relax, you can taste the salt in the air. Droplets of ocean seem to fall on you as you hear the pounding of the surf and it ever-so-gently rolling back to sea. Everything seems light and yellow and tan and blue. The sun's bright yellow on the sand's relaxing tan contrasted with the ocean's vivid blue seem just the right combination of serenity. You decide to close your eyes and take in all the sensations through other senses.

The sun seems to move over your body. First your arms warm up from the intensity of the sun's rays. You can feel the heat pass through them, and the feeling is one of relaxation. Next your legs become caressed by the sun as they too become warm. The sun moves to warm your chest now and your whole chest area becomes heated and relaxed. But it doesn't stop there. The sun moves to your abdomen bringing its relaxing warmth there. And, as though you've willed it, the sun next moves to your forehead bringing warmth and relaxation there. Your whole body now feels warm and relaxed. Your muscles are relaxed and your body feels as though it's sinking into the sand. Your body feels warm and heavy. Your body tingles from the sun's warmth.

You hear the sea gulls as you relax. They are flying over the ocean. They are free and light and peaceful. As they fly out to sea, they are carrying your problems and worries with them. You are relieved of your problems and worries and relaxed. You think of nothing but your body's heaviness and warmth and tingling sensation. You are totally relaxed.

You have relaxed all day like this, and now the sun is setting. As you feel the sun leaving, you slowly open your eyes feeling wonderfully relaxed and content. You have no worries, you have no cares. You look at the sea gulls who have left your problems and worries out at sea and you thank them. Feeling alert, you stand and stretch feeling the still warm—but yet cooling—sand between your toes, and you feel terrific. You feel so good that you know the car ride home will be pleasant. You welcome the time to be alone, in your car, at peace, without problems or cares. You fold your blanket and leave your piece of beach taking with you your relaxation and contentment. You say goodbye to your beach as you walk from it knowing you can return anytime you desire.

Remember, imagery has been shown to be extremely effective in either eliciting the stress or the relaxation response;[29,30] so use it to your advantage.

An Autogenic Training Experience

The six initial stages and the phases of autogenic meditation already described take a good deal of time to work through. A set of instructions follows that will take you through a modified autogenic training experience. Note that each of the six initial stages are presented at one sitting and that visualization is also a part of this exercise. For relaxation purposes, my students and others for whom I have conducted relaxation training report these instructions to be effective.

This exercise should be practiced at least once daily but preferably twice: once upon waking and once just before dinner. You can either memorize the phrases below, ask someone to read them to you, or recite them into a tape recorder. In any case, these phrases should be presented calmly, softly, and with sufficient pause between them for you to be able to bring about the sensations to which each phrase refers.

Now, assuming you're ready and haven't just eaten or ingested a stimulant, are located in a relatively quiet, comfortable environment, and have approximately thirty minutes for relaxation, position yourself in one of the three autogenic positions previously described. Repeat the phrases below:

I am calm.

It is quiet.

I am relaxed.

My right arm (if right-handed) is heavy. (Repeat four or five times)

My right arm is warm. (Repeat four or five times)

My right arm is tingly.

My right arm is heavy and warm.

My right arm is weighted down and feels warm.

My left arm is heavy. (Repeat four or five times)

My left arm is warm. (Repeat four or five times)

My left arm is tingly.

My left arm is heavy and warm.

My left arm is weighted down and warm.

Both my arms are heavy and warm. (Repeat four or five times)

(Repeat the phrases above for the legs, beginning with the dominant leg.)

My heart is beating calmly.

I am relaxed.

My heart is calm and relaxed. (Repeat four or five times)

My breathing is regular.

My breathing is calm.

My breathing is calm and relaxed. (Repeat four or five times)

It breathes me. (Repeat four or five times)

My solar plexus is warm. (Repeat four or five times)

I feel warmth throughout my abdomen. (Repeat four or five times)

My forehead is cool. (Repeat four or five times)

I am calm.

I am relaxed.

I am quiet.

Now think of a relaxing scene.

(Refer to the scene you identified earlier in this chapter as relaxing for you.)

Imagine yourself there.

See this scene clearly.

Experience it.

Be one with it.

Hear the sounds.

See the colors.

This scene relaxes you.

You are calm.

You are quiet.

You are at peace.

Your mind is quiet.

Your whole body is quiet, heavy, warm, and relaxed.

Your thoughts are of your quiet, heavy, warm body and of your scene.

Tell yourself you feel quiet, you feel relaxed, you feel calm.

Now prepare to leave your scene.

Count backward from five.

With each number you will be more alert.

With each number you will be closer to opening your eyes.

Five.

You are leaving your scene.

You wave goodbye.

Four.

You are back in this room.

You are seated (or reclined).

You know where you are.

Three.

Prepare to open your eyes.

Think of what you will see when you open your eyes.

Two.

Open your eyes.

Focus upon one object in the room.

Take a deep breath.

One.

Focus on objects about the room.

Take several deep breaths.

When you feel ready, stretch your arms and legs.

Now stand and stretch.

Take several more deep breaths.

Now proceed with your regular activities knowing that you are refreshed and revitalized.

The Relaxation Technique Rating Scale

Practice autogenic training as suggested and regularly. After at least a one-week trial period, answer each of the questions below using the following scale.

1 = very true
2 = somewhat true
3 = I'm not sure
4 = somewhat untrue
5 = very untrue

_____ 1. It felt good.
_____ 2. It was easy to fit into my schedule.
_____ 3. It made me feel relaxed.
_____ 4. I handled my daily chores better than I usually do.
_____ 5. It was an easy technique to learn.
_____ 6. I was able to close out my surroundings while practicing this technique.
_____ 7. I did not feel tired after practicing this relaxation technique.
_____ 8. My fingers and toes felt warmer directly after trying this relaxation technique.
_____ 9. Any stress symptoms I had (headache, tense muscles, anxiety) before doing this relaxation technique disappeared by the time I was done.
_____ 10. Each time I concluded this technique, my pulse rate was much lower than when I began.

Now sum up the values you responded with for a total score. Save this score and compare it with scores for other relaxation techniques you try. The lower the score, the more appropriate a particular relaxation skill is for you.

Summary

1. Autogenic training is a relaxation technique that consists of a series of exercises designed to bring about body warmth and heaviness in the limbs and torso. In addition, relaxing images are employed to expand physical relaxation to the mind.

2. Autogenic training results in the trophotropic response. Autogenic means self-generating and refers to the fact that it is self-induced.

3. Autogenics have been used in the treatment of Raynaud's disease, migraine headaches, insomnia, hypertension, bronchial asthma, constipation, writer's cramp, indigestion, ulcers, hemorrhoids, tuberculosis, diabetes, and lower back pain.

4. Prerequisites for doing autogenics include high motivation, a measure of self-direction, maintenance of the recommended body position, blocking out the external environment, focusing inward, and giving up ego boundaries.

5. Autogenic training can be done lying down or in a seated position. Cushion parts of your body that feel uncomfortable and let your body relax.

6. The six initial stages of autogenic training are focusing on heaviness in the limbs, warmth in the limbs, heaviness and warmth in the area of the heart, regular breathing, sensations of warmth in the abdomen, and sensations of coolness in the forehead.

7. Sometimes called autogenic meditation, visualization of relaxing images begins by rotating the eyeballs inward and upward. The next step involves choosing one color to visualize and then numerous colors. Next, visualization of abstract images and then of people follows.

Notes

1. Daniel A. Girdano and George S. Everly, Jr., *Controlling Stress and Tension: A Holistic Approach* (Englewood Cliffs, N.J.: Prentice-Hall, 1986), 175.

2. Johannes Schultz, *Das Autogene Training* (Stuttgart: Geerg-Thieme Verlag, 1953).

3. Wolfgang Luthe, ed., *Autogenic Therapy,* 6 vols. (New York: Grune and Stratton, 1969).

4. Wolfgang Luthe, "Method, Research and Application of Autogenic Training," *American Journal of Clinical Hypnosis* 5(1962):17–23.

5. Johannes Schultz and Wolfgang Luthe, *Autogenic Training: A Psychophysiologic Approach to Psychotherapy* (New York: Grune and Stratton, 1959).

6. Phillip L. Rice, *Stress and Health: Principles and Practice for Coping and Wellness* (Monterey, Calif.: Brooks/Cole, 1987), 281.

7. J. F. Keefe, R. S. Surwit, and R. N. Pilon, "Biofeedback, Autogenic Training, and Progressive Relaxation in the Treatment of Raynaud's Disease: A Comparative Study," *Journal of Applied Behavior Analysis* 13(1980):3–11.

8. Edward Taub, "Self-regulation of Human Tissue Temperature," in *Biofeedback: Theory and Practice,* ed. Gary E. Schwartz and J. Beatty (New York: Academic Press, 1977).

9. B. V. Silver, "Temperature Biofeedback and Relaxation Training in the Treatment of Migraine Headaches," *Biofeedback and Self-Regulation* 4(1979):359–66.

10. T. J. Coates and C. E. Thoreson, "What to Use Instead of Sleeping Pills," *American Medical Association Journal* 240(1978):2311–12.

11. Edward B. Blanchard and Leonard H. Epstein, *A Biofeedback Primer* (Reading, Mass.: Addison-Wesley, 1978), 69–72.

12. J. Kamiya, "Conscious Control of Brain Waves," *Psychology Today* 1(1978):57–60.

13. Kenneth Lamott, *Escape from Stress: How to Stop Killing Yourself* (New York: G. P. Putnam's Sons, 1974), 151.

14. C. O. Simonton and Stephanie Simonton, "Belief Systems and Management of the Emotional Aspects of Malignancy," *Journal of Transpersonal Psychology* 7(1975):29–48.

15. N. B. Anderson, P. S. Lawrence, and T. W. Olson, "Within-Subject Analysis of Autogenic Training and Cognitive Coping Training in the Treatment of Tension Headache Pain," *Journal of Behavioral Therapy and Experimental Psychiatry* 12(1981):219–23.

16. B. Gorton, "Autogenic Training," *American Journal of Clinical Hypnosis* 2(1959):31–41.

17. Shoshana Shapiro and Paul M. Lehrer, "Psychophysiological Effects of Autogenic Training and Progressive Relaxation," *Biofeedback and Self-Regulation* 5(1980):249–55.

18. Malcomb Carruthers, "Autogenic Training," *Journal of Psychosomatic Research* 23(1979):437–40.

19. Martha Davis, Matthew McKay, and Elizabeth Robbins Eshelman, *The Relaxation and Stress Reduction Workbook* (Richmond, Calif.: New Harbinger Publications, 1980), 82.

20. Jack A. Gerschman et al., "Hypnosis in the Control of Gagging," *Australian Journal of Clinical and Experimental Hypnosis* 9(1981): 53–59.

21. Jon D. Boller and Raymond P. Flom, "Behavioral Treatment of Persistent Post-traumatic Startle Response," *Journal of Behavior Therapy and Experimental Psychiatry* 12(1981):321–24.

22. Tansella Zimmerman, "Preparation Courses for Childbirth in Primipara: A Comparison," *Journal of Psychosomatic Research* 23(1979):227–33.

23. Patricia S. Cowing, "Reducing Motion Sickness: A Comparison of Autogenic-Feedback Training and an Alternative Cognitive Task," *Aviation, Space, and Environmental Medicine* 53(1982):449–53.

24. Kenneth R. Pelletier, *Mind as Healer, Mind as Slayer* (New York: Dell Publishing Co., 1977), 241.

25. Ibid., 232.

26. Davis, McKay, and Eshelman, *Workbook,* 88.

27. Kamiya, *Psychology Today.*

28. Edward A. Charlesworth and Ronald G. Nathan, *Stress Management: A Comprehensive Guide to Wellness* (Houston, Tex.: Biobehavioral Publishers, 1982).

29. A. A. Sheikh, *Imagery: Current Theory, Research, and Application* (New York: Wiley, 1983).

30. A. A. Sheikh, *Imagination and Healing* (Farmingdale, N.Y.: Baywood Publishing Company, 1984).

10

Progressive Relaxation

I'll never forget my first lesson in downhill skiing. Having been selected the most valuable player on my college basketball team and having found success at some local tennis tournaments, I considered myself an accomplished athlete. Well, an accomplished skier I was not and never became; and as I prepare to relate the story of my skiing lesson, I'm reminded of the poem by A. E. Housman, from the collection entitled *A Shropshire Lad* in which he talks "To an Athlete Dying Young":

Runners whom renown outran
And the name died before the man.

The area where I learned to ski (that is, attempted to learn to ski) had three slopes: beginner, intermediate, and advanced. My first lesson, this first day ever on a pair of skis, consisted of one hour of falling, learning how to rise (no easy task in snow with long thin objects protruding fore and aft from my feet), and snowplowing. Well, believing my entry on the Olympic team as a downhill slalom racer assured after this lesson, I immediately attacked the intermediate course. With ineffective snowplowing to avoid some skiers and a loud "Watch Out!" that worked even better to avoid a crash with most of the others, I managed to get to the bottom of the slope without even getting snow on my ski outfit (consisting of my army long johns, tennis socks, jeans, and an old sweatshirt). As I waited for the lift to return me to the top so I could break the downhill speed record, I was awed by the grace and ease with which the more accomplished skiers appeared to be floating downhill. Effortlessly, it seemed, they moved left, then right, then tucked, then stopped smoothly at the bottom. Well, I never learned to ski well. In fact, the very next (and last) time I was silly enough to find myself at the top of a series of ski slopes and recklessly let my fragile body begin sliding downward, I found that my snowplowing was good enough to get me about one-third down a zigzagging slope, though I wound up a little further and further behind each successive curve. The one-third point was where I attempted to save my body from the oncoming woods by turning to the left, only to learn that it was too late and my skills were too few. Using my brains as the only way out, I sat down and skidded just short of a threatening blue spruce. Recalling something about wisdom being the better part of valor, I removed my skis, smacked the snow off my derrière, and marched downhill to spend the rest of the day in what was for me a more natural habitat—the fireplace-warmed lodge.

Bracing

I relate this embarrassing story because what I really want to discuss is the grace and effortlessness I observed in the good skiers. The reason they appeared this way is that they were using proper *form*. Some of you have probably had lessons in tennis, golf, or another sport during which you were taught the proper form. Proper form means moving the body to accomplish the task most effectively—with the least amount of energy. Proper form allows you to be effective and efficient. What has always been interesting to me is that too much muscular contraction can often interfere with using proper form. The approach of Tim Galway in teaching tennis is to prevent the mind from scaring the body into tensing so much that proper form is impossible.[1] For example, Galway instructs players to try to read the writing on the ball as it comes toward them rather than worry about having to hit a backhand return.

Doing things effectively and efficiently is important for our daily routines as well. Too often we use too much muscular contraction with the consequences being backache, headache, pains in the neck or shoulders, and other illnesses. In chapter 1 you were asked to freeze and inspect your body for unnecessary muscular contraction. You may have found your shoulders raised, your hands holding something too tightly, your forearm muscles tensed, or your abdominal muscles sort of squeezing you in. These are all signs of bracing. The muscles are contracted to ready the body for some action that the body seldom takes.

The next time you drive an automobile, notice how tightly you grasp the steering wheel. With the power steering of most modern cars, the steering wheel need only be held gently. To do otherwise is to be bracing.

The next time you take notes during a lecture, notice how tightly you hold the pen or pencil. If you hold too tightly or press down too hard you are bracing.

The next time you visit a dentist, notice how you cling to the arms of the chair. Since the chair will probably not move, your grip on it is unnecessary. You are bracing.

On numerous occasions we use muscular contraction inefficiently, and the result is poor health. However, we can learn to use our muscles in a more healthy manner through a relaxation technique called **progressive relaxation.**

What Is Progressive Relaxation?

Progressive relaxation is a technique used to induce nerve-muscle relaxation. Developed by Edmund Jacobson and described in his book *Progressive Relaxation,* this technique was originally designed for hospital patients who appeared tense.[2] Jacobson, a physician, observed that tense patients, as evidenced by such small muscle movement as frowning or wrinkling the forehead, did not recuperate quickly or well. Seeking to intervene in this residual muscle tension syndrome, Jacobson taught his patients a series of exercises that first required them to contract a muscle group, then relax it, moving (or progressing) from one muscle group to another. The purpose of first contracting the muscle is to teach people to recognize more readily what muscle tension feels like.[3] At first glance this appears unnecessary, but remember our discussion of bracing. The purpose of the relaxation phase is to become familiar enough with this sensation so that it can be voluntarily induced. The idea, then, is to sense more readily when we are muscularly tense and, on those occasions, to be able to relax those muscles.

Sometimes termed **neuromuscular relaxation** (since the nerves control muscular contraction) or **Jacobsonian relaxation** (named after its developer), progressive relaxation starts with one muscle group, adds another when the first is relaxed, and progresses through the body until total body relaxation occurs. It starts with the distal muscle groups (the feet and legs) and moves to the proximal muscle groups (the head and trunk) afterward.[4] Like autogenic training, progressive relaxation relaxes the mind by first relaxing the body. However, unlike autogenic training and meditation, progressive relaxation does not produce a hypnotic state.[5] Like the other relaxation techniques presented in this book, progressive relaxation should be practiced regularly, and you should expect to become more proficient as you gain experience with the technique.

This relaxation technique has proven effective in helping people relax and does not require any special equipment. In addition, although it takes several years of practice as originally described by Jacobson, benefits can result in several weeks of three daily practice sessions of just five minutes each.[6] In addition, progressive relaxation has been shown to have both physiological and psychological benefits.

Benefits of Progressive Relaxation

Physiological Effects

In describing Jacobson's research on the effects of progressive relaxation, Brown states that learned relaxation of skeletal muscles can be generalized to smooth muscles, causing relaxation of the gastrointestinal and cardiovascular systems.[7] Other researchers have found progressive relaxation effective in treating tension headaches[8-10] and migraine headaches.[11,12] In addition, backache sufferers have been helped with progressive relaxation.[13] It appears that conditions resulting from bracing or ineffective muscular tension can be alleviated,[14] or at least their symptoms diminished, with regular practice of progressive relaxation—even writer's cramp.[15]

Psychological Effects

Progressive relaxation has been demonstrated to have wide-ranging effects upon psychological well-being as well as upon behavioral change. For example, college students with poor self-concepts improved their perceptions of themselves through training in progressive relaxation.[16] Further, both depression[17] and anxiety[18,19] were lessened in people trained in progressive relaxation. Even insomniacs were helped to sleep by using this relaxation technique.[20] Alcoholism,[21] drug abuse,[22] and even batting slumps[23] were aided by regular practice of progressive relaxation. When baseball players were taught progressive relaxation, they were better able to perform (bat) under stress than their teammates who did not practice relaxation techniques. They had higher batting averages. This should not be surprising, since we know that stress (up at the plate or before an audience) can interfere with performance. In the stress management classes I teach, several students have been performers (a singer and a violinist come to mind) who reported performing better when using stress management techniques.

It should be noted that virtually every form of relaxation has the potential of eliciting anxiety.[24] However, progressive relaxation, though no exception to this rule, is less likely than other relaxation techniques to generate anxiety.[25] It is therefore recommended when anxiety is of particular concern to the person seeking relaxation.

How to Do Progressive Relaxation

As with the other relaxation techniques, learning progressive relaxation necessitates several prerequisites as well as learning the appropriate body position for performing the exercises.

Cues Identifying Tension

First of all, it is helpful to recognize that you are tense. You may have aches in your shoulders, back, neck, or head. Your body may feel stiff. You may sense that you are generally holding yourself too tightly or rigidly. You may have difficulty sitting comfortably, or your hands may tremble.

As you become more experienced with regular practice of progressive relaxation, you will more readily recognize these signs of tension and be better prepared to relax them away. In addition, regular practice will help prevent these signs of tension from occurring in the first place.

Figure 10.1
Reclining position for
progressive relaxation
exercise

Look for these signs of tension and use them as cues to doing progressive relaxation. A good idea is to check for these cues just prior to meals so you can relax them away before eating. As we've discussed earlier, food in your stomach results in the blood flow increasing to that area of your body. This makes it more difficult to bring about relaxation, since the relaxation response includes increasing the blood flow to the arms and legs.

Prerequisites

When learning progressive relaxation, seek a relatively quiet, distraction-free environment. That means any telephones must be removed from the room or the receiver removed from the cradle and muffled with a towel. The lights should be dimmed and the threat of cats, dogs, kids, or roommates disturbing you eliminated. If, after making adjustments in your environment, the noise is still impeding your learning, you might try headphones or cotton in your ears to block out the noise. Make sure you remove or loosen any tight clothing or jewelry and that the room is warm. It is difficult to relax in a cold environment, since the blood doesn't readily travel to cold extremities. Removing your shoes is also advisable.

Lastly, approach the exercises knowing that any discomfort, muscle cramping, or pain can quickly be eliminated by just stopping the exercise. Proceed slowly and carefully. Learning is designed to proceed slowly, so don't expect to be proficient at progressive relaxation after only a few sessions. Don't contract a muscle that is strained, pained, or cramped. There's always another day.

Body Position

To do progressive relaxation, stretch out on the floor (see fig. 10.1). The idea is to have your body supported by the floor rather than by your muscles. Once lying on your back, let your arms and legs go. You can rest your hands on your abdomen or at your sides, and your legs and feet will most likely rotate outward. Just relax. You can support your neck with a pillow (small enough to fit behind your neck between your shoulders and where your head is resting on the floor); you may also find that a pillow placed under your knees feels comfortable. Make sure you are comfortable before starting. If not, rearrange your body so that you are. After you have more experience with progressive relaxation, you will be able to relax particular muscle groups when seated or even when standing in line (for example, those muscles in the neck). However, it is best to learn these exercises while reclined.

After you become proficient, you can eliminate the contraction phase and focus totally on relaxation. It may take several weeks or months of regular practice, though, to develop the "muscle sense" that the contraction phase teaches.

Since this phase teaches you to recognize muscle tension, it is important not to rush to eliminate it. But, as you will soon find out, it is the relaxation phase that is most pleasant and has the most health-related benefits. If you are having difficulty with progressive relaxation, you can even work with a partner.[26]

Exercises

There have been several different variations of muscle relaxation exercises developed by stress management experts. For example, Forman and Myers suggest contracting a muscle group by pushing against an immovable object.[27] They recommend pushing down with the fingertips on a desk top, for instance. Their reasoning is that this resistance technique requires more muscular contractions which, in turn, increases the ability to recognize the difference between the contracted and relaxed states. Smith, on the other hand, recommends eleven isometric squeeze exercises: hand squeeze, arm squeeze, arm and side squeeze, back squeeze, shoulder squeeze, back and neck squeeze, face squeeze, front of neck squeeze, stomach and chest squeeze, leg squeeze, and foot squeeze.[28] (After all those squeezes, you're probably entitled to squeeze someone you love.) Smith argues that too often students of progressive relaxation are taught to stretch the muscles too quickly during the contraction phase. He believes isometric contractions will be experienced as more pleasurable, thereby being more effective in teaching relaxation.

The exercises that follow are simple enough to learn and yet powerful enough to be used for the control of stress and tension. Try them several times a day for at least a week. Then complete the relaxation technique rating scale to evaluate progressive relaxation's benefits to you compared to the other relaxation techniques you have tried.

The following instructions, which were developed by Jenny Steinmetz, can be read to you, memorized, or recited into a tape recorder. Follow each instruction carefully and completely. Don't skip any part of the body (unless injured) and don't skip any exercises. Also make sure that you spend twice as much time relaxing a muscle as you do tensing that muscle.

Relaxation of the arms (four or five minutes)
Settle back as comfortably as you can and let yourself relax to the best of your ability.
Now, as you relax, clench your right fist.
Clench it tighter and tighter, and study the tension as you do so.
Keep it clenched and feel the tension in your right fist, hand, and forearm.
Now relax . . .
Let the fingers of your right hand become loose . . .
Observe the contrast in your feelings.

Now, let yourself go and try to become more relaxed all over.
Once more, clench your right fist really tight.
Hold it, and notice the tension again.
Now, let go, relax, let your fingers straighten out . . .
Notice the difference once more.

Now repeat that with your left fist.
Clench your left fist while the rest of your body relaxes.
Clench that fist tighter and feel the tension.
And now relax . . . again, enjoy the contrast.
Repeat that once more, clench the left fist, tight and tense.
Now do the opposite of tension—relax and feel the difference . . .
Continue relaxing like that for awhile.

Clench both fists tighter and tighter, both fists tense, forearms tense.
Study the sensations . . . and relax . . .
Straighten out your fingers and feel that relaxation . . .
Continue relaxing your hands and forearms more and more.

Now bend your elbows and tense your biceps.
Tense them harder and study the tension feeling.
All right, straighten out your arms . . .
Let them relax and feel the difference again . . .
Let the relaxation develop.
Once more, tense your biceps.
Hold the tension and observe it carefully.
Straighten the arms and relax . . .
Relax to the best of your ability . . .
Each time pay close attention to your feelings when you tense up and when you relax.

Now straighten your arms, straighten them so that you feel most tension in the triceps
    muscles along the back of your arms.
Stretch your arms and feel the tension.
And now relax . . .
Get your arms back into a comfortable position . . .
Let the relaxation proceed on its own . . .
The arms should feel comfortably heavy as you allow them to relax.
Straighten the arms once more so that you feel the tension in the triceps muscles.
Feel that tension . . . and relax.
Now let's concentrate on pure relaxation in the arms without any tension . . .
Get your arms comfortable and let them relax further and further . . .

Continue relaxing your arms even further . . .
Even when your arms seem fully relaxed, try to go that extra bit further . . .
Try to achieve deeper and deeper levels of relaxation.

Relaxation of the face, neck, shoulders, and upper back (four or five minutes)

Let all your muscles go loose and heavy.
Just settle back quietly and comfortably.
Wrinkle up your forehead now, wrinkle it tighter.
And now stop wrinkling up your forehead.
Relax and smooth it out . . .
Picture the entire forehead and scalp becoming smoother, as the relaxation increases.
Now frown and crease your brows and study the tension.
Let go of the tension again . . .
Smooth out the forehead once more.
Now, close your eyes.
Keep your eyes closed, gently, comfortably, and notice the relaxation.

Now clench your jaws, push your teeth together.
Study the tension throughout the jaws.
Relax your jaws now . . .
Let your lips part slightly . . .
Appreciate the relaxation.
Now press your tongue hard against the roof of your mouth.
Look for the tension.
All right, let your tongue return to a comfortable and relaxed position.
Now purse your lips, press your lips together tighter and tighter.
Relax the lips . . .
Notice the contrast between tension and relaxation . . .
Feel the relaxation all over your face, all over your forehead, and scalp, eyes, jaws, lips,
    tongue, and throat . . .
The relaxation progresses further and further.

Now attend to your neck muscles.
Press your head back as far as it can go and feel the tension in the neck.
Roll it to the right and feel the tension shift . . .
Now roll it to the left.
Straighten your head and bring it forward.
Press your chin against your chest.
Let your head return to a comfortable position and study the relaxation . . .
Let the relaxation develop.

Shrug your shoulders right up.
Hold the tension.
Drop your shoulders and feel the relaxation . . .
Neck and shoulders relaxed.
Shrug your shoulders again and move them around.
Bring your shoulders up and forward and back.
Feel the tension in your shoulders and in your upper back.
Drop your shoulders once more and relax . . .
Let the relaxation spread deep into the shoulders right into your back muscles.
Relax your neck and throat, and your jaws and other facial areas, as the pure
    relaxation takes over and grows deeper . . . deeper . . . even deeper.

Relaxation of the chest, stomach, and lower back (four or five minutes)

Relax your entire body to the best of your ability.
Feel that comfortable heaviness that accompanies relaxation.
Breathe easily and freely in and out . . .
Notice how the relaxation increases as you exhale . . .
As you breathe out, just feel that relaxation.
Now breathe right in and fill your lungs.
Inhale deeply and hold your breath.
Study the tension.
Now exhale, let the walls of your chest grow loose, and push the air out automatically.
Continue relaxing and breathe freely and gently . . .
Feel the relaxation and enjoy it.

With the rest of your body as relaxed as possible, fill your lungs again.
Breathe in deeply and hold it again.
Now breathe out and appreciate the relief, just breathe normally . . .

Continue relaxing your chest and let the relaxation spread to your back, shoulders, neck, and arms . . .

Merely let go and enjoy the relaxation.

Now let's pay attention to your abdominal muscles, your stomach area.

Tighten your stomach muscles, make your abdomen hard.

Notice the tension.

And relax, let the muscles loosen and notice the contrast.

Once more, press and tighten your stomach muscles.

Hold the tension and study it.

And relax, notice the general well-being that comes with relaxing your stomach.

Now draw your stomach in.

Pull the muscles right in and feel the tension this way.

Now relax again . . . let your stomach out . . .

Continue breathing normally and easily and feel the gentle massaging action all over your chest and stomach.

Now pull your stomach in again and hold the tension.

Once more pull in and feel the tension.

Now relax your stomach fully . . .

Let the tension dissolve as the relaxation grows deeper.

Each time you breathe out, notice the rhythmic relaxation both in your lungs and in your stomach . . .

Notice how your chest and your stomach relax more and more . . .

Try to let go of all contractions anywhere in your body.

Now direct your attention to your lower back.

Arch up your back, make your lower back quite hollow, and feel the tension along your spine.

Now settle down comfortably again, relaxing the lower back.

Just arch your back up and feel the tensions as you do so.

Try to keep the rest of your body as relaxed as possible.

Try to localize the tension throughout your lower back area.

Relax once more, relaxing further and further . . .

Relax your lower back, relax your upper back, spread the relaxation to your stomach, chest, shoulders, arms, and facial area . . .

These parts relaxing further and further and further and even deeper.

Relaxation of the hips, thighs, and calves (four or five minutes)

Let go of all tensions and relax.

Now flex your buttocks and thighs.

Flex your thighs by pressing down your heels as hard as you can.

Relax and notice the difference.

Straighten your knees and flex your thigh muscles again.

Hold the tension.

Relax your hips and thighs . . .

Allow the relaxation to proceed on its own.

Press your feet and toes downward, away from your face, so that your calf muscles become tense.

Study that tension.

Relax your feet and calves.

This time, bend your feet toward your face so that you feel tension along your shins.
Bring your toes right up.
Relax again . . . keep relaxing for awhile . . .
Now let yourself relax further all over . . .
Relax your feet, ankles, calves and shins, knees, thighs, buttocks, and hips . . .
Feel the heaviness of your lower body as you relax still further.
Now spread the relaxation to your stomach, waist, and lower back.
Let go more and more deeply . . .
Make sure no tension has crept into your throat.
Relax your neck and your jaws and all your facial muscles.
Keep relaxing your whole body like that for awhile . . .
Let yourself relax.
Now you can become twice as relaxed as you are merely by taking in a really deep
    breath and slowly exhaling, with your eyes closed, so that you become less aware
    of objects and movements around you, and thus prevent any surface tensions from
    developing.
Breathe in deeply and feel yourself becoming heavier.
Take in a long, deep breath and exhale very slowly . . .
Feel how heavy and relaxed you have become.
In a state of perfect relaxation, you should feel unwilling to move a single muscle in
    your body.
Think about the effort that would be required to raise your right arm.
As you think about that, see if you can notice any tensions that might have crept into
    your shoulders and arm.
Now you decide not to lift the arm, but to continue relaxing . . .
Observe the relief and the disappearance of the tension.
Just carry on, relaxing like that . . . continue relaxing . . .
When you wish to get up, count backwards from four to one.
You should now feel fine and refreshed, wide-awake and calm.

Other Short Exercises

There may be occasions when you choose not to devote as much time to relaxation
as the exercises just presented require. In those instances, you can still practice
a modified, simplified, and quick version of progressive relaxation. For example,
you may be working at your desk and notice that your shoulder muscles are tense.
To relax them you can tense them further—raising your shoulders as high as you
can get them—and then let them relax. Focus on the sensations of your relaxed
shoulder muscles, paying particular attention to any warm and tingly sensations.

Another quick exercise you can do involves your abdominal muscles. Make
these muscles tense by keeping your abdominal area flat but tight. Notice how
you breathe with these muscles tensed—with the expansion of your chest muscles
alone. Be aware of the sensations of breathing this way. Now relax your abdominal muscles and let your abdominal area stick out. Breathe by the expansion and
contraction of your abdominal area rather than your chest. To help breathe this
way, place the palm of your hand on your abdomen. Let your hand rise and fall
as your abdomen rises when you inhale and falls when you exhale. Notice how
relaxed you feel breathing in this manner.

You can improvise your own quick, modified version of progressive relaxation by identifying any particular muscle group that feels tense and then tensing it further. Next, relax that muscle group and focus upon the feelings of relaxation. After approximately five minutes of such an exercise, you can begin to feel less tense and more relaxed—and better able to proceed with the rest of your day. You might even do such exercises on schedule each day, considering that five minutes as a "vacation period" in which you leave your daily cares to travel to a more relaxed state.

The Relaxation Technique Rating Scale

Practice progressive relaxation as suggested and regularly. After at least a one-week trial period, answer each of the questions below using the following scale.

1 = very true
2 = somewhat true
3 = I'm not sure
4 = somewhat untrue
5 = very untrue

____ 1. It felt good.
____ 2. It was easy to fit into my schedule.
____ 3. It made me feel relaxed.
____ 4. I handled my daily chores better than I usually do.
____ 5. It was an easy technique to learn.
____ 6. I was able to close out my surroundings while practicing this technique.
____ 7. I did not feel tired after practicing this relaxation technique.
____ 8. My fingers and toes felt warmer directly after trying this relaxation technique.
____ 9. Any stress symptoms I had (headache, tense muscles, anxiety) before doing this relaxation technique disappeared by the time I was done.
____ 10. Each time I concluded this technique, my pulse rate was much lower than when I began.

Now sum up the values you responded with for a total score. Save this score and compare it with scores for other relaxation techniques you try. The lower the score, the more appropriate a particular relaxation skill is for you.

Summary

1. People often use more muscular contraction than necessary. This can lead to backache, headache, or pains in the shoulders and neck.

2. Muscular tension that prepares the body for action that is never taken is termed bracing. Raising your shoulders throughout the day is an example of bracing.

3. Progressive relaxation is a technique used to induce nerve-muscle relaxation. It involves contraction of a muscle group and then relaxation of it, progressing from one muscle group to another throughout the body.

4. The contraction phase of progressive relaxation is designed to help people better recognize when they are bracing. The relaxation phase is designed to help people recognize and bring on a relaxed state when they choose.

5. Progressive relaxation has been used to treat tension headaches, migraine headaches, backaches, and other conditions. It has also been used to treat psychological conditions, such as poor self-concept, depression, anxiety, insomnia, and others.

6. When learning progressive relaxation, seek a distraction-free environment and lie on your back. Proceed slowly and carefully, stopping if you experience muscle cramping or pain.

7. It may take several weeks or months of regular practice of progressive relaxation before you develop the "muscle sense" that the contracting phase teaches, but the relaxation will benefit you much sooner.

Notes

1. W. Timothy Galway, *The Inner Game of Tennis* (New York: Random House, 1974).

2. Edmund Jacobson, *Progressive Relaxation* (Chicago: University of Chicago Press, 1938).

3. David Pargman, *Stress and Motor Performance: Understanding and Coping* (Ithaca, N.Y.: Mouvement Publications, 1986), 183.

4. D. A. Berstein and B. Given, "Progressive Relaxation: Abbreviated Methods," in *Principles and Practice of Stress Management,* ed. R. Woolfolk and P. Lehrer (New York: Guilford Press, 1984).

5. Edmund Jacobson, *You Must Relax* (New York: McGraw-Hill Book Co., 1970).

6. John D. Curtis and Richard A. Detert, *How To Relax: A Holistic Approach to Stress Management* (Palo Alto: Mayfield, 1981), 102.

7. Barbara B. Brown, *Stress and the Art of Biofeedback* (New York: Harper & Row, 1977), 45.

8. D. J. Cox, A. Freundlich, and R. G. Meyer, "Differential Effectiveness of Electromyographic Feedback, Verbal Relaxation Instructions, and Medication Placebo with Tension Headaches," *Journal of Consulting and Clinical Psychology* 43(1975):892–98.

9. S. N. Haynes et al., "Electromyographic Biofeedback and Relaxation Instructions in the Treatment of Muscle Contraction Headaches," *Behavior Therapy* 6(1975):672–78.

10. Leon Otis et al., "Voluntary Control of Tension Headaches" (Paper presented at the Biofeedback Research Society Meeting, Colorado Springs, Colo., 1974).

11. Edward B. Blanchard and Leonard H. Epstein, *A Biofeedback Primer* (Reading, Mass.: Addison-Wesley, 1978), 80–81.

12. K. R. Mitchell and D. M. Mitchell, "Migraine: An Exploratory Treatment Application of Programmed Behavior Therapy Techniques," *Journal of Psychosomatic Research* 15(1971):137–57.

13. Cynthia D. Belar and Joel L. Cohen, "The Use of EMG Feedback and Progressive Relaxation in the Treatment of a Woman with Chronic Back Pain," *Biofeedback and Self-Regulation* 4(1979):345–53.

14. Phillip L. Rice, *Stress and Health: Principles and Practice for Coping and Wellness* (Monterey, Calif.: Brooks/Cole, 1987), 240.

15. Daniel A. Girdano and George S. Everly, *Controlling Stress and Tension: A Holistic Approach* (Englewood Cliffs, N.J.: Prentice-Hall, 1986), 145.

16. Maureen Dion, "A Study of the Effects of Progressive Relaxation Training on Changes in Self-Concepts in Low Self-Concept College Students," *Dissertation Abstracts International* 37(1977):4860.

17. C. Kondo, A. Canter, and J. Knott, "Relaxation Training as a Method of Reducing Anxiety Associated with Depression" (Paper presented at the Biofeedback Research Society Meeting, Monterey, Calif., 1975).

18. M. Raskin, G. Johnson, and J. Rondestvedt, "Chronic Anxiety Treated by Feedback-Induced Muscle Relaxation," *Archives of General Psychiatry* 23(1973):263–67.

19. S. Breeden et al., "EMG Levels as Indicators of Relaxation" (Paper presented at the Biofeedback Research Society Meeting, Monterey, Calif., 1975).

20. T. D. Berkovec and D. C. Fowles, "Controlled Investigation of the Effects of Progressive and Hypnotic Relaxation on Insomnia," *Journal of Abnormal Psychology* 82(1973):153–58.

21. Brown, *Biofeedback,* 89.

22. Ibid.

23. Kenneth J. Kukla, "The Effects of Progressive Relaxation Training upon Athletic Performance during Stress," *Dissertation Abstracts International* 37(1977):6392.

24. E. J. Heide and T. D. Borkovec, "Relaxation-Induced Anxiety: Mechanisms and Theoretical Implications," *Behaviour Research and Therapy* 22(1984):1–12.

25. P. M. Lehrer and R. L. Woolfolk, "Are Stress Reduction Techniques Interchangeable, or Do They Have Specific Effect?: A Review of the Comparative Empirical Literature," in *Principles and Practice of Stress Management,* ed. R. L. Woolfolk and P. M. Lehrer (New York: Guilford, 1984).

26. John D. Curtis et al., *Teaching Stress Management and Relaxation Skills: An Instructor's Guide* (La Crosse, Wis.: Coulee Press, 1985), 167.

27. Jeffrey W. Forman and Dave Myers, *The Personal Stress Reduction Program* (Englewood Cliffs, N.J.: Prentice-Hall, 1987), 72.

28. Jonathan C. Smith, *Relaxation Dynamics: Nine World Approaches to Self-Relaxation* (Champaign, Ill.: Research Press, 1985), 65.

Biofeedback and Other Relaxation Techniques

My friend and colleague Dr. Jack Osman goes around the country offering his lecture, "Fat Is Where It's At." A good speaker, creative, and well-informed, Jack is always looking for new ways to have his audience appreciate that the charts listing how much you should weigh for your sex and height (and sometimes body build) are invalid. We were sitting in my office one day when Jack described his latest motivational device, soon to be tested on an unsuspecting audience. "I'm going to purchase old bathroom scales from junkyards. They'll probably cost a dollar apiece. Then I'll get a sledgehammer. The first thing I'm going to do after I'm introduced to the audience is use that sledgehammer to whack the hell out of a scale. I'll hit that sucker until it begs for mercy."

Being the gentleman that he is (really), Jack cares about those he educates. He wants them to know that weight charts do not consider body fat, but rather total weight. A well-developed weight lifter, for instance, may weigh more than the weight chart advises but not be "overfat."

What Is Biofeedback?

Biofeedback has been defined as "the use of instrumentation to mirror psycho-physiological processes of which the individual is not normally aware and which may be brought under voluntary control."[1] That's just a fancy way of saying biofeedback is receiving information about what is occurring in your body at a particular time and then helping you to control that occurrence. A biofeedback instrument is just a tool used to obtain the measure about the part of your body in which you are interested. Consequently, a basal body thermometer is a biofeedback instrument—albeit slow and not as accurate as more sophisticated equipment—since it gives you information about a parameter of the body (its core temperature).

To better understand the concept of biofeedback and biofeedback instrumentation, tape a basal body thermometer to your middle finger, making sure the sensitive bulb of the thermometer is against the skin of your finger. In a short period of time (five minutes) the thermometer will stabilize at a reading indicating the temperature at the surface of that finger. Record that temperature below.

_____ °F

Your task now is to increase the temperature at the surface of that finger by increasing the peripheral blood flow. As you should recall, either meditation or autogenic training will result in more blood flowing to the arms and legs (and fingers and toes). Therefore, use either of these relaxation techniques for ten or fifteen minutes to accomplish your task and then record the temperature of the surface of your finger below.

_____ °F

Biofeedback, however, is also a process. It has been determined, and more than adequately validated, that once people are fed back information about their body processes, they can be taught to control these processes. Biofeedback has been defined as:

a process in which a person learns to reliably influence physiological responses of two kinds: either responses which are not ordinarily under voluntary control or responses which ordinarily are easily regulated but for which regulation has broken down due to trauma or disease.[2]

Biofeedback really involves three phases:

1. *Measuring* the physiological parameter. (The sensitive mercury in the bulb of the thermometer senses temperature.)
2. *Converting* this measurement to some understandable form. (The mercury in the thermometer rises in a tube calibrated by degrees Fahrenheit, allowing the temperature of the finger to be determined visually.)
3. *Feeding back* of this information to the person who is learning to control his or her body processes.

Before this system could be developed, however, researchers had to demonstrate that body processes previously believed to be involuntary could, in fact, be brought under voluntary control. The early research in biofeedback was directed toward demonstrating this fact. It was shown, for instance, that subjects could change their heart rate,[3-5] the electrical conductance of their skin (galvanic skin response),[6-8] the dilation of their blood vessels,[9] and the brain waves they emitted.[10,11] Numerous other physiological parameters can also be controlled by biofeedback training: muscle tension, blood pressure, penile erection, and secretion of hydrochloric acid in the stomach, to name a few. Although it has still not been determined *how* people control their physiology, that they can is no longer questioned.

Benefits of Biofeedback

Biofeedback has many benefits, not the least of which is the demonstration (objectively and physiologically) that we have much greater control of ourselves than most of us realized. If we can demonstrate through measurable means that we can control blood pressure and brain waves, shouldn't we be able to control cigarette smoking and exercise behavior? If we can increase or decrease heart rate or the amount of stomach acid we secrete, how difficult could it be to conquer stage fright or an alcohol problem? Biofeedback demonstrates to us that our behavior, as well as our physiology, is pretty much our own doing. That being the case, we must accept responsibility for our behavioral choices. Remind you of the internal locus of control presented earlier?

Other general benefits of biofeedback include the following:

1. The doctor-patient interaction that has heretofore been dominated by the physician or psychologist now is at least partially—if not more than that—controlled by the patient. The patient must "do the work" of healing with the doctor assisting as he or she can, rather than the patient being relegated to a passive recipient of "a laying on of hands" by the know-it-all doctor.
2. Psychologists and other mental health experts can monitor physiological reactions to identify sensitive issues affecting their patients. This can significantly shorten the time needed to determine the issues with which counseling should be concerned.
3. Patients learn they can depend on their own inner resources rather than having to rely on medication or the therapist. This realization can result in greater self-care when that is appropriate, thereby decreasing unnecessary expenditures for medical care.

In addition, biofeedback has specific physiological and psychological benefits. These benefits are presented next. It should be stated at the outset, however, that not all experts agree that the benefits as described here have been conclusively demonstrated. This point will be elaborated upon in the sections following.

Physiological Effects

As we shall soon see, biofeedback has been used to improve the physical health of many people. However, an interesting point is made by Elmer Green and his associates:

> In actuality, there is no such thing as training in brain wave control, there is training only in the elicitation of certain subjective states. . . . what are detected and manipulated (in some as yet unknown way) are subjective feelings, focus of attention, and thought processes.[12]

Once again the relationship between mind and body is demonstrated. Changes in subjective states result in changes in physiology during biofeedback practice.

In any case, **electromyographic (EMG) biofeedback** alone, which focuses upon muscle tension, has been effective in treating the following conditions:

asthma	ulcers
hypertension	muscle spasms
bruxism	nerve-muscle injuries (stroke, paralysis)
hyperkinesia	spasmodic torticollis
spasticity	tinnitus
cerebral palsy	migraine headache
dystonias	tension headache
dysphonia	colitis

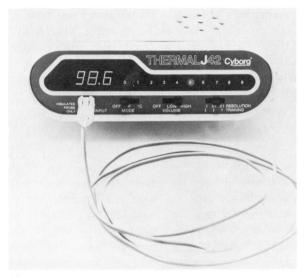

(a)

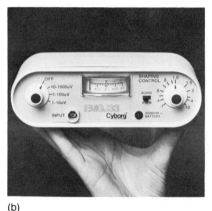

(b)

(c)

Biofeedback instrumentation comes in various forms and measures various physiological parameters. Included are (a) a thermal (temperature) instrument, (b) an electromyographic instrument, and (c) a galvanic skin response (electrical conductivity) instrument.

Thermal (temperature) **biofeedback** has been successful in treating Raynaud's disease (a condition resulting in too little blood flowing into the fingers), migraine headaches, and hypertension.[13]

Even scoliosis—an S-shaped curvature of the spine—is being remedied through biofeedback. To correct this curvature of the spine, many patients wear a body brace, which may be uncomfortable and psychologically disturbing. Since this condition occurs most often in adolescent girls, a body brace can be particularly bothersome during this developmental period. Neal Miller and Barry Dworkin have recently developed an alternative to the typical body brace.[14] This new harness is made of a nylon fiber, which makes it lightweight and not as cumbersome as most braces now in use. Its supports run both vertically and horizontally. A sensor determines when the wearer is not standing straight and a tone then sounds. Such innovative uses of biofeedback are the wave of the future.

However, researchers have found contradictory results regarding some of these benefits and uses of biofeedback. For example, whereas Litt,[15] Fentress,[16] and Sargent[17] found that biofeedback helped subjects in their studies reduce the pain of migraine headaches, Chapman found no benefit of biofeedback in treating migraines.[18] Whereas Blanchard[19] and Collet[20] found biofeedback helpful for the treatment of tension headaches, Callon[21] and Lacroix[22] found it to be ineffective. When Szekely studied the use of biofeedback to treat headaches resulting from menstrual pain he did not find it to be an effective treatment.[23]

Psychological Effects

Biofeedback has been used to help people improve their psychological health and make changes in their health-related behavior. Phobias, anxiety, stage fright, insomnia, alcoholism, drug abuse, depression, and hyperactivity in children have been successfully treated with biofeedback. Tension headaches, sexual dysfunction, pain, and even stuttering have responded to biofeedback as well.[24-28]

Summarizing the research pertaining to biofeedback's effectiveness and usefulness, Rice perhaps best describes the current state of the art by posing and then answering three questions:

The first is whether biofeedback can be used to teach a person how to alter a specific internal process. The answer seems to be an unqualified yes. The second question is whether biofeedback is useful for treating a variety of stress and health problems. The answer seems to be a qualified maybe. The third question is whether the positive outcomes are a result of some unique property of biofeedback not present in other procedures. The answer is mostly no. In fact, the more biofeedback is studied, the more it appears to share common elements with both relaxation and cognitive stress management procedures.[29]

One comprehensive review of biofeedback research concluded that biofeedback has not demonstrated any particular superiority over the other relaxation techniques and cognitive coping strategies, which are less costly and require less expertise and effort than does biofeedback.[30]

Limitations of Biofeedback

At this point you know that no one relaxation technique is a panacea. In addition to questionable effectiveness, the limitations of biofeedback relate to its availability, cost, and the way it is used.

Availability

Biofeedback equipment (the effective kind) is usually not sold directly to the public. Believed to be an adjunct to medical or psychological care, this equipment is usually restricted to physicians, physical therapists, psychologists, psychiatrists, researchers, and hospital and university personnel. The idea is that biofeedback training cannot be done correctly without the assistance of a qualified trainer. As a matter of fact, the Biofeedback Society of America has recently developed certification procedures for biofeedback trainers. Consequently, even if you wanted to train on biofeedback equipment, you'd have to depend on someone else to work with you.

This raises some ethical questions. There are those who argue that biofeedback equipment should be available to anyone who can pay for it. These people believe the restricted sale of this instrumentation is designed to create business for the professionals to whom the equipment is sold. On the other hand, some believe biofeedback can be harmful if not supervised by a trained and qualified professional. How will a layperson know what kind of feedback, and at what level, is appropriate, and how many cases will not be referred to more traditional modes of treatment that should be? You can see that this question of the availability of biofeedback equipment is far from being resolved.

The limited access to biofeedback equipment leads to the next limitation—cost. If you have to pay a health professional to supervise the training, the expense may be more than you can afford. Even if you could purchase the equipment, for the most part it is very expensive. The expense is related to two important characteristics of effective biofeedback equipment:

Cost

1. Feedback must be instantaneous (in fractions of a second) so that when the machine indicates that your muscle tension is at a particular level, and you attempt to associate your thoughts, images, and sensations of *that moment* with that level of muscular contraction, you are not being misled. If the feedback is too slow, as was the thermometer described earlier, the equipment may be telling you not what your body *is* doing, but what it *was* doing. The sensations you are experiencing at a particular moment, then, may not be related to the feedback provided at that moment, but rather to the feedback soon to be provided. Sound confusing? Well, with poor equipment it usually is!
2. Feedback must be highly accurate. The error factor must be small enough that you can have confidence in the feedback.

You can purchase inexpensive biofeedback equipment, but it probably will not feed back information rapidly enough or accurately enough.

Biofeedback equipment is not designed to be used during the routine stressful moments we all experience daily. Rather, it is a training device. Biofeedback is used to train people to gain greater control of their physiological processes. You can't walk around all day long attached to some biofeedback apparatus or "hook up" whenever you are stressed. The equipment is used to teach you the sensations of relaxation and its physiological correlates: decreased muscle tension, heart rate, respiratory rate, blood pressure, and so forth. The hope is that once you are able to control more of your physiological responses to stressors, you will not react to stress dysfunctionally.

The Use of Biofeedback Equipment

Since you cannot remain connected to biofeedback equipment forever, another relaxation technique is usually taught to you and used in conjunction with biofeedback for purposes of stress management. Autogenic training, meditation, and progressive relaxation have all been employed in this manner. In one respect, the biofeedback equipment just objectively verifies that the other relaxation technique has been learned. It also, of course, may facilitate such learning by serving as a reinforcer and quickly identifying what is and what is not working.

An example of how I used biofeedback with one of my students will illustrate this last point. After teaching several different types of relaxation techniques to my students and providing them with sufficient time for practice of these techniques, I found one of my students frustrated. It seems he felt that none of the techniques helped him to relax. He said he really didn't remember relaxing much during his fifty-odd years of life. When we worked with the biofeedback equipment, however, it was a different story. With electromyographic biofeedback, this student was able to demonstrate a remarkably low frontalis (forehead) muscle tension. Since the frontalis muscle is believed to be a mirror to general body relaxation, I was glad to see this student finally achieve a deep state of relaxation. Afterward we spoke, and he told me that, for some reason, whenever he imagined a tunnel with black walls with purple blotches on them, the equipment reported he was at a very low level of muscular tension. He never saw that tunnel before, nor could he associate it with any symbolic meaning. However, the vision of it relaxed him. The biofeedback training, then, served this student well because it helped him to identify an image that he could recall whenever he chose to and relax.

How to Do Biofeedback Training

In spite of the limited availability of biofeedback equipment, its high cost, and the frequent need to also learn another relaxation technique, you can still do biofeedback training if you're cagey enough. Seek out the psychology, counseling, health education, or a similar department on a college campus, and you'll often find biofeedback equipment. Next, make yourself available to faculty and graduate students who need subjects for their biofeedback research. I know we are often looking for subjects to use in this manner. Perhaps there's even a course that employs biofeedback as a component. If so, enroll in it.

In addition to universities, hospitals often have biofeedback equipment. Perhaps you can qualify for third-party payment (health insurance) for biofeedback training. Perhaps the hospital personnel are also conducting biofeedback research and need subjects.

Lastly, you might write to biofeedback instrument manufacturers to ask them where or how you can get training or equipment; or write to the Biofeedback Society of America, Department of Psychiatry C268, University of Colorado Medical Center, 4200 East Ninth Avenue, Denver, Colorado 80220.

Other Relaxation Techniques

There are relaxation techniques other than the ones already presented; however, space dictates only a brief discussion of them. References are provided to assist you to learn more about these techniques should your interest be sparked.

For conducting studies with biofeedback equipment, researchers use more sensitive instrumentation capable of measuring several physiological responses at the same time.

Even when you are tense, there is some part of your body which feels relaxed. Body scanning[31] requires you to search for that part and, once identifying it, spread that sensation to the more tense parts of yourself. For example, if you pay attention to your bodily sensations you may find that your calf muscles feel particularly relaxed. You would then focus upon the feelings in your calf muscles, becoming aware of the sensations experienced there. Then you would attempt to transfer these sensations to other parts of your body which are more tense—for example, your shoulder muscles. The relaxed sensation can be imagined to be a warm ball which travels to various bodily locations warming and relaxing them.

Body Scanning

When distressed, your breathing becomes rapid, shallow, and stems from your chest. When more relaxed, you breathe slowly, with deep and regular breaths, and your breath comes from your stomach area expanding rather than your chest. Relaxed breathing has been termed *diaphragmatic breathing*[32] since it results from the expansion of the diaphragm, whereas distressed breathing has been termed *thoracic breathing* since it results from expansion of the chest wall that is brought about by contractions of muscles in the chest area. To practice diaphragmatic breathing, lie on your back with the palms of your hands placed on your lower stomach area. As you breathe, expand your chest area while keeping your stomach flat. Become aware that this is thoracic breathing and learn to recognize it as such. Next, expand your abdomen so that your stomach rises and

Diaphragmatic Breathing

falls with each breath while your chest size remains relatively constant (it will expand some). Recognize this type of breathing as diaphragmatic breathing. Practice it at various times of the day (when seated doing school work, for instance).

Massage and Acupressure

Massage[33,34] has a way of relaxing the muscles of a tense body. Various forms of massage exist, but acupressure—pressing down on points of the body where knots or bands of muscle tension frequently occur—appears to be one of the more popular forms. Although any object can be used to employ pressure, most often it is the hands which are used for massaging. The procedure involves warming a massage lotion (such as vitamin E or body lotion) and employing one of several techniques: caressing, gliding, and/or kneading. Never press directly on the vertebrae, just on their sides; and never apply hard pressure on the neck or lower back region. To use acupressure correctly you should obtain a chart of acupressure points.

Yoga and Stretching

Yoga[35] comes from a root word that has many meanings: to bind, join, attach, and yoke; to direct and concentrate one's attention; or communion with God.[36] Actually yoga should more accurately be called "yogas" since there are so many types: Prana Yoga, Brahma Yoga, Kriya Yoga, Kundalini Yoga, Raja Yoga, Tantra Yoga, and the most widely known in the western world, Hatha Yoga (involving stretching exercises). It is no wonder, therefore, that yoga is proposed to serve many different functions: from cleansing the body, to activating the nervous system, to improving one's intelligence or sex life. The stretching involved in yoga can be quite relaxing, and the prescribed yoga positions (called asanas) encourage this benefit. However, be careful not to stretch in a way that is uncomfortable—remember, you're trying to relax—or in a way in which you will injure yourself. Although space does not allow a complete description of the yogic stretching positions here, there are many other sources you can consult if you wish to learn more about Hatha Yoga.[37,38]

Summary

1. Biofeedback is the use of instrumentation to receive information about occurrences within the body. People fed back such information can learn to control these body processes.
2. Biofeedback involves three phases: measuring the physiological parameter, converting this measurement to some understandable form, and feeding back this information to the person learning to control his or her body processes.
3. Biofeedback has been used to help people control their heart rates, skin's electrical conductance, blood vessels' dilation, and brain waves. Biofeedback has also been used to control muscle tension, blood pressure, penile erection, and secretion of hydrochloric acid.

4. Electromyographic biofeedback has been used to treat asthma, hypertension, ulcers, muscle spasms, migraine and tension headaches, colitis, cerebral palsy, and other conditions.

5. Thermal biofeedback has been used to treat Raynaud's disease, migraine headaches, and hypertension.

6. The limitations of the use of biofeedback relate to the availability and cost of the instrumentation and the expense of engaging a trained professional to work with the person using the equipment.

7. When used for relaxation purposes, biofeedback is often employed in conjunction with another relaxation technique. Oftentimes, autogenics or meditation are the other techniques used during biofeedback training.

8. There are many different types of relaxation techniques other than meditation, autogenic training, progressive relaxation, and the use of biofeedback instrumentation. Among these are body scanning, diaphragmatic breathing, massage and acupressure, and yoga and stretching.

Notes

1. George D. Fuller, *Biofeedback: Methods and Procedures in Clinical Practice* (San Francisco: Biofeedback Press, 1977), 3.

2. Edward B. Blanchard and Leonard H. Epstein, *A Biofeedback Primer* (Reading, Mass.: Addison-Wesley, 1978), 2.

3. D. W. Shearn, "Operant Conditioning of Heart Rate," *Science* 137 (1962):530–31.

4. T. W. Frazier, "Avoidance Conditioning of Heart Rate in Humans," *Psychophysiology* 3(1966):188–202.

5. Neal E. Miller, "Learning of Visceral and Glandular Response," *Science* 163(1969):434–45.

6. H. D. Kimmell and F. A. Hill, "Operant Conditioning of the GSR," *Psychological Reports* 7(1960):555–62.

7. H. D. Kimmel, "Instrumental Conditioning of Autonomically Mediated Behavior," *Psychological Bulletin* 67(1967):337–45.

8. W. A. Greene, "Operant Conditioning of the GSR Using Partial Reinforcement," *Psychological Reports* 19(1976):571–78.

9. L. V. DiCara and Neal E. Miller, "Instrumental Learning of Vasomotor Responses by Rats: Learning to Respond Differentially in the Two Ears," *Science* 159(1968):1485.

10. Joseph Kamiya, "Conscious Control of Brain Waves," *Psychology Today* 1(1968):57–60.

11. Barbara B. Brown, "Recognition Aspects of Consciousness through Association with EEG Alpha Activity Represented by a Light Signal," *Psychophysiology* 6(1970):442–52.

12. Elmer E. Green, A. M. Green, and E. D. Walters, "Voluntary Control of Internal States: Psychological and Physiological," *Journal of Transpersonal Psychology* 2(1970):1–26.

13. David G. Danskin and Mark A. Crow, *Biofeedback: An Introduction and Guide* (Palo Alto, Calif.: Mayfield, 1981), 24–28.

14. Neal E. Miller, "RX: Biofeedback," *Psychology Today,* February 1985, 54–59.

15. Mark D. Litt, "Mediating Factors in Non-Medical Treatment for Migraine Headache: Toward an Interactional Model," *Journal of Psychosomatic Research* 30(1986):505–19.

16. David W. Fentress et al., "Biofeedback and Relaxation-Response Training in the Treatment of Pediatric Migraine," *Developmental Medicine and Child Neurology* 28(1986):139–46.

17. Joseph Sargent et al., "Results of a Controlled, Experimental, Outcome Study of Nondrug Treatments for the Control of Migraine Headaches," *Journal of Behavioral Medicine* 9(1986):291–323.

18. Stanley L. Chapman, "A Review and Clinical Perspective on the Use of EMG and Thermal Biofeedback for Chronic Headaches," *Pain* 27(1986):1–43.

19. Edward B. Blanchard et al., "Two, Three, and Four Year Follow-Up on the Self-Regulatory Treatment of Chronic Headache," *Journal of Consulting and Clinical Psychology* 55(1987):257–59.

20. L. Collet, "MMPI and Headache: A Special Focus on Differential Diagnosis, Prediction of Treatment Outcome and Patient: Treatment Matching," *Pain* 29(1987):267–68.

21. Eleanor W. Callon et al., "The Effect of Muscle Contraction Headache Chronicity on Frontal EMG," *Headache* 26(1986):356–59.

22. J. Michael Lacroix et al., "Physiological Changes after Biofeedback and Relaxation Training for Multiple-Pain Tension-Headache Patients," *Perceptual and Motor Skills* 63(1986):139–53.

23. Barbara Szekely, "Nonpharmacological Treatment of Menstrual Headache: Relaxation-Biofeedback Behavior Therapy and Person-Centered Insight Therapy," *Headache* 26(1986):86–92.

24. T. H. Budzynski, J. M. Stoyva, and C. Adler, "Feedback-Induced Muscle Relaxation: Application to Tension Headache," *Journal of Behavior Therapy and Experimental Psychiatry* 1(1970):205–11.

25. G. A. Eversaul, "Psycho-physiology Training and the Behavioral Treatment of Premature Ejaculation: Preliminary Findings," *Proceedings of the Biofeedback Research Society* (Denver, Colo., 1975).

26. Kenneth R. Pelletier, *Mind as Healer, Mind as Slayer* (New York: Dell Publishing Co., 1977), 289.

27. B. Guitar, "Reduction of Stuttering Frequency Using Analogue Electromyographic Feedback," *Journal of Speech and Hearing Research* 18(1975):672–85.

28. Edward B. Blanchard et al., "Three Studies of the Psychologic Changes in Chronic Headache Patients Associated with Biofeedback and Relaxation Therapies," *Psychosomatic Medicine* 48(1986):73–83.

29. Phillip L. Rice, *Stress and Health: Principles and Practice for Coping and Wellness* (Monterey, Calif.: Brooks/Cole, 1987), 313.

30. D. C. Turk, Donald H. Meichenbaum, and W. H. Berman, "Application of Biofeedback for the Regulation of Pain: A Critical Review," *Psychological Bulletin* 86(1979):1322–38.

31. John D. Curtis and Richard A. Detert, *How to Relax: A Holistic Approach to Stress Management* (Palo Alto, Calif.: Mayfield, 1981), 80–81.

32. Jeffrey W. Forman and Dave Myers, *The Personal Stress Reduction Program* (Englewood Cliffs, N.J.: Prentice-Hall, 1987), 31–36.

33. G. Downing, *Massage Book* (Berkeley, Calif.: Book Works Publishing Co., 1972). Distributed by Random House, Inc.

34. See the *Massage Therapy Journal* available from the American Massage Therapy Association, P.O. Box 1270, Kingsport, TN 37662.

35. Maxine Tobias and Mary Stewart, *Stretch and Relax: A Day by Day Workout and Relaxation Program* (Tucson, Ariz.: The Body Press, 1975).

36. Jonathan C. Smith, *Relaxation Dynamics: Nine World Approaches to Self-Relaxation* (Champaign, Ill.: Research Press, 1985), 83.

37. B. K. S. Iyengar, *Light on Yoga* (New York: Schocken Books, 1965).

38. Kriyananda, *Yoga Postures for Self-Awareness* (San Francisco: Ananda Publications, 1967).

PART IV

▼

General
Applications:
Physiological
Arousal and
Behavior Change
Interventions

Physiological Arousal Interventions—Exercise

I'm ashamed to admit it, and yet it makes a point. I'm referring to the time that I was in the upstairs bathroom and my son, who was four, was being a pain in the neck. As I was applying a very sharp razor to my very soft skin, Todd was using me as a tackling dummy. After repeatedly beseeching him to control his aggression, and after about half a pint of my red corpuscles had spilled into the sink, I was totally frustrated. Reacting reflexively, I did the only mature thing available to me at the moment—I kicked him. Well, Todd had never even experienced a spanking in his first four years of life and, in fact, his mother and I emphasized that hitting was an inappropriate manner of solving problems. We stated that with such conviction and so often that when I kicked Todd, he looked like his world had collapsed. Now mind you, this was not child abuse. The kick was pretty gentle, while making its point. A court of law need only have looked at my mangled face to declare self-defense. But disappointed Todd was anyhow. Staring at me with eyes wide open, Todd asked, "Why did you do that?" Without hesitation, I admitted, "Because it felt good." A few apologies, hugs, and kisses later, both of us realized we had acted selfishly and vowed to learn from that situation.

Haven't you experienced situations where you, too, would have liked to strike out at someone or something? A friend of mine punched a wall, only to find it surprisingly softer than his knuckles. The repair of his swollen hand occurred several weeks prior to the repair of the hole in his wall.

When emotions build up, we seek physical outlets. It feels good to "let it out," so we slam doors, throw dishes, or kick four-year-olds. Now that you are familiar with the stress response and recognize that the body has been physiologically prepared to do something physical (fight or flight), you can appreciate the value of using your body in some active way.

Now, there are more socially acceptable ways of using the stress products than those described above. I don't mean to make too light of having kicked my son, because that was wrong. It was so wrong that, as I said when I introduced that story, I'm embarrassed by it. Some people beat up their spouses because they are distressed. Others beat up their children. Still others act violently in other ways. The idea is to use stress products in a *positive* manner—a manner that will make you feel better and not violate anyone else's rights.

Let me tell you about Dick. Dick and I played tennis together, and Dick never won. Our talents were not dissimilar, but Dick seemed invariably to hit the ball harder than necessary and, consequently, could not control it as I did. One day I suggested to him that he hit easier but try to control the ball better. You know, it's not how hard you hit it but where it goes? Dick's response taught me an important lesson. He said that the ball represented his boss, his wife, or anyone else he was upset with at the moment. No way was he going to hit that "sucker" easier! I was concerned about winning; Dick was concerned about his health. I was frustrated when I hit a poor shot; as long as Dick got "good wood" on that ball, he was satisfied. Dick used physical exercise to alleviate stressful feelings and the buildup of stress products.

That is what this chapter is about—how to use exercise to manage stress. In particular, exercise is presented as a means of *using* the stress products—increased heart and respiratory rates, blood fats, muscle tension, and so forth—so they are not able to affect your health negatively. In addition, exercise can redirect your attention from stressors to the exercise.

Exercise and Health

Exercise is not only good for your physical health but for your psychological health as well. These benefits of exercise are described in the following sections.

Physical Health

When people speak of health, most often they are referring to physical health. Physical health is the status of your body and its parts. Vigorous exercise does the following:

1. Improves the functioning of the lungs and circulatory system so that transportation of food and oxygen to cells is facilitated
2. Provides the lungs with greater elasticity to breath in more air by expanding more
3. Delays the degenerative changes of aging
4. Increases the production of red blood cells in the bone marrow, resulting in a greater ability to transport oxygen to the parts of the body where it is needed
5. Helps to maintain normal blood pressure in normotensives and lower blood pressure in hypertensives
6. Results in a quicker recovery time from strenuous activity
7. Strengthens the heart muscle the way other muscles are strengthened—by exercising it
8. Results in a lower pulse rate, indicating that the heart is working more efficiently
9. Burns calories, thereby helping to prevent hypertension, heart disease, diabetes, and other conditions related to excess body fat
10. Accelerates the speed and efficiency with which food is absorbed

11. Tones muscle to improve strength and create a more visually appealing physique
12. Increases endurance
13. Improves posture
14. Decreases low-density lipoproteins (associated with heart disease) and serum cholesterol
15. Raises high-density lipoproteins (protective against heart disease)

Most of us know that regular exercise can improve our physical fitness, but many of us do not know what that term actually means. **Physical fitness,** the ability to do one's work and have energy remaining for recreational activities, is comprised of several components:

1. *Muscular strength:* the absolute maximum force that a muscle can generate
2. *Muscular endurance:* the ability to do continuous muscular work[1]
3. *Cardiorespiratory endurance:* the ability of the circulatory system (heart, lungs, and blood vessels) to supply oxygen to the muscles and remove waste products of muscular contraction[2]
4. *Flexibility:* the ability to move the joints of the body through their fullest range of motion
5. *Body composition:* the proportion of lean body mass (bones and muscles) to the percentage of body fat
6. *Agility:* the ability to move with quickness, speed, and balance[3]

Figure 12.1 Physical fitness scorecard for selected sports and exercises.

A rating of 21 indicates maximum benefit. Ratings were made on the basis of regular (minimum of four times per week), vigorous (duration of thirty minutes to one hour per session) participation in each activity.

	Jogging	Bicycling	Swimming	Skating (ice or rolling)	Handball/Squash	Skiing—Nordic	Skiing—Alpine	Basketball	Tennis	Calisthenics	Walking	Golf*	Softball	Bowling
Physical Fitness														
Cardiorespiratory endurance (stamina)	21	19	21	18	19	19	16	19	16	10	13	8	6	5
Muscular endurance	20	18	20	17	18	19	18	17	16	13	14	8	8	5
Muscular strength	17	16	14	15	15	15	15	15	14	16	11	9	7	5
Flexibility	9	9	15	13	16	14	14	13	14	19	7	8	9	7
Balance	17	18	12	20	17	16	21	16	16	15	8	8	7	6
General Well-being														
Weight control	21	20	15	17	19	17	15	19	16	12	13	6	7	5
Muscle definition	14	15	14	14	11	12	14	13	13	18	11	6	5	5
Digestion	13	12	13	11	13	12	9	10	12	11	11	7	8	7
Sleep	16	15	16	15	12	15	12	12	11	12	14	6	7	6
Total	148	142	140	140	140	139	134	134	128	126	102	66	64	51

*Ratings for golf are based on the fact that many Americans use a golf cart and/or caddy. If you walk the links, the physical fitness value moves up appreciably.

Physical fitness, however, does not develop from just any physical activity. Certain activities are better than others. Figure 12.1 depicts the benefits of several sports and exercises, and table 12.1 gives the energy required by various activities (the amount of calories used). Your attention is directed not only to the total physical fitness rating for each of these sports, but to the individual fitness component scores. If you have a particular need, certain sports will be better than others. For example, if you need to lose weight, you'd be advised to jog (it gives you a score of 21). On the other hand, if flexibility is your concern, you'd be better off doing calisthenics or playing handball or squash (they give you scores of 19 and 16, respectively).

If you exercise, you will be more sensitive to your body. For example, you will more readily recognize muscle tension. Further, with an exercised body you will improve your physical self-esteem. In these ways, exercise will serve to help you to be less stressed. In addition, exercising will allow you to focus on something other than your daily problems as well as use the products of stress such as increased blood glucose, heart rate, and muscle tension.

Table 12.1
Energy Expenditure by a 150-pound Person in Various Activities

Activity	Gross Energy Cost (cal per hr)
A. Rest and Light Activity	50–200
Lying down or sleeping	80
Sitting	100
Driving an automobile	120
Standing	140
Domestic work	180
B. Moderate Activity	200–350
Bicycling (5½ mph)	210
Walking (2½ mph)	210
Gardening	220
Canoeing (2½ mph)	230
Golf	250
Lawn mowing (power mower)	250
Bowling	270
Lawn mowing (hand mower)	270
Fencing	300
Rowboating (2½ mph)	300
Swimming (¼ mph)	300
Walking (3¾ mph)	300
Badminton	350
Horseback riding (trotting)	350
Square dancing	350
Volleyball	350
Roller skating	350
C. Vigorous Activity	over 350
Table tennis	360
Ditch digging (hand shovel)	400
Ice skating (10 mph)	400
Wood chopping or sawing	400
Tennis	420
Water skiing	480
Hill climbing (100 ft per hr)	490
Skiing (10 mph)	600
Squash and handball	600
Cycling (13 mph)	660
Scull rowing (race)	840
Running (10 mph)	900

Source: President's Council on Physical Fitness and Sports, *Exercise and Weight Control* (Washington, D.C.: President's Council on Physical Fitness and Sports, 1976), 8.

Strenuous physical work that both takes your mind off problems and uses built-up stress products is best for relieving tension.

Endorphins

Researchers have found a chemical substance released by the brain that is like morphine. Endorphins can numb pain and produce a feeling of well-being. These substances are in greater abundance during exercise than otherwise and are suspected of being related to the "jogger's high"—a euphoric, relaxed state reported by long distance runners.

The psychological benefits of exercise, therefore, may have a physiological and chemical basis. At this point in your reading, this conclusion should come as no surprise.

Psychological Health

The benefits of exercise for psychological health include the following:

1. Having more self-esteem due to feeling fit and feeling good about your body
2. Being more positively perceived by others, since a more attractive physical appearance leads other people to consider you more poised, sensitive, kind, sincere, and more socially and occupationally successful[4]
3. Feeling more alert and able

Physical exercise can help manage stress by using built-up stress products.

4. Being a better worker, since healthy men and women miss fewer days of work, have less illness, are involved in less accidents, and have a better attitude toward work[5]
5. Decreasing feelings of depression[6] and anxiety[7]
6. Being better able to manage stress, with a resulting decrease in stress-related behaviors[8]

The Healthy Way to Exercise

Have you ever seen someone jogging on a hot summer day wearing a rubberized sweat suit? Any time you overdress for exercise you are endangering your health. Your body needs to cool itself, and the evaporation of perspiration is its primary method. If you interfere with this cooling process, you can be overtaxing your heart or courting heatstroke or heat exhaustion. The result could even be death.

Sounds ridiculous, doesn't it? You think you're doing something *for* your health and instead you're doing something *against* it. People don't flirt with rubberized sweat suits because they want to see how far they can tempt the gods. They are probably just trying to lose a little more weight and think the more they perspire, the more weight they will lose. They don't know that the fluid lost through perspiration will be replenished by drinking water and by urinating less. They don't know of the dangers they are inviting. The problem is a lack of knowledge.

This section will describe how to exercise in a healthy manner. Among the topics discussed will be what to do before exercise, which exercises are appropriate, how fatigued you should get, and competition. In addition, a sample exercise program will be offered. All of this is designed to aid you in making exercise an effective stress management technique.

Before Exercising: Medical Screening

Several professional organizations and medical and sports specialists have cautioned those about to embark on an exercise program to obtain a medical evaluation first. In particular, those over forty years old or those who have been relatively inactive should be screened by their physicians before exercising vigorously. Table 12.2 includes questions people should ask themselves prior to beginning exercise programs. The American Medical Association recommends an even more extensive medical evaluation for potential exercisers when the following conditions are present:

1. Acute or chronic infectious disease
2. Diabetes that is not well controlled
3. Marked obesity
4. Psychosis or severe neurosis
5. Central nervous system disease
6. Musculoskeletal disease involving the spine and lower extremities
7. Active liver disease
8. Renal disease with nitrogen retention
9. Severe anemia
10. Significant hypertension (diastolic)
11. Angina pectoris or other signs or symptoms of myocardial insufficiency
12. Cardiomegaly
13. Arrhythmia
    a. Second degree AV block
    b. Ventricular tachycardia
    c. Atrial fibrillation
14. Significant disease of the heart valves or larger blood vessels
15. Congenital heart disease without cyanosis
16. Phlebothrombosis or thrombophlebitis
17. Current use of drugs such as
    a. Reserpine
    b. Propranolol hydrochloride
    c. Guanethidine sulfate
    d. Quinidine sulfate, nitroglycerin, and other vascular dilators
    e. Procainamide hydrochloride
    f. Digitalis
    g. Catecholamines (e.g., adrenalin)
    h. Ganglionic blocking agents
    i. Insulin
    j. Psychotropic drugs

Table 12.2
Exercise Screening Questions

I. Hidden or overt heart disease[a]

A. Has a doctor ever said you had heart trouble?

B. Have you ever had rheumatic fever, growing pains, twitching of the limbs called St. Vitus' dance, or rheumatic heart disease?

C. Did you ever have or do you now have a heart murmur?

D. Have you ever had a real or suspected coronary occlusion, myocardial infarction, coronary attack, coronary insufficiency, heart attack, or coronary thrombosis?

E. Do you have angina pectoris?

F. Have you ever had an abnormal electrocardiogram or ECG?

G. Have you ever had an electrocardiogram taken while you were exercising (such as climbing up and down steps) which was *not* normal?

H. Have you ever had pain or pressure or a squeezing feeling in the chest which came on during exercise or walking or any other physical or sexual activity?

I. If you climb a few flights of stairs fairly rapidly, do you have tightness or pressing pain in your chest?

J. Do you get pressure or pain or tightness in the chest if you walk in the cold wind or get a cold blast of air?

K. Have you had bouts of rapid heart action, irregular heart action, or palpitations?

L. Have you ever taken digitalis, quinidine or any drug for your heart?

M. Have you ever been given nitroglycerin, sometimes labeled TNG or NTG, or any tablets for chest pain which you use by placing them under the tongue?

II. Other heart attack risk factors[a]

A. Do you have diabetes, high blood sugar, or sugar in the urine now?—at any time in the past?

B. Have you ever or do you now have high blood pressure or hypertension?

C. Have you been on a diet or taken medications to lower your blood cholesterol?

D. Are you more than 20 pounds heavier than you should be?

E. Has there been more than one heart attack or coronary attack or person with heart trouble in your family before age 60 (blood relative)?

F. Do you now smoke more than a pack and a half of cigarettes per day?

III. Further limiting conditions[a]

A. Do you have any chronic illness?

B. Do you have asthma, emphysema, or other lung condition?

C. Do you get very short of breath on activities which don't make other people similarly short of breath?

D. Have you ever gotten or do you now get cramps in your legs if you walk several blocks?

E. Do you have arthritis, rheumatism, gout or gouty arthritis, or a predisposition to gout? Has the uric acid in your blood been found to be high?

F. Do you have any condition limiting the motion of your muscles, joints, or any part of the body which could be aggravated by exercise?

Source: Beyond Diet: Exercise Your Way to Fitness and Heart Health, by Lenore R. Zohman, M.D., CPC International, Englewood Cliffs, New Jersey.

[a]If you answer "yes" to any of these questions, consult your physician *before* beginning an exercise program.

The American College of Sports Medicine (ACSM), the leading organizational authority regarding exercise and sports, also offers guidelines for when it is necessary for someone embarking on an exercise program to undergo medical screening. Their recommendations are related to the health, status, and age of the participant. ACSM separates individuals into three categories:[9]

1. *Apparently healthy:* those who are apparently healthy and have no major coronary risk factors
2. *Individuals at higher risk:* those who have symptoms suggestive of possible coronary disease and/or at least one major coronary risk factor
3. *Individuals with disease:* those with known cardiac, pulmonary, or metabolic disease

Based upon this classification, the American College of Sports Medicine recommendations appear in table 12.3.

Principles of Exercise

Intensity, Frequency, and Duration

For strenuous exercise to have a beneficial cardiovascular effect, it should be done with the heart rate raised to 60–80 percent of its maximum. To indirectly determine your maximal heart rate, subtract your age in years from 220. Take 60–80 percent of that number, and that is how fast your heart should be beating during strenuous exercise. For example, if you are thirty, your maximal heart rate is 190 beats per minute. You should, therefore, exercise so that your heart is beating between 60 and 80 percent of 190 (114–152 beats per minute). This is called your **target heart rate** and should be at the 60 percent level when beginning an exercise program and gradually increase to the 80 percent level as your physical fitness improves. A good rule to follow is to take your pulse—every five minutes if just beginning to exercise and every fifteen minutes if more experienced—during exercise to determine if you are not working hard enough or if you are working too hard. The pulse rate should be taken for six seconds and multiplied by ten to get its one-minute rate (see chapter 1 for how to do this).

For a training effect to occur, you should exercise twenty to thirty minutes for three or four days each week. Since cardiorespiratory endurance decreases after forty-eight hours, you should make sure to exercise at least every other day. You might want to schedule your exercise as you do other events in your life. In this way you might view it as a commitment and be more apt to do the exercise, rather than assuming you'll exercise when you have the time and finding yourself continually postponing it.

Aerobic and Anaerobic Exercise

The exercises we have been referring to so far in this chapter are of relatively long duration, use large muscle groups, and do not require more oxygen than you can take in. These are called **aerobic** exercises.[10] Exercises of short duration, done "all out," and for which the oxygen taken in is not sufficient are called **anaerobic** exercises. Aerobic exercises include jogging, bicycling, long-distance swimming,

Table 12.3
Guidelines for Exercise Testing

	Apparently Healthy		Higher Risk		With Disease	
	Below 45	45 and Above	Below 35 (No Symptoms)	35+ (No Symptoms)	35+ (Symptoms)	Any Age
Maximal exercise test recommended prior to an exercise program	no	yes	no	yes	yes	yes
Physician attendance recommended for maximal testing	no (under 35)	yes	no	yes	yes	yes
Physician attendance recommended for submaximal testing	no	no	no	yes	yes	yes

Source: American College of Sports Medicine, *Guidelines for Exercise Testing and Prescription* (Philadelphia: Lea and Febiger, 1986) 7.

walking, and rope jumping. Anaerobic exercises include sprinting and short swimming races. Aerobic exercise is the kind that builds up cardiovascular endurance; however, both aerobic and anaerobic exercise are effective for managing stress and using stress products. Either form of exercise helps you use your body physically—which is what the fight-or-flight response prepares you for—as well as focus your attention away from stressors you would otherwise be thinking about.

Types of Training

Regular exercise (training) can be conducted a number of different ways. The three basic forms of training are the following:

1. *Interval training:* bouts of hard exercise are separated by periods of light exercise with no pause for rest.
2. *Continuous training:* exercise is maintained at a constant level of intensity for a fairly long and uninterrupted period.
3. *Circuit training:* a round of exercise is completed (called a circuit) consisting of various activities. The circuit is completed at less than maximum capacity and may be repeated as often as desirable. Par (fitness) courses located in many parks throughout the United States are examples of circuits.

Assessing Your Fitness

Many exercise programs focus on cardiorespiratory endurance. The publicity surrounding the benefits of exercise for the nation's leading killer (heart disease) is probably responsible for the emphasis on improving the functioning of the heart, circulatory system, and lungs. If you were to concentrate on only one component of fitness, this is the best one to choose. Exercises that overload the oxygen-transport system (aerobic exercise) lead to an increase in cardiorespiratory endurance and often an increase in strength for selected large muscle groups.[11]

Cardiorespiratory Fitness

A tried and true way of estimating your cardiorespiratory fitness is by employing the Harvard Step Test.[12] All you need is an 18-inch bench or stool (or something sturdy and close to that height) and a wristwatch with a second hand. Here is the procedure:

1. Step on the bench with one foot and then the other until you are standing erect, and then down with one foot and then the other.
2. Step at a cadence that will result in thirty such repetitions each minute for four minutes for females and five minutes for males.
3. When the stepping is completed (being sure to straighten the knees), be seated.
4. After one minute of sitting, take your pulse for thirty seconds (if you can get a partner to do this test with you, have your partner take your pulse) and record that number.
5. Wait thirty seconds more, and then take your pulse for the next thirty seconds and record that number.
6. Last, wait thirty more seconds and then take your pulse for the next thirty seconds and record that number. In other words, you will have taken your pulse between 1 and 1½ minutes after stepping, 2 and 2½ minutes after stepping, and 3 and 3½ minutes after stepping.
7. Using the three pulse counts, compute the following formula:

$$\text{index} = \frac{\text{duration of exercise in seconds} \times 100}{2 \times \text{sum of the 3 pulse counts in recovery}}$$

Your cardiorespiratory fitness can then be judged using this scale:

Below 55	Poor
55–64	Low average
65–79	Average
80–89	Good
90 and above	Excellent

I'1 the laboratory, muscular strength—or the absolute maximum force that a muscle can generate—can be measured using elaborate and expensive equipment. Dynamometers, cable tensiometers, and force transducers and recorders have all been used this way. A more practical means of measuring your muscular strength is available, however. The problem is that you need to obtain weight training equipment because measuring muscular strength requires you to lift weights to assess that strength. In terms of the best use of space in this book, it doesn't seem warranted to provide a detailed prescription for assessing your muscular strength. If you do seek to perform this measurement, you can find detailed instructions in another one of my books, *Physical Fitness: A Wellness Approach* (see Notes section at the conclusion of this chapter). Suffice it to say you will need to demonstrate strength through such exercises as the bench press, standing press, curl, half-squat, and leg press, which test various muscle groups throughout the body.

Muscular Strength

There is a big difference between muscular endurance and muscular strength. Strength is the maximum that can be done, whereas endurance is the ability to do continuous muscular work. We will use three tests of muscular endurance: the sit-up, the pull-up, and the flexed-arm hang.

Muscular Endurance

The sit-up test measures the endurance of the abdominal muscles and needs a partner to hold your feet. Lying on your back with your feet drawn back to your buttocks until they are flat on the floor and your hands clasped across your chest, sit up until your lower back is perpendicular to the floor. Then gently return to the starting position. Your partner should keep count of how many sit-ups you can do in two minutes.

If you are a man, the *pull-up* test is used to measure the muscular endurance of the muscles in the arms, shoulders, and upper back. A bar approximately 1.5 inches in diameter is placed high enough for you to hang from with the arms fully extended and your feet not touching the ground. Grasp the bar with the overhand grip (palms facing away), and hang with the arms and legs fully extended (see fig. 12.2). Next, raise your body until your chin is above the bar and then lower yourself so that your arms are once again fully extended. Record the maximum number of pull-ups you can do.

Some studies have found the pull-up to be a poor measure of muscular endurance in women. Consequently, the *flexed-arm hang* is used to measure the endurance of the arms, shoulders, and upper back muscles in women. A bar similar to that used for the pull-up, and at the same height, is grasped with the overhand grip. In this case, however, your body is initially positioned so that it is stationary, with the chin just above the bar (see fig. 12.3). Your score is determined by the length of time (in seconds) you can remain in this position.

Use table 12.4 to interpret your muscular endurance scores.

Figure 12.2 Pull-up

Figure 12.3 Flexed-arm hang

Table 12.4
Muscular Endurance Interpretations

	Sit-ups (no.) Men/Women	Pull-ups (no.)	Flexed-Arm Hang (sec.)
Above average	69 + /58 +	9 +	27 +
Average	44–68/40–57	3–8	15–26
Below average	0–44/0–40	0–2	0–14

Flexibility

A doctoral student once submitted a draft of her dissertation that was replete with spelling errors. Becoming upset and embarrassed about all the corrections, she shouted, "It's a small mind that can spell a word only one way!" Well, the story may be *stretching* the point (pun intended), but flexibility is an important part of our needs—and certainly of our fitness needs. *Flexibility* is the ability to move the body throughout a range of motion and concerns the stretching of the muscles and tissues around skeletal joints. We will measure flexibility with three tests: shoulder reach, trunk flexion, and trunk extension.

To measure shoulder reach, stand against a pole or a projecting corner, raise the right arm, and reach down behind your back as far as you can. At the same time, reach up from behind with the left hand and try to overlap the palm of the right hand (see fig. 12.4). Have a partner measure the overlap, or by how much you miss overlapping, to the nearest half-inch. If you overlap, place a plus sign in front of the amount of overlap; if you are short of touching fingers, place a minus sign in front of the amount of the gap between the fingers of one hand and those of the other. If the fingers of one hand just barely touch those of the other, score that a zero. Repeat this test with the arms reversed; that is, the one that reached down over the shoulder now reaches up from behind the back. Record both scores.

Figure 12.4
Shoulder reach

To measure the ability to flex the trunk and to stretch the back and the backs of the thigh muscles, sit with your legs straight and your feet flat against a box set against a wall. Place a ruler on top of the box and then stretch over the box (and the ruler) as far as you can (see fig. 12.5). Your score is the number of inches beyond the edge of the box you can stretch (a plus sign in front of that value) or the number of inches short of the edge of the box you can reach (a minus sign in front of that value). Just to the edge of the box is a zero score. You must, however, maintain the stretched position for three seconds. Record your score.

To determine trunk extension (the flexibility of your back), lie face down on the floor with a partner holding your legs and buttocks down (see fig. 12.6). Clasp your hands behind your neck and raise your head and chest off the ground (for three seconds) as high as you can. Have another partner measure the distance (to the nearest inch) between your chin and the floor. Record that value.

Use table 12.5 to interpret your flexibility scores.

Figure 12.5 Trunk flexion

Figure 12.6 Trunk extension

Table 12.5
Flexibility Interpretations

	Shoulder Reach (R up/L up)	Trunk Flexion	Trunk Extension
Men:			
Above average	6 + /3 +	11 +	15 +
Average	4–5/0–2	7–10	8–14
Below average	below 4/below 0	below 7	below 8
Women:			
Above average	7 + /6 +	12 +	23 +
Average	5–6/0–5	7–11	15–22
Below average	below 5/below 0	below 7	below 15

Agility

If you're really into the measurement of components of physical fitness, you might even want to include an assessment of your agility. To begin, mark off a course as shown in figure 12.7. Use chairs or cones where the four squares are marked (ten feet apart from each other). Start by lying on the floor on your stomach, with your hands placed on the floor just under your shoulders. At the signal, jump to your feet and follow the course, completing it as quickly as possible. Your score is the time it takes to complete the course (to the nearest tenth of a second). Record that value. Make sure not to touch the chairs as you go around them. To interpret your agility score, use the following classifications:

1. Above-average agility—17.0 seconds or less
2. Average agility—17.5–21.5 seconds
3. Below-average agility—more than 22 seconds

Body Composition

Measurement of body composition requires an assessment of the percentage of body fat you possess. This measurement can best be done by use of underwater weighing devices (hydrostatic weighing) or some proxy measure such as skinfold measurements. These procedures are too complex to describe here. If you are interested in reading more about this sort of measurement, consult the previously mentioned book, *Physical Fitness: A Wellness Approach.*

Starting an Exercise Program

Assuming you have determined you're a candidate for exercise, how do you begin? **Slowly!** If you have been sedentary, a good way to start is by walking. Walking can be quite enjoyable when you notice the surroundings—the foliage, the sounds, the buildings, the people, the sky, the colors. If you walk briskly, it can also be good exercise. After years of trying, I finally convinced my father to get off the bus one stop sooner on the way home from work and walk the rest of the way. He told me he never felt better. His body felt limber, he had a sense of accomplishment, and he felt less stressed.

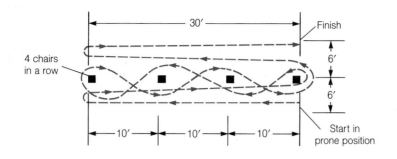

Figure 12.7 Illinois agility run

Source: T. K. Cureton, *Physical Fitness Workbook*, Urbana, Ill.: Stipes Publishing Co., 1944, p. 24.

Swimming or bicycle riding are other good ways to begin exercise programs if done moderately. If your body's like mine, you probably don't qualify to play the role of Tarzan anyhow, so take it easy. Since your body is supported by water when swimming and by the seat when biking, if you begin slowly, these are excellent beginning activities. Swimming and biking can also be done more strenuously when you get in better shape.

You should remember several points when exercising. First, keep in mind that exercise *trains,* too much exercise *strains.* I never cease being amazed at friends of mine who jog long distances but are always complaining about a knee that hurts, an Achilles tendon that is tender, or the presence of shinsplints. They approach running as a religion rather than as exercise for leisure and health. Do you exercise at a pace and with a frequency that makes it healthy and fun rather than harmful? Have a fun run, not strain and pain.

How to Exercise

Warm-up and Cool-down

Do's and Don't's

Research has indicated that beginning exercise too abruptly can cause cardiac rhythm problems.[13] Since these problems have the potential to result in heart attacks (even in an otherwise healthy heart), a ten- or fifteen-minute warm-up is recommended before any strenuous exercise. The warm-up will also help to stretch the muscles and decrease the chance of muscle strains during the exercise itself.

After exercising vigorously there is the possibility of too much blood pooling in the veins. This can lead to fainting. Though this possibility is somewhat remote, you should take a five- or ten-minute cool-down period after strenuous exercise. The cool-down will also help rid the muscles of lactate—a waste product of exercise—which in turn will decrease residual soreness in the muscles. Walking and stretching exercises serve as a good cool-down.

Clothing

Light-colored clothing that reflects the sun's rays is cooler in the summer, and dark clothes are warmer in the winter. When the weather is very cold, it's better to wear several layers of light clothing than one or two heavy layers. The extra layers help trap heat, and it's easy to shed one of them if you become too warm.

You should wear something on your head when it's cold, or when it's hot and sunny. Wool watch caps or ski caps are recommended for winter wear, and some form of tennis or sailor's hat that provides shade and can be soaked in water is good for summer.

Don't wear rubberized or plastic clothing. Such garments interfere with evaporation of perspiration and cause body temperature to rise to dangerous levels.

If you dress properly, you can exercise in almost any weather, but it's advisable not to exercise outdoors when it's extremely hot and humid. On such days, plan to exercise early in the morning or in the evening.

Fluids
Drink plenty of water before and after exercising. Also drink fluids during exercising if possible.

Equipment
Use appropriate equipment. Poor-fitting sneakers or a tennis racket with too large a grip can lead to injury and more stress rather than less.

Know Your Body
Become aware of how your body usually feels so you can recognize when it doesn't feel right. The following may be signs of overtraining and may indicate you should cut down on your exercise:

1. Soreness in muscles and joints
2. Heaviness in arms and legs
3. Inability to relax
4. Persistent tiredness
5. Loss of appetite
6. Loss of weight
7. Constipation or diarrhea
8. Repeated injury

Competition and Enjoyment

When I first started long-distance running, I was very competitive. Each time I went out, I tried to beat my best personal record. My wristwatch was as important a piece of equipment as my running shorts and shoes. Pretty soon I stopped enjoying running. It became a thing I had to do. Running became discouraging, since there was a day I ran so well that subsequent runs could never be as fast. I started developing aches in my legs and stiffness in my knees.

It was at that point that I decided to make a change. From that day on I have never worn a wristwatch while jogging and never had anyone else time me. I run at a pace that affords me a training effect and is comfortable. If someone attempts to pass me or if I am about to pass someone else, I'll try to carry on a brief conversation. "Nice day for a run, isn't it? How far are you going? Do you like those running shoes?" I now pay attention to the color of the trees (what a great time of year autumn is for running), hear the sound of my running shoes crunching the snow (what a great time of year winter is for running), notice the budding of flowers (what a great time of year spring is for running), and actually enjoy the feel of the sun on my body (what a great time of year summer is for running). Get the picture? For me, jogging has now become an enjoyable and stress-reducing technique rather than a pain and a stressor.

Competition, either with others or just with ourselves, often changes a recreational activity into one that does not re-create. Now, competition can be positive. It often takes competition for us to realize our potential. For example, you'll never know how good your return of service is in tennis unless your opponent hits a good serve for you to return. Too often, though, competition means we are comparing ourselves with others or with some idealized self. When we come off second best (or even worse), we often do not enjoy the activity, or develop a diminished sense of self-worth, or both. Further, we plug our satisfaction into an end result rather than enjoying the experience regardless of the outcome. All of this can add to stress reactivity rather than help to manage stress.

If you can use competition in a healthy manner to actualize your potential, more power to you. Continue what you're doing. However, if you're like my friend Don, who one day—after missing a return of serve—flung his tennis racket over a fence and several trees into a creek and then had the nerve to ask if I would help him get it before it floated too far downstream, you'd be advised to approach sports and exercise differently. Realize you're not a professional athlete and that sports and exercise should be fun. Do your best, try hard, but enjoy the effort in spite of how it turns out. Use sports and exercise to manage stress, not create it.

Choosing an Exercise Program

There are many different types of exercise programs. In this section, several exercise possibilities are described and addresses provided where you can get information about others. Also consult the sources listed in the Notes section at the chapter's conclusion for still more information about options for exercise.

Swimming

It may surprise you to know that as of January 1980 there were almost two million in-ground swimming pools in the United States and another two million above the ground. Obviously, swimming is a viable exercise for many of us. Swimming can provide benefits similar to other exercises but has one decided advantage: it diminishes the chances of athletic injury since, when submerged up to the neck, the water supports 90 percent of your weight.[14] Therefore, your feet and legs need only support 10 percent of your body weight and will not be injured as easily as during weight-bearing exercises (for example, basketball).

Many people use lap swimming to keep fit and to manage stress. Others do not have access to pools large enough to swim laps but can still use the water to obtain adequate exercise. These people can participate in aquadynamics. **Aquadynamics** is a program of structured exercises conducted in limited water areas involving standing water drills (for example, alternate toe touching, side-straddle hopping, toe bouncing, and jogging in place); poolside standing drills (such as stretching the arms out, pressing the back flat against the wall, and raising the knees to the chest); gutter-holding drills (such as knees to chest; hop-twisting; front, back, and side flutter kicking; bobbing; and treading water). If you have your own pool and feel it is too small for lap swimming, you might want to write to the President's Council on Physical Fitness and Sports, Washington, D.C. 20201, for the *Aqua Dynamics* booklet. Another good source is an article entitled "The W.E.T. Workout" by Jane Katz.[15]

Rope Jumping

Rope jumping is another excellent exercise. When I was thirteen, my friend Steven and I both fell head over heels in love with twelve-year-old, blonde-haired, adorable, vivacious (yes, even at that age) Jill. I'm talking about the heart-pounding, palm-perspiring, any-spare-time-spent-with-her love. Steven and I would do anything for Jill. We even spent hours playing *Who Stole the Cookie from the Cookie Jar?* while our friends played baseball or basketball. That was the summer I learned to jump rope, the whole time made frantic by the thought that this was a "sissy" activity. If my other friends had seen me, I would have died.

Well, I'm no longer crippled by that thought because I have since learned that the gender you were born with need not stop you from engaging in an enjoyable activity. I have also learned that rope jumping is an excellent way to develop cardiorespiratory endurance, strength, agility, coordination, and a sense of wellness. Fortunately, many other people have learned a similar lesson, and rope jumping has become very popular. Here are some pointers for jumping rope:

1. Determine the best length for your rope by standing on the center of the rope. The handles should then reach from armpit to armpit.
2. When jumping, keep your upper arms close to your body with your elbows almost touching your sides. Have your forearms out at right angles, and turn the rope by making small circles with your hands and wrists. Keep your feet, ankles, and knees together.
3. Relax. Don't tense up. Enjoy yourself.
4. Keep your body erect with your head and eyes up.
5. Start slowly.
6. Land on the balls of your feet, bending your knees slightly.
7. Maintain a steady rhythm.
8. Jump just one or two inches from the floor.
9. Try jumping to music. Maintain the rhythm of the music.
10. When you get good, improvise. Create new stunts. Have fun.

The American Heart Association recommends the rope jumping stunts shown in figure 12.8. Try them out yourself.

Figure 12.8 Rope jumping stunts*

1. Side swing
1. Twirl rope to one side
2. Repeat on the opposite side
3. Twirl rope alternately from side to side

Teaching Hints: Keep hands together, keep feet together.

2. Basic bounce (single bounce)
1. Jump on both feet
2. Land on balls of feet

Teaching Hints: Keep feet, ankles, and knees together.

3. Double side swing and jump
1. Twirl rope to left side
2. Twirl rope to right side
3. Jump over rope

Teaching Hints: Keep hands together on side swings, keep feet together.

4. Single side swing and jump
1. Twirl rope to left side   3. Twirl rope to right side
2. Jump over rope   4. Jump over rope

Teaching Hints: Keep hands together on side swings, keep feet together.

5. Skier (side to side)
1. Jump left
2. Jump right

Teaching Hints: Feet move laterally 4–6″ to each side, keep feet together.

6. Bell (forward and backward)
1. Jump forward
2. Jump backward

Teaching Hints: Feet move 4–6″ forward and backward as a bell clapper, keep feet together.

*Reproduced with permission. Stunt descriptions only. © American Heart Association.

Figure 12.8 *(continued)*

7. Side straddle (spread together)
   1. Jump to a straddle position
   2. Return to basic bounce
Teaching Hints: Spread feet shoulder width apart.

8. Forward straddle (scissors)
   1. Jump to stride position with left foot forward
   2. Jump and reverse position of feet
Teaching Hints: Feet 8–12″ apart.

9. X motion (straddle, cross)
   1. Jump to straddle position
   2. Jump to crossed legs
Teaching Hints: Feet shoulder width apart.

10. Wounded duck (alternate toes/heels together)
   1. Jump, toes and knees touch, heels spread
   2. Jump, heels touch, toes and knees spread
Teaching Hints: Alternate toes touching and heels touching.

11. Criss cross (cross arms)
   1. Cross arms and jump
   2. Open rope, basic bounce
Teaching Hints: Cross right arm over left, cross left arm over right.

12. Full turn (one complete circle with rope in front)
   1. Turn body left, with right turn of rope
   2. Side swing right, body turns right
   3. Full turn, body makes full turn to right
   4. Jump rope forward
Teaching Hints: Follow rope, rope and body may turn left.

13. Heel to Heel
   1. Jump and touch left heel
   2. Jump and touch right heel
Teaching Hints: Heel touches are forward.

Figure 12.8 *(continued)*

14. Toe to toe (alternate toe touch)
  1. Hops on left foot, touch right toe
  2. Hops on right foot, touch left toe
Teaching Hints: Keep body over weighted foot.

15. Forward 180 (half turn rotating rope from forward
  position to backward jumping position)
    1. Side swing left, half turn of body right
    2. Jump over backward turning rope
Teaching Hints: Follow rope, rope and body may turn to left.

16. Backward 180 (turn keeping rope in front of face)
  1. Jump backward, turning rope
  2. Half turn of body left, facing rope
  3. Jump rope forward
Teaching Hints: Follow rope, rope and body may turn left.

17. Heel-toe (alternate heel-toe touch)
  1. Hop on left foot, touch right heel forward
  2. Hop on left foot again, touch right toe backward
  3. Repeat on opposite side
Teaching Hints: Heel-toe as in a polka.

18. Kick swing (alternate kick or swing feet, forward,
  sideways, backward)
    1. Hop on left foot, swing right leg forward
    2. Hop on right foot, swing left leg forward
Teaching Hints: Repeat directions sideways and backward.

19. Peek-a-boo (alternate toe touch sideways)
  1. Hop on left foot, touch right toe right
  2. Hop on right foot, touch left toe left
Teaching Hints: Keep feet close to floor.

20. Double peek-a-boo (double toe touch sideways)
  1. Hop on left foot, touch right toe right about 6″
  2. Hop on left foot again, touch right toe right about 12″
Teaching Hints: Keep feet close to floor.

Figure 12.8 *(continued)*

---

21. 360 (combine forward 180 and backward 180)
1. Execute numbers 15 and 16 in a continuous sequence
2. Repeat 2 or more times
Teaching Hints: Follow rope.

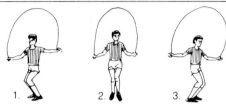

---

22. Twist (rotate hips from side to side)
1. Jump and rotate hips right
2. Basic jump
3. Jump and rotate hips left
Teaching Hints: Advanced twist, execute nos. 1 & 3 in a continuous sequence.

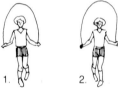

---

23. Can Can (knee-up–touch kick)
1. Hop on right foot, left knee up
2. Hop on right foot, touch left toe
3. Hop on right foot, kick left leg
4. Basic jump
Teaching Hints: Knee lift and kick are waist high, repeat on opposite leg.

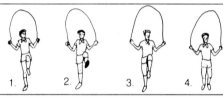

---

24. Shuffle (side step and touch)
1. Step sideways to the right, touch left toe beside right foot
2. Step sideways to the left, touch right toe beside left foot
Teaching Hints: Keep feet close together.

---

25. Side swing criss cross (alternate side turn— cross—side turn—cross)
1. Twirl rope on right side   3. Twirl rope on left side
2. Criss cross (number 11)   4. Criss cross
Teaching Hints: On criss crosses, number 2 right arm crosses over left, number 4 left arm crosses over right.

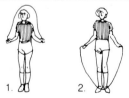

---

26. Double under (2 rotations of rope with one jump)
1. Whip rope to increase speed
2. Rope passes under feet twice during one jump
Teaching Hints: Jump higher than normal at first.

---

27. Grapevine
1. Step right on right foot
2. Left foot crosses behind right
3. Step right on right foot
4. Kick the left leg forward right
Teaching Hints: Each step is taken over the rope, repeat to the left, have students say "step, behind, step, kick."

Note: All the above stunts can be performed with the rope turning backward as well as forward.

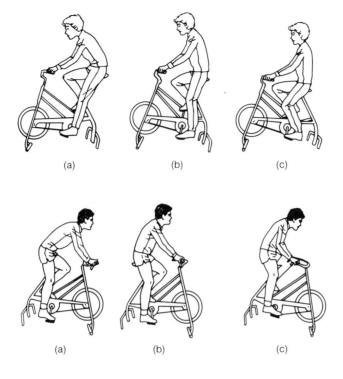

Figure 12.9 Correct and incorrect seat heights: (*a*) too high, (*b*) correct, (*c*) too low.

Figure 12.10 Correct and incorrect handlebar adjustment: (*a*) too far forward, (*b*) correct, (*c*) too far back.

(a)   (b)   (c)

(a)   (b)   (c)

Bicycling

Biking can take place on the road or in your room. Either road or stationary biking can use the built-up stress products and help you develop physical fitness if done regularly and at the proper intensity. To bike on the road you need a bicycle with gears; they vary greatly in cost. A good ten-speed bike will cost approximately $300. If you shop around or buy a secondhand bicycle, you can probably get a good ten-speed for half the cost of a new one. You will also need a helmet (approximately $50), gloves with padded palms (about $10), and pant clips or special clothing. Of course, many people bike with less sophisticated equipment and still get the benefits of the exercise.

Another alternative is to bike and never go anywhere; this is especially appealing on a snowy day. For this you need a stationary bicycle. While riding a stationary bicycle, you need to pay attention to adjusting it correctly. In particular, you should make sure the handlebars and the seat are where they should be. The seat needs to be adjusted so that your knee is just slightly bent when the pedal is in its lowest position (see fig. 12.9). The handlebars need to be set so you are relaxed and leaning slightly forward (see fig. 12.10).

Jogging

Running is very popular. Surveys show that more than seventeen million adult Americans are running regularly and over fifty thousand Americans have completed at least one marathon (26 miles, 385 yards).[16] Running is such a good form of exercise because it requires a minimum of equipment (the only expense is a good pair of running shoes), it can be done almost anywhere, anytime, and it does not require a special skill.

In most sports we are taught to run for speed and power. In running for fitness, the objectives are different and so is the form. Here are some suggestions to help you develop a comfortable, economical running style:

1. Run in an upright position, avoiding excessive forward lean. Keep back as straight as you comfortably can and keep head up. Don't look at your feet.
2. Carry arms slightly away from the body, with elbows bent so that forearms are roughly parallel to the ground. Occasionally shake and relax arms to prevent tightness in shoulders.
3. Land on the heel of the foot and rock forward to drive off the ball of the foot. If this proves difficult, try a more flat-footed style. Running only on the balls of your feet will tire you quickly and make your legs sore.
4. Keep your stride relatively short. Don't force your pace by reaching for extra distance.
5. Breathe deeply with mouth open.

The American Podiatry Association recommends the following running program:[17]

1–6 weeks

Warm up with walking and stretching movement.

Jog 55 yards, walk 55 yards (four times)

Jog 110 yards, walk 110 yards (four times)

Jog 55 yards, walk 55 yards (four times)

Pace: 110 yards in about 45 seconds

6–12 weeks

Increase jogging and reduce walking.

Pace: 110 yards in 30–37 seconds

12–24 weeks

Jog a nine-minute mile. (However, since you need to work out aerobically for 20–30 minutes to gain cardiorespiratory endurance, you should add other exercise as well.)

30+ weeks

The second workout each week, add variety—continuous jogging, or running and walking alternately at a slow varying pace for distances up to two miles.

Walking is an excellent lead-in to other more vigorous physical fitness activities, but usually it is not a sufficient stimulus for young people to raise their heart rates high enough for a training effect.[18] However, for the deconditioned, overweight, or elderly person who is beginning an exercise program, walking is recommended; or for younger people, if they increase the pace sufficiently to reach their target heart rate. If you take up walking, use the following rule to gauge your readiness to progress to other, more vigorous forms of fitness activities: once you can walk three miles in forty-five minutes, you are ready.

Of course, we are referring to natural-gait walking. Race walking or speed walking is another story altogether. These forms of exercise are excellent means of using the built-up stress by-products, as well as means to develop an increased level of physical fitness. In race walking the lead foot must be on the ground when your trailing leg pushes off and you must keep your knee straight as your body passes over that leg.[19] What is surprising to many people is that a race walker burns off more calories than does a jogger. For example, whereas a jogger at a twelve-minute-a-mile pace will burn off 480 calories per hour, a race walker at the same pace will burn off 530 calories per hour.[20] To perform race walking correctly, remember the following guidelines:

1. Keep your back straight and walk tall.
2. Point your feet straight and plant them at a 40° angle to the ground.
3. As you pull forward with one leg, push straight back with the other leg until the toe of that leg is off the ground.
4. Stretch your hips forward rather than from side to side.

If you are interested in learning more about walking or have decided to participate in this activity, there are a couple of organizations you may want to contact. The Walkers Club of America, 445 East 86th Street, New York, NY 10128 and the Rockport Walking Institute, P.O. Box 480, Marlboro, MA 01752 can provide advice and encouragement for your walking program. The Walking Association (listed at the conclusion of this chapter) can also be of assistance.

One of the best fitness activities is dance. Just look at the bodies of dancers! They are remarkably muscularly developed, incredibly supple, and ready to meet the demands strenuous exercise places on their hearts, circulatory systems, and respiratory systems.

Aerobic Dance

In recent years a different form of dance has swept the country—aerobic dance. Aerobic dance combines calisthenics and a variety of dance movements, all done to music. Aerobic dance, a term coined by Jacki Sorenson in 1979,[21] involves choreographed routines that include walking, jumping, hopping, bouncing, kicking, and various arm movements designed to develop cardiorespiratory endurance, flexibility, and muscular strength and endurance. What's more, it's fun. Dancing to music is an enjoyable activity for many people who would not otherwise seek to exercise. And since aerobic dance is often done in groups, the social contact makes it even more enjoyable. Its potential for using up stress by-products as well as its potential for developing a social support network make aerobic dance an excellent fitness activity for stress management.

To maximize the fitness benefits of aerobic dance, you should maintain the dancing for approximately thirty-five to forty-five minutes and work out three or four times a week. In addition, you should check periodically to see if you are maintaining your target heart rate. Since many communities offer aerobic dance classes (some may be called Dancercize or Jazzercise) through YM/YWCAs, colleges, and local schools, and even on morning television programs, maintaining a regular dance regimen should not be difficult. The only equipment you will need is a good pair of aerobic dance shoes with good shock absorbency, stability, and outer sole flexibility; and clothes to work out in. One caution: Don't dance on a concrete floor since the constant pounding could result in shinsplints. A wooden floor is preferred.

Low Impact Aerobic Dance

Several factors associated with aerobic dance have led some experts to question the manner in which it is usually conducted. A study by the American Aerobics Association found 80 percent of its teachers and students were getting injured during workouts, and another questionnaire administered to aerobics instructors found 55 percent reported significant injuries.[22] Among the causes of these injuries are bad floors (too hard), bad shoes (too little shock absorbency and stability), and bad routines offered by poorly trained instructors.[23] With the popularity of aerobics, it is not surprising what is done in its name. Even a "pet aerobics" routine has been developed for that pudgy dog or cat. It is therefore no surprise that many aerobics instructors are poorly trained and teach routines that are inappropriate and injury-producing, using surfaces which result in high-impact injuries.

To respond to these concerns, several developments have occurred. One is the certification of aerobics instructors. Organizations such as the American College of Sports Medicine, the Aerobics and Fitness Association of America, International Dance and Exercise Association, Ken Cooper's Aerobics Way, and the Aerobic Center have all instituted certification for aerobics instructors. Unfortunately, the requirements for certification by these organizations vary greatly. However, some form of certification is probably better than none. If you decide to participate in aerobic dance, you would be wise to check to see if the instructor is certified.

Another attempt at limiting the injuries from aerobics is the development of **low impact** aerobic routines. Low impact aerobics features one foot on the ground at all times and the use of light weights. The idea is to cut down on the stress to the body caused by jumping and bouncing while at the same time deriving the muscle toning and cardiorespiratory benefits of high impact aerobics. These routines have become more and more popular as the risk of injury from high impact aerobics has become better known. Something called "chair aerobics" has even been developed.[24] It involves routines done while seated in a chair. However, low impact aerobics is not risk-free. Injuries to the upper body caused by the circling and swinging movements with weights are not infrequent.[25] However, many of these injuries can be treated at home and are not serious. With any form of physical activity there is always the chance of injury. However, the benefits for managing stress and to the cardiorespiratory system and the rest of the body can be significant.

Stretching is an excellent stress reduction technique. In fact, a form of stretching is used during Hatha Yoga exercises. A word of caution: Never stretch a muscle that has not been warmed up. To do so courts injury since the muscle may tear or strain. Also, don't bounce or strain into the stretch. A gradual stretching motion is what feels best and *is* best in terms of preventing injury. The stretching exercises diagrammed in figures 12.11 through 12.21 can become a regular part of your exercise routine, thereby enhancing your flexibility and, if you focus on the sensations and the position of your body, can be effective in helping you manage stress.

Stretching

If you want more detailed information about a particular sport or physical fitness activity, you can write to the appropriate organization listed below (provided by the Office of Disease Prevention, Department of Health and Human Services).

Where to Get More Information

Basketball

Amateur Basketball Association of the United States of America (ABAUSA), 1750 East Boulder St., Colorado Springs, CO 80909. (303)636–7687. The ABAUSA serves as the national governing body for the sport of basketball. They will respond to requests for information on their programs.

Bicycling

Bicycle Touring Group of America, P.O. Drawer 330976, Coconut Grove, FL 33133. (305)661–8846. The Bicycle Touring Group is an industry-sponsored association to promote noncompetitive recreational bicycling.

Bikecentennial, the Bicycle Travel Association, P.O. Box 8308, Missoula, MT 59807. (406)721–1776. Bikecentennial is a national service organization for touring bicyclists. The organization's efforts are aimed at educating the public in bicycle use and safety, and researching and mapping bicycle touring routes. A publications list is available and questions are answered on all aspects of bike touring.

Figure 12.11 Standing reach

Starting position:
Stand erect, feet shoulder width apart, arms extended over head.

Action:
Stretch as high as possible, keeping heels on ground. Hold for 15–30 counts.

Figure 12.12 Alternate knee pull

Starting position:
Lie on back, feet extended, hands at sides.

Action:
Pull one leg to chest, grasp with both arms, and hold for 5 counts. Repeat with opposite leg.

Repeat 7–10 times with each leg.

Figure 12.13 Flexed-leg back stretch

Starting position:
Sit with feet shoulder width apart, arms at sides.

Action:
Slowly bend over, touching the ground between the feet. Hold for 15–30 counts. If at first you can't reach the ground, touch the top of your shoe line.

Repeat 2–3 times.

Figure 12.14 Double knee pull

Starting position:
Lie on back, feet extended, hands at sides.

Action:
Pull both legs to chest, lock arms around legs, and pull buttocks slightly off ground. Hold for 20–40 counts.

Repeat 7–10 times.

Figure 12.15 Side-lying leg lift

Starting position:
Lie on right side, legs extended.

Action:
Count 1—Raise left leg as high as possible.
Count 2—Lower to starting position.
Repeat on opposite side.

Suggested repetitions: 10–15

Figure 12.16 Back leg swing

Starting position:
Stand erect behind chair, feet together, hands on chair for support.

Action:
Count 1—Lift one leg back and up as far as possible.
Count 2—Return to starting position.
Repeat equal number of times with other leg.
Do not accentuate the back arch.

Suggested repetitions: 20

Figure 12.17 Heel raises

Starting position:
Stand erect, hands on hips, feet together.

Action:
Count 1—Raise body on toes.
Count 2—Return to starting position.

Suggested repetitions: 20

Figure 12.18 Straddle stretch

Sit on floor and spread straight legs about twice shoulder width. Slowly lean forward from waist, sliding hands along floor, as far forward as you can. Hold for 30 seconds.

Return to starting position. Slowly stretch forward over right leg, sliding both hands down to right ankle. Try to keep knee straight and touch chin to right kneecap. Hold for 30 seconds.

Return to starting position. Repeat second step of exercise to left side.

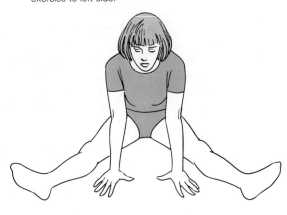

Figure 12.19 Leg stretcher

Sit in same position as in preceding exercise. Rest left hand on left thigh and grasp inside of right foot with right hand. Keep back straight and slowly straighten right leg, letting it raise to about a 45 degree angle. Hold position for 30 seconds.

Repeat exercise with other leg.

Figure 12.20 Achilles tendon and calf stretcher

Stand facing wall approximately three feet away. Lean forward and place palms of hands flat against wall. Keep back straight, heels firmly on floor, slowly bend elbows to hands, and tuck hips toward wall. Hold position for 30 seconds.

Repeat exercise with knees slightly flexed.

Figure 12.21 Thigh stretcher

Stand arm's length from wall with left side toward wall. Place left hand on wall for support. Grasp right ankle with right hand and pull foot back and up until heel touches buttocks. Lean forward from waist as you lift. Hold for 30 seconds.

Repeat exercise with opposite hand and foot.

League of American Wheelmen, P.O. Box 988, Baltimore, MD 21203. (301)727–2022. The League answers inquiries on topics such as where to ride, what to take along, routes, how to plan and conduct bicycle events, and safety.

United States Cycling Federation, 1750 East Boulder St., Colorado Springs, CO 80909. (303)632–5551. The governing body for amateur and professional cycling in the United States, and an organization concerned with the preservation, development, and administration of bicycle racing.

Bowling

American Bowling Congress (ABC) and Women's International Bowling Congress (WIBC), 5301 South 76th St., Greendale, WI 53129. (414)421–6400. These two groups are the primary organizations promoting bowling for men and women. Direct your questions on bowling to the public relations department of the appropriate organization (men should write to the ABC, and women should write to the WIBC).

Dancing

Aerobic Dancing, Inc., 18907 Nordhoff St., Box 6600, Northridge, CA 91328. (213)885–0032. Aerobic dancing is a fitness program originated by Jacki Sorenson, consisting of vigorous dances designed to improve physical fitness. Contact Aerobic Dancing at the above address for a location near you, or check your local telephone directory.

Jazzercise, Inc., 2808 Roosevelt St., Carlsbad, CA 92008. (619)434–2101. Jazzercise is a dance and fitness program of simple jazz dance movements set to a variety of music. Contact Jazzercise at the above address for classes near you.

Hiking/Backpacking

Forest Service, U.S. Department of Agriculture, Information Office, P.O. Box 2417, Washington, DC 22013. (202)447–3957. The Information Office of the Forest Service will provide a list of Forest Service field offices and addresses. They request that inquirers contact the field offices to obtain information on recreation opportunities in the national forests.

National Campers and Hikers Association (NCHA), 7172 Transit Rd., Buffalo, NY 14221. (716)634–5433. The NCHA will answer questions on hiking and camping. This organization is dedicated to camping fellowships, the preservation of our natural heritage, and the strengthening of family bonds through activities in the out-of-doors.

Sierra Club, 530 Bush St., San Francisco, CA 94108. (415)981–8634. The Sierra Club is dedicated to the principles of wilderness conservation. The national office will answer inquiries on hiking, camping, backpacking, canoeing, and other outdoor activities.

Racquetball

American Amateur Racquetball Association (AARA), 815 North Weber St., Colorado Springs, CO 80903. (303)635–5396. The AARA promotes the sport of racquetball and is a member of the U.S. Olympic Committee. They will respond to requests for information on racquetball.

Running/Jogging

American Running and Fitness Association (ARFA), 2420 K St. NW, Washington, DC 20037. (202)965–3430. The American Running and Fitness Association serves as a clearinghouse of information on running and jogging. They promote healthful running by physically qualified people. Their Runner's Referral Service will match you with a runner of similar ability in your area. To be included in the referral service, a runner can complete an information form and file it with the ARFA.

Road Runners Club of America (RRCA), 1226 Orchard Village, Manchester, MO 63011. (314)391–6712. The RRCA promotes long-distance running on an amateur basis. They can answer requests on organizing a running club or a running competition.

Skating

Ice Skating Institute of America, 1000 Skokie Blvd., Wilmette, IL 60091. (312)256–5060. The goals of the Ice Skating Institute are to improve the ice rink business and to increase public interest in ice skating. They can respond to requests for information on ice skating.

Roller Skating Rink Operators Association (RSROA), P.O. Box 811846, Lincoln, NE 68510. (402)489–8811. RSROA's membership consists of almost 2,000 roller skating rinks across the country. It promotes and popularizes the sport of roller skating. Publications on skating are available, but they cannot respond to specific requests for information. These questions should be directed to your local rink.

United States Figure Skating Association, 20 First St., Colorado Springs, CO 80906. (303)635–5200. The U.S. Figure Skating Association is the governing body for amateur figure skating in the United States. Information will be provided by mail on local clubs and on learning to ice skate.

Skiing

American Water Ski Association, P.O. Box 191, Winter Haven, FL 33880. (813)324–4341. The American Water Ski Association promotes competitive and noncompetitive water skiing in the United States. It acts as a clearinghouse for information on water skiing.

Ski Touring Council, c/o Lewis Polak, 32 Harmony Rd., Spring Valley, NY 10976. (914)356–9376. The Ski Touring Council is a nonprofit organization founded to promote ski touring or noncompetitive cross-country skiing. They will answer mail or telephone inquiries on cross-country skiing, but will not answer questions on snow conditions or similar subjects.

United States Ski Association (USSA), P.O. Box 100, Park City, UT 84060. (801)649–6935. The USSA is the national governing body for organized skiing. Information services include answers to mail or telephone inquiries on cross-country skiing, alpine skiing, and ski jumping. Information on cross-country skiing for older people is also available.

Soccer

United States Soccer Federation (USSF), 350 Fifth Ave., Room 4010, New York, NY 10118. (212)736–0915. The United States Soccer Federation is the national governing body for the sport of soccer. They serve as a clearinghouse for information, publications, and audiovisuals on soccer.

Softball

Amateur Softball Association of America, 2801 NE 50th St., Oklahoma City, OK 73111. (405)424–5266. The Amateur Softball Association of America develops and promotes the sport of softball on an organized basis. It will answer inquiries on all aspects of softball.

Swimming

International Amateur Swimming Federation (IASF), 200 Financial Center, Des Moines, IA 50309. (515)244–1116. The IASF promotes and encourages the development of amateur swimming, diving, water polo, and synchronized swimming. They will respond to mail and telephone requests for information on swimming.

United States Swimming, Inc. (USS), 1750 East Boulder St., Colorado Springs, CO 80909. (303)578–4578. The USS is the national governing body for amateur competitive swimming. They offer a variety of programs geared to all levels of swimmers. They will answer requests for information on their programs.

Tennis

United States Tennis Association Education and Research Center, 729 Alexander Rd., Princeton, NJ 08540. (609)452–2580. The objective of the United States Tennis Association is to develop tennis as a means of healthful recreation and physical fitness. It serves as a clearinghouse for information on recreational tennis.

Volleyball

United States Volleyball Association, 1750 East Boulder St., Colorado Springs, CO 80909. (303)632–5551, ext. 3331. The U.S. Volleyball Association is the national governing body for the sport of volleyball. It will refer inquirers to an appropriate regional director.

Walking

Walking Association, 4113 Lee Highway, Arlington, VA 22207. (703)527–5374. The Walking Association is concerned with all matters related to walking, including its health and recreational aspects. It will respond to inquiries on walking but suggests that inquirers first check their local libraries.

Exercise can help you manage stress by using the products of stress: muscle tension, serum cholesterol and increased heart and respiratory rate. This chapter has provided you with the information you need to begin an exercise program. Unfortunately, many people who begin exercising regularly do not keep at it. For one reason or another they stop exercising or do it so infrequently as to make it detrimental. For this reason, the next chapter presents techniques for influencing behavior. Before beginning your exercise program, read that chapter. Application of the techniques presented there will go a long way toward helping you stick to your program.

**Exercise—
Keeping It Going**

You can do it. You can exercise regularly and improve your physical and psychological health. You can use those stress products before they result in illness or disease. You are in control of your exercise behavior and you can exercise (no pun intended) that control.

Summary

1. Vigorous exercise improves the functioning of the lungs and circulatory system, delays the degenerative changes of aging, increases ability to transport oxygen to body parts, strengthens the heart muscle, burns calories, and lowers serum cholesterol.
2. Physical fitness consists of several components: muscular strength, muscular endurance, cardiorespiratory endurance, flexibility, body composition, and agility.
3. The psychological benefits of exercise include improved self-esteem, being perceived more positively by others, feeling more alert, having a better attitude toward work, decreased feelings of depression and anxiety, and being better able to manage stress.
4. Endorphins are released by the brain during exercise and produce a euphoric, relaxed state.
5. The American College of Sports Medicine has developed recommendations regarding the need for testing prior to commencing an exercise program. They recommend that for individuals who are younger than forty-five and apparently healthy and individuals younger than thirty-five with some risk factors but no symptoms of disease, a stress test is unnecessary. However, those over forty-five, those with some symptoms of disease (cardiac, pulmonary, or metabolic), or those actually having one of these types of diseases should be given a stress test before they begin an exercise program.
6. The intensity, frequency, and duration of exercise are important considerations if cardiorespiratory endurance is the goal.
7. Aerobic exercise is of relatively long duration, uses large muscle groups, builds cardiovascular fitness, and does not require more oxygen than you can take in. Anaerobic exercise is of short duration, high intensity, and requires more oxygen than you can take in.
8. Training can be conducted in three primary ways: interval training, continuous training, or circuit training.

9. You can assess your level of physical fitness by determining your cardiorespiratory endurance with the Harvard Step Test; your muscular strength by lifting weights with various muscle groups; your muscular endurance by doing sit-ups, pull-ups, and flexed-arm hangs; your flexibility by doing a shoulder reach, trunk flexion, and trunk extension; your agility by running an agility course; and your body composition by either hydrostatic weighing or skinfold measurements.

10. When exercising, do warm-up and cool-down routines, wear clothing appropriate to the weather, drink plenty of fluids, use properly fitted equipment, and recognize when your body is telling you you're overdoing it.

11. An exercise program can consist of a number of activities such as swimming, rope jumping, bicycling, jogging, walking, aerobic dance, low impact aerobic dance, or stretching.

12. There are many organizations from which you can obtain more information about specific physical fitness activities or a particular sport.

Notes

1. Richard A. Berger, *Applied Exercise Physiology* (Philadelphia: Lea and Febiger, 1982), 240.

2. George B. Dintiman et al., *Discovering Lifetime Fitness: Concepts of Exercise and Weight Control* (St. Paul: West, 1984), 6–7.

3. Bud Getchel, *Physical Fitness: A Way of Life* (New York: John Wiley, 1983), 64.

4. Jane E. Brody, "Effects of Beauty Found to Run Surprisingly Deep," *New York Times,* 1 September 1981, C1–C3.

5. President's Council on Physical Fitness and Sports, *Building a Healthier Company* (Washington, D.C.: President's Council on Physical Fitness and Sports, n.d.).

6. Charles B. Corbin and Ruth Lindsey, *Concepts of Physical Fitness with Laboratories,* 6th ed. (Dubuque, Iowa: Wm. C. Brown, 1988), 13.

7. P. Mikevic, "Anxiety, Depression and Exercise," *Quest* 33(1982):140–53.

8. William J. Stone, *Adult Fitness Programs: Planning, Designing, Managing, and Improving Fitness Programs* (Glenview, Ill.: Scott, Foresman and Company, 1987), 34–35.

9. American College of Sports Medicine, *Guidelines for Exercise Testing and Prescription,* 3d ed. (Philadelphia: Lea and Febiger, 1986), 2.

10. Kenneth H. Cooper, *The Aerobics Way: New Data on the World's Most Popular Exercise Program* (New York: M. Evans, 1977).

11. Jerrold S. Greenberg and David Pargman, *Physical Fitness: A Wellness Approach,* 2d ed. (Englewood Cliffs, N.J.: Prentice-Hall, 1989).

12. Lucien Brouha, "The Step Test: A Simple Method of Testing the Physical Fitness of Boys," *Research Quarterly* 14(1943):23.

13. Linda S. Lamont and Mary T. Reynolds, "Developing an Individualized Program for Physical Fitness," *Occupational Health Nursing* 28(1980):16–19.

14. President's Council on Physical Fitness and Sports, *Aqua Dynamics* (Washington, D.C.: President's Council on Physical Fitness and Sports, 1981), 1.

15. Jane Katz, "The W.E.T. Workout: A Swimmer's Guide to Water Exercise Techniques," *Shape,* June 1986, 82–88+.

16. President's Council on Physical Fitness and Sports, *An Introduction to Running: One Step at a Time* (Washington, D.C.: President's Council on Physical Fitness and Sports, 1980).

17. American Podiatry Association, *Jogging Advice from Your Podiatrist* (Washington, D.C.: American Podiatry Association, n.d.).

18. Frank D. Rosato, *Fitness and Wellness: The Physical Connection* (St. Paul, Minn.: West, 1986), 253.

19. Stephen Kiesling, "Loosen Your Hips: Walkshaping," *American Health,* October 1986, 62–67.

20. Ibid., 62.

21. Jacki Sorenson, *Aerobic Dancing* (New York: Rawson, Wade, 1979).

22. Jean Rosenbaum, "Aerobics without Injury," *Medical Self-Care,* Fall 1984, 30–33.

23. Beth Schwinn, "Burned in Pursuit of the Burn," *Washington Post, Health,* 14 August 1986, 12.

24. Tim Green, "My Favorite Routine: Chair Aerobics," *Shape,* June 1986, 150–53.

25. Gail Weldon, "The ABC's of Aerobics Injuries," *Shape,* September 1986, 86–90+.

Strategies for Reducing Stressful Behaviors

Why can't I stop smoking? Why did I drink too much at the party last Saturday night? Why can't I learn to relax? How many times do we say we wish we had or had not done something? Some of the activities or actions that we *take* or *fail to take* cause us stress. For example, we say to ourselves we are going to go out and meet new people, but somehow we never get around to doing it; we are going to go on a diet but do not stick to it. We worry about our inability to change our behavior. We feel less in control of ourselves. Consequently our self-esteem may decline. In sum, we may experience a fight-or-flight response when we cannot behave as we would like to. The focus of this chapter is to present a number of behaviors that cause us stress either because we want to give them up and cannot, or because we want to adopt them but have been unable to. It also describes methods that will help us make changes in these behaviors. With greater control of our behaviors, we will be better at managing our stress.

Life-style and Health Behaviors

We will look at two types of behaviors: health behaviors and life-style behaviors. Health behaviors are considered a subclass of life-style behaviors and are differentiated for emphasis. Health behaviors are defined as activities undertaken by people who believe themselves to be healthy for the purpose of preventing disease or detecting it in an asymptomatic stage.[1] Examples of health behaviors are limiting sugar and salt in your diet, avoiding smoking cigarettes, using a seat belt, engaging in physical exercise, limiting your use of alcoholic beverages, and practicing relaxation techniques. Life-style behaviors encompass the whole host of activities in which people engage. Examples of life-style behaviors include everyday activities like doing chores, going to school or work, and enjoying leisure times. Examples of other less common life-style behaviors are asking someone for assistance, writing a letter to a friend, listening intently to a speaker, and meeting new people.

This chapter was written by Robert Feldman, Ph.D., of the Department of Health Education, University of Maryland, College Park, Maryland.

A few years ago, I decided that I wanted to follow a "healthy diet." I had read some newspaper and magazine articles and books on nutrition, and heard experts speak about healthy diets, but somehow I never got around to doing anything about it. I was busy and could not find the time to diet properly. I also found it difficult to find the foods I wanted to buy. When I did find these foods, I also found them to be expensive and inconvenient to use. That is, a number of barriers—mainly psychological and, to some extent, economic—stood in the way of my taking action. I did finally make changes in my diet and will discuss how I did that later in this chapter. The point I want to make is that many times numerous barriers prevent those of us with the best of intentions from behaving as we would otherwise choose to behave.

I had a friend who always wanted to play the piano but, as a child, never had a piano or took piano lessons. He regretted his piano-deprived childhood but felt that as an adult he would finally have the time to sit down at the piano and learn to play. But he never seemed to have the time. It distressed him. He would see other people play and think that someday he, too, would play. But to this day, as far as I know, he still does not know how to play the piano.

Why can we not do what we want to do? How do we overcome these barriers that keep us from learning to play the piano or following a healthy diet? To help you to understand the relationship between the difficulty in changing our behavior and the stress that it causes, let us look at two behavioral scales.

Health-Behavior Assessment

Before you can go about changing your health-related behaviors, you should first identify which behaviors need changing. The purpose of the health-behavior questionnaire is to tell you how well you are doing at staying healthy. Since few of us live completely healthy lives, we all could profit from some changes in our health-related behaviors. The questionnaire will inform you of the areas that need improvement. The questionnaire is distributed by the Office of Disease Prevention and Health Promotion of the Public Health Service, Department of Health and Human Services.

This is not a pass-fail test. Its purpose is simply to tell you how well you are doing to stay healthy. The behaviors covered in the test are recommended for most Americans. Some of them may not apply to persons with certain chronic diseases or disabilities. Such persons may require special instructions from their physician or other health professional.

You will find that the test has six sections: smoking, alcohol and drugs, nutrition, exercise and fitness, stress control, and safety. Complete one section at a time by circling the number corresponding to the answer that best describes your behavior (for example, two for "almost always," one for "sometimes," and zero for "almost never"). Then add the numbers you have circled to determine your score for that section. Write the score on the line provided at the end of each section. The highest score you can get for each section is ten.

If you never smoke, enter a score of 10 for this section and go to the next section on alcohol and drugs.

Smoking

	Almost always	Some-times	Almost never
1. I avoid smoking cigarettes.	2	1	0
2. I smoke only low tar and nicotine cigarettes *or* I smoke a pipe or cigars.	2	1	0

Smoking score: _____

Alcohol and drugs

	Almost always	Some-times	Almost never
1. I avoid drinking alcoholic beverages *or* I drink no more than one or two drinks a day.	4	1	0
2. I avoid using alcohol or other drugs (especially illegal drugs) as a way of handling stressful situations or the problems in my life.	2	1	0
3. I am careful not to drink alcohol when taking certain medicines (for example, medicine for sleeping, pain, colds, and allergies).	2	1	0
4. I read and follow the label directions when using prescribed and over-the-counter drugs.	2	1	0

Alcohol and drugs score: _____

Source: "Health Style: A Self-Test" Washington, D.C., United States Department of Health and Human Services, Public Health Service, PHS 81–50155, 1981.

Eating habits

	Almost always	Some- times	Almost never
1. I eat a variety of foods each day, such as fruits and vegetables, whole grain breads and cereals, lean meats, dairy products, dry peas and beans, and nuts and seeds.	4	1	0
2. I limit the amount of fat, saturated fat, and cholesterol I eat (including fat on meats, eggs, butter, cream, shortenings, and organ meats such as liver).	2	1	0
3. I limit the amount of salt I eat by cooking with only small amounts, not adding salt at the table, and avoiding salty snacks.	2	1	0
4. I avoid eating too much sugar (especially frequent snacks of sticky candy or soft drinks).	2	1	0

Eating habits score: _____

Exercise/fitness

	Almost always	Some- times	Almost never
1. I maintain a desired weight, avoiding overweight and underweight.	3	1	0
2. I do vigorous exercises for fifteen to thirty minutes at least three times a week (examples include running, swimming, and brisk walking).	3	1	0
3. I do exercises that enhance my muscle tone for fifteen to thirty minutes at least three times a week (examples include yoga and calisthenics).	2	1	0
4. I use part of my leisure time participating in individual, family, or team activities that increase my level of fitness (such as gardening, bowling, golf, and baseball).	2	1	0

Exercise/fitness score: _____

Stress control

	Almost always	Some-times	Almost never
1. I have a job or do other work that I enjoy.	2	1	0
2. I find it easy to relax and express my feelings freely.	2	1	0
3. I recognize early, and prepare for, events or situations likely to be stressful for me.	2	1	0
4. I have close friends, relatives, or others whom I can talk to about personal matters and call on for help when needed.	2	1	0
5. I participate in group activities (such as community organizations) or hobbies that I enjoy.	2	1	0

Stress control score: _____

Safety

	Almost always	Some-times	Almost never
1. I wear a seat belt while riding in a car.	2	1	0
2. I avoid driving while under the influence of alcohol and other drugs.	2	1	0
3. I obey traffic rules and the speed limit when driving.	2	1	0
4. I am careful when using potentially harmful products or substances (such as household cleaners, poisons, and electrical devices).	2	1	0
5. I avoid smoking in bed.	2	1	0

Safety score: _____

Your Health-Behavior Scores

After you have figured your scores for each of the six sections, circle the number in each column of figure 13.1 that matches your score for that section of the test.

Remember, there is no total score for this test. Consider each section separately. You are trying to identify aspects of your health behavior that you can improve in order to be healthier and to reduce the risk of illness. So let's see what your scores reveal.

General Applications: Physiological Arousal and Behavior Change Interventions

Cigarette Smoking	Alcohol & Drugs	Eating Habits	Exercise & Fitness	Stress Control	Safety
10	10	10	10	10	10
9	9	9	9	9	9
8	8	8	8	8	8
7	7	7	7	7	7
6	6	6	6	6	6
5	5	5	5	5	5
4	4	4	4	4	4
3	3	3	3	3	3
2	2	2	2	2	2
1	1	1	1	1	1
0	0	0	0	0	0

Figure 13.1 Your health-behavior scores

Scores of 9 and 10

Excellent! Your answers show that you are aware of the importance of this area to your health. More importantly, you are putting your knowledge to work for you by practicing good health habits. As long as you continue to do so, this area should not pose a serious health risk. It's likely that you are setting an example for your family and friends to follow. Since you got a very high score on this part of the test, you may want to consider other areas where your scores indicate room for improvement.

Scores of 6 to 8

Your health practices in this area are good, but there is room for improvement. Look again at the items you answered with a "sometimes" or "almost never." What changes can you make to improve your score? Even a small change can often help you achieve better health.

Scores of 3 to 5

Your health risks are showing! Would you like more information about the risks you are facing and about why it is important for you to change these behaviors? Perhaps you need help in deciding how to successfully make the changes you desire. In either case, help is available.

Scores of 0 to 2

You may be taking serious and unnecessary risks with your health. Perhaps you are not aware of the risks and what to do about them. You can easily get the information and help you need to improve.

To assist you in making changes in your health behaviors, choose two health behaviors that you would like to change. We will return to these two health behaviors after we look at the broader range of selected life-style behaviors.

Selected Life-style Behaviors

Below is a selected list of life-style activities that some people find stressful. The purpose of the questionnaire is to help you identify life-style behaviors that you would like to adopt. Feel free to choose other life-style activities that are not on this selected list that you would like to adopt or change. In any case, it is important to identify these behaviors, because it is our inability to engage in these activities that worries us and causes us distress.

Selected Life-style Behavior Questionnaire

2 = almost always
1 = sometimes
0 = almost never

____ 1. I go out and meet new people.
____ 2. I am able to ask for help from others.
____ 3. I listen intently to other people.
____ 4. I am able to communicate with others.
____ 5. I avoid needless arguments.
____ 6. I am able to say I am sorry.
____ 7. I spend time with friends.
____ 8. I am punctual in writing friends.
____ 9. I play a musical instrument.
____ 10. I participate in artistic activities.
____ 11. I participate in sports.
____ 12. I travel to different places.
____ 13. I am involved with hobbies.
____ 14. I do volunteer work for worthwhile causes.
____ 15. I am not afraid to try something new.
____ 16. I enjoy talking in front of groups of people.
____ 17. I am on time for meetings and appointments.
____ 18. I do my work/studying on time.
____ 19. I punctually do my day-to-day chores.
____ 20. I am able to save money.

Now that you have completed this questionnaire, examine those items for which you chose 0. From those items, choose two life-style behaviors that may cause you stress and that you would like to change. Later in this chapter we will present a number of techniques that you can use to change these behaviors, thereby eliminating stress in your life. However, before we look at strategies to change life-style and health behaviors, there are a few more sets of factors that need to be considered: the first is barriers to action.

Good intentions are abundant. How often we have good intentions! Yes, I plan to write to you. Yes, I plan to stop smoking, lose weight, save money, or get involved. But somehow I never have the time. It is too hot to jog today. I will start running tomorrow. I am embarrassed to speak in front of a group of people. I will do it another time. I really want to develop hobbies, but I have so many other obligations. Excuses, excuses.

It would be more fruitful to consider these "excuses" **barriers.** That is, barriers that we perceive as preventing us from engaging in a number of activities. To the dieting person whose spouse brings home a high-calorie dessert, the lack of family support is a barrier to maintaining a diet. A series of rainy days is a barrier to the novice jogger. A heavy work or school schedule is a barrier to getting involved in worthwhile causes. The lack of availability of low-salt foods is a barrier to reducing one's intake of salt. In other words, to help you understand ways to change health and life-style behaviors, it is useful to identify the barriers in the way of adopting the behavior you want to adopt.

Barriers to Action

Sometimes people are unable to engage in certain health and life-style behaviors. Figure 13.2 lists a number of possible factors that may have kept *you* from engaging in these activities.[2] Choose one health or life-style behavior you would like to change, and for each item on the questionnaire, circle a number from 1 to 7 that represents the degree to which that factor is a barrier to your adopting this behavior.

You now have information concerning some barriers and obstacles that have impeded your adopting certain health and life-style behaviors. The items for which you circled 7, 6, or 5 are major obstacles to performing the particular behavior that you are interested in changing. We will use this information when we examine methods of changing behaviors that are stressful to you.

Barriers-to-Action Questionnaire

The next aspect of health and life-style behavior change concerns the issue of personal control. In chapter 7, the *locus of control* concept was presented. Although locus of control can be a generalized perception of the control you have over events that affect your life, it can also be specific to parts of your life. For example, you may believe you can control your social life and events that affect it—for example, going out and meeting people—but you may believe that your health is a matter of chance or luck: "It's who you're born to, not what you do." The locus of control for health is the focus of this section.

Some people feel that it's their physician's responsibility to keep them well: "That's what I'm paying 'em for." Yet, a growing number of people feel that they actually do have control over their health and other life outcomes: "Yes, I can prevent illness from stress." "Yes, I can maintain a desired weight."

Locus of Control

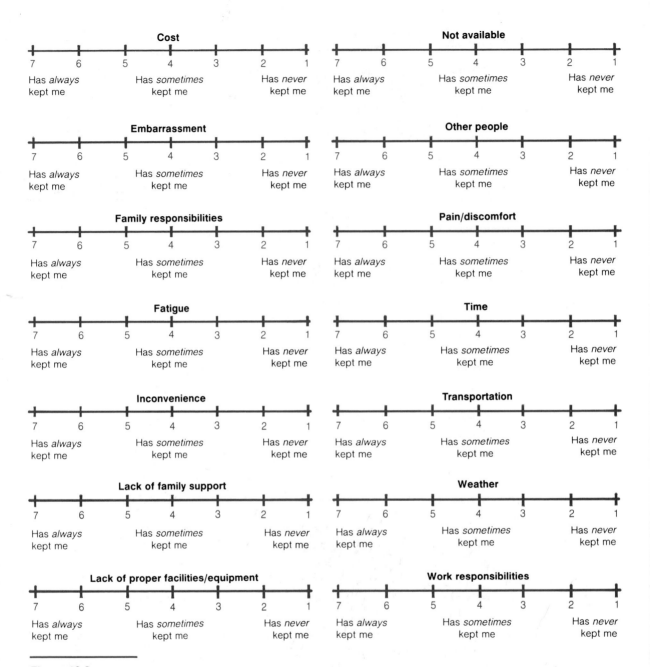

Figure 13.2
Barriers-to-action
questionnaire

Now it is your turn to find out whether you feel you have control over your health—that is, your health locus of control. Below is a questionnaire adapted from the Multidimensional Health Locus-of-Control Scales. Choose a number from one to five. The questionnaire is made up of three subscales:

1. Internal health locus-of-control scale (I):
   This subscale measures whether you feel that you have personal control over your health.
2. Powerful others health locus-of-control scale (P):
   This subscale measures whether you feel that powerful individuals (e.g., physicians) control your health.
3. Chance health locus-of-control scale (C):
   This subscale measures whether you feel that your health is due to luck, fate, or chance.

5 = strongly agree
4 = agree
3 = neither agree nor disagree
2 = disagree
1 = strongly disagree

Multidimensional
Health Locus-of-
Control Scales

Internal Health Locus of Control

_____ 1. If I get sick, it is my own behavior that determines how soon I get well.
_____ 2. I am in control of my health.
_____ 3. When I get sick, I am to blame.
_____ 4. The main thing that affects my health is what I myself do.
_____ 5. If I take care of myself, I can avoid illness.
_____ 6. If I take the right actions, I can stay healthy.

Powerful Others Health Locus of Control

_____ 1. Having regular contact with my physician is the best way for me to avoid illness.
_____ 2. Whenever I don't feel well, I should consult a medically trained professional.
_____ 3. My family has a lot to do with my becoming sick or staying healthy.
_____ 4. Health professionals control my health.
_____ 5. When I recover from an illness, it's usually because other people (e.g., doctors, nurses, family, and friends) have been taking good care of me.
_____ 6. Regarding my health, I can only do what my doctor tells me to do.

Chance Health Locus of Control

____ 1. No matter what I do, if I am going to get sick, I will get sick.
____ 2. Most things that affect my health happen to me by accident.
____ 3. Luck plays a big part in determining how soon I will recover from an illness.
____ 4. My good health is largely a matter of good fortune.
____ 5. No matter what I do, I'm likely to get sick.
____ 6. If it's meant to be, I will stay healthy.

Scoring Locus-of-Control Scales

To obtain your score for a subscale, add the numbers you chose in that subscale.

1. A score of 23–30 on any subscale means you have a strong inclination to that particular dimension. For example, a high C score would indicate you hold strong beliefs that your health is a matter of chance.

2. A score of 15–22 means you are moderate on that particular dimension. For example, a moderate P score would indicate you have moderate belief that your health is due to powerful others.

3. A score of 6–14 means you are low on that particular dimension. For example, a low I score means that you generally do not believe that you personally control your health.

Therefore, if you scored *high* on the internal health locus-of-control scale and low or moderate on the powerful others and chance scales, you are a person who feels that your health is basically under your control. If you scored *moderately* on internal health locus of control, you are a person who feels that sometimes your health is under your control and sometimes it is not. For the moderately internal individual, the scores on the powerful others and chance scales would determine the relative weight of these other two dimensions.

If you scored *low* on the internal health locus-of-control scale, you are a person who feels that you do not have control over your own health. Your scores on the powerful others and chance scales would determine the relative influence of these other two dimensions. If you scored relatively high on the powerful others scale and moderate to low on the other two scales, you are a person who feels that powerful others (e.g., physicians) control your health. If you scored relatively high on the chance scale and moderate to low on the other two scales, you are a person who feels that chance, fate, or luck determines your health status.

Based on the Multidimensional Health Locus-of-Control Scales, you should have gained some insight into your perceptions of control over your health. As you saw in chapter 7, we neither have complete control nor lack of complete control over life outcomes. As we learn how to gain greater control over aspects of our environment, we will be able to make changes in stressful behaviors. Techniques for doing this appear later in this chapter.

You have now completed four questionnaires:

1. Health-behavior questionnaire
2. Life-style-behavior questionnaire

3. Barriers-to-action questionnaire
4. Multidimensional Health Locus-of-Control Scales

These questionnaires should assist you in determining the following:

1. What health behaviors you need to change to reduce your risk of illness and injury
2. Which life-style changes you are *distressed* about and would like to change
3. What barriers are preventing you from carrying out these changes in health and life-style activities
4. Your perceptions of control over your health

Now we are ready to examine ways of making changes in your health and life-style behaviors.

One day I decided that I wanted to lose weight. This time I was going to do it! I was determined to keep to a strict diet and lose weight. I started on Monday morning. I began by writing a **contract**—a set of rules that I agreed to follow during my dieting.

I have known myself to finish off a dessert while deeply involved in a book, unaware of what or how much I was eating. Now, I separated the two activities and gained control over my eating habits. No more eating while doing something else. I discussed these plans with my wife, who agreed to give me encouragement and approval for adhering to my diet.

I also used a smaller plate. The smaller portions filled up the plate and I did not feel that I was depriving myself. In addition, I increased the portions of the lower calorie foods, such as salads and vegetables, and decreased the portions of the higher calorie foods, such as meats and certain starches. If I snacked during the day, it was a piece of low-calorie fruit. If I was able to successfully follow the rules that I set down in my contract, I would reward myself with a tape at the end of the week.

The account above describes a diet plan that includes a number of psychological and behavioral techniques that can be used to change and modify health and life-style behaviors. In this section of the chapter, we will examine some frequently used methods of reducing stressful behaviors. These methods include:

1. Self-monitoring
2. Tailoring
3. Material reinforcement
4. Social reinforcement
5. Self-contracting
6. Contracting with significant others
7. Shaping
8. Reminders
9. Self-help groups
10. Professional help

Some of these techniques overlap and have procedures in common. However, they are listed separately in order to give emphasis to different aspects of the techniques.

Techniques for Reducing Stressful Behaviors

Self-monitoring   One aspect common to many of these methods involves the monitoring of behavior. **Self-monitoring** is a process of observing and recording your own behavior.[3] For example, suppose you are a person who tends to be late to meetings
and appointments. You have good intentions, but somehow you are not able to
make it on time. You may not realize how often you are late or how late you are
to appointments and meetings. Self-monitoring is a method to increase your
awareness of your behavior. Every time you have an appointment or a meeting,
note whether you arrived on time. If you are late, note how many minutes (or
hours?!) you were late. This will help you avoid being late by making you aware
of just how much of a problem this behavior is. In addition, self-monitoring will
provide you a benchmark to compare your behavior at the point at which you
began your behavioral change program with the change you have actually made.
In this manner, your progress becomes, in itself, reinforcing.

Tailoring   Programs that are adapted to the specific routines, life-styles, abilities, and unique
circumstances of an individual are said to be "tailored" to that individual.[4] For
example, let us say you find yourself under a lot of pressure and are having difficulty relaxing. You decide that you will begin a relaxation program. Someone
suggests that you awake a half hour earlier and do your relaxation exercises in
the morning. You awake the following Monday a half hour earlier and do your
relaxation exercises. You feel tired Monday evening but continue on Tuesday,
Wednesday, and Thursday morning. You feel tired on these evenings as well and
oversleep on Friday morning. The following week you oversleep on Thursday and
Friday mornings and feel discouraged. What you need is tailoring.

Since you are not a "morning person," it would make sense to do your relaxation exercises after school or work. The program should be adapted to your
particular schedule. It should be tailored to your unique characteristics and circumstances. Programs that are tailored to the specific characteristics of a person
tend to be more effective. For example, if Sunday evening is a quiet time in your
weekly schedule, then that would be a good time to write those letters you have
put off writing.

Before you initiate a behavior change program, examine your schedule and
life-style. When is the best time to do your chores? What time must you leave
in order to be on time for your appointments and meetings? When should you
exercise? When is the best time to engage in relaxation?

If you consistently brush your teeth twice a day (e.g., early morning and late
at night), relaxation techniques could be practiced at that time. In other words,
relaxation techniques would be *paired* with teeth brushing behavior. If you do
not consistently brush your teeth twice a day, then relaxation techniques could
be embedded into another part of your schedule (e.g., after work or before dinner).
Tailoring offers you a way to maximize your success in a behavior change program by allowing you to fit the change into your particular circumstances.

An important component in programs to increase healthy behavior is reinforcement or reward.[5,6] If you remember, I stayed with my diet all week and therefore rewarded myself with a tape. The tape is, of course, material reinforcement. You could reward yourself (self-reward) or you could be rewarded by another. If I refrain from smoking for a week, I could buy myself a book or magazine. Or I could be in a smoking-cessation program in which I receive five dollars a week for not smoking. Other examples of material reinforcement include bonuses, commissions, clothes, tickets for a show or concert, antiques, or any other items of value. Both material and social reinforcement increase the probability of the behavior being repeated. A point to note: what is reinforcing for Jack may not be reinforcing for Jill. If a person does not like to attend folk concerts, then tickets to a folk concert are *not* a reinforcer. A reinforcer is something of value to a particular individual. Money is a powerful and useful reinforcer since it can be exchanged for a countless number of objects that are rewarding and valued.

Reinforcement may also take the form of social reinforcement. Another person (a friend, roommate, spouse, or coworker) can be a source of encouragement and can assist you in overcoming various hurdles that you encounter. Also, this person can be a source of social reinforcement. That is, the significant other can tell you that you are doing a good job and give you praise. Acknowledgment, praise, a pat on the back, and even a smile are forms of social reinforcement. Research supports the observation that social reinforcement increases the frequency of the behavior that it follows.[7-9]

Imagine you are trying to stop smoking. You go a full day without smoking and your roommate says, "That's great." That statement from your roommate is an example of social reinforcement. Or suppose you are at work, and you take on a new assignment. The assignment turns out well, and your boss pats you on the back. You feel good about the completed assignment and take on another new assignment. In our interactions with other people, we sometimes tell others they are doing a good job. These forms of social reinforcement are useful methods of encouraging people to continue what they are doing.

However, a word of caution should be added. What you are doing is for yourself. Therefore, do not expect a pat on the back every time you do a good job or a good deed. Your own sense of satisfaction may be all you need to continue the behavior. If you engage in regular practice of some relaxation technique, for instance, the sensation obtained and the knowledge that you are doing something that is healthy may be enough to encourage the continuation of this behavior.

Once you have established a base rate for a particular behavior (e.g., I am late two out of three times), then you can create a set of rules for changing that behavior and set up a contract.[10] A contract takes the form of an "if-then" rule. For example, *if* I am on time to a meeting, *then* I will watch TV tonight. "Being

Material
Reinforcement

Social
Reinforcement

Self-contracting

on time to a meeting" is the behavior of interest and "watching TV tonight" is the reward or consequence of the behavior. In addition, if I am *not* on time to a meeting today, then I will *not* watch TV tonight. I did not exhibit the desired behavior; therefore, I did not reap the reward. **Self-contracting** means that you administer your own rewards. As part of this procedure, then, you must list things that you would consider rewarding. Obviously, different things will be rewarding for different people. Contracting with another person may be even more successful.

Contracting with a Significant Other

Mahoney and Thoresen suggest five principles for contracts:

1. The contract should be fair.
2. The terms of the contract should be very clear.
3. The contract should be generally positive.
4. Procedures should be systematic and consistent.
5. At least one other person should participate.[11]

Contracts have the value of involving people in the planning of their lifestyle changes. When you actually write down what behaviors will be tied to what rewards or consequences, you will be less likely to forget about it. In addition, contracting with significant others makes the contract a *public* commitment. A **significant other** may be a spouse, a roommate, a friend, or a relative. The significant other does not necessarily have to live under the same roof. A significant other is a person who has meaning to you, in whom you can confide, and to whom you can be made accountable.

For example, you decide that you want to initiate an exercise program. (For a detailed look at exercise, see chapter 12.) You plan to jog vigorously for twenty minutes at a time, three times a week: Monday, Wednesday, and Friday. If you successfully carry out this exercise program, you will buy yourself a tape on Saturday. You write up a contract specifying what activity (jogging for twenty minutes), how frequently (three times a week: Monday, Wednesday, and Friday), and what reward (a tape) you will receive if you successfully complete the activity. Since you are contracting with a significant other, you show your spouse or close friend your contract. You discuss the contract with your significant other, actually sign the contract in his or her presence (known as a public behavioral commitment), and may have the significant other sign the contract (a witness) as well. In general, contracting has been found to be a useful technique in a variety of health and life-style situations.[12,13]

Shaping

It is difficult to go "cold turkey"—stopping the undesired behavior all at once. Therefore, shaping programs have been established to "shape" desired behaviors. **Shaping** refers to the process of introducing components of a program sequentially as the individual learns and performs prior steps in the sequence.[14] The steps are graded in order of difficulty for the person. For example, if you want to reduce your caloric intake by 1000 calories a day, you may begin by reducing your dinner by 250 calories. Once you have successfully completed this part of the program, you may then reduce your lunch by 250 calories a day. If you want to start an exercise program, you can begin by exercising once a week for twenty minutes. Once you are able to carry out this task, you could increase your program to twice a week for thirty minutes, then three times a week for thirty minutes. This procedure of shaping has been widely used in a variety of behavioral programs.

Reminders

If you were going to save money this pay period but forgot, why not place a note on each payday on your kitchen calendar. Then place a check mark on the calendar *after* you have put money into your savings each pay period. That is, set up a **reminder system.** A calendar that you look at each day is an ideal place to put reminder messages: write Joe on Friday, exercise on Monday at 4:30 P.M., call Mom on Saturday. In some cases, you could ask a significant other to remind you (as long as it does not lead to arguments or antagonisms).

Self-help Groups

Many people with alcoholic problems have found successful solutions to their problems with self-help groups such as Alcoholics Anonymous. Other self-help groups include Gamblers Anonymous, Weight Watchers, Overeaters Anonymous, self-help drug programs, self-help psychiatric groups, self-help divorce groups, and self-help groups for battered and abused spouses and children. The self-help movement has generated numerous groups to assist people with common problems. You may be able to locate a self-help group where you live that deals with your particular concern.

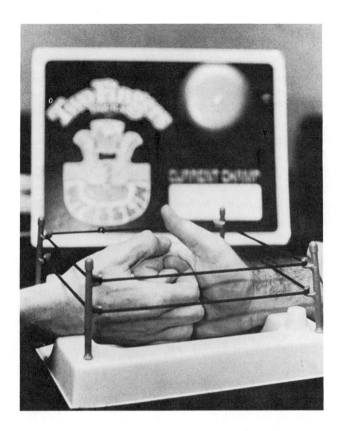

Professional Help

If a self-help group is not available, then professional help is an alternative. Physicians, nurses, psychiatrists, psychologists, therapists, social workers, counselors, and health educators are available in almost every community and can assist you in health and life-style behavior changes.

Application of Behavior Change Techniques

To better understand the variety of techniques used to modify the stressful behaviors decribed in this chapter and integrate the material presented, illustrative examples follow.

Example 1:
Exercise

Exercise can be considered a health behavior and a life-style behavior. We have included it among the health behaviors because of its importance to health in such areas as cardiovascular health and weight control.

Let us say that you completed the health-behavior questionnaire, and exercise/fitness was one of the behaviors you were distressed about not engaging in regularly. You decided to change that behavior. Next, you turned to the barriers-to-action questionnaire. The greatest barriers to exercise were time, inconvenience, and fatigue. Now you are ready to turn to the section on techniques to reduce stressful behaviors. The first thing that you need to know is how often you exercise. If you do not exercise at all, then you already know the answer. However, if you exercise occasionally, then you need to *self-monitor* your exercise behavior. Observe and record the duration, frequency, and intensity of your exercise.

The next step is to write a *contract*. For example, you can state, "I will vigorously jog twenty minutes from 6:00–6:20 P.M. on Monday, Wednesday, and Friday." The contract can either be a *self-contract* or a *contract with a significant other*. Contracts with significant others are more effective since they make you accountable to another person. Therefore, let us assume that you show the contract to your spouse, roommate, or a close friend.

To overcome the three barriers of time, inconvenience, and fatigue, you need to *tailor* your exercise schedule to your unique circumstances. Three twenty-minute periods a week is only one hour a week. Given your time constraints, can you spare one hour a week? After or before work, you can set aside time to engage in your thrice-weekly exercise activity.

To increase the probability that you will succeed in your exercise program, *social and/or material reinforcement* should follow your exercise. Your spouse, roommate, or close friend could tell you how well you are doing, and at the end of the week, you could treat yourself to a tape, book, movie, or other rewarding experience.

If you have difficulty initiating and maintaining a thrice-weekly exercise schedule, then shaping might help. That is, start with one day a week. Once that has been successfully maintained, then increase your exercise to twice a week. After that has been established, then initiate a thrice-weekly program.

To maintain the program over time, use *reminders*. A note on your calendar, by your bed, dresser, or even taped to the bathroom mirror could be used to remind you that today is exercise day. You could also use another person to remind you that today is exercise day. If all else fails, you might ask *self-help* and *professional help groups* for assistance.

This example has included all the methods of reducing stressful behaviors: self-monitoring, self-contracting, contracting with a significant other, tailoring, social reinforcement, material reinforcement, shaping, reminders, self-help groups, and professional groups. Let us now turn to another example.

After examining the life-style behavior questionnaire, you decided that being late for meetings and appointments was one of the behaviors that caused you stress and that you would like to change. You turn to the barriers-to-action questionnaire to determine the major obstacles to your being on time. You decide that time factors and added family and work responsibilities are making it difficult for you to be on time. Basically, you have a time-management problem.

First, you need to know how often you are late for meetings and appointments. Are you late 100 percent of the time or 50 percent of the time? Are you late five minutes, ten minutes, or forty-five minutes? You need to *monitor* your meeting and appointment-keeping behavior. At the beginning of the week, you can make a list of the scheduled times of all your meetings and appointments.

Example 2: Being on Time for Appointments and Meetings

Then, as they occur, write down the time that you arrive. This will give you a base measure of how often you are late and how late you are to meetings and appointments.

Then set up a *contract*. *A contract with a significant other* would be more effective in changing your behavior than a *self-contract*. For example, you can state: I will be on time to 50 percent of my meetings and appointments and no later than five minutes late to the remaining 50 percent. A more ambitious program would be to state that you will be on time 100 percent of the time.

To overcome the barriers of time factors and family and work responsibilities, you need to *tailor* your time commitments. You may be taking on more responsibilities than you can effectively manage. Determine how much time each of your activities is consuming. Then, set priorities. Decide which activities are of primary importance and which are of secondary importance. Based upon your set of priorities, you can decide which activities are essential and which are optional. This should assist you in better managing your time commitments.

To increase the probability that you will succeed in managing your time, you should incorporate *social and/or material reinforcement* into your program. A significant other could praise you for being on time. In addition, if you are successful in maintaining your contract for one week, you could reward yourself by going out for dinner, going to a movie, or some other rewarding experience.

If you have difficulty initiating and maintaining a punctual schedule, you could use shaping. Start the first week being on time 25 percent more often than you usually are. If you are now on time 30 percent of the time, make it your goal to be on time 55 percent of the time (30 percent + 25 percent). If you are successful at the end of week one, increase your goal for week two to 80 percent (55 percent + 25 percent), and so forth.

To maintain the program over time, use *reminders*. Make a schedule each day of your meetings and appointments. Figure out how much time you need to arrive at a particular meeting, and allow yourself some extra time for unforeseen events. A watch with an alarm mechanism would also be helpful as a reminder.

If all else fails, then you could contact *self-help* and *professional help groups*. A word about self-help groups: If a self-help group does not exist in your community for a particular problem, you can always start one yourself. You will be surprised at the number of people who also have similar health and life-style problems they find stressful.

The information in this chapter can help you be less distressed over behaviors you wish to change but have not been able to eliminate. Try these methods. Modify them to fit your particular circumstances, and continue your search for better health and a satisfying life-style.

To assist you in making changes in your behaviors, use this guide, which is based on the material in this chapter.

1. Behavior I would like to change _____
   _____

2. What barriers are preventing me from making these changes?
   _____
   _____

3. Techniques to reduce stressful behaviors
   a. Self-monitoring: How often do I do this behavior? _____
   b. Contract: If I do this behavior— _____
      then I will receive this reward— _____
   c. Significant other: Who will be witness to this contract?
      _____

   d. Tailoring: When is the best time to do this behavior?
      _____

      Where is the best place to do this behavior? _____
   e. Social reinforcement: Who will reward me?
      _____

      How will that person socially reward me?
      _____

   f. Material reinforcement: What type of material rewards?
      _____

   g. Shaping: I will change my behavior in steps. List the steps:
      (1) _____
      (2) _____
      (3) _____
      (4) _____
   h. Reminders: What aids can I use to remind me to do this behavior (e.g., calendar)?
      _____

   i. Self-help groups: What self-help groups are available for my particular concern?
      _____

   j. Professional help: Do I need professional help with my problem? If so, where is it available? _____
      _____

Summary

1. By reducing stressful behaviors and increasing healthy behaviors, you can better manage the stress in your life.
2. To reduce stressful behaviors it is useful to identify the barriers that prevent changing these behaviors. Once the barriers are identified, strategies can be developed to eliminate or reduce them.
3. Perceptions of control over your health influence whether you engage in healthy behaviors. If you perceive you have control over your health, you will be more apt to engage in healthy behaviors than if you believe your health is a function of luck, chance, fate, or powerful others.
4. Self-monitoring is observing and recording your behavior. Self-monitoring health and life-style behaviors can increase your awareness of your behavior, which is the first step in reducing stressful behaviors.
5. Tailoring a health-behavior program offers a way to maximize your success by allowing you to fit the program into your particular circumstances.
6. The use of material and social reinforcement or rewards increases the likelihood that healthy behaviors will be repeated.
7. Self-contracting and contracting with a significant other formalizes a commitment to engage in a particular behavior. Contracts have proven to be an effective means of reducing stressful behaviors.
8. Shaping a behavior is the gradual introduction of various components of a program. This technique is particularly helpful when a person has difficulty carrying out a total program—for example, a weight control or exercise program. A reminder system can also be helpful.
9. Self-help groups have been formed to offer emotional support and information to individuals with similar health and life-style problems. Professional help has also been found valuable in assisting people to reduce their stressful behavior.

Notes

1. Stanislav V. Kasl and Sidney Cobb, "Health Behavior, Illness Behavior, and Sick-Role Behavior," *Archives of Environmental Health* 12 (1966):246–66.
2. Melody P. Noland and Robert H. L. Feldman, "An Empirical Investigation of Exercise Behavior in Adult Women," *Health Education* 16(1985):29–33.
3. Marc Belisle, Ethel Roskies, and Jean-Michel Levesque, "Improving Adherence to Physical Activity," *Health Psychology* 6 (1987):159–72.

4. Jerrold S. Greenberg and David Pargman, *Physical Fitness: A Wellness Approach,* 2d ed. (Englewood Cliffs, N.J.: Prentice-Hall, 1989).

5. Melbourne F. Hovell, Beverly Calhoun, and John P. Elder, "Modification of Students' Snacking: Comparison of Behavioral Teaching Methods," *Health Education* 19 (1988):26–37.

6. Robert H. L. Feldman, "The Assessment and Enhancement of Health Compliance in the Workplace," in *Occupational Health Promotion: Health Behavior in the Workplace,* by George S. Everly and Robert H. L. Feldman (New York: John Wiley & Sons, 1985), 33–46.

7. D. Cairns and J. A. Pasino, "Comparison of Verbal Reinforcement and Feedback in the Operant Treatment of Disability Due to Chronic Low Back Pain," *Behavior Therapy* 8 (1977):621–30.

8. K. D. Brownell et al., "The Effect of Couples Training and Partner Cooperativeness in the Behavior Treatment of Obesity," *Behavior Research Therapy* 16 (1978):323–33.

9. Marshall H. Becker and Lawrence W. Green, "A Family Approach to Compliance with Medical Treatment—A Selective Review of the Literature," *International Journal of Health Education* 18 (1975):1–11.

10. Mark J. Kittleson and Becky Hageman-Rigney, "Wellness and Behavior Contracting," *Health Education* 19 (1988):8–11.

11. M. J. Mahoney and C. E. Thoresen, *Self-Control: Power to the Person* (Monterey, Calif.: Brooks/Cole, 1974).

12. M. Dinoff, N. C. Rickard, and J. Colwick, "Weight Reduction through Successive Contracts," *American Journal of Orthopsychiatry* 42 (1972): 110–13.

13. R. A. Mann, "The Behavior-Therapeutic Use of Contingency Contracting to Control an Adult-Behavior Problem: Weight Control," *Journal of Applied Behavioral Analysis* 5 (1972):99–109.

14. Jess Feist and Linda Brannon, *Health Psychology: An Introduction to Behavior and Health* (Belmont, Calif.: Wadsworth, 1988).

PART V

▼

Specific
Applications

14

Occupational Stress

It was over dinner in a seafood restaurant with fishnets and lobster cages on the walls that my father-in-law was bemoaning his choice of professions. Witnessed by a stuffed marlin looking at us from across the room, he was expressing his envy of his physician friends who "made $300,000 a year, worked three days a week, and played golf the rest of the time." I was surprised to hear him speak this way because he always seemed to me to be excited about his law practice and proud that he was a second-generation attorney in business with his son. "If I had to do it all over again, I'd be a physician," he said as his eyes wandered upward and his mind visualized how delightful that kind of life would have been. When he lowered his eyes, they fell upon me and the inevitable question fell from his lips. "What would you be if you had to do it all over again?" Well, that was ten years ago and today Ralph is retired. He still looks back wondering how life might have been. In spite of the ten-year interval, though, my answer to his question remains the same. "I'd do just what I am doing now." Upon some study I learned that my answer is not uncommon among my fellow college professors. It seems that "professoring" is consistently reported to be a satisfying profession by its practitioners. Being a professor is accompanied by certain traits associated with low-stress occupations. This chapter will discuss these characteristics in particular and occupational stress in general.

By the way, what would you do if you could start all over?

Before proceeding, answer the following questions to get a better handle on oc-cupational stress. If you are presently employed, answer these questions as they relate to your job. If you are not now working but have worked, answer these questions as they relate to your last job. If you have never worked, write me immediately to let me know your secret. In the meantime, answer these questions as you think they relate to a loved one who is presently working.

Occupational Stress Scale

Now, before you get to the questions I need to make one point. When I talk with groups of people about occupational stress, inevitably a woman raises her hand to say she's never worked and therefore can't answer these questions. Upon further investigation we find she worked very hard but never received an outright salary. She mothered, wifed, laundered, cleaned, arranged car pools, and counseled. If you are a woman and work at home, answer these questions for that occupation.

Okay, here they are. For each question below, place the number that represents your answer in the space provided. These questions were developed by Weiman.

1 = never
2 = seldom
3 = sometimes
4 = frequently
5 = nearly all the time

_____ 1. How often do you feel that you have too little authority to carry out your responsibilities?

_____ 2. How often do you feel unclear about just what the scope and responsibilities of your job are?

_____ 3. How often do you not know what opportunities for advancement or promotion exist for you?

_____ 4. How often do you feel that you have too heavy a work load, one that you could not possibly finish during an ordinary workday?

_____ 5. How often do you think that you will not be able to satisfy the conflicting demands of various people around you?

_____ 6. How often do you feel that you are not fully qualified to handle your job?

_____ 7. How often do you not know what your superior thinks of you, how he or she evaluates your performance?

_____ 8. How often do you find yourself unable to get information needed to carry out your job?

_____ 9. How often do you worry about decisions that affect the lives of people that you know?

_____ 10. How often do you feel that you may not be liked and accepted by people at work?

_____ 11. How often do you feel unable to influence your immediate supervisor's decisions and actions that affect you?

_____ 12. How often do you not know just what the people you work with expect of you?

_____ 13. How often do you think that the amount of work you have to do may interfere with how well it is done?

_____ 14. How often do you feel that you have to do things on the job that are against your better judgment?

_____ 15. How often do you feel that your job interferes with your family life?

To score this occupational stress scale, add up your answers and divide by fifteen. The higher the score, the more occupational stress.

Stress score group	N	% group	Average number risks/patient				
			0.2	0.4	0.6	0.8	1.0
1.0–1.3	70	4.5					
1.4–1.6	148	9.6					
1.7–1.9	314	20.4					
2.0–2.2	308	20.0					
2.3–2.5	328	21.3					
2.6–2.8	222	14.4					
2.9–3.1	115	7.5					
3.2–3.4	24	1.6					
3.5–3.7	9	0.6					
3.9–4.0	2	0.1					
	1540	100.0					

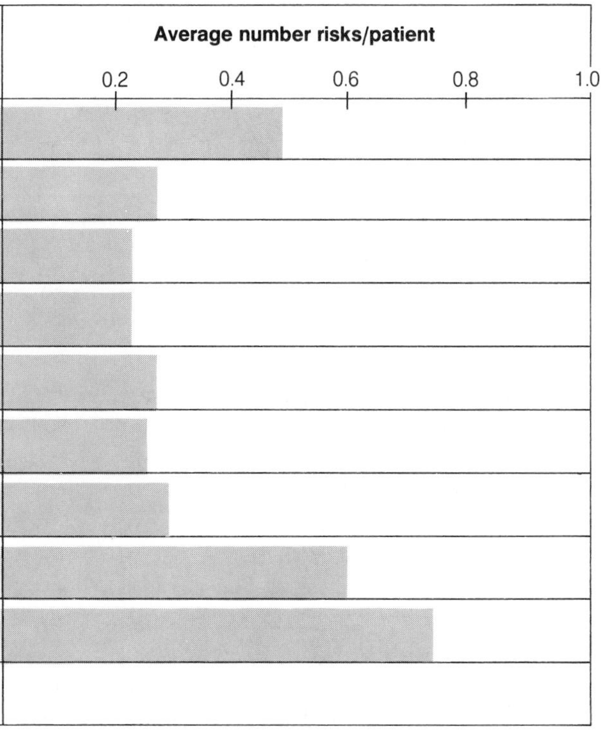

Figure 14.1
Percentage distribution of stress scores

Figure 14.1 depicts the relationship between the scores on this scale and the incidence of disease when 1,540 workers were studied.[1] The expectation that a large amount of stress would be associated with a greater incidence of disease was supported. However, a small amount of stress was also associated with a greater incidence of disease. In other words, there was an optimal amount of stress (not too little and not too much) that was found to be healthiest. Several hypotheses can be offered to explain this finding. However, the one I think most plausible is that low scores on this instrument mean these respondents felt underutilized and unneeded. They felt little responsibility and believed their jobs were not very important. They could easily be replaced. Believing this created a great deal of stress rather than a little, but this type of stress was not measured by the scale. Further support for this interpretation can be found later in this chapter.

What Is Occupational Stress?

Occupational stress is an extremely difficult construct to define. Obviously, it is stress on the job; but stress on the job occurs in a person. Here is where we run into problems, since any worker brings to the job a level of predisposition to be stressed. One way to depict the complexity of occupational stress is shown in figure 14.2.

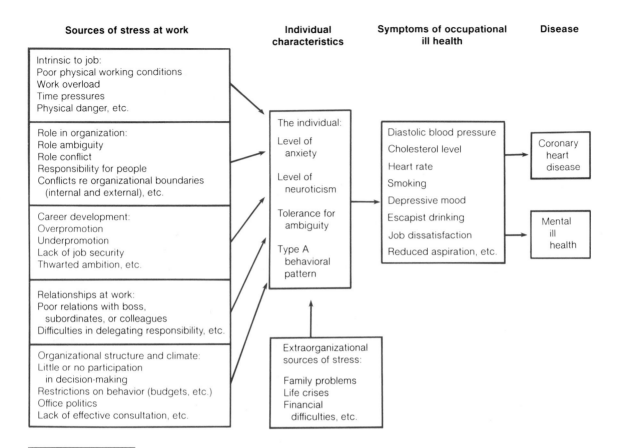

Sources of stress at work

Intrinsic to job:
Poor physical working conditions
Work overload
Time pressures
Physical danger, etc.

Role in organization:
Role ambiguity
Role conflict
Responsibility for people
Conflicts re organizational boundaries
    (internal and external), etc.

Career development:
Overpromotion
Underpromotion
Lack of job security
Thwarted ambition, etc.

Relationships at work:
Poor relations with boss,
    subordinates, or colleagues
Difficulties in delegating responsibility, etc.

Organizational structure and climate:
Little or no participation
    in decision-making
Restrictions on behavior (budgets, etc.)
Office politics
Lack of effective consultation, etc.

Individual characteristics

The individual:

Level of
    anxiety

Level of
    neuroticism

Tolerance for
    ambiguity

Type A
behavioral
pattern

Extraorganizational
sources of stress:

Family problems
Life crises
Financial
    difficulties, etc.

Symptoms of occupational ill health

Diastolic blood pressure
Cholesterol level
Heart rate
Smoking
Depressive mood
Escapist drinking
Job dissatisfaction
Reduced aspiration, etc.

Disease

Coronary
heart
disease

Mental
ill
health

Figure 14.2
Occupational stress
model

We shall soon consider some of the sources of work stress in detail. For now, note that several sources of occupational stress exist. Some of these stressors are intrinsic to the job, some are related to the employee's role within the organization, some to career development, some to relationships at work, and some to the structure and climate of the organization.

Interacting with these work stressors are the individual's characteristics. These are brought to the workplace rather than being a function of it, but they are important ingredients in occupational stress nevertheless. These characteristics include the worker's levels of anxiety and neuroticism, tolerance of ambiguity, Type A behavior pattern, and others.

Added to this brew are the sources of stress that come from outside the workplace and outside the worker. These extraorganizational sources of stress stem from family problems, life crises, financial matters, and environmental factors. Mix it all up and out come symptoms of occupational health problems that may develop into full-blown disease.

This model of occupational stress, as complex as it appears, is simplified by limiting the examples of stress at work, individual characteristics, and extraorganizational sources of stress. Many others could be included. Further, the interaction between these three factors is depicted as evenly weighted. In actuality, different workplaces have different levels of intrinsic job stressors and career development stressors. Different workers have differing levels of anxiety and tolerances of ambiguity, and different workers experience differing amounts of family and financial problems. To assume that all of these ingredients can be quantified is naive.

Another way of looking at occupational stress utilizes the Occupational Stress Evaluation Grid.[2] This grid, presented in table 14.1, recognizes that occupational stressors occur in different contexts—sociocultural, organizational, work setting, interpersonal, psychological, biological, and physical/environmental. The grid identifies formal and informal means of intervening for each of these levels of stressors. As with the model of occupational stress presented in figure 14.2, the Occupational Stress Evaluation Grid recognizes occupational stress to be a more complex construct than merely inclusive of some sources of stress at work.

Why Is Occupational Stress of Concern?

One of the reasons that occupational stress has been receiving so much attention of late is that businesses are genuinely beginning to care about employee welfare. You don't buy that? Well, how about this? Work stress is costing businesses billions of dollars. Sounds more plausible, doesn't it?

It has been estimated that stress on the job for executives alone costs businesses between 10 and 19 billion dollars per year.[3] These costs include salaries for sick days, costs of hospitalization and outpatient care, and costs related to the deaths of these executives. Other stress-related factors are catching the eyes of business leaders. Over the past twenty-five years, health-benefit costs to employers have increased more than 800 percent.[4]

Employees trained over a long period of time, at great cost, may break down when stressed on the job. They may make poor decisions, miss days of work, begin abusing alcohol and other drugs, or die and have to be replaced by other workers who need training. All of this is costly.

Job stress has been estimated to cost American industry 150 billion dollars each year.[5] The Metropolitan Life Insurance Company estimated that an average of one million workers are absent on any given day largely due to stress disorders,[6] and a study by the American Academy of Family Physicians found that job stress was considered the greatest cause of poor health habits.[7]

These effects of occupational stress have resulted in stress management programs being the highest priority for industry;[8] and why not? The PA Medical Corporation found a 14 percent decline in absenteeism due to their stress reduction program.[9] Kenecott Copper saved 75 percent in sickness and accident costs when they offered a stress management program.[10] When the effects of stress management programs were evaluated in an extensive analysis it was concluded that "the data suggest that stress reduction programs at the worksite are effective in reducing both physiological and psychological indications of stress."[11]

Table 14.1
Occupational Stress Evaluation Grid (OSEG)

Levels	Stressors	Interventions	
		Formal	Informal
Sociocultural	Racism; sexism	Elections	Grass roots organizing
	Ecological shifts	Lobbying/political action	Petitions
	Economic downturns	Public education	Demonstrations
	Political changes	Trade associations	Migration
	Military crises		Spouse employment
Organizational	Hiring policies	Corporate decision	Social activities
	Plant closings	Reorganization	Contests; incentives
	Layoffs, relocation	New management model	Manager involvement and ties
	Automation, market shifts,	Management consultant	with workers
	retraining	(inservice/retraining)	Continuing education
	Organizational priorities		Moonlighting
Work setting	Task (time, speed, autonomy,	Supervisor meetings	Slow down/speed up
	creativity)	Health/safety meetings	Redefine tasks
	Supervision	Union grievance	Support of other workers
	Coworkers	Employee involvement	Sabotage, theft
	Ergonomics	Quality circles	Quit, change jobs
	Participation in decision	Job redesign	
	making	Inservice training	
Interpersonal	Divorce, separation, marital	Legal/financial services	Seek social support/advice
	discord	Leave of absence	Seek legal/financial assistance
	Conflict, family/friend	Counseling, psychotherapy	Self-help groups
	Death, illness in family	Insurance plans	Vacation/sick days
	Intergenerational conflict	Family therapy	Child care
	Legal/financial difficulties	Loans/credit unions	
	Early parenthood	Day care	
Psychological	Neurosis, mental illness	Employee assistance (referral/	Seek support from friends,
	Disturbance of affect,	in house)	family, church
	cognition, or behavior	Counseling, psychotherapy	Self-help groups/books
	Ineffective coping skills	Medication	Self-medication
	Poor self-image	Supervisory training	Recreation, leisure
	Poor communication	Stress management	Sexual activity
	Addictive behavior	Workshop	"Mental health" days
Biological	Disease, disability	Preplacement screening	Change sleep/wake habits
	Sleep, appetite disturbance	Counseling	Bag lunch
	Chemical dependency	Medical treatment	Self-medication
	Biochemical imbalance	Health education	Cosmetics
	Pregnancy	Employee assistance	Diets, exercise
		Maternity leave	Consult physician
Physical/	Poor air, climate	Protective clothing/equipment	Own equipment, decoration
environmental	Noise exposure	Climate control	Walkman, radio
	Toxic substance exposure	Health/safety committee	Consult personal physician
	Poor lighting	Interior decoration	Letters of complaint
	Radiation exposure	Muzak	
	Poor equipment design	Union grievance	
	Bad architecture		

Source: M. J. Smith et al., "A Review of NIOSH Psychological Stress Research—1977," *NIOSH Proceedings of Occupational Stress Conference* (Cincinnati, Ohio: National Institute of Occupational Health and Safety, March, 1978), pp. 27–28.

Concern for workers in other countries, most particularly Japan, has resulted in greater productivity and increased profits.[12] American businesses have taken note of these employer-employee relationships. Fear of government regulation in support of employee health has led some businesses to act now rather than "under the gun" later. In an attempt to attract the best employees, some businesses have beefed up their fringe-benefit packages. Programs to reduce occupational stress and promote physical fitness are included as such inducements.

Another reason why business has become interested in their employees' health is because they may be held liable for a worker's ill health resulting from occupational stress. For example, state worker compensation laws are increasingly adding injury resulting from stress on the job as being eligible for compensation. Furthermore, there has been a tremendous rise in employee compensation lawsuits that claim occupational stress as the cause of workers' emotional and physical disabilities.[13,14] Observers of these developments have noted that "situations involving sudden emotional shock, protracted stress, or what is called 'wear and tear' are the basis for thousands of stress-illness claims now being filed in courts throughout the United States."[15] In addition, these courts are creating a clear trend in the direction of liberal compensation for plaintiffs in these lawsuits. You can see that responding to occupational stress is not only ethical; it is also good business.

Occupational Stress and Disease

The link between occupational stress and disease is a difficult one to prove, since this relationship is complicated by the workers' characteristics and stressors outside of the workplace. There is, however, evidence that supports the conclusion that occupational stress is related to illness and disease. This evidence falls into two categories: evidence of the physiological effects of occupational stress and evidence of disease states associated with occupational stress.

Physiological Effects

Several studies have shown that physiological arousal accompanies occupational stress.[16,17] Airplane pilots have been found to have an elevated heart rate and military pilots elevated blood pressure during takeoff and landing.[18,19] Pilots of planes landing on aircraft carriers were found to have increased levels of serum cholesterol while landing.[20]

Granted, flying airplanes may produce more than just ordinary occupational stress. However, blue-collar jobs that are paced by machines (assembly line work, for example) have also been found to be physiologically arousing.[21] Further, jobs that involve a hurried pace and relative lack of control over that pace by the worker lead to increased heart and blood pressure rates.[22,23] Increases in epinephrine, uric acid, serum cholesterol, glucose, and total blood lipids were found when day workers switched to night shifts.[24]

An interesting finding is that the amount of work does not seem as critical to health as the control the worker has over the work rate or related work processes. For example, workers in jobs with higher work load and pacing demands, and very little control of these demands, have increased rates of coronary heart disease and higher blood pressure than workers in jobs not so characterized.[25]

Disease States

Many studies have implicated occupational stress in the development of illness and disease. Russek and Russek found that heart-disease patients could be differentiated from healthy control subjects by occupational stress more than any other heart-disease risk factor (e.g., high blood pressure, serum cholesterol, smoking cigarettes, or obesity).[26] The relationship of cardiovascular disease to occupational stress has been a fairly consistent finding among researchers.[27,28]

In addition to coronary heart disease, work stress has been related to hypertension, diabetes, and peptic ulcers.[29] Occupational stress may, in fact, lead to any of the stress-related diseases discussed in chapter 3. The consequence of contracting such diseases has been early retirement because of disability.[30] The impact of work stress can be so devastating that at least one researcher has found higher rates of heart attacks on "back-to-work" Mondays than any other day of the week, and fewest heart attacks on Fridays (TGIF).[31] Why ruin the weekend?

Psychological Effects

Occupational stress also has consequences for your psychological health. For example, it has been found that some occupational stressors can result in low self-confidence, increased job tension, and lower job satisfaction.[32] A summary of ninety-six other studies of the psychological effects of occupational stress has also found that absenteeism and poor job performance are related to stress on the job.[33]

Occupational Stressors

Workers report more occupational stress when work objectives are unclear, when they have conflicting demands placed upon them, when they have too little or too much to do, when they have little input into decisions that affect them, and when they are responsible for other workers' professional development.[34] Among blue-collar workers, occupational stressors can be categorized in four ways:

1. *Compensation.* Purchasing power is eroded by inflation, and the remedy might result in unemployment.
2. *Health and safety hazards.* Inadequately tested components and processes create hazards in the workplace. The exaggeration of these hazards by the media on the one hand and the evasion of governmental regulations by employers on the other create stress.
3. *Work setting.* The workplace may be poorly ventilated or lit, or it may be noisy and smelly. The difference between blue-collar and white-collar work settings in the same organization may create jealousy and a lack of pride on the part of the blue-collar workers.
4. *Work loss.* Looking over your shoulder at the spectre of unemployment leads to a heightened sense of anxiety and insecurity.[35]

Wellness in the Factory

You work in a factory.

Your day begins at 7:30 A.M. You arrive on time and cheerfully greet your fellow workers. At the sound of a small whistle, you take your place—and begin a twenty-minute session of stretching and limbering exercises. At 8 o'clock you head for the assembly line, fresh, invigorated, alert.

At midmorning, you take a short break, then join your quality control circle. You talk about your line's productivity, about possible improvements, about any potential new policies that might be forthcoming from management. Then back to work.

At noon, you eat a moderate, nutritious lunch, then head out to the athletic area for a quick game of tennis, volleyball, or softball. After a ninety-minute break, you return to the line.

Sound like another world? It's not. It's simply a picture of everyday worklife in Japan. It's no coincidence that productivity in Japan is increasing at 10 percent a year, while productivity in the United States has been declining.

The enlightenment of Japanese business management with regard to employee health may well have significant implications for workers in this country. American corporate executives, who are making jet-age pilgrimages to the Asian Mecca of productivity, are returning from Japan with newfound respect for the importance of employee health and fitness. No matter what the product, good health is good business.

Source: Charles Jennings and Mark J. Tager, "Good Health is Good Business" in *Medical Self-Care,* Summer 1981, p. 17. © 1981 Medical Self-Care. Reprinted by permission.

To appreciate the difficulty involved in identifying occupational stressors, however, one need only look at McLean's list of societal changes influencing attitudes toward work.[36] McLean argues that the level of occupational stress is affected by such changes as the following:

Societal Changes

1. *Contemporary economic problems.* Slow economic growth, high unemployment, the energy crisis, reduction in productivity, reduced exports, inflation, and increased social costs to support the nonworking population are among current economic problems.

2. *The era of rising entitlements.* More people hold the expectation of an ever-increasing standard of living, consumer appetites for more and more, and the belief that families should be protected against economic hardship, illness, or aging through social service programs.

3. *Increased educational opportunity.* More people are acquiring more education, but the economy does not allow for their skills to be used.

4. *Challenge to authority.* Seventy percent of young workers state they need not follow a supervisor's orders if they disagree. Workers are no longer blindly adhering to job demands.

5. *Decline of confidence in institutions.* Business, government, labor, churches, and the military have lost the public's trust. This lack of trust has resulted in feelings of insecurity and suspicion.

6. *Resistance to change.* Change breeds insecurity. Change in occupations is viewed as directed toward increasing productivity and reducing costs rather than responding to workers' needs. Technological change may mean layoffs and is therefore resisted.

7. *Changing attitudes toward work.* In 1967 over 50 percent of American students answered yes when asked if hard work paid off. In 1975 only 25 percent answered yes.

8. *The changing family.* More divorces and dual-career families create new pressures. Whether to relocate for one spouse's job when the other's job doesn't permit relocation is a decision that may lead to distress. How to keep business and family needs from serving as excuses to avoid each other is also a concern.

9. *Society is changing faster than the workplace.* The large bureaucracies that organizations become remain resistant to change. The changes that are adopted are often made begrudgingly. They may even be forced upon the organization by workers or government regulation.

Lack of Participation

One of the factors of the workplace and the organization's modus operandi that is related to stress is the degree of participation. Workers' perceptions of the degree of participation in the decision-making process, the degree to which they are consulted on issues affecting the organization, and their involvement in establishing rules of behavior at work have proven to be related to job satisfaction, job-related feelings of threat, and feelings of self-esteem.[37,38] Others have found that nonparticipation is related to overall poor physical health, escapist drinking, depression, dissatisfaction with life, low motivation to work, intention to leave the job, and absenteeism.[39] Figure 14.3 depicts the effects of high participation on the job. Low participation can be expected to have the opposite effect.

Role Problems

A clear sense of your role in an organization and a sense that you can "play the part" are important in keeping stress at a minimum. A variety of role-related problems may arise for workers who lack these feelings.

Role Overload
When job demands are so great that the worker feels an inability to cope, stress will develop. You can imagine the feeling of having too much to do in too little time.

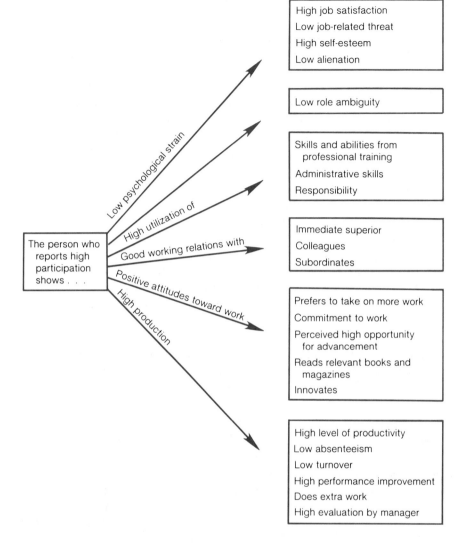

Figure 14.3 The effect of participation on work-related criteria measures

The person who reports high participation shows . . .

Low psychological strain

High job satisfaction
Low job-related threat
High self-esteem
Low alienation

High utilization of

Low role ambiguity

Skills and abilities from professional training
Administrative skills
Responsibility

Good working relations with

Immediate superior
Colleagues
Subordinates

Positive attitudes toward work

Prefers to take on more work
Commitment to work
Perceived high opportunity for advancement
Reads relevant books and magazines
Innovates

High production

High level of productivity
Low absenteeism
Low turnover
High performance improvement
Does extra work
High evaluation by manager

Role Insufficiency

When workers lack the training, education, skills, or experience to accomplish the job, they will feel stressed. A poor fit between workers' talents and the organization's expectations will create disharmony and dissatisfaction.[40]

Role Ambiguity

When aspects of the job and workplace are unclear, frustration and stress are likely to develop. Workers should know the criteria for career advancement, the priorities of the organization, and generally what is expected of them.

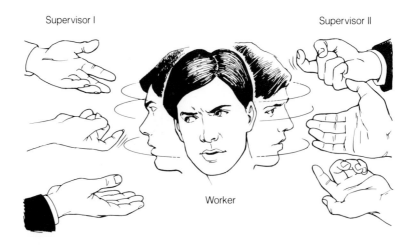

Figure 14.4 Role conflict: Which demands to meet?

Supervisor I   Supervisor II

Worker

Role Conflict

Sometimes workers get caught in a bind. Two supervisors each expect something different. The worker may be faced with conflicting demands (see fig. 14.4). This is the "damned if you do, damned if you don't" dilemma. Such a situation is a factor in occupational stress.

Job Dissatisfaction

The factors that are typically thought related to dissatisfaction on the job are salary and conditions of the workplace (e.g., noise, poor lighting, poor ventilation, crowding, etc.). However, even if workers were paid well and worked in hygienic conditions, they might still be dissatisfied. A class of work-related factors, called **motivational factors,** can affect job satisfaction. These factors include the degree of stimulating tasks involved, the amount of recognition for jobs done well, relationships with fellow workers, and the amount of encouragement to take on responsibility (see fig. 14.5). Unfortunately, many unions ignore these factors when negotiating a contract. Obviously, some of these motivational factors would be difficult to assure in writing. They're important enough, however, to try for.

The Work Environment

Some places of work include hazards that can create stress. Dangerous tasks or work settings, toxic chemicals, high noise levels, dust, overcooling, unpleasant odors, and other stressful factors can lead to illness or disease. An interesting source you might want to consult if you are interested in this aspect of occupational stress is a book entitled *Office Work Can Be Dangerous to Your Health.*[41]

Self-realization needs	Job-related satisfiers
Reaching your potential	Involvement in planning your work
Independence	Freedom to make decisions affecting work
Creativity	
Self-expression	Creative work to perform
	Opportunities for growth and development

Esteem needs	Job-related satisfiers
Responsibility	Status symbols
Self-respect	Merit awards
Recognition	Challenging work
Sense of accomplishment	Sharing in decisions
	Opportunity for advancement

Social needs	Job-related satisfiers
Companionship	Opportunities for interaction with others
Acceptance	
Love and affection	Team spirit
Group membership	Friendly coworkers

Safety needs	Job-related satisfiers
Security for self and possessions	Safe working conditions
	Seniority
Avoidance of risks	Fringe benefits
Avoidance of harm	Proper supervision
Avoidance of pain	Sound company policies, programs, and practices

Physical needs	Job-related satisfiers
Food	Pleasant working conditions
Clothing	Adequate wage or salary
Shelter	Rest periods
Comfort	Laborsaving devices
Self-preservation	Efficient work methods

Figure 14.5 Human needs and their job-related satisfiers

The Workaholic

Too much work, even if you enjoy it, can itself be an occupational stressor. There are some of us who either enjoy our work so much or find so little pleasure in our nonworking lives that we immerse ourselves in our jobs. They consume us. If you've ever wondered whether you're a **workaholic**—or if you think you might be working or living with one—take this test and see.

Are You a Workaholic?

	Yes	No	

_____ _____   1. *Do you get up early, no matter how late you go to bed?*
As one management consultant confessed, "I'd get home and work until [about] 2 A.M., and then get up at 5 A.M. and think, 'Gee, aren't I terrific!' "

_____ _____   2. *If you are eating lunch alone, do you read or work while you eat?*
Robert Moses, New York's longtime Parks Commissioner, reportedly considered lunches a bore and a bother because he couldn't bear to interrupt work. He used a large table as a desk so lunch could be served right there.

_____ _____   3. *Do you make daily lists of things to do?*
Ever-present appointment books and cluttered calendars are a hallmark of workaholics. Indeed, their main way of wasting time, admits Dr. Elizabeth Whelan, a Harvard University epidemiologist, may be looking for lost lists!

_____ _____   4. *Do you find it difficult to "do nothing"?*
It was claimed that David Mahoney, the handsome, hardworking chairman of Norton Simon, Inc., abandoned transcendental meditation because he found it impossible to sit still for twenty minutes.

_____ _____   5. *Are you energetic and competitive?*
President Johnson once asked Doris Kearns, then a White House Fellow, if she were energetic. Kearns replied, "I hear you need only five hours of sleep, but I need only four, so it stands to reason that I've got even more energy than you."

_____ _____   6. *Do you work on weekends and holidays?*
In *Working,* author Studs Terkel related that the president of a Chicago radio station confessed that he regularly works in his home on weekends. But, he added, "When I do this on holidays, like Christmas, New Year's, and Thanksgiving, I have to sneak a bit so the family doesn't know what I'm doing."

_____ _____   7. *Can you work anytime and anywhere?*
Two associates at Cravath, Swaine and Moore, one of Manhattan's most prestigious law firms, were said to have bet about who could bill the most hours in a day. One worked around the clock, billed twenty-four, and felt assured of victory. His competitor, however, having flown to California in the course of the day and worked on the plane, was able to bill twenty-seven.

Yes	No

8. *Do you find vacations "hard to take"?*
George Lois, the art director who heads Lois Pitts Gershon, an advertising agency, had to think a while when I asked him when he had taken his last vacation. Finally, he recalled when it was: 1964—almost fourteen years before!

9. *Do you dread retirement?*
After retiring from the ad agency where she had created such classic slogans as Clairol's "Does she . . . or doesn't she?" Shirley Polykoff started her own advertising agency. As president of Shirley Polykoff Advertising in New York she still—some six years later—has no plans to slow up or step down. She says, "I'm doing more now than I've ever done. I don't know how you retire if you're still healthy and exuberant about living. They'll have to carry me out in a box!"

10. *Do you really enjoy your work?*
As Joyce Carol Oates, the Canadian novelist, once told the *New York Times,* "I am not conscious of working especially hard, or of 'working' at all. . . . Writing and teaching have always been, for me, so richly rewarding that I do not think of them as work in the usual sense of the word."

If you answered "yes" to eight or more questions, you, too, may be a workaholic.

In a study of workaholics, Marilyn Machlowitz found that they exhibited the following characteristics:

1. Tend to be intense and energetic
2. Sleep less than most people
3. Have difficulty taking vacations
4. Spend most of their waking time working
5. Frequently eat while they work
6. Prefer work to play
7. Work hard at making the most of their time
8. Tend to blur the distinction between work and play
9. Can and do work anywhere and everywhere[42]

To combat "workaholism," try these suggestions:

1. Focus on the work you most love doing, and try to find ways to stop doing, delegate, or minimize the parts of your work you dislike.
2. Ask yourself: "What work would I do for free?" Then try to evolve your work in that direction.

3. Use your time; don't let it use you. Decide how much time you want to spend working, then limit your work time accordingly. For example, you might arrange to stop working at 5:30 P.M. by making a commitment to go running with a friend every workday at 5:45. Arrangements like these help workaholics return to feeling more refreshed—and more productive.

4. Build friendships at work. Arrange to spend quality time with coworkers.

5. Schedule open time into your work life. If, for instance, you now schedule work-related appointments every thirty minutes, try to evolve toward scheduling them every forty-five minutes instead.

6. Learn to say no to new demands on your time. If this is difficult, say that you'd like some time to think about it, then say no later.

7. Decorate your workplace to create an environment that pleases you. You deserve it.

8. Try to stay in touch with the positive aspects of your work: the pleasure of doing work that fulfills you, the freedom, the opportunity to be of service to others, or other aspects of your work you find rewarding.

9. Heavy involvement in work usually entitles you to have a good deal to say about the way you work. How might you change or restructure your work to make it feel more fulfilling?

In addition to these suggestions, remember that the workaholic enjoys work and therefore might not notice the harm it is doing. The family often suffers more than the workaholic since time is taken away from them, and family responsibilities added to them, because of the workaholic's work style. To intervene between workaholism and poor family health, therefore, time should be scheduled for family activities that will get the workaholic away from the telephone and job commitments. Hiking and backpacking are useful for this purpose.

Burnout

Too much work or frequent frustration at work can lead to a syndrome of physical and emotional exhaustion. This syndrome is called **burnout.** Burnout is "an adverse work stress reaction with psychological, psychophysiological, and behavioral components. Moreover, burnout appears to be a major factor in low worker morale, high absenteeism and job turnover rates, physical illness and distress, increased alcohol and drug use, marital and family conflict, and various psychological problems."[43] The symptoms of burnout include the following:

1. *Diminished sense of humor:* inability to laugh at daily, on-the-job situations

2. *Skipping rest and food breaks:* continually having no time for coffee or lunch breaks to restore stamina

3. *Increased overtime and no vacation:* indispensable to the organization; reluctant to say no to working on scheduled off-days

4. *Increased physical complaints:* fatigue, irritability, muscle tension, stomach upset, and susceptibility to illness

5. *Social withdrawal:* pulling away from coworkers, peers, family members

6. *Changed job performance:* increased absenteeism, tardiness, use of sick leave, and decreased efficiency or productivity

7. *Self-medication:* increased use of alcohol, tranquilizers, and other mood-altering drugs

8. *Internal changes:* emotional exhaustion, loss of self-esteem, depression, frustration, and a "trapped" feeling

In addition, burnout may be characterized by pessimism, paranoia, rigidity, callousness,[44] feelings of loneliness and guilt,[45] and difficulty in making and explaining decisions.[46]

Burnout in women has been of recent interest. In a recent book by Freudenberger and North, an argument is made that businesswomen experience a high degree of burnout.[47] However, they are less prone to admit to its existence than are men because of their concern about it being construed as weakness. Even women aerobic instructors are experiencing burnout, and this burnout is resulting in physical injury.[48]

A different way of looking at how burnout develops involves a progressive five-stage approach:

Stage one (the honeymoon). At this stage, the worker is usually satisfied with the job and the tasks involved, and remains enthusiastic toward the work. However, as this stage continues, the tasks become unenjoyable and the worker loses energy.

Stage two (fuel shortage). At this stage, fatigue sets in, and the worker may respond by abusing drugs. Difficulty sleeping is another symptom of this stage.

Stage three (chronic symptoms). At this stage, overwork leads to physical effects that include constant exhaustion and susceptibility to disease, and psychological effects that include acute anger and feelings of depression.

Stage four (crisis). At this stage, actual illness can develop that results in the worker not being able to attend to the job. Relationships at home may also be affected due to a sense of pessimism, self-doubt, and/or obsession with problems.

Stage five (hitting the wall). At this stage, the physical and psychological problems can become severe enough to cause illness that is life-threatening. The worker now has so many problems at work that his or her career is actually threatened.

Brownout Inventory

Are you suffering from burnout, or are you only partway there (**brownout**)? Complete the brownout inventory below and find out. For each statement below, write a *T* if that statement is true for you or an *F* if it isn't.

_____ 1. Is your efficiency at work declining?
_____ 2. Have you lost some of your initiative at work?
_____ 3. Have you lost interest in your work?
_____ 4. Does work stress get to you more than it used to?
_____ 5. Do you feel fatigued or run-down?
_____ 6. Do you get headaches?
_____ 7. Do you get stomachaches?
_____ 8. Have you lost weight recently?
_____ 9. Do you have trouble sleeping?
_____ 10. Do you experience shortness of breath?
_____ 11. Do you have frequently changing or depressing moods?
_____ 12. Are you easy to anger?
_____ 13. Do you get frustrated easily?
_____ 14. Are you more suspicious than you used to be?
_____ 15. Do you feel more helpless than you used to?
_____ 16. Are you using too many mood-altering drugs (e.g., tranquilizers or alcohol)?
_____ 17. Are you becoming more inflexible?
_____ 18. Are you becoming more critical of your own and others' competencies?
_____ 19. Are you working more but feeling that you're getting less done?
_____ 20. Have you lost some of your sense of humor?

If you answered *true* for more than half of these statements you may be experiencing brownout. If you answered *true* for fifteen or more of these statements, you may be burning out (or already burnt out). Recognize, however, that you can remedy this situation by employing the stress management suggestions described in this chapter.

Well, what can one do about burnout? An expert in this field suggests the following:

1. *"What do I work for?"* List all things—material and abstract—that you get out of your job. Identify your motivations, the value and meaning of your job.

2. *"I really want to do that."* List all activities you like and rank them in order of importance. Then note the last time you engaged in each.

3. *Create a support group.* Friends and/or coworkers meet on a regular basis.

4. *Start a physical self-care program.* Include exercise, nutrition, and elimination of destructive habits such as smoking.

5. *Start a psychological self-care program.* Include training in relaxation, negotiation, time management, and assertiveness.

6. *Do something silly every day.* Roller skate, play tiddlywinks, blow bubbles, or make a funny face . . . relax, smile, and avoid taking yourself too seriously.[49]

Have you had it with school? With work? Are you near burnout? If so, will you do something about it? You're in control of yourself and your feelings. You can exercise this control. You don't have to suffer from burnout if you choose not to.

The Victims of Occupational Stress

Although occupational stress may strike any worker, certain jobs generally tend to be more stressful than others. Police officers, nurses, air traffic controllers, bus drivers, accountants, and auto assembly workers have been frequently cited as particularly prone to occupational stress. Table 14.2 presents results from a study of 22,000 workers in 130 occupations. As you can see, some jobs generally tend to be more stressful than others. However, anyone can suffer from occupational stress; we all need to pay attention to keep it from leading to poor health.

Interventions

Using our stress model, we know we can intervene between occupational stress and its negative consequences by changing life situations, our perceptions or cognitive appraisal of those situations, our emotional reactions, or by doing something physical to use up the stress by-products. This section will describe how to specifically apply these interventions.

Table 14.2
Occupations with Low and High Incidences of Stress-related Diseases

Low-stress Occupations	High-stress Occupations
Sewers	Laborers
Checker, examiner	Secretary
Stockhandler	Inspector
Craftsman	Clinical lab technician
Maid	Office manager
Farm laborer	Foreman
Heavy equipment operator	Manager/administrator
Freight handler	Waitress/waiters
Child care worker	Operatives
Packer, wrapper	Farm owner
College/university professor	Mine operatives
Personnel/labor relations	Painter (not artist)
Auctioneer/huckster	Health technology technician
	Practical nurse (LPN)
	Nurses' aide
	Musician
	Dental assistant
	Teacher aide
	Computer programmer
	Bank teller
	Health aide
	Social worker
	Registered nurse
	Telephone operator
	Hairdresser
	Warehouseman
	Sales manager
	Clergy
	Sales representative
	Police
	Railroad switchman
	Meat cutter
	Electrician
	Fireman
	Plumber
	Structural metal craftsman
	Guard/watchman
	Machinist
	Mechanic
	Public relations

Source: M. J. Smith et al., ''A Review of NIOSH Physical Stress Research—1977,'' *NIOSH Proceedings of Occupational Stress Conference* (Cincinnati, Ohio: National Institute of Occupational Health and Safety, March 1978), 27–28.

If you dislike your job and it is causing you to either feel ill or behave in ways that are detrimental to your career and/or your home life, you can always quit that job. Short of that you can ask for a change in job responsibilities, or you can request a less stressful job within the same organization. If you are experiencing burnout, you desperately need to reread the section on time management in chapter 6. Learn to organize your time better and to say "no" when asked to take on additional responsibilities. In addition, some stress reducing rules might help:

Life-Situation
Interventions

1. Don't take work home.
2. Take a full lunch hour.
3. Do not discuss business over lunch.
4. Discuss your feelings about occupational stress with whomever is close by whenever those feelings develop.

Recognizing that your perceptions of your occupational stress are as important as the actual events precipitating that stress, you will need to intervene in these perceptions. These suggestions should help:

Perception
Interventions

1. *Look for the humor in your stressors at work.* A resourceful teacher, frustrated by inane memos from the principal with which she was repeatedly and unmercifully bombarded, kept a file of these memos and eventually wrote a very humorous and successful book based upon them. The principal may not have found humor in this teacher's survival technique, but she sure did; and besides, she had tenure anyhow.
2. *Try to see things for what they really are.* Here's an example, but keep this between us. Publishers are notorious for requesting manuscripts from authors by certain *firm* deadline dates. Unfortunately, too often these manuscripts sit on some editor's desk before being processed. Through some bitter experiences, I have learned that publishers' *deadlines* are really not deadlines. Rather, they are dates *close to* when they would like to receive a manuscript and, knowing that many authors will be late with their submissions, these editors have selected dates with a margin for delay. I have learned to allow myself more time to get a job done when I have been able to perceive that I really have more time to complete that work than I first thought. You can use that strategy as well. Perhaps you too have "deadlines" which really aren't deadlines.
3. *Distinguish between need and desire.* For example, "I *must* get this task completed" might be more truthfully stated as "I *wish* I could get this task completed."
4. *Separate your self-worth from the task.* If you fail at a task, it does not mean *you* are a failure.

5. *Identify situations and employ the appropriate style of coping.* Lazarus and Folkman have differentiated between **problem-focused coping** and **emotion-focused coping.**[50] Problem-focused coping is the use of activities specific to getting the task accomplished, whereas emotion-focused coping is the use of activities to feel better about the task. If you employed problem-focused coping for a task which was beyond your accomplishment (for example, turning in a two hundred page treatise on the migratory habits of aardvarks for tomorrow's class), you would only frustrate yourself and become distressed. Given such an impossible task you would do better to joke about it, discuss your feelings with a friend, or leave a real aardvark in your professor's mailbox with a note instructing him or her to observe this creature's migratory habits and get back to you. Conversely, if a task can be accomplished but you dillydally by joking and partying with friends, you are employing emotion-focused coping when you should have engaged in activities to get the task done (problem-focused coping). Perceiving what is called for in a particular situation will allow you to better determine which method of coping is most appropriate.

Emotional Arousal Interventions

The relaxation techniques described in previous chapters, if done regularly, can help prevent occupational stress from making you ill, creating disharmony in your relationships at work or at home, or leading to your abuse of alcohol or other drugs, as well as prevent the other harmful consequences of occupational stress which we have previously discussed. I have had participants in my classes and workshops tell me they have found out-of-the-way places at work where they meditate during part of their lunch hour or during breaks in the workday. Others have had to leave the work site but have found nearby parks or golf courses where they too practice a relaxation technique. Still others have been able to get their companies to establish one area as the relaxation area—usually an infrequently used lounge or work area. You can use a relaxation technique to intervene at this level if you choose to. Be ingenious, be assertive, be committed to caring for you.

Physiological Arousal Interventions

As with other stressors, exercise is an excellent way of using up the stress products that are created by occupational stress. Recognizing this, many businesses have built gymnasiums and/or outside exercise areas (for example, running tracks or par courses). If you are fortunate to have these facilities at work, use them. If not, you can join an exercise club (if you need the company of others) or exercise on your own. Remember to follow the guidelines provided in chapter 12 so that your exercise program reduces stress rather than causes it.

Managing Occupational Stress

In conclusion, occupational stress may be difficult to define and measure because of the personal stressors people bring to their jobs and their varying personality characteristics, but we all know when we are experiencing it. Fortunately, we can manage occupational stress by using the stress model presented in chapter 4 to set up roadblocks between occupational stress and illness and disease. We can change jobs (life-situation intervention), perceive the stressors associated with our jobs as challenges rather than burdens to bear (perception intervention), practice relaxation techniques regularly (emotional arousal intervention), or exercise regularly to use up the accumulated products of stress (physiological arousal intervention). But whether we do anything is our own choice. "Grinning and bearing it" won't help; neither will always complaining about our jobs or our bosses. Help is available and a reading of this book is a good start.

Summary

1. Too little occupational stress is almost as unhealthy as too much occupational stress. There is an optimal level of occupational stress that is desirable.

2. Occupational stress consists of a mix of work site stressors, the individual's characteristics, and extraorganizational stressors. These stressors can lead to symptoms of occupational ill health or actual disease.

3. Businesses have become interested in occupational stress because it costs them money to ignore it due to employees' ill health, poor decision making, or absenteeism. In addition, stress management programs are used to attract prospective employees whom the company is recruiting.

4. Workers report more occupational stress when work objectives are unclear, when they have conflicting demands placed upon them, when they have too little or too much to do, when they have little input in decisions that affect them, and when they are responsible for other workers' development.

5. Role problems that can result in occupational stress include role overload, role insufficiency, role ambiguity, and role conflict.

6. Workaholics spend much of their time working, often eat while working, prefer work to play, and can and do work anytime and anywhere. They are intense and energetic, and have difficulty sleeping and taking vacations.

7. Burnout is a syndrome of physical and emotional exhaustion; it is an adverse work stress reaction with psychological, psychophysiological, and behavioral components. Symptoms include diminished sense of humor, skipping rest and food breaks, increased overtime and no vacations, increased physical complaints, social withdrawal, diminishing job performance, self-medication, and psychological changes such as depression or a "trapped" feeling.

Notes

1. Clinton G. Weiman, "A Study of the Occupational Stressor and the Incidence of Disease/Risk," *NIOSH Proceeding: Reducing Occupational Stress* (Cincinnati, Ohio: National Institute for Occupational Safety and Health, April 1978), 55.

2. Jefferson A. Singer, Michael S. Neale, and Gary E. Schwartz, "The Nuts and Bolts of Assessing Occupational Stress: A Collaborative Effort with Labor," in *Stress Management in Work Settings,* ed. Lawrence R. Murphy and Theodore F. Schoenborn (Washington, D.C.: National Institute for Occupational Safety and Health, 1987), 3–29.

3. James W. Greenwood, "Management Stressors," *NIOSH Proceeding: Reducing Occupational Stress* (Cincinnati, Ohio: National Institute for Occupational Safety and Health, April 1978), 41.

4. Charles Jennings and Mark J. Tager, "Good Health Is Good Business," *Medical Self-Care*, Summer 1981, 14.

5. J. S. J. Manuso, "Stress Management in the Workplace," in *Health Promotion in the Workplace,* ed. M. P. O'Donnell and T. Ainsworth (New York: John Wiley & Sons, 1984), 362–90.

6. Paul J. Rosch and Kenneth R. Pelletier, "Designing Worksite Stress Management Programs," in *Stress Management in Work Settings,* ed. Lawrence R. Murphy and Theodore F. Schoenborn (Washington, D.C.: National Institute for Occupational Safety and Health, 1987), 69.

7. American Academy of Family Physicians, *A Report on Lifestyles/ Personal Health Care in Different Occupations* (Kansas City: American Academy of Family Physicians, 1979).

8. Kenneth R. Pelletier, *Healthy People in Unhealthy Places: Stress and Fitness at Work* (New York: Delacorte Press/Seymour Lawrence, 1984).

9. George S. Everly and Daniel A. Girdano, *The Stress Mess Solution: The Causes of Stress on the Job* (Bowie, Md.: Robert J. Brady, 1980), 4.

10. R. Egdahl and D. Walsh, *Mental Wellness Programs for Employees* (New York: Springer-Verlag, 1980).

11. K. R. McLeroy et al., "Assessing the Health Effects of Health Promotion in Worksites: A Review of the Stress Program Evaluations," *Health Education Quarterly* 11(1984):379–401.

12. Wm. Ouchi, *Theory Z* (Reading, Mass.: Addison-Wesley, 1981).

13. Daniel B. Moskowitz, "Workers' Compensation Awards for Job Stress on the Rise," *Washington Post, Business,* 14 October 1985, 39.

14. Robert Byrd, "Job-Stress Illness Up, Report Says; More Injury Claims Cite Mental Anxiety," *Washington Post,* 3 October 1986, F2.

15. John M. Ivancevich, Michael T. Matteson, and Edward P. Richards III, "Who's Liable for Stress on the Job," *Harvard Business Review,* March–April 1985, 66.

16. D. B. Baker, "The Study of Stress at Work," *Annual Review of Public Health* 6(1985):367–81.

17. J. J. Hurrell and M. J. Colligan, "Psychological Job Stress," in *Environmental and Occupational Medicine,* ed. W. N. Rom (Boston: Little, Brown, 1982), 425–30.

18. H. P. R. Smith, "Heart Rate of Pilots Flying Aircraft on Scheduled Airline Routes," *Aerospace Medicine* 38(1967):1117–19.

19. J. A. Roman, "Cardiorespiratory Functioning in Flight," *Aerospace Medicine* 34(1963):322–37.

20. R. T. Rubin, "Biochemical and Endocrine Responses to Severe Psychological Stress," in *Life Stress And Illness,* ed. E. K. E. Gunderson and Richard H. Rahe (Springfield, Ill.: Charles C. Thomas, 1974).

21. M. Frankenhauser and B. Gardell, "Underload and Overload in Working Life: Outline of a Multidisciplinary Approach," *Journal of Human Stress* 2(1976):35–46.

22. J. Chadwick et al., "Psychological Job Stress and Coronary Heart Disease," NIOSH report under contract no. CDC-99-74-42 (National Institute for Occupational Safety and Health, 1979).

23. David C. Glass, "Stress Behavior, Patterns, and Coronary Disease," *American Scientist* 65(1977):177–87.

24. T. Theorell and T. Akerstedt, "Day and Night Work: Changes in Cholesterol, Uric Acid, Glucose, and Potassium in Serum and in Circadian Patterns of Urinary Catecholamine Excretion—A Longitudinal Cross-Over Study of Railroad Repairmen," *Acta Medicine Scandinavia* 200(1976):47–53.

25. R. A. Karasek, J. Schwartz, and T. Theorell, *Job Characteristics, Occupation, and Coronary Heart Disease,* final report on contract no. R-01-0H00906 (Cincinnati, Ohio: National Institute for Occupational Safety and Health, 1982).

26. Henry I. Russek and Linda G. Russek, "Is Emotional Stress an Etiological Factor in Coronary Heart Disease?" *Psychosomatics* 17(1976):63.

27. T. Theorell and B. Floderus-Myrhed, "Workload and Myocardial Infarction—A Prospective Psychosocial Analysis," *International Journal of Epidemiology* 6(1977):17–21.

28. S. G. Haynes and M. Feinleib, "Women at Work and Coronary Heart Disease: Prospective Findings from the Framingham Heart Study," *American Journal of Public Health* 70(1980):133–41.

29. S. Cobb and R. M. Rose, "Hypertension, Peptic Ulcer, and Diabetes in Air Traffic Controllers," *Journal of the American Medical Association* 224(1973):489–92.

30. Anne Chase, "Police Psychologist: Post Remains Vacant for 9 Months Despite Growing Stress in Department," *Prince George's Journal,* 14 March 1980, A4.

31. S. Rabkin and F. Matthewson, "Chronobiology of Cardiac Sudden Death in Men," *Journal of the American Medical Association* 244 (1980): 1357–58.

32. Joseph Hurrell, "An Overview of Organizational Stress and Health," in *Stress Management in Work Settings,* ed. Lawrence R. Murphy and Theodore F. Schoenborn (Washington, D.C.: National Institute for Occupational Safety and Health, 1987), 34.

33. S. Jackson and R. Schuler, "A Meta-Analysis and Conceptual Critique of Research on Role Ambiguity and Role Conflict in Work Settings," *Organizational Behavior and Human Decision* 36(1985):16–28.

34. Christopher T. Cory, "The Stress-Ridden Inspection Suite and Other Jittery Jobs," *Psychology Today,* January 1979, 13–14.

35. Arthur B. Shostak, *Blue-Collar Stress* (Reading, Mass.: Addison-Wesley, 1980), 33–34.

36. Alan A. McLean, *Work Stress* (Reading, Mass.: Addison-Wesley, 1979), 49–53.

37. J. R. P. French and R. D. Caplan, "Psychosocial Factors in Coronary Heart Disease," *Industrial Medicine* 39(1970):383–97.

38. V. A. Beehr and J. E. Newman, "Job Stress, Employee Health, and Organizational Effectiveness: A Facet Analysis, Model, and Literature Review," *Personnel Psychology* 31(1978):665–99.

39. B. L. Margolis, W. H. Kroes, and R. P. Quinn, "Job Stress: An Unlisted Occupational Hazard," *Journal of Occupational Medicine* 16 (1974): 654–61.

40. Samuel H. Osipow and Arnold R. Spokane, "Occupational Environment Scales" (Unpublished scales, University of Maryland, 1980).

41. Jeanne Stellman and Mary Sue Henifen, *Office Work Can Be Dangerous to Your Health* (New York: Pantheon, 1983).

42. Marilyn Machlowitz, *Workaholics: Living with Them, Working with Them* (Reading, Mass.: Addison-Wesley, 1980).

43. John W. Jones, "A Measure of Staff Burnout among Health Professionals" (Paper presented at the annual meeting of the American Psychological Association, Montreal, September 1980).

44. Deanna S. Forney, Fran Wallace-Schutzman, and T. Thorn Wiggers, "Burnout among Career Development Professionals: Preliminary Findings and Implications," *Personnel and Guidance Journal* 60(1982):435–39.

45. William Eldridge, Stanley Blostein, and Virginia Richardson, "A Multi-Dimensional Model for Assessing Factors Associated with Burnout in Human Service Organizations," *Public Personnel Management* 12(1983):315.

46. David F. Gillespie, "Correlates for Active and Passive Types of Burnout," *Journal of Social Service Research* 4(Winter 1980–81):1–16.

47. Herbert J. Freudenberger and Gail North, *Women's Burnout* (New York: Doubleday & Co., 1985).

48. "Aerobic Instructor Burnout," *Reebok Instructor News* 1(1988):1, 4–5.

49. Pamela K. S. Patrick, *Health Care Worker Burnout: What it Is, What to Do about It* (Chicago: Blue Cross Association, Inquiry Books, 1981), 87–111.

50. Richard S. Lazarus and Susan Folkman, *Stress, Appraisal, and Coping* (New York: Springer, 1984).

15

Stress and the College Student

Jack's best friend put a gun to his own head and pulled the trigger. Aside from feeling a deep sense of loss, Jack was angry and disappointed. "I was his best friend. Why didn't he talk with me about this? Why did he have to kill himself?" It seemed that much of Jack's day was preoccupied by such questions. His schoolwork and his job outside of school were both affected.

Kim was a student from Taiwan who was sent, at great expense to her family, to the United States to attend college. What with the difficulty she had with studying in a second language and the pressure she felt to succeed in school (her parents sacrificed to send her to school in the United States), she was just keeping her head above water. She barely passed several courses and had to take incompletes in others. Her concern and frustration about her schoolwork overflowed into her social life. She found herself being angry and argumentative with friends and devoting so much time to her studies that she soon had no friends. Alone and lonely in a foreign country, not doing well in school, Kim was experiencing a great deal of stress.

Bill was a postman who was attending college at night to prepare for another career when he retired from the postal service. He was having problems with his marriage, his job, and his schooling. There never seemed enough time for any of these. His wife and daughter complained that with being at work and school he was seldom home, and when he was, he was always doing schoolwork. His supervisor at the post office claimed he always seemed tired and grouchy, and this was affecting his job performance. His professors told Bill that he was not turning in his work on time, nor was it of sufficient quality to pass his courses. When Bill finally left his family (his domestic problems became more and more serious), he brooded so much that he had less time, instead of more, to concentrate on the other aspects of his life.

These are but a few of the students enrolled in my stress management classes during *one semester*. They came to me to discuss these problems and to get guidance regarding how to manage them. Too often the life of the college student is depicted as "rah-rah," fraternity row, and football games. These are carefree and fun years for many students. For many others, though, college is just another life change to which they must adapt. They may be young and experiencing the

Although college is fraught with stress, many students believe the reward at the end makes it all worthwhile. What do you believe?

growing and developing pains of youth; they may be older students with too many other responsibilities to enjoy their schooling; or they may experience unique situations during the time they are supposed to be concentrating on their studies. In any case, college is very stressful for a large number of students.

There is plenty of evidence to support this view. Did you know that the average college student gains nine pounds during the freshman year?[1] Or that the biggest worry of college students is their study habits?[2] As you might expect, studies have found college students experience a lot of life change.[3,4] In fact, some experts believe the college years to be the most stressful in our lives.[5] On my own campus, a recent survey of the top health issues found stress to be second only to fitness and exercise. What do you think students on your campus would rate as the top three health issues? I'll bet stress is one of them.

The Younger College Student

The younger college student—one who enters college from high school or shortly thereafter—experiences stressors such as the dramatic life-style change from high school to college, grades, course overload, making friends, love and sex stressors, shyness, jealousy, and breakups.

Life-style Change

In chapter 5, the concept of life changes and their relationship to stress was presented. We discussed how the more life changes you experience, the more stress you will feel and the more likely it is that illness and disease will result. Just imagine all the life changes associated with attending college for the first time!

You attend high school while living at home, under the supervision of your parents, and usually without the need to work. There is plenty of time to meet friends after school, to do homework, and to relax. After all, the laundry is done by someone else, the meals are prepared by someone else, and the car may even be filled with gas by someone else. Food somehow, miraculously, appears in the refrigerator and cupboards, and the dust on the furniture and floors periodically vanishes.

Although many high school students do take on household responsibilities and do have jobs, generally the high school years are comfortable ones. When college begins, however, a dramatic change takes place. Time must be set aside for shopping, cooking, cleaning, doing the laundry, and a myriad of other routine chores. For the first time in many students' lives, they must assume responsibilities they never had to assume before. Further, no one keeps asking if they've done their homework. They must remember to fit this in between all their other activities.

However, in addition to all of the above, other changes are dictated by college life. Usually it requires finding an apartment or choosing a dormitory in which to live. A whole new network of same-sex and opposite-sex friends must be established. Schoolwork seems excessive, and it seems that not enough time is available to accomplish it. The fear of flunking permeates the air.

As though all of this weren't enough, the younger college student is confronted with several important tasks during that time of his or her life:

1. The development of competence
2. The management of emotions
3. The freeing of interpersonal relationships
4. The development of purpose
5. The development of integrity
6. The development of identity
7. The development of autonomy[6]

Considering all the changes listed above and the effects of stress on the immunological system, it is no small wonder that influenza epidemics and bouts of mononucleosis are frequent visitors to college campuses. Of course, the close living quarters exacerbate this situation. We also should not be surprised to learn that suicide is the second leading cause of death on college campuses.

Grades

The old story of the college professor who tossed the term papers down the stairs and graded those landing on the top three steps an *A*, those on the next three steps a *B*, and so on serves to emphasize the confusion about grading. Grades—students have to get them and professors have to give them. Unfortunately, both groups seem to gear too much of their behavior to them. Students see their goal as getting good grades instead of learning as much as they can. Professors see their goal as accurately differentiating between an *A* student and a *B* student rather than teaching as much as they can. As with all such generalizations, there are numerous exceptions. However, I think anyone associated with a college campus will agree that too much emphasis is placed upon grades. Levine's findings that only one in eight students reported not being interested in grades and that prospective employers do indeed peruse job candidates' files for grades support this conclusion.[7]

Students may even link their self-worth with their grades. For example, "Boy am I dumb. I flunked English." Instead, they'd be better off saying, "Boy I guess I didn't study long enough or well enough. I'll have to remember that for the next test."

Let's not kid ourselves, though. Grades are very important. They are important to students who want to go to graduate school or whose prospective employers consider them prior to hiring. They are also important to the university that wants its graduates considered competent and well educated. The university will use grades to weed out those who will not reflect well upon it. However, I have seen students so preoccupied by grades that they have let their physical health deteriorate. They give up exercise, don't have enough time to prepare balanced meals, or pull "all-nighters" so frequently that they walk around with bags under their eyes. I have seen other students so grade-conscious that they don't have a social life—they're always studying.

Course Overload

Related to the issue of grades is **course overload.** When we discussed role overload in the preceding chapter on occupational stress, we defined it as having too much to do and too little time in which to do it. Course overload is having too many courses or courses that are too difficult to do well during any one semester. In today's goal-oriented, rush-rush society, the more you accomplish in the shortest period of time, the better. The result is people rushing through their lives and experiencing very little. They achieve a lot of goals, but don't enjoy the trip to those goals.

Course overload results in a similar predicament. If I had a dollar for every student who, upon graduation, told me "I wish I had taken more courses I enjoyed" or "I wish I had devoted more time to my studies" or "I wish I had taken fewer courses each semester and learned more in the ones I did enroll in," I'd be wealthy today. Hoping to graduate in the shortest time possible, too many students overload themselves and suffer physically, psychologically, socially, and educationally for it. They may get physically ill, their emotions may be ready to explode, they may not have time for friends, and while taking more courses, they actually learn less. In this case, more is less.

Friendship

Giving up or changing old friendships and developing new ones is often a stressful activity associated with college life. Will people like me? Will I find someone with similar interests? How about boyfriends and girlfriends? Will people want to date me? All of these questions and many others are of concern during this phase of life. Old friends were accompanied by old routines—you knew just how much you could tell whom. Since friendship is a function of the degree of self-disclosure friends are willing to share, new friends require a period of testing to see just how much self-disclosure feels comfortable with this new person. To demonstrate this point, complete the task in the accompanying questionnaire on friendship and "acquaintanceship."

Think of a casual acquaintance and one of your closest friends. First circle the number of the statements below that you discuss with your friends in private conversation. Next, list the same set of statements you would discuss with a casual acquaintance.

1. Whether or not I have ever gone to a church other than my own (2.85)
2. The number of children I want to have after I am married (5.91)
3. How frequently I like to engage in sexual activity (10.02)
4. Whether I would rather live in an apartment or a house after getting married (3.09)
5. What birth control methods I would use in marriage (9.31)
6. What I do to attract a member of the opposite sex whom I like (8.54)
7. How often I usually go on dates (5.28)
8. Times that I have lied to my girlfriend or boyfriend (8.56)
9. My feelings about discussing sex with my friends (7.00)
10. How I might feel (or actually felt) if I saw my father hit my mother (9.50)
11. The degree of independence and freedom from family rules that I have (had) while living at home (5.39)
12. How often my family gets together (2.89)
13. Who my favorite relatives (aunts, uncles, and so on) are and why (5.83)
14. How I feel about getting old (6.36)
15. The parts of my body I am most ashamed for anyone to see (8.88)
16. My feelings about lending money (4.75)
17. My most pressing need for money right now (outstanding debts, some major purchases that are needed or desired) (6.88)
18. How much I spend for my clothes (7.17)
19. Laws that I would like to see put in effect (3.08)
20. Whether or not I have ever cried as an adult when I was sad (8.94)
21. How angry I get when people hurry me (5.33)
22. What animals make me nervous (3.44)
23. What it takes to hurt my feelings deeply (9.37)
24. What I am most afraid of (8.25)
25. How I really feel about the people I work for or with (7.29)
26. The kinds of things I do that I don't want people to watch (8.85)

The amount of disclosure is shown by the number of statements circled for each person. Intimacy of disclosure is found by adding up the numbers in parentheses for the circled statements, divided by the total number of statements circled. For instance, if you have circled statements 1, 4, 12, 19, and 22 for an acquaintance,

5 indicates the amount you would disclose, and 3.07 (2.85 + 3.09 + 2.89 + 3.08 + 3.44 = 15.35 ÷ 5) would be the intimacy of disclosure figure—not very much in this case.*

As you can see by the results of the friendship and acquaintanceship questionnaire you just completed, self-disclosure is a vital ingredient in friendship. Without self-disclosure of a significant degree, your relationship stops at the acquaintance level. Although acquaintances may help alleviate our loneliness they don't provide the social support that friends do, which we have learned can act as a buffer for our stress.

Love

With old friends and family back home, many students fill the void by new love relationships. These relationships themselves, however, may create new stresses. Any new relationship requires a new set of rules and standards. How often do we see each other? How often do we telephone? Where should we go on dates? Who should pay? With whose friends should we hang out?

In addition, some love relationships involve two people who are different types of lovers. To understand this point better, complete the following scale from *The Colours of Love* by John Lee. If you are now involved in a love relationship, perhaps you'll want your lover to complete the scale as well.

To find out what type of lover you are, answer each question as it applies to your boyfriends, girlfriends, lovers, or spouse.

A = almost always
U = usually
R = rarely
N = never (or almost never)

___ 1. You have a clearly defined image of your desired partner.
___ 2. You felt a strong emotional reaction to him or her on the first encounter.
___ 3. You are preoccupied with thoughts about him or her.
___ 4. You are eager to see him or her every day.
___ 5. You discuss future plans and a wide range of interests and experiences.
___ 6. Tactile, sensual contact is important to the relationship.
___ 7. Sexual intimacy was achieved early in the relationship.
___ 8. You feel that success in love is more important than success in other areas of your life.
___ 9. You want to be in love or have love as security.
___ 10. You try to force him or her to show more feeling and commitment.
___ 11. You declared your love first.
___ 12. You are willing to suffer neglect and abuse from him or her.
___ 13. You deliberately restrain frequency of contact with him or her.

Source: D. A. Taylor and I. Altman, "Intimacy-Scaled Stimuli for Use in Research on Interpersonal Exchange" (Naval Medical Research Institute Technical Report No. 9, MF 022, o1.03–1002, May 1966).

_____ 14. You restrict discussion and display of your feelings with him or her.

_____ 15. If a breakup is coming, you feel it is better to drop the other person before being dropped.

_____ 16. You play the field and have several persons who could love you.

_____ 17. You are more interested in pleasure than in emotional attachment.

_____ 18. You feel the need to love someone you have grown accustomed to.

_____ 19. You believe that the test of time is the only sure way to find real love.

_____ 20. You don't believe that true love happens suddenly or dramatically.

If you answered A or U to 1–8 you are probably an erotic lover. If you answered A or U to 3–4 and 8–12, your love style tends to be manic. If you answered A or U to 13–17 and R or N to the other questions, you are probably a ludic lover. If you answered A or U to 17–20, together with R or N for the other statements, your love style tends to be storgic.

Some researchers have identified four basic types of love: erotic, ludic, storgic, and manic. **Erotic love (eros)** is a passionate, all-enveloping love. The heart races, a fluttering appears in the stomach, and there's a shortness of breath when erotic lovers meet. **Ludic love (ludus)** is a playful, flirtatious love. It involves no long-term commitment and is basically for amusement. Ludic love is usually played with several partners at once. **Storgic love (storge)** is a calm, companionate love. Storgic lovers are quietly affectionate and have goals of marriage and children for the relationship. **Manic love (mania)** is a combination of erotic and ludic love. A manic lover's needs for affection are insatiable. He or she is often racked with highs of irrational joy, lows of anxiety and depression, and bouts of extreme jealousy. Manic attachments seldom develop into lasting love.

Imagine that a ludic lover is in a love relationship with a storgic lover. One is playing games with no intention of a lasting or exclusive relationship, and the other is thinking marriage and children. Love relationships on college campuses may be stressful because of misunderstandings regarding the types of love involved.

Sex

One of the assignments in my undergraduate stress management class is for students to keep a journal of stressors they encounter. Invariably, several female students will describe the pressure they are receiving—from their female friends as well as their boyfriends—to engage in sexual intercourse. It's the talk of the dorm or sorority house. Although no male student has ever described a similar stressor, I'm convinced that the pressure to be sexually active is at least as great for male students as it is for female students. Why else would young males feel compelled to exaggerate their sexual experiences or describe an enjoyable, relaxing evening as a Roman orgy? I believe that males are just less apt to admit that they feel stressed by pressure to be sexually active.

To compound this stressor, the older public looks at college students as a promiscuous, pill-popping, irresponsible group of rascals and only tolerates them because they are young and soon will learn better. At age nineteen, however, approximately one-half of the females have never experienced sexual intercourse. Yet even college students tend to exaggerate the sexual experience of their compatriots.

To determine just how much you really know about sexuality and about the sexual behavior of your peers, and how any misconceptions affect the degree of stress you experience, answer the true-false questions below.

___ 1. By the time they graduate from college, just about all students have masturbated.

___ 2. Almost all college graduates have experienced sexual intercourse at least once.

___ 3. Masturbation is a habit of the young and is eliminated as one becomes an adult.

___ 4. Any sexual behavior between consenting adults done in private is legal.

___ 5. As long as "safe sex" is practiced, both pregnancy and sexually transmitted diseases can be prevented.

___ 6. Masturbation can result in either physical illness or psychological harm.

___ 7. Sexual fantasies are wishes you have for participation in sex.

___ 8. Oral-genital sex is abnormal and perverse.

All of the statements above are false. Let's look more closely at them one at a time.

1. Most researchers have found that approximately 90 percent of men and 60 percent of women have masturbated at some time. Stated another way, approximately 10 percent of men and 40 percent of women have *not* had masturbatory experience.

2. As stated earlier, about 50 percent of nineteen-year-old women and a little over 70 percent of nineteen-year-old men have experienced sexual intercourse. Obviously, this number will increase by the time students are old enough to graduate. However, when I studied college students' sexual behavior I found that 14 percent of seniors had never engaged in coitus.[8]

3. Masturbation is engaged in throughout one's life. Whether because one's sexual partner is unavailable, pregnant, or ill, or just for the pleasure of it, masturbation is practiced by adults at all ages.

4. There are sodomy laws in many states which specifically outlaw certain sexual behaviors, even if those engaging in these behaviors consent to them and perform them in private. Oral-genital sex, anal sexual intercourse, and homosexual activities are usually the sex acts prohibited. However, coitus between unmarried people is also against the law in many states.

5. We shall discuss sexually transmitted diseases, and AIDS in particular, shortly. For now you should know that there is no such thing as safe sex. Anytime coitus occurs, for instance, there is the chance of a pregnancy resulting (there is no *100 percent* effective means of birth control) and the

possibility of contracting one of several sexually transmitted diseases. However, there are ways to engage in "safer" sex; that is, decreasing the chances of conception or of disease occurring—for example, using a condom.

6. Experts agree that the only danger of masturbation is the psychological harm resulting from guilt, shame, or embarrassment one associates with it. If people were to learn how prevalent masturbation is, how it doesn't interfere with normal relationships or the ability to sometime later be sexually functional, and that it usually continues throughout one's life (albeit at a lesser frequency), masturbation might not be associated with guilt and other negative feelings and thereby not create any harm at all.

7. Because you fantasize about something doesn't necessarily mean you would actually like to experience that fantasy. For example, when you become angry with a professor, you might dream about slashing the tires on his or her car. However, most of us would not do that even if we knew we wouldn't get caught (at least I hope my students reading this agree!). Likewise, sexual thoughts and fantasies may or may not be events we would like to experience. We shouldn't feel guilty or embarrassed about our sexual thoughts; that can only do us harm. However, we should be held accountable for our sexual *behavior.*

8. Approximately 60 percent of college students report they have engaged in oral-genital sexual activities at least once. Whether one chooses to view oral-genital sex as perverse depends on one's values. However, given its frequency, it certainly cannot be considered abnormal.

When I studied the sexual behavior of college students, I found the results that appear in table 15.1. Although that data might appear to be outdated, the results are remarkably consistent with other researchers. For example, sociologists John DeLamater and Patricia MacCorquodale[9] studied 1,141 students at the University of Wisconsin and found that 75 percent of the male students and 60 percent of the female students had experienced sexual intercourse; and Arafat and Cotton[10] found that approximately 89 percent of male college students and 61 percent of female college students have masturbated.

Do these results surprise you? Does the information regarding sexual myths surprise you? If so, don't worry. You are probably in good company, with significant numbers of your classmates also believing many of the same myths about the sexual behavior of college students. Given the misconceptions you have regarding how sexually active you "should be" if you were "normal," the pressure for you to engage in sex can be intense. This pressure comes from both outside yourself as well as from within; for example, "If I were normal. . . ." The pressure might lead to stress that interferes with your health, grades, and interpersonal relationships. Hopefully, a more realistic perception of the sexual behavior of your classmates will help you see yourself as not unusual in your own sexual behavior, and thereby help you to better deal with the pressure to be sexually active whether you are experienced sexually or inexperienced. (Remember, in either case you are in the company of a large number of other college students.)

Table 15.1
College Students' Sexual Behavior

Independent Variable	Number	Incidence of Masturbation (%)	Frequency[a] of Masturbation	Incidence of Sexual Intercourse (%)
1. Sex				
male	52	84.62	6.73	76.93
female	75	52.00	1.82	69.33
2. Marital status				
married	21	61.90	2.81	100.00
not married	106	66.04	4.04	72.45
3. Class in school				
Freshman				
male		80.00		
female		33.33		
total	27	51.85	4.07	51.85
Sophomore				
male		100.00		
female		50.00		
total	29	55.17	1.62	72.41
Junior				
male		90.48		
female		57.14		
total	42	73.81	3.86	76.19
Senior				
male		75.00		
female		76.92		
total	29	75.86	5.79	86.21
4. Race				
Negro	7	33.33	0.57	55.56
Caucasian	111	76.24	4.17	80.20
other	9	42.86	2.22	85.71

Source: Jerrold S. Greenberg, "The Masturbatory Behavior of College Students," *Psychology in the Schools* 9(1972):427–32. © 1972 Clinical Psychology Publishing Co., Brandon, VT. Reprinted by permission.

[a]Frequency of masturbation given as the number of times per month.

AIDS

There is a good deal of concern both on and off college campuses regarding the spread of sexually transmitted diseases—in particular, acquired immune deficiency syndrome (AIDS). This section describes the causes, treatments, and means of prevention of AIDS with the hope that knowledge will aid in alleviating undue stress regarding your sexual behavior and will help you prevent AIDS from developing in the first place.

Acquired immune deficiency syndrome is caused by a virus called the human immunodeficiency virus (HIV). AIDS results in an ineffectiveness of the immunological system so that its victims develop opportunistic infections that eventually lead to death. The Centers for Disease Control reports that as of April 25, 1988, over 60,000 Americans have died of AIDS.

There is no known cure for AIDS, although there are some drugs which can slow the course of the disease and prolong the life of the AIDS victim. The most effective of these drugs is azidothymidine (AZT).

HIV is transmitted through bodily fluids such as blood and semen. High-risk groups are homosexuals, intravenous drug users, and infants born to women with the virus in their bloodstream. However, public health officials would rather direct attention to high-risk *behaviors* rather than high-risk *groups* since membership in the group is immaterial—it's what you *do* that can give you AIDS, not what group you belong to. If you share needles with others (as I.V. drug users are prone to do), if you engage in oral or genital sex without using a condom or in anal sex even if you do use a condom, or if you have multiple sex partners, you are more likely to contract AIDS than if you didn't engage in these high-risk behaviors. In spite of some widespread misconceptions, AIDS is not transmitted casually; that is, it cannot be contracted by touching a person with AIDS, or sharing eating utensils, or swimming in the same swimming pool, or being in the same classroom, or being stung by a mosquito, or kissing.[11] You also cannot acquire AIDS by giving blood; and since 1985, the blood supply has been screened so that contracting AIDS through a blood transfusion is only a remote possibility. AIDS is a *sexually* transmitted disease.

To alleviate some distress you may have regarding AIDS, engage in behaviors that can make you less prone to contracting it. There are several things you can do to protect yourself. The best approach in terms of prevention is to abstain from sex: oral sex, coitus, and anal sex. If you decide that alternative is not acceptable to you, the next best approach is to maintain a monogamous sexual relationship with someone you know to be AIDS-free. The problem here, though, is determining that someone is AIDS-free. The test for AIDS actually tests for the presence of antibodies that you develop when having come in contact with HIV. Since the test may not identify the presence of these antibodies for anywhere up to a year after exposure, even if someone had a negative AIDS test today, if that person had sex with someone else within the past year, he or she may still possess the virus. What the experts say is really true: When you sleep with someone, you are sleeping with that person's previous sexual partners and those previous partners' sexual partners. In any case, should you engage in sex, always use a condom made of latex rather than animal skin (such as lambskin) since the animal skin condom may be too porous to prevent the virus from penetrating.

It should be noted that AIDS is only one of several sexually transmitted diseases (STDs) that are threats to health. Syphilis, gonorrhea, chlamydia, herpes genitalis, and pelvic inflammatory disease are others which also need to be paid attention to.[12] Many of the same preventive measures we've discussed regarding AIDS are also effective against the other STDs.

This little bit of knowledge should help you take greater control of preventing AIDS and other sexually transmitted diseases. This is one instance when an internal locus of control can actually save your life! Use this information and AIDS will be less of a stressor for you.

Shyness

Since entering college is a new experience, and the people and surroundings are new, it is not surprising to find many students feeling and acting shy. Shyness can be a significant stressor for some college students, but it is one, as we shall see later, that can be effectively responded to.

To be shy is to be afraid of people, especially people who for some reason are emotionally threatening: strangers because of their novelty or uncertainty, authorities who wield power, members of the opposite sex who represent potential intimate encounters.

Shyness can be a mental handicap as crippling as the most severe of physical handicaps, and its consequences can be devastating:

Shyness makes it difficult to meet new people, make friends, or enjoy potentially good experiences.

It prevents you from speaking up for your rights and expressing your own opinions and values.

Shyness limits positive evaluations by others of your personal strengths.

It encourages self-consciousness and an excessive preoccupation with your own reactions.

Shyness makes it hard to think clearly and communicate effectively.

Negative feelings like depression, anxiety, and loneliness typically accompany shyness.[13]

College students may experience stress due to their shyness with professors, club leaders, or people whom they would like to date. This shyness is uncomfortable and, as cited above, may have severe consequences.

Jealousy

College students need to make new friends—both same-sex and opposite-sex ones. Making new friends is ego-threatening ("What if they don't want to be friends with me?"), requires a risk, takes time, and takes a good deal of energy. After all of that, friendship becomes comfortable. We know who we can go places with, who we can confide in, and who we can receive love from. It is understandable, then, that we should value these friendships greatly and become protective and defensive when they are threatened. Even if the threat is only a perceived one—not a real one—jealousy may result.

Jealousy is the fear of losing our property, whether that be our lover, friend, status, or power. It has two basic components: (1) a feeling of battered pride and (2) a feeling that our property rights have been violated.[14] We respond to jealousy by either protecting our egos—for example, arguing with our friends or trying to get even—or by trying to improve the relationship. Obviously the second way is preferable.

Jealousy is a stressor some college students experience. It becomes stressful whether we are jealous ourselves or our friends or lovers are the jealous ones.

Breakups

Jealousy sometimes becomes so stressful that it results in a breakup of the relationship. One study found that almost half of steadily dating couples in college split up.[15] Sometimes relationships break up because the partners are too dissimilar (one may be interested in sports and the other in the theatre) or because they have different expectations of the relationship (one may be a ludic lover and the other a storgic lover). Since younger college students are at a stage of life in which they are experimenting with different kinds of relationships, it is not surprising that many of these relationships do not become permanent. Younger college students usually experience several breakups of relationships during the college years, and these breakups can be quite stressful.

The Older College Student

Many college students are not in their early twenties. More and more, college student populations include a large percentage of older students. In fact, the Census Bureau reports that during the 1980–81 academic year the majority of college students were twenty-two or older. Students aged twenty-five to twenty-nine increased from 11.4 percent in 1970 to 14.2 percent in 1981, and the proportion of students aged thirty to thirty-four doubled between 1970 and 1981 (from 5 percent to 9.9 percent).[16] These older students have been in the armed services, or developed careers, or raised families, or were engaged in some other activities that led them to postpone their college educations. Those other responsibilities well-managed or completed, they are now entering college. These students experience stressors similar to those experienced by younger college students: grades, course overload, jealousy, and breakups. However, they also experience some stressors that are unique to them. We shall briefly discuss three of these: mixing career and school, handling family and school responsibilities concurrently, and doubting about their abilities to do well in college.

Career and School

The year was 1964, and I was teaching in a high school in New York City. The students were from Harlem and had problems that were foreign to me. Still, I was very concerned with responding to their needs and, within the limits that existed, helping them to improve the qualities of their lives. In other words, I was committed to my job. As the last period of the school day ended, however, I had to rush to the subway to take a thirty-minute train ride to C.C.N.Y., where I was taking twelve credits toward my master's degree. My classes were over at about 9:30 P.M., which is when I rushed to the subway to take a one-hour train ride back to my apartment in Brooklyn.

This situation is not unique. Now that I teach on a college campus, I see many students experiencing what I experienced. I recall one student, for example, whose job required her to be in Europe Thursday through Sunday—she was an airline flight attendant—but she was taking several college courses on Monday and Tuesday. Others have had careers that they were committed to—students of mine who were social workers, accountants, and police officers come to mind—but were enrolled in college, too. The need to do well with a career may cause stress, and the need to do well at school may also cause stress. Even though each of these stressors may be manageable alone, when they coexist there may be an overload. The result may be illness or disease.

Family and School

Not only are many older college students working, but many have family responsibilities as well. A number of students have discussed with me the problem of what to do with after-work time. Should they work on their term paper? Study for an exam? Read next week's chapter? Or should they play with their kids or spend time with their spouses? Will the in-laws understand if they don't visit because they're doing schoolwork?

It takes a very understanding spouse to provide psychological support for a student who has family and work responsibilities too. It is tiring and often frustrating to have so much to do in a day. It is stressful and may be unhealthy as well. A spouse who can provide those extra few minutes with the kids that the student-parent can't, who can take on more than his or her share of the household chores, and who can provide a shoulder to lean on and an ear to listen, can go a long way in intervening between stress and illness for the older college student.

Not to be forgotten in this discussion is the financial investment necessary to attend college. Older students who must support a family must decide if the investment in education is worthwhile. There will be a payoff down the road—either in increased income or in improved life-style that a more enjoyable or less demanding job may afford. Often, however, a financial sacrifice is required by the student and his or her family while the schooling takes place. This sacrifice is easier to bear if the whole family believes it worthwhile and is willing to put off immediate pleasures to achieve long-range goals. If the older student has to continually justify the expense of college, or if the family's sacrifice is periodically brought up to make him or her feel guilty, the stress associated with college will be greater than otherwise.

Self-doubt

Some colleges are recognizing that returning college students—those who dropped out years ago—and older, first-time college students have all sorts of doubts about their ability to be successful in their studies. Consequently, they are offering counseling programs for these students. These self-doubts are understandable, since our society too often perceives learning as a young person's activity. How can I compete with young, bright people? How can I do well when I'm also working full-time? How can I pass my courses when I need to devote time to my family? How will I be able to spend as much time at the library as students who live on campus? I don't have someone to study with or professors to consult with frequently as does the student living on campus. I've forgotten how to study; I haven't taken an exam in ages. These are some of the stressful concerns of the older college student.

Interventions

Interventions can diminish the stress of college for both the younger and older student. These interventions can be at the levels of life situation, perception, emotional arousal, or physiological arousal.

Life-Situation Interventions

Students entering college are bombarded with numerous life changes. To prevent adding to these needed adjustments, other aspects of life should be made as routine as possible. Since more life changes mean more stress, entering college is not the time to take on added job responsibilities, to have a baby, or to break up old relationships. I've long suspected that the large number of college dropouts

is more a function of stress than of grades. When we consider that most students enter college, move out of their homes, leave old friends, make new friends, accept new responsibilities, live in a new town, it is not surprising that all of these life changes would be stressful to them. Recognizing this situation, at least two suggestions seem sensible: (1) that high schools teach stress management and (2) that colleges offer stress management workshops during orientation sessions for entering students. More and more of this is occurring, but still not enough. High school graduates are not only entering college; some are entering the military, some are taking full-time jobs, and some are raising families. In spite of what they do when they leave high school, their lives change dramatically and swiftly. They should be helped to deal with this change by managing the stress accompanying it.

Another life-situation intervention responds to the need to make new friends. The more people you meet, the more likely you are to find a new friend. Joining clubs, participating in intramurals, going to parties and dances, and working with other students to improve campus life are all good ways to meet people. Remember, however, that the idea is to improve your health—psychological and physical—so don't engage in unhealthy or dysfunctional activities just to be part of a group. I've had several students talk with me about their problem with abusing alcohol because "all" their friends spend their time drinking at an off-campus hangout. When we looked more closely at the situation, we found that not "all" the friends drank and that friendships could be maintained with those who did drink without having to get drunk oneself. Once students realized that it was they, not their friends, who were responsible for their drinking, they were better able to control it.

Fifteen Steps to a More Confident You

To respond to stressors associated with shyness and self-doubt, try some of the following suggestions. These suggestions come from one of the country's authorities on shyness and the director of the Stanford University Shyness Clinic.

1. Recognize your strengths and weaknesses and set your goals accordingly.
2. Decide what you value, what you believe in, what you realistically would like your life to be like. Take inventory of your library of stored scripts and bring them up to date, in line with the psychological space you are in now, so they will serve you where you are headed.
3. Determine what your roots are. By examining your past, seek out the lines of continuity and the decisions that have brought you to your present place. Try to understand and forgive those who have hurt you and not helped when they could have. Forgive yourself for mistakes, sins, failures, and past embarrassments. Permanently bury all negative self-remembrances after you have sifted out any constructive value they may provide. The bad past lives on in your memory only as long as you let it be a tenant. Prepare an eviction notice immediately. Give the room to memories of your past successes, however minor.
4. Guilt and shame have limited personal value in shaping your behavior toward positive goals. Don't allow yourself to indulge in them.
5. Look for the causes of your behavior in physical, social, economic, and political aspects of your current situation and not in personality *defects* in you.
6. Remind yourself that there are alternative views to every event. "Reality" is never more than shared agreements among people to call it the same way rather than as each one separately sees it. This enables you to be more tolerant in your interpretation of others' intentions and more generous in dismissing what might appear to be rejections or put-downs of you.
7. Never say bad things about yourself; especially, never attribute to yourself irreversible negative traits, like "stupid," "ugly," "uncreative," "a failure," "incorrigible."
8. Don't allow others to criticize *you* as a person; it is your *specific actions* that are open for evaluation and available for improvement—accept such constructive feedback graciously if it will help you.

9. Remember that sometimes failure and disappointment are blessings in disguise, telling you the goals were not right for you, the effort was not worth it, and a bigger letdown later on may be avoided.

10. Do not tolerate people, jobs, and situations that make you feel inadequate. If you can't change them or yourself enough to make you feel more worthwhile, walk on out, or pass them by. Life is too short to waste time on downers.

11. Give yourself the time to relax, to meditate, to listen to yourself, to enjoy hobbies and activities you can do alone. In this way, you can get in touch with yourself.

12. Practice being a social animal. Enjoy feeling the energy that other people transmit, the unique qualities and range of variability of our brothers and sisters. Imagine what their fears and insecurities might be and how you could help them. Decide what you need from them and what you have to give. Then, let them know that you are ready and open to sharing.

13. Stop being so overprotective about your ego; it is tougher and more resilient than you imagine. It bruises but never breaks. Better it should get hurt occasionally from an emotional commitment that didn't work out as planned than get numbed from the emotional insulation of playing it too cool.

14. Develop long-range goals in life, with highly specific short-range subgoals. Develop realistic means to achieve these subgoals. Evaluate your progress regularly and be the first to pat yourself on the back or whisper a word of praise in your ear. You don't have to worry about being unduly modest if no one else hears you boasting.

15. You are not an object to which bad things just happen, a passive nonentity hoping, like a garden slug, to avoid being stepped on. You are the culmination of millions of years of evolution of our species, of your parents' dreams, of God's image. You are a unique individual who, as an active actor in life's drama, can make things happen. You can change the direction of your entire life any time you choose to do so. With confidence in yourself, obstacles turn into challenges and challenges into accomplishments. Shyness then recedes, because, instead of always preparing for and worrying about how you will live your life, you forget yourself as you become absorbed in the living of it.

For jealousy-related stress, Walster and Walster recommend three steps.[17] The first step involves finding out exactly what is making you jealous. Key questions to ask are "What was going on just before you started feeling jealous?" and "What are you afraid of?" As we discussed earlier, you're probably afraid of losing something (for example, love, self-esteem, property, status, or power). The second step asks you to put your jealous feeling in proper perspective. Is it really so awful that your friend is interested in someone else? Aren't you interested in other people as well? Is your jealousy irrational? What's the difference between *having* to have this person love you and *wishing* this person loved you? Is it really true that you couldn't stand to lose this person's love? Or is it that you'd *like* not to?

Lastly, you can negotiate a "contract" with the other person. This contract should help you be less jealous but must not be too restrictive on the other person. To expect your friend to lunch only with you might be unfair. To expect your friend to lunch with you on Tuesdays and Thursdays, on the other hand, might assure you're spending time together while allowing each of you the freedom to spend time with other people.

Other life-situation interventions are listed below.

1. Limit the courses in which you enroll to a number you can handle without overloading yourself.
2. Improve your communication with lovers so both of you have the same expectations for, and understanding of, the relationship.
3. The best way to manage a breakup is to seek out new relationships. Get involved with other people—and not only romantically, by the way.
4. To coordinate family and school responsibilities, schedule each of these. Working out specific times for schoolwork with your family will assure you're getting your work done and your family is not being disappointed you're not with them. Working out specific times to be with your family will assure that you do not overlook their needs.

When intervening at the life-situation level, don't forget some obvious resources. You can consult with your professor, seek assistance from personnel at the campus health center, speak with your advisor, or get help from the community health department. These and other resources have proven valuable to many of my students and I believe they will for you as well. Help is all around you if you look and ask for it.

| Perception Interventions | As we've stated many times in this book, as important as external events are in relation to stress, so is your perception of those events. The following are some ways to perceive the stressors of college life as less distressing. |

1. Use the self-talk described in chapter 7 to perceive shyness and jealousy as less threatening. Questions such as "What am I really afraid of? How probable is it that this thing I fear will happen? How bad is it if it does happen?" will help to view the shyness or jealousy more realistically.
2. Use selective awareness to focus upon the positive aspects of college. The opportunity to learn new things, meet new people, prepare for a future you are looking forward to, and the opportunity to find out how capable you really are should occupy your thoughts rather than how difficult or time-consuming it is or how much time it requires away from your family and your job.

3. Smell the roses along the way—literally and figuratively. I love the look and smell of my campus. Whether it be winter or summer, spring or fall, the trees, bushes, buildings, and grounds have a pleasing nature. I sometimes walk off the path to hear the crunch of snow under my feet, and I've been known to walk right up to a flowering crab apple tree to smell its fragrance. Maybe your campus isn't as pretty as mine, or maybe it's prettier. In any case, there are things about your campus that, if you paid attention to them, would make the time you spend there more pleasant.

4. When looking at all of your responsibilities, you might feel overloaded. However, if you were to write a schedule for them, you would probably recognize that you do have enough time for it all. Only when viewed collectively do they appear overwhelming.

Emotional Arousal Interventions

As with other stressors, college-related ones can be managed at the emotional level by regular practice of relaxation techniques. Chapters 8, 9, and 10 describe some relaxation techniques that you can use. When I mention this to groups of people who have so little time (for example, students who work full-time and also have family responsibilities) I'm frequently told that there just aren't forty minutes a day for relaxation. I tell them that if they don't have the time then they, in particular, need the regular relaxation. The paradox is that those without the time probably need the practice more than those who can fit it in. At this point in your reading, you should recognize that we all have the time; we just choose to use it for something else. You can rearrange how you use your time so you can practice a relaxation technique regularly. It's up to you!

Physiological Arousal Interventions

Regular exercise will use the stress products you build up. The body is prepared to do something physical, and exercise will afford it a healthy way to make use of this preparation. Read chapter 12 if you are unsure about how to begin a regular exercise program.

College students are more fortunate than others relative to physiological arousal intervention since they usually have access to exercise facilities and equipment. They can join intramural teams, participate in recreational sports hours (these usually occur during the noon hour or late afternoon or evening), or do exercise alone (for example, jog around campus or shoot baskets).

College life can be made less stressful with attention paid to managing college-related stressors. You're probably tired of reading this, *but* whether it's stressful or not is really up to you.

Summary

1. College life can be quite stressful because it requires adapting to a dramatic life change. College life involves assuming greater responsibility for one's life, making new friends, a great deal of study, and learning about a new environment.

2. Specific stressors experienced by college students include striving for good grades, coping with a greater amount of schoolwork, making friends, managing pressure to be sexually active, being shy, becoming jealous, and breaking up with a dating partner.

3. The typical college student today is older than the college student of past years. The majority of college students are over twenty-two years of age.

4. Older college students experience stressors unique to their situations. They must juggle career, school, and family responsibilities.

5. Older college students often doubt their abilities to return to school, achieve academically, or interact well with classmates who may be much younger.

6. Colleges and high schools need to offer stress management educational experiences to their students to help them manage the degree of change that occurs upon graduating from high school and entering college.

7. To manage jealousy-related stress, determine what makes you jealous, put your jealous feelings in proper perspective, and/or negotiate a contract with the other person.

Notes

1. "On the Pulse," *Washington Post,* 6 February 1985, 5.

2. Jim Pond, "Survey Shows Studying Freshmen's Top Worry," *The Diamondback,* 15 April 1985, 1, 3.

3. Jerrold S. Greenberg, "A Study of the Effects of Stress on the Health of College Students: Implications for School Health Education," *Health Education* 15(1984):11–15.

4. Jerrold S. Greenberg, "A Study of Stressors in the College Student Population," *Health Education* 12(1981):8–12.

5. F. O'Brien and K. Sothers, "The UW-SP Stress Management Program," *Health Values* 8(1984):35–40.

6. Nicholas J. Long and Jody Long, *Conflict and Comfort in College* (Belmont, Calif.: Wadsworth, 1970), 6.

7. A. Levine, *When Dreams and Heroes Died* (San Francisco: Jossey-Bass, 1983).

8. Jerrold S. Greenberg, "The Masturbatory Behavior of College Students," *Psychology in the Schools* 9(1972):427–32.

9. John DeLamater and Patricia MacCorquodale, *Premarital Sexuality: Attitudes, Relationships, Behavior* (Madison: University of Wisconsin Press, 1979).

10. I. Arafat and W. L. Cotton, "Masturbation Practices of Males and Females," *Journal of Sex Research* 10(1974):293–307.

11. C. Everett Koop, *Understanding AIDS: A Message from the Surgeon General* (Washington, D.C.: Department of Health and Human Services, 1988).

12. Jerrold S. Greenberg et al., *Sexuality: Insights and Issues,* 2d ed. (Dubuque, Iowa: Wm. C. Brown, 1989).

13. Philip G. Zimbardo, *Shyness: What It Is and What to Do about It* (Reading, Mass.: Addison-Wesley, 1977), 12.

14. Elaine Walster and G. William Walster, *A New Look at Love* (Reading, Mass.: Addison-Wesley, 1978), 87.

15. C. Hill, Z. Rubin, and L. Peplau, "Breakups before Marriage: The End of 103 Affairs," in *Divorce and Separation,* eds. G. Levinger and O. Moles (New York: Basic Books, 1979).

16. Keith B. Richburg, "College Students' Average Age Rises," *Washington Post,* 14 August 1985, A4.

17. Walster and Walster, *A New Look at Love,* 91–93.

CHAPTER

▽
16
▽

Stress and Sex Roles

A father and his son were involved in a car accident in which the father was killed, and the son was seriously injured. The father was pronounced dead at the scene of the accident and his body taken to a local mortuary. The son was taken by ambulance to a local hospital and was immediately wheeled into an operating room. A surgeon was called. Upon seeing the patient, the attending surgeon exclaimed, "Oh, my God, it's my son." Can you explain this? (Keep in mind the father who was killed in the accident is not a stepfather, nor is the attending physician the boy's stepfather.) The answer appears at the bottom of the page.*

The bank was a typical one: leather upholstered chairs, wooden gates with swinging doors, red carpet, caged-in tellers, and cheap replicas of attractive paintings on the walls. It didn't look like a studio setting, yet a TV camera hanging conspicuously in the corner of the room recorded all the exciting goings-on. I was there with my wife seeking approval of a mortgage well beyond our means but just this side of our aspirations. The bank manager who, to her credit, sized up the situation quickly, was asking all the usual embarrassing questions—"How much did you make last year? Can you prove it? Whom do you owe money? Is your car paid for?"

Well, the trouble was just beginning. It soon came time for my wife to answer the same questions. The first one did it—"Do you work?" How innocent those three little words sounded. Nevertheless, I knew what to expect as I leaned back in my chair in an unconscious nonverbal expression that said, "I don't want any part of this one!" "I most certainly do," was my wife's answer.

"How much do you earn?"
"I don't earn anything. I work at home."
"Oh, you're just a housewife."
"No I'm not *just* a housewife."
"Sorry, I didn't mean any offense."

*The surgeon was the boy's mother.

Sorry or not the damage was done. Had I bothered to, I'm sure I could have objectively verified what I knew to be my wife's biomedical condition—elevated blood pressure, increased heart rate, rapid and shallow breathing, and tense muscles. By now you recognize the stress response.

Women experience stressors, such as the one just described, that are based in sex-role stereotyping. Their work in the home is not valued, they earn less than they should earn when working outside the home, or they are expected to be "superwomen"; that is, excellent lovers, wives, mothers, and employees. However, men, too, experience stress as a result of sex-role stereotyping. Do you think it's easy being ashamed to show fear? Men are supposed to be strong, and many consider fear a sign of weakness. Don't you think it stressful to have the responsibility of being the "breadwinner"? How do you think the "breadlosers" feel?

Both males and females, then, suffer from sex-role stereotyping. The accompanying box on stereotyping describes what we all are doing to one another. As you read it, see if you recognize yourself or others you know.

The point of the box on sex-role stereotyping is that we are often shackled by others' conceptions of who and what we *should* be (our sexuality), rather than allowed to evolve into who we are *naturally*. The root of the word naturally (nature) is important here. If we do not develop into who we naturally are, we become unnatural.

This chapter will look at stressors associated with sex roles and how these stressors can be managed. We will consider how sex roles are learned, the effects of working outside and inside the home, and the contribution of sexual stressors to our sense of well-being.

Sex-Role Stereotyping

He is playing masculine. She is playing feminine. She is playing feminine because he is playing masculine. He is playing masculine because she is playing feminine.

He is playing the kind of man that he thinks the kind of woman she is playing ought to admire. She is playing the kind of woman that she thinks the kind of man he is playing ought to desire.

If he were not playing masculine, he might well be more feminine than she is—except when she is playing very feminine. If she were not playing feminine, she might well be more masculine than he—except when he is playing very masculine.

So he plays harder. And she plays—softer.

He wants to make sure that she could never be more masculine than he. She wants to make sure that he could never be more feminine than she. He therefore seeks to destroy the femininity in himself. She therefore seeks to destroy the masculinity in herself.

She is supposed to admire him for the masculinity in him that she fears in herself. He is supposed to desire her for the femininity in her that he despises in himself.

He desires her for her femininity, which is his femininity, but which he can never lay claim to. She admires him for his masculinity, which is her masculinity, but which she can never lay claim to. Since he may only love his own femininity in her, he envies her femininity.

Since she may only love her own masculinity in him, she envies him his masculinity.

The envy poisons their love.

Learning Sex Roles

My son Todd was eight years old and in the third grade when he brought home a worksheet from school that included these fill-in statements (the correct answers appear in parentheses):

The boy (climbed) the tree to look in the nest.

John was (pushed) in the mud when children were playing.

Mary (washed) the dishes for mother.

Something girls wear. (apron)

He was being taught, albeit unintentionally, that boys are active (they climb and push) and that girls wash dishes and wear aprons. There are, however, many male dishwashers and many men who wear aprons—for example, carpenters and butchers—as well as many active women.

He, coveting her unattainable femininity, decides to punish her. She, coveting his unattainable masculinity, decides to punish him. He denigrates her femininity—which he is supposed to desire and which he really envies—and becomes more aggressively masculine. She feigns disgust at his masculinity—which she is supposed to admire and which she really envies—and becomes more fastidiously feminine. He is becoming less and less what he wants to be. She is becoming less and less what she wants to be. But now he is more manly than ever, and she is more womanly than ever.

Her femininity, growing more dependently supine, becomes contemptible. His masculinity, growing more oppressively domineering, becomes intolerable. At last she loathes what she has helped his masculinity to become. At last he loathes what he has helped her femininity to become.

So far, it has all been very symmetrical. But we have left one thing out.

The world belongs to what his masculinity has become.

The reward for what his masculinity has become is power. The reward for what her femininity has become is only security, which his power can bestow upon her. If he were to yield to what her femininity has become, he would be yielding to contemptible incompetence. If she were to acquire what his masculinity has become, she would participate in intolerable coerciveness.

She is stifling under the triviality of her femininity. The world is groaning beneath the terrors of his masculinity.

He is playing masculine. She is playing feminine.

How do we call off the game?

Our periodontist was looking at my daughter Keri's bite. We asked his advice about whether she needed braces. "It's borderline," was the answer. "If she were a boy, I'd say no. Boys can live with some teeth less straight than others. In her case though, she'll probably want straight teeth when she becomes interested in the opposite sex. I'd say she needs them."

For years our relatives have been telling us not to be concerned with Keri's height, since it's okay for a girl to be short. We are lucky, they said, that it wasn't Todd who was short. We haven't bothered to discuss Keri's teeth with them.

You have encountered similar situations. We all have. Sex-role expectations are learned at a very young age, whether they are taught purposely or incidentally. The natural place to seek evidence of such learning is where we are *supposed* to learn—in school. In a study of sex-role stereotyping in schools, the texts used to learn reading were inspected.[1] Table 16.1 reports the results of this study.

Table 16.1
Analysis of Reading Texts

	Allyn & Bacon	American Book Co.	Bank Street	Ginn	Harper and Row	D.C. Heath	Houghton-Mifflin	Laidlaw	Lyons & Carnahan	MacMillan	Open Court	Science Research Associates	Scott Foresman	New S.F. Reading System	Singer/Random House	Sullivan	Totals
Number books read	3	6	7	10	6	7	9	5	9	9	2	10	13	12	5	21	134
Total number stories	85	175	116	361	130	176	151	81	100	165	81	221	321	110	94	393	2,760
Featuring boys	31	42	43	107	40	49	63	10	34	48	4	62	116	28	30	116	823
Featuring girls	7	25	17	31	13	12	24	1	6	13	3	17	42	11	0	99	319
Featuring adult males	1	10	7	7	8	3	21	4	3	12	7	24	0	2	8	2	119
Featuring adult females	0	2	2	7	4	2	9	0	0	1	2	5	1	2	0	0	37
Boy and girl	8	16	18	79	6	20	5	3	10	15	4	13	76	9	3	105	390
Male animal	2	6	1	12	1	20	3	21	4	8	24	2	1	6	14	1	126
Female animal	3	0	2	14	2	7	1	2	1	5	7	5	1	1	3	1	55
Male folk fantasy	7	17	2	34	16	21	9	22	6	16	14	15	6	7	12	6	210
Female folk fantasy	1	4	1	6	2	4	3	6	3	0	15	4	1	0	4	3	57
Male biography	16	11	1	9	18	12	6	7	13	17	0	15	22	16	6	0	169
Female biography	3	3	0	3	4	0	0	0	0	5	0	2	5	1	1	0	27
Other: science, neuter animal, social, etc.	6	39	22	52	16	26	7	5	20	25	1	57	50	27	13	60	426
Occupations shown for men	22	25	24	24	26	30	29	14	13	33	*	21	33	35	13	25	
Occupations shown for women	7	7	5	2	2	3	9	3	2	5	*	5	5	11	2	7	

Source: Women on Words & Images, *Dick and Jane as Victims* (Princeton, N.J.: Women on Words & Images, 1975), 56. Reprinted by permission.
*Not listed

Of the 134 books studied and 2,760 stories analyzed, the following was found:

1. Thirty percent featured boys and only 12 percent featured girls.
2. Four percent featured adult males and only 1 percent featured adult females.
3. Even more male animals were featured than female animals (126 to 55).
4. More male folk fantasy was featured than female folk fantasy (210 to 57).
5. For every biography of a female in these reading books, there were six biographies of males.
6. Each publisher studied averaged twenty-four males shown working outside the home and only five females.

Are you, or do you know, a "macho man"? Toughness is often a burden men have labored with but a facade they are increasingly abandoning. Sensitivity is in!

*"Sure I'll play doctor.
But you have to be the
nurse and I'll be the
doctor!"*

One might conclude that, in addition to reading, these books were teaching that boys and men are more interesting than girls and women and that men contribute more to society than do women. In summarizing their findings, the researchers reported that males were depicted in reading texts as more ingenious, clever, industrious, problem-solving, strong, brave, heroic, adventuresome, and imaginative than females. Females were more passive, dependent, altruistic, incompetent, and victimized by the opposite sex than were males. Which set of traits would you prefer to have? No wonder women feel stressed about their societal role.

An even more recent study found teachers stereotyping the sexes in a most disturbing way.[2] Boys were praised more than girls, boys were given more academic help, and teachers accepted boys' comments to a greater extent than girls' comments during classroom discussions. The result is boys are eight times more likely to call out answers; that is, they develop more self-confidence regarding their academic abilities than do girls.

However, there are differences that do exist between males and females. Table 16.2 lists some of these. It also indicates those abilities and traits generally believed to be more characteristic of one sex than the other for which clear, convincing evidence is lacking. Do any of these surprise you? They surprised me.

Well, it's now easy to see that we learn much of our sex-role expectations and stereotypes from our schooling. We also learn about sex roles from our parents and the roles they adopt. Does Dad cook, clean, or do laundry? Does Mom? Does Dad tune up the car, write out the checks, or play baseball with the children? Does Mom? The media, too, depict males and females in ways that influence our perceptions. The "media families" in many ongoing television programs, for example, often show women and men in stereotypical roles.

Table 16.2
Gender-linked Differences in Abilities and in Physical and Psychological Traits

	Males Tend to Be Higher	No Difference, or Differences Not Established with Conflicting Evidence	Females Tend to Be Higher
Abilities[a]	Physical size, strength, and fleetness Mathematical skills (but not arithmetical) Visual-spatial skills Gross-muscle movements	Intelligence Creativity Rote-learning ability Analytic ability[b] (males are higher in analytic ability involving spatial relations)	Verbal skills[c] Resistance to illness and disease Tactile sensitivity Fine muscle movements (manual dexterity)
Psychological traits	Aggression Activity (males tend to be more active in boisterous play; girls' activity tends to be quieter)	Dominance Assertiveness Emotionality Passivity Competitiveness Compliance Timidity Self-esteem Achievement-orientation Suggestibility Erotic responsiveness	Nurturance[b] (although this is a very difficult trait to measure, many authorities believe that women are genetically *predisposed* to nurturant behavior, so that they develop this potential more easily than men) Sociability[b] Empathy[b]

Source: Lloyd Saxton, *The Individual, Marriage, and the Family,* 4th ed. © 1980 by Wadsworth, Inc. Reprinted by permission of Wadsworth Publishing Company, Belmont, California 94002. Pages 47, 87–88.

[a]Gender-linked abilities not indicated here are the four biological imperatives (gestation, lactation, and menstruation in the female, and sperm production in the male).

[b]These abilities and traits are especially controversial. Men tend to be superior in analyzing problems that have to do with manipulating objects in space; some authorities find that more women than men are predisposed to being nurturant by their genetic programming; some authorities find that women are superior in personal relations, empathy, or sociability—judging emotions and expressions better than men.

[c]It is curious that although most writers, orators, and newscasters are men, girls score higher on tests of verbal ability, and remedial reading and writing programs enroll far more boys than girls. Either verbal ability in children is not related to later professional verbal skills, or cultural factors (opportunity and expectation) must explain this phenomenon.

The sum total of these influences places barriers all around us: we can go here and do this, but not there and do that. This lack of freedom may be quite stressful. The embarrassment felt when we go beyond the boundaries—I'll never forget the looks I received from my teenaged male friends when they found out that I played Mah-Jongg with my cousin and her female friends—also causes stress. Thankfully, much of this is changing, but as we discussed earlier, change, too, can be stressful.

Women and Work Outside the Home

Before proceeding further it may be interesting to see just how much you know about women's economic roles. To determine that, answer the accompanying questionnaire.

Women's Economic Role

Decide which of the following statements are true and which are false.

___ 1. The wealth of our nation is mainly in the hands of women.
___ 2. Women are frequently sick and miss too many workdays.
___ 3. Women are not worth hiring where any training or investment is involved, since they just get married or pregnant or quit.
___ 4. Women lack the physical strength for many highly skilled and well-paid manual jobs, especially in the crafts.
___ 5. Women are better off today, in terms of job opportunities and pay, than they were a generation ago.

Stress and the Male Role

Lest male readers feel insulated from the stress derived from sex-role stereotyping, read on. Psychologist Sidney Jourard (1971) provides one of the best descriptions of the effects of masculinity on health in a chapter ominously entitled "Some Lethal Aspects of the Male Role." Jourard finds manliness associated with the following:

1. *Low self-disclosure.* Men typically reveal less information about themselves than do women. Another way of describing this situation is that men have more secrets about themselves than women do. Keeping these secrets, and the threat that they might be exposed, makes men tense, continually alert, and restless. "All this implies that trying to seem manly is a kind of work, and work imposes stress and consumes energy. Manliness, then, seems to carry with it a chronic burden of stress and energy expenditure which could be a factor related to man's relatively shorter life span."

2. *Lack of insight and empathy.* Due to men's low self-disclosure, they lack insight into their own selves (low self-insight) and into others (low empathy). Furthermore, men are taught to ignore their own feelings and be objective in making decisions. Ignoring their own feelings leads men to be less sensitive to signs of their own ill health. Studies have found women more likely to consult a physician. "Men, by contrast, fail to notice these 'all is not well signals' of weaker intensity and do not stop work or take to their beds until the destructive consequences of their manly way of life have progressed to the point of a 'stroke' or a total collapse."

Women have demonstrated many behaviors thought to be exclusively characteristic of males. Courage is but one of these.

3. *Incompetence at loving.* Not only do men disclose less about themselves to others than do women; in general, women are the *recipients* of more disclosure from others than are men. Consequently, men are less adept at understanding other people. This leads to men making mistakes in their relationships with others due to not having enough experience in having others disclosing themselves to them. Furthermore, not disclosing themselves to their loved ones—it is not manly to do so—results in those loved ones not understanding their men. Not being understood means they cannot be loved as well. "That is, it will be difficult for a woman or another man to know the immediate present state of the man's self, and his needs will thereby go unmet. Some men are so skilled at dissembling, at 'seeming,' that even their wives will not know when they are lonely, anxious, or hungering for affection. And the men, blocked by pride, dare not disclose their despair or need. . . . If love is a factor that promotes life, then handicap at love, a male characteristic, seems to be another lethal aspect of the male role."

4. *Dispiritation.* Men see the meaning and value of their lives in the work that they do. When they can no longer work or they retire, their lives lose meaning—they become dispirited—and it is not unusual for them to become ill and soon die. "If men can see themselves as manly, and life as worthwhile, only so long as they engage in gainful employment, or are sexually potent or have enviable social status, then clearly these are tenuous bases upon which to ground their existence. It would seem that women can continue to find meaning and raisons d'etre long after men feel useless and unneeded."

So you see, sex-role stereotyping is also unhealthy for men.

If you answered that all five statements were false, you get an honorary membership in the Burbank Friends of Truth about Women Museum; and if you answered that all were true, you get a stuffed male chauvinist pig for Christmas or Chanukah.

Saxton describes five myths about women's economic roles.*

There are many widely believed myths regarding women's economic roles in our society. Until these myths are dispelled, even the fairest and best-intentioned observers of male-female relations must necessarily base their conclusions on misconceptions.

1. *Myth One: The wealth of our nation is mainly in the hands of women.* This is simply not true. Only about one-third of the population regarded as "wealthy" are women. In addition, these women acquire their wealth at a much older age than men, primarily through widowhood. Moreover, the financial holdings of many of the younger women in this group are in the form of assets assigned them in name only for tax purposes, while a father or husband retains the actual control.

2. *Myth Two: Women are frequently sick and miss too many days of work.* The fact is that men miss more work than women for chronic sickness. Women average 5.3 and men 5.4 sick days in the course of the year.

3. *Myth Three: Women are not worth hiring where any training or investment is involved, since they just get married or pregnant or quit.* Women do indeed quit jobs more often than men, and frequently they give family-related reasons. However, women are more frequently hired for menial, routine, duller jobs than men (or jobs for which they are "overqualified," such as college-educated women working as clerk typists), and turnover rates among these jobs are very high. For example, auto assembly, a dull, routine job, has the highest job turnover rate of all, even though it is overwhelmingly male. When occupational level and income are held constant, men and women do not differ significantly in turnover rates.

4. *Myth Four: Women lack the physical strength for many highly skilled and well-paid manual jobs, especially in the crafts.* Given current machinery, most such jobs rarely entail more physical exertion than that involved in carrying a sixty-pound child or transporting a desk typewriter from one office to another, both tasks done frequently by a large number of women. Moreover, it is clear that some men are physically weaker than most women, whereas some women are stronger than most men.

5. *Myth Five: Women are much better off today, in terms of job opportunities and pay, than they were a generation ago.* Nothing could be further from the truth. As we have seen, the proportion of women in prestigious occupations is no higher than in past decades, nor has the income of women relative to men improved.

Although women are working outside the home in greater numbers than in the past (see fig. 16.1), they are still predominantly employed in traditional women's jobs. As shown in figure 16.2, nurse, dental hygienist, cashier, secretary, waitress, child-care worker, and dressmaker are occupations still made up of over

*From *The Individual, Marriage, and the Family,* 4th edition, by Lloyd Saxton, © 1980 by Wadsworth, Inc. Reprinted by permission of Wadsworth Publishing Company, Belmont, California 94002. Pages 47, 87–88.

Number of women in the labor force, in millions

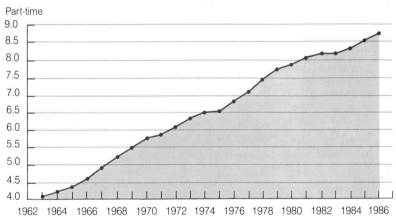

Part-time

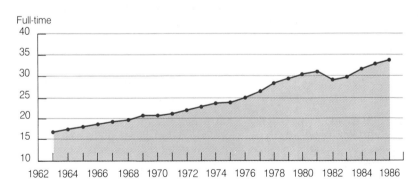

Full-time

Figure 16.1 Full-time or part-time?

Source: U.S. Bureau of Labor Statistics.

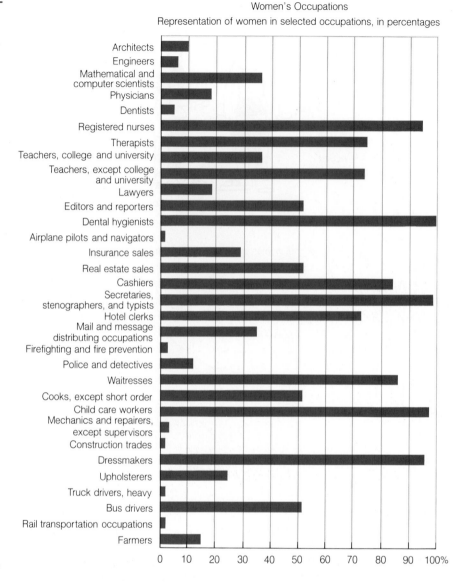

Figure 16.2
Women's occupations

Source: U.S. Bureau of Labor Statistics.

Women's Occupations
Representation of women in selected occupations, in percentages

80 percent women. Some believe this situation may be changing. As evidence for this conclusion they offer data such as that in figure 16.3, which depicts the increase in the number of doctoral degrees awarded to women in science and engineering. However, evidence to the contrary also exists. Thirty percent of recent women college graduates majored in education, while only 9 percent of men graduates did. Whereas 27 percent of male graduates majored in business or economics, only 17 percent of female graduates majored in these disciplines.

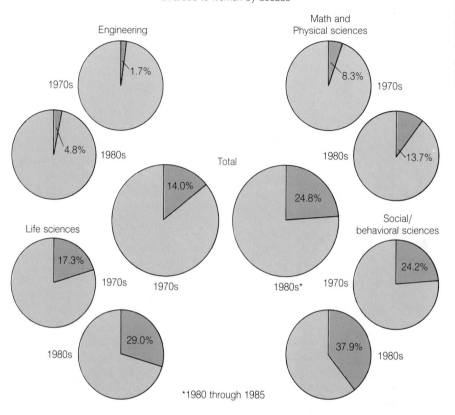

Percentage of
science and engineering doctorate degrees
awarded to women by decade

Engineering

1970s   1.7%

1980s   4.8%

Life sciences

1970s   17.3%

1980s   29.0%

Total

14.0%   1970s

24.8%   1980s*

*1980 through 1985

Math and
Physical sciences

8.3%   1970s

1980s   13.7%

Social/
behavioral sciences

24.2%   1970s

37.9%   1980s

Figure 16.3
Percentage of science and engineering doctorate degrees awarded to women by decade.

Source: National Research Council Doctorate Records File.

Proportionately twice as many male graduates majored in law, medicine, or dentistry (6 percent) than did female graduates (3 percent). And, relative to nursing, pharmacy, and health technologies, 9 percent of female graduates studied these areas, whereas only 1 percent of male graduates majored in these fields of study.[3]

Just as stressful is the fact that women earn less than men in almost all job categories (see fig. 16.4). Table 16.3 shows the percentage of male salaries earned by females for the same jobs. As noted in table 16.3, this situation has not changed dramatically from what it was in 1979, even when work experience is the same (see table 16.4).

Further, even when they have the same level of education as men, women earn less. Female workers with four or more years of college education had an average income slightly above that of men who had only one to three years of high school. They earned $14,679 and $12,117, respectively, in 1983. Female high school graduates (with no college) working full-time year round had a lower average income than fully employed men who had completed less than eight years of elementary school—$13,787 and $14,093, respectively.[4] For a comparison of earnings by sex and ethnicity, see figure 16.5.

Figure 16.4
Earnings: women's vs.
men's

Source: U.S. Bureau of Labor
Statistics.

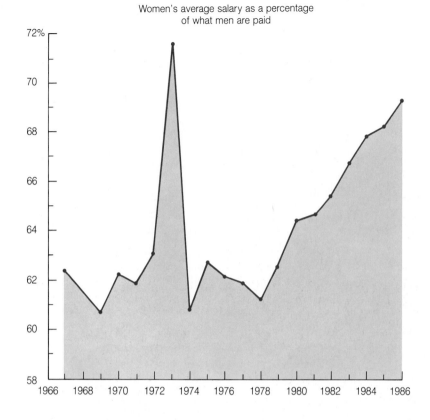

Women's average salary as a percentage
of what men are paid

Figure 16.5 Median
weekly earnings of
full-time wage and
salary workers, by sex
and ethnicity, 1988.

Source: Office of Information
and Public Affairs. *Women
and Work*. Washington, D.C.:
Department of Labor, August,
1988.

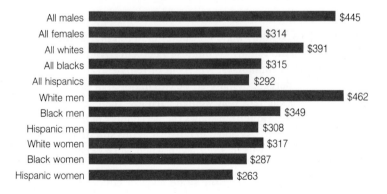

All males	$445
All females	$314
All whites	$391
All blacks	$315
All hispanics	$292
White men	$462
Black men	$349
Hispanic men	$308
White women	$317
Black women	$287
Hispanic women	$263

Table 16.3

Characteristics of Selected Occupations in 1979 and 1986: Females as a Percent of All Full-Time Workers and Relative Earnings of Females

Occupation	Females as a Percent of All Full-Time Workers		Ratio of Female to Male Earnings (Full-Time Workers)	
	1979	1986	1979	1986
Secretaries	98.8	99.2	.58	(B)[2]
Registered nurses	94.6	92.7	.82	(B)
Bookkeepers, accounting and auditing clerks	88.1	93.0	.66	.74
Nursing aides, orderlies, and attendants	85.1	88.3	.72	.81
Cashiers	77.7	79.8	.71	.75
Computer operators	56.6	63.8	.69	.73
Assemblers	47.2	42.1	.71	.75
Accountants and auditors	34.0	44.7	.60	.72
Computer programmers	28.0	39.7	.80	.81
Supervisors and proprietors, sales occupations	22.4	26.6	.57	.55
Managers and administrators, n.e.c.[1]	22.1	28.9	.51	.61
Computer systems analysts	20.4	29.7	.79	.83
Janitors and cleaners	15.3	21.0	.74	.69
Lawyers	10.4	15.2	.55	.63
Sales representatives, mining, manufacturing, and wholesale	10.1	13.4	.62	.72
Electrical and electronic engineers	4.4	9.4	.75	(B)
Truck drivers, heavy	1.5	1.5	.71	(B)
Carpenters, except apprentices	1.1	0.5	.71	(B)
Automotive mechanics, except apprentices	0.9	0.6	.86	(B)

Source: U.S. Bureau of the Census, Current Population Reports, Series P-70, No. 10, *Male-Female Differences in Work Experience, Occupations, and Earnings: 1984* (Washington, D.C.: U.S. Government Printing Office, 1987), 5.

Note: Data for 1979 are from the 1980 census of population. Data for 1986 are from the March 1987 Current Population Survey.

[1]Not elsewhere classified.

[2](B) Too few cases to analyze.

Lastly, women who work outside the home must also work inside the home. When children are involved, the stress associated with working can be magnified. And yet, more and more women with young children are entering the labor force.

Regardless of their reasons—to earn more, to achieve a sense of self-worth, or to respond to pressure from others who may not find value in work at home—more and more women are working outside the home (see fig. 16.6). It is not surprising, therefore, that more and more women are developing afflictions that were previously the exclusive domain of men—for example, coronary heart disease.

Let us not forget the men in this picture. With the economic "belt-tightening" in the early 1980s, businesses have been forced to decrease their payrolls.

Table 16.4
Earnings Per Hour, by Tenure on Current Job

Characteristic	All Workers			Full-Time Workers		
	Male	Female	Female to Male Ratio	Male	Female	Female to Male Ratio
Workers 21 to 64 years	$10.53	$7.13	.68	$10.82	$7.52	.70
Tenure on current job						
Less than 2 years	8.22	5.73	.70	8.46	6.03	.71
2 to 4 years	9.32	6.73	.72	9.38	6.78	.72
5 to 9 years	10.62	7.70	.73	10.42	7.56	.73
10 years or more	12.66	8.66	.68	12.38	7.91	.64
Years of work experience by tenure on current job						
Experience less than 5 years	6.83	5.48	.80	7.19	5.88	.82
On job less than 2 years	6.64	5.23	.79	7.07	5.72	.81
On job 2 years or more	7.07	5.85	.83	7.33	6.07	.83
Experience 5 to 9 years	8.15	6.62	.81	8.35	6.95	.83
On job less than 2 years	7.49	5.95	.79	7.74	6.36	.82
On job 2 to 4 years	8.33	6.67	.80	8.45	6.91	.82
On job 5 years or more	8.70	7.20	.83	8.89	7.45	.84
Experience 10 to 19 years	10.77	7.78	.72	10.95	8.07	.74
On job less than 2 years	9.17	6.17	.67	9.50	6.56	.69
On job 2 to 4 years	10.22	7.36	.72	10.39	7.69	.74
On job 5 to 9 years	11.07	8.43	.76	11.15	8.71	.78
On job 10 years or more	11.94	8.49	.71	12.01	8.53	.71
Experience 20 years or more	12.22	7.80	.64	12.41	8.15	.66
On job less than 2 years	9.73	5.65	.58	10.20	6.12	.60
On job 2 to 4 years	11.02	6.79	.62	11.27	6.92	.61
On job 5 to 9 years	11.82	7.16	.61	11.96	7.42	.62
On job 10 years or more	12.95	8.81	.68	13.02	9.10	.70

Source; U.S. Bureau of the Census, Current Population Reports, Series P-70, No. 10, *Male-Female Differences in Work Experience, Occupations, and Earnings: 1984* (Washington, D.C.: U.S. Government Printing Office, 1987), 4.

Note: Universe is all workers.

Figure 16.6 Top ten U.S. cities with most working women

Source: U.S. Bureau of Labor Statistics.

City	% of women who work	% of women among all workers
Washington	62.7%	47.6%
Dallas–Fort Worth	62.7%	44.0%
San Francisco	60.7%	45.6%
Boston	57.0%	44.6%
Houston	54.8%	38.0%
Chicago	54.4%	43.3%
Los Angeles	54.3%	43.0%
Philadelphia	51.1%	44.1%
Detroit	51.1%	42.2%
New York	45.4%	43.3%

Table 16.5
Overall Response Rates to Coping Mechanisms

Coping	Never (%)	Sometimes (%)	Often or Always (%)
Exercise	20.2	43.9	35.9
Engage in a hobby	26.2	46.65	27.2
Drink alcohol	42.5	42.9	14.6
Take drugs or medicine	70.33	21.55	8.14
Act as though nothing much happened	20.8	49.3	29.95
Keep it to yourself	19.55	45.55	34.9
Apologize even though you were right	38.6	48.0	13.4
Take it out on or blame others	41.25	50.64	8.13
Blow off steam	13.44	53.9	32.7
Talk to a friend	6.09	37.4	56.5
Take action	4.43	45.1	50.5
Smoke cigarettes	70.6	6.8	22.6
Drink more coffee or soda or eat more	17.7	40.2	42.15
Get away from it all	17.3	61.9	20.8

Source: *9-to-5 National Survey of Women and Stress* (Cleveland, Ohio: 9-to-5, National Association of Working Women, 1983).

Unemployment rates have soared. Men have begun complaining that women have taken jobs they would have had—not a very healthy relationship between the sexes. Further, men whose wives work outside the home often participate more in the work inside the home. They may clean, cook, do laundry, pick up the kids, shop, and do any other household chores that need doing. When these chores are undertaken by young men who are beginning relationships or marriages, they are easier to adapt to than when ongoing relationships are adjusted in this way. Again, change is stressful. When, after ten or more years of marriage, the wife begins to work outside the home and the husband must assume a greater share of the household work, both of them are experiencing stress.

Frustration is growing among working women regarding the division of labor in the home. A study conducted by the Institute for Social Research found that wives working outside the home do less housework than wives who work inside the home, but they still do the majority of the housework.[5] Husbands take on some added burden of housework, but it is in no way comparable to what one would expect. So women argue that they are being abused and treated unfairly by their spouses. Score another point for the stress response.

How do women cope with stress on the job? Table 16.5 shows that several coping mechanisms are frequently employed.

Table 16.6
Health Effects Frequently Experienced by Women
in Relation to Difficult Job Conditions

	Always Pressure Without Clout (%)	Never Make Decisions on My Own (%)	Never Find Work Challenging (%)	All Respondents (%)
Eyestrain	31.7	34.0	27.8	20.2
Headache	38.4	33.3	35.3	24.0
Nausea	11.96	12.4	12.94	6.2
Insomnia	29.2	25.5	24.25	17.6
Muscle pain	55.5	54.9	48.25	38.7
Fatigue	58.52	54.25	51.75	40.0
Digestive problems	32.0	29.6	28.9	18.9
Chest pain	11.7	11.85	7.84	6.0
Anxiety	53.2	48.03	43.8	27.5
Anger	46.7	43.4	46.9	27.5
Depression	36.0	34.23	41.2	20.0

Source: 9-to-5 National Survey of Women and Stress (Cleveland, Ohio: 9-to-5, National Association of Working Women, 1983).

Women and Stress: From 9-to-5

9-to-5 (the National Association of Working Women) has done more than just have a movie made of itself. They conducted perhaps the most extensive study of the stress experienced by working women. By the way, homemakers were part of the sample of working women that 9-to-5 studied. Sixty-two percent of the women described their jobs as "somewhat stressful" and one-third described their jobs as "very stressful." More women in their thirties described their work as "very stressful" than other age groups.

Regarding particular stressors, 72 percent of the women who reported their jobs as "very stressful" said they had too much work to do; 61 percent said they were required to work too fast; and 57 percent said they had a lot of responsibility and pressure without enough authority to make decisions. For the homemakers, 25 percent reported they never take time to get "away from it all," and 19 percent stated they *always* drink more coffee or soda or eat more as a way of coping with the stress they encounter.

As table 16.6 indicates, various ill states of health (physical as well as psychological) are associated with particular job conditions.

For a copy of 9-to-5's report, write to them at 1224 Huron Road, Cleveland, Ohio 44115.

Sexual harassment at work has typically meant sexual advances made by someone of power or authority who threatens firing, lack of promotion, or some other sanction if sexual activity is declined. A sexual advance at work that is politely made and that carries no threat of sanction is not sexual harassment, although some offended workers have interpreted such advances that way. The problem area in sexual harassment pertains to a sexual advance from someone of a higher job status to someone of a lower job status. The person of lower job status may feel pressured to say yes even though no job sanction has been made explicit.

However, sexual advances are not the only criteria for sexual harassment. If jokes and sexual innuendos permeate the workplace so that workers feel uncomfortable, unable to perform well, and suffer in their careers as a result, that in itself qualifies as sexual harassment. Furthermore, even if the company is unaware that such harassment is occurring, the Supreme Court ruled in *Meritor Savings Bank v. Vinson* in 1986 that the company is still legally liable for the results of such harassment. It is for this latter reason that businesses have instituted educational programs to notify supervisors that sexual harassment will not be tolerated in their organizations.

Both men and women are victims of sexual harassment. However, women experience such harassment to a greater extent than men—especially young, inexperienced women holding low-paying clerical or subprofessional jobs.[6] Further, most of the harassment, though not all, comes from male bosses. A *Redbook* survey found 92 percent of working women had experienced harassment. Fifty percent either quit, were fired, or knew someone else who had quit or been fired as a result of sexual harassment; and 75 percent believed that nothing would be done if they complained to a supervisor.[7] When federal workers were studied by the Merit System Protection Board in 1980, it was found that nearly 25 percent of almost 2 million workers (42 percent females, 15 percent males) experienced some type of sexual harassment.[8] Since 1981, complaints of sexual harassment to the Equal Employment Opportunity Commission have increased by 70 percent.[9]

In 1988, the Merit System Protection Board again reported on a survey of sexual harassment among governmental workers. Although incidents of rape and assault declined from the 1980 results, touching, teasing, and joking remained high. The 1988 data disclosed that 42 percent of the women surveyed experienced sexual harassment within the last two years. That is the same percent as reported sexual harassment seven years earlier—this despite attempts to educate federal workers and their supervisors so as to discourage sexual harassment. (The average federal worker has received one to two hours of training on sexual harassment.)

The effects of sexual harassment are varied. Some people have been fired or had promotions withheld when they didn't make themselves sexually available. Others have felt guilty and wondered what they did to encourage the sexual advance. Many have felt helpless. In a study of sexually harassed women, 78 percent said they were affected emotionally or physically.[10] Loss of self-esteem;

Sexually Harassed
on the Job?
YOU'RE NOT ALONE!

In surveys conducted in various parts of the U.S., 70%–88% of women workers report that they experience some form of sexual harassment at work.
YOU DON'T HAVE TO TAKE IT!
Courts are beginning to handle the issue and women are beginning to speak up.

Contact AASC (the Alliance Against Sexual Coercion) for:
• legal options & referrals
• unemployment compensation information & referrals
• emotional support
• vocational counseling referrals
• educational program referrals
617-547-1176
P.O. Box 1 Cambridge, MA 02139

Figure 16.7 One organization's calling card. Other groups have also been formed to help the sexually harassed.

feelings of fear and helplessness; headaches, backaches, and neck pains; gastrointestinal illness; and chronic depression have all been associated with sexual harassment.[11]

Remedies have been developed to be used by those who have been sexually harassed. Grievance procedures in many businesses or colleges have been established to deal with such complaints. Educational campaigns are being conducted at work and school sites.[12] And women's groups have counseled the sexually harassed regarding their legal options (see fig. 16.7).

Domestic Engineering— Working in the Home

One of the stressors women experience is the denigration of their homemaking role. My wife's term—domestic engineer—is an accurate one. Full-time homemaking is difficult, tiring, and requires a great deal of skill, time, effort, creativity, and commitment. Although there is nothing that makes them more suited for this role than men, tradition has made full-time homemaking a job done predominantly by women. In recent years more attention has been paid to men who occupy this role, and their designation—househusband—is as demeaning as the female version—housewife. Men and women who work as full-time homemakers are certainly not married to the house, and their priorities aren't there either. Rather, their homemaking role is designed to make themselves and those with whom they live feel comfortable. They organize car pools, umpire baseball games, place Band-Aids on wounds that heal better for their loving care, and do other varied and meaningful tasks such as watching over the family's health and nutrition.

That some people, men and women, downplay the significance and value of homemaking is unfortunate. Certainly this role is not one that everyone would choose, but it is a role that many women and some men occupy by choice and perform exceptionally well. It is an extremely important role that can be divided by members of the family or performed by one person.

The stressors associated with domestic engineering are similar to other occupational stressors: too much to do in too little time (role overload), not being specifically trained for many of the tasks (role insufficiency), having to answer to too many different family members' demands (role conflict), and not being clear on all that is expected (role ambiguity). When the denigration of the role is added to these stressors, the load may become too much to bear, and illness and disease may occur.

Women with children face another stressor—the empty-nest syndrome. One day, after years of mothering, the last child has moved out. Some women feel their value is diminished at this point, since they feel less needed than before. Even for women who see this as an opportunity to do things that they didn't have time to do before, obstacles present themselves. Absurd as it is, some employers have been known to view such applicants as lacking experience. Career counselors, however, have been helping women market themselves as well-trained and abundantly experienced in organizational skills, time management, interpersonal relationships, problem solving, and purchasing. How many employers would not want to hire an applicant who has demonstrated an ability to handle tiresome, difficult chores requiring a great deal of skill, time, effort, creativity, and commitment? These are the traits that I used several paragraphs earlier to describe homemaking.

In figure 16.8 there appear nine dots. Before reading further, try to connect those nine dots with four straight lines made without lifting your pencil off the paper or retracing any line. Come on now. Don't read any further until you've tried.

The solution to figure 16.8 appears in figure 16.9. As you can see, the solution lies in going beyond the dots. When drawing the horizontal line at the bottom, you must go beyond the last dot, and when drawing the next line up, you must go beyond the top middle dot.

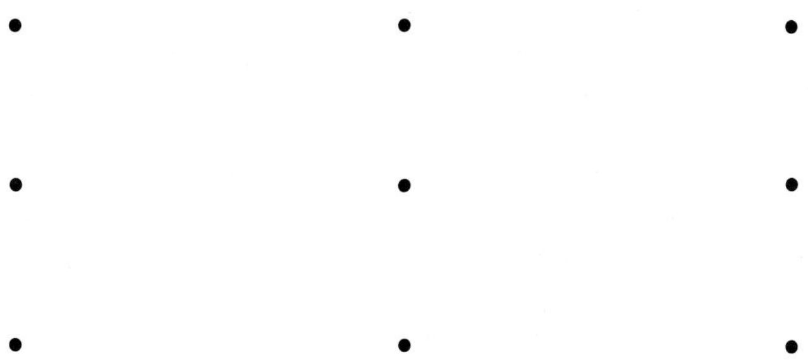

Stress and Sexuality

Figure 16.8 Connect the dots with four straight lines without lifting your pencil from the paper or retracing any line.

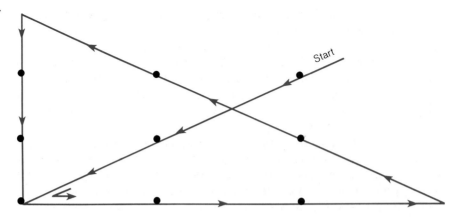

Figure 16.9 Solution to figure 16.8

Issue: Is Sex-Role Stereotyping Less Stressful Than Open-Ended Sex Roles?

Some people believe that well-defined, traditional sex roles provide guidance. When growing up and learning these roles, we know what to study for. We are clear about what our future holds and therefore focus our early years to prepare for that future. Confusion, and thereby stress, are diminished by this clear focus.

Others argue that the limits on our options are stressful in themselves. How can traditional roles in which the male is empowered and the female subservient not be stressful? With the male's power came an awesome burden of responsibility and with the female's subservience came a diminished sense of self-worth—both extremely stressful.

What do you think?

It seems that today's sexuality has gone beyond the dots, or boundaries, as well. Because the limits no longer seem limiting, confusion about how to behave sexually abounds. Let's take extramarital sex as an example. Nearly one-half of married men have extramarital sex at least once in their lives, and approximately 20 percent of all married women do.[13] Further, when asked their attitudes about extramarital sex, between 80 and 98 percent of both women and men stated they would object to their spouses engaging in sex with someone else. One might conclude, then, that a lot of people are "cheating" on their spouses and hiding it from them because they know their spouses would object. That creates a good deal of stress both for the adulterer, the suspecting spouse, and the third party.

Even for the unmarried, our changing sexual standards and roles are stressful. Some of my male students tell me that they don't know whether to light a female's cigarette or open a car door for her. If they don't, they may be considered rude, and sometimes when they do, the female objects to being considered help-less. My female students, on the other hand, tell me that they don't know whether to wait in the car until the male gets out, comes around the car, and opens the door for them or to open it themselves. Though seemingly a trivial concern, the lack of standards is stressful. Does the female call the male for a date? Who initiates the sexual activity? Who's responsible for contraception? Is oral-genital behavior acceptable? Is it expected? How about vibrators? What's kinky and what's standard in today's society?

Some might argue that society is changing, and more and more it is appro-priate, for example, for *either* a male or a female to initiate dates and sexual activity. True, and because of that it is stressful. It is the changing nature of sexuality in society that results in the stress. Rather than a clear "Anyone can," there seems to be confusion about "Should I?"—"Am I expected to?"—"Will he (she)?"

Interventions

As with other stressors, interventions can be set up to prevent sex-role stressors from resulting in illness or disease. These interventions can relate to life situa-tions, perceptions, emotions, or physiological arousal.

Life-Situation Interventions

To eliminate sex-related stressors at the life-situation level, apply the information and skills learned in chapters 5 and 6. First, look at the things routinely stressing you in this area of your life and eliminate any that aren't worth the hassle. For example, rather than having to decide each time you're in a car whether you will wait to have someone open the door for you, make that decision now. Then each time that situation arises, it will no longer be distressing, since you've already decided how to handle it. If you are periodically sexually harassed at work, devise a plan to respond to the harassment and follow that plan whenever it is needed. The plan may start with a verbal response: "I am not interested in you sexually and would prefer that you not broach the subject again. If you do, I will consider it sexual harassment and file grievance procedures. If you don't ever treat me this way again, I'm willing to forget this incident." The discussion in chapter 6 on assertiveness will help you develop your verbal response. Have a second step planned; that is, what you will do if the verbal response doesn't stop the sexual harassment. Perhaps you'll decide to report the incident, or maybe you'll try an-other, more threatening verbal response. In any case, you'll be prepared, and each time you are sexually harassed, you will be confident of your ability to handle it. As a result, sexual harassment, while still disturbing, will be less stressful.

A very important life-situation intervention is to improve communication be-tween you and the person who stresses you. If the lack of societal standards and rules is disturbing you, work out your own with your partner. Discuss who will be responsible for contraception, which sexual activities are acceptable and which aren't, and which chores you will be responsible for and which your partner will be responsible for. With more effective communication, you and the other person can short-circuit stress that might otherwise result from recurring situations. The following are some hints to get you started improving your sexual communication:

1. Make sure you have plenty of time for your discussion. Don't be cut short because either of you needs to run off somewhere.
2. Don't allow others to interrupt your discussion with phone calls or by barging in on you.
3. Accept all feelings, and the right to the verbal expression of these feelings. For example, it's appropriate to say, "I feel angry when . . ."
4. Take a risk and really describe your thoughts and needs. You can't expect your partner to guess what they are unless you get them out.
5. Approach the discussion with mutual understanding that the goal is to improve your relationship rather than to see who can shock whom.
6. Don't expect miracles overnight. Sexual communication requires continued dialogue. You might want to seek the help of other family members, friends, members of the clergy, or others who can contribute to your ability to sexually communicate. Sexual counselors can also assist.[14]

All the work to improve your sexual communication will, in the long run, be well worth it. You will develop a deeper trust in your partner, a greater sense of intimacy, and a feeling of adventure. In short, your sexual life will be greatly improved, and you can expect a positive carryover to other aspects of your relationship.

| Perception Interventions | Chapter 7 presents several perception interventions that will work well for sexual stressors. Selective awareness is one of these. If you are a full-time homemaker, you can choose to be aware of the negative aspects of that role—it's boring and doesn't have much status—or you can focus upon its positive aspects—it's important to your family and allows you to be at home more often than if you worked elsewhere. Regarding the lack of societal sexual standards, you can choose to view that as exciting and free as opposed to upsetting and confusing. If you experience bias because of your gender, you can always prevent yourself from having a stress response by feeling sorry for the person expressing the bias. You are the one who makes the choice regarding which aspects of each situation you will focus upon. |

Another useful perception intervention is to use the anxiety management techniques described earlier. If sexual situations make you anxious, you might try self-talk, relabeling, environmental planning, thought stopping, or systematic desensitization. Reread chapter 7 for a detailed description of how to use these interventions.

The regular use of relaxation techniques will help you manage sexual stressors. Be it meditation, autogenic training, or progressive relaxation, you will learn the relaxation response and be able to call upon it when encountering a stressor. Chapters 8, 9, and 10 present various ways in which to practice these interventions.

Emotional Arousal Interventions

As with relaxation techniques, for exercise to be effective and healthy, it needs to be done regularly. If you have already experienced the sensation of being stressed and then exercised strenuously, you know the therapeutic value of exercise. I recall that on a number of occasions when I was either overworked or heard some upsetting news, I went out and practiced serving tennis balls or jogged. Afterward, I felt much better. I used the stress products I had built up. You, too, can better manage stressors, in this case sexual ones, by exercising. Chapter 12 describes how to exercise properly so it will be helpful rather than harmful.

Physiological Arousal Interventions

Summary

1. Both males and females suffer from sex-role stereotyping since both are limited in their behavior and options because of such stereotyping.
2. Schools teach sex-role stereotyping to children at very young ages, albeit unintentionally. They do this through reading books, exam questions, funding priorities, and teacher behavior.
3. Certain traits are gender-linked. Males tend to be higher in physical size and strength, visual-spatial skills, gross muscle movements, and aggression; females tend to be higher in verbal skills, tactile sensitivity, fine muscle movements, nurturance, sociability, and empathy.
4. Certain traits seem not to be gender-linked. These include intelligence, creativity, analytic ability, dominance, assertiveness, competitiveness, self-esteem, suggestibility, and erotic responsiveness.
5. Although more women are working than ever before, they are still predominantly employed in traditionally female jobs. Nurse, dental hygienist, cashier, secretary, waitress, child-care worker, and dressmaker are occupations still made up of over 80 percent women. More women are earning doctorates in science and engineering than previously; however, proportionately more women still major in education, nursing, pharmacy, and health technologies than do males and more males major in business, law, medicine, and dentistry than do females.
6. Women earn less than men regardless of the job, even when they have comparable work experience and education. However, since 1978 the earnings gap between female and male workers has decreased.
7. Women who work outside the home must also work inside the home. Consequently, the stress associated with having to maintain home and outside work responsibilities has resulted in women developing afflictions previously the exclusive domain of men—for example, coronary heart disease.

8. Commonly used means of coping with work stress as reported by women workers are acting as though nothing much happened, keeping it to themselves, blowing off steam, taking action, and getting away from it all. However, significant numbers of women workers employ such dysfunctional coping measures as drinking alcohol, taking drugs, or drinking coffee in attempting to deal with stress related to the job.

9. Sexual harassment at work involves sexual advances made by someone of power or authority who threatens firing, lack of promotion, or some other sanction if sexual activity is declined. In addition, creating an uncomfortable or unproductive work environment by repeatedly telling jokes of a sexual nature or by any other means is also legally defined as sexual harassment. Both men and women suffer from sexual harassment, although women are more likely to be its victims.

10. The stress associated with domestic engineering (homemaking) can be similar to the stress resulting from other jobs. Such components of occupational stress as role overload, role conflict, role insufficiency, and role ambiguity may be present in the homemaking situation, just as they can be associated with many jobs outside the home.

11. Life-situation, perception, and emotional and physiological arousal interventions can be effective in managing sex-role stress.

Notes

1. Women on Words & Images, *Dick and Jane as Victims* (Princeton, N.J.: Women on Words & Images, 1975).

2. Myra Sadker and David Sadker, "Sexism in the Schools of the '80s," *Psychology Today,* March 1985, 54–57.

3. U.S. Bureau of the Census, *Current Population Reports, Series P-70, No. 10, Male-Female Differences in Work Experience, Occupations, and Earnings: 1984* (Washington, D.C.: U.S. Government Printing Office, 1987).

4. Women's Bureau, *Facts on Women Workers* (Washington, D.C.: U.S. Department of Labor, 1984), 3.

5. Ann Crittendon, "We 'Liberated' Mothers Aren't," *Washington Post,* 5 February 1984, D4.

6. "Sleeping with the Boss," *Forum,* December 1979, 7.

7. Claire Safran, "What Men Do to Women on the Job: A Shocking Look at Sexual Harassment," *Redbook,* November 1976, 149, 217–24.

8. Merit System Protection Board report on sexual harassment in the workplace (given before the Subcommittee on Investigations, Committee on the Post Office and Civil Service, U.S. House of Representatives, September 1980).

9. Sharon Warren Walsh, "Confronting Sexual Harassment at Work," *Washington Post, Business,* 21 July 1986, 16–17.

10. Catherine Mac Kinnon, *Sexual Harassment of Working Women* (New Haven, Conn.: Yale University Press, 1979).

11. P. Somers and J. Clementson-Mohr, "Sexual Extortion in the Workplace," *The Personnel Administrator,* April 1979, 23–28.

12. Patricia Riddle and Geraldine A. Johnson, "Sexual Harassment: What Role Should Educators Play?" *Health Education* 14(1983):20–23.

13. Morton Hunt, *Sexual Behavior in the 1970s* (Chicago: Playboy Press, 1974), 258, 261.

14. Jerrold S. Greenberg, Clint E. Bruess, and Doris Sands, *Sexuality: Insights and Issues* (Dubuque, Iowa: Wm. C. Brown, 1986).

17

Family Stress

I'll never forget the voice breaking with emotion, the tears being held back, as he eulogized his forty-two-year-old brother after his premature death:

> My brother need not be idealized or enlarged in death beyond what he was in life. To be remembered simply as a good and decent man who saw wrong and tried to right it, who saw suffering and tried to heal it, who saw war and tried to stop it. Those of us who loved him and who take him to his rest today, pray that what he was to us, what he wished for others, may come to pass for all the world. As he said many times in many parts of this nation, to those he touched and who sought to touch him: Some men see things as they are. I dream things that never were and say, why not?

These words were spoken in New York City's St. Patrick's Cathedral in early June of 1968 as the nation stopped to mourn with Edward Kennedy the death of his brother Robert. As I listened to the eulogy and participated in the funeral, albeit from afar, I could not help thinking of *my* two brothers, Stephen and Mark. Stephen, the businessman bent on making a million dollars, and Mark, the musician and artist, are as different from me as they are from each other. And yet, we are family. We grew up sharing one bedroom, fought with each other regularly, and shared the sorrows and joys accompanying twenty-some-odd years of life under one roof.

This chapter is about such bonds—family bonds—and how the changes in family life can be stressful. It describes ways to intervene between family stress and illness and disease.

The Family

A family is a set of intimate and personal relationships. These relationships may be legal (as in marriage) or extralegal (as in communal family groups). We speak of *a family of friends*, fraternity *brothers*, sorority *sisters*, and kissing *cousins*, using family-related terms to communicate the intimacy of these relationships. Our discussion, however, will be limited to the **nuclear family**—a married couple and their children—and the **extended family**—relatives other than spouses and children.

One of the functions of a family is to provide "social control of reproduction and child rearing."[1] Although there are some marriage partners who do not have children—by choice or anatomical condition—for those who do have them, the societal expectation is that these children will be raised within a family structure of some sort. This family may take many forms, and although some single women choose to conceive children, the social expectation is still that a child will be born to a married couple.

The family also provides economic support. Food, clothing, and shelter are provided for by family members who assist one another in their various tasks and functions. For example, one family member might cook the food that another family member earns money to buy, or both marriage partners may take jobs outside the home to earn money to eat out. While children are growing up, they are supported by the more self-sufficient family members (parents, older siblings, or other relatives) and their physiological, safety, and security needs are provided for.

Lastly, the family provides for many emotional needs. It provides love, eliminates feelings of isolation, fosters a sense of belonging, and teaches you that others are concerned about and care for you. In a family you can really be yourself—even your worst self—and usually still feel you belong to the group. Your family may not like your behavior or your decisions, but you'll still be welcome for Thanksgiving dinner, so to speak. Families can also serve you well in times of crisis. As we noted earlier in this book, having people with whom you can discuss your problems (social support) can help prevent you from becoming ill from those problems.

These words describing the needs satisfied by families can only convey the role of the family in an academic, intellectual sense. We all have experienced family life, however, and therefore have an effective, emotional sense of the function of families. We have been made to feel safe and secure, we have been made to feel loved, and we have been helped to feel as though we belonged. I'm reminded of a story I recently read in the newspaper of an automobile accident in which a family of five were involved. The car crash killed the father, mother, and two young children, but the two-year-old youngest daughter, who wore a seat belt, survived. As I read the story, my heart went out to this child, and I felt her loss. By that, I do not mean that I was concerned about who would care for her, feed her, or shelter her. Rather, I was feeling her *irreplaceable* loss—the loss of her blood relatives whose connection with her could never be totally compensated. There's something about the family bond that makes it unique.

The discussion of needs satisfied by the family pertains to effective families. Certainly there are families in which some of these needs are not met. For example, a family in which a child is physically abused or sexually molested is not one in which safety and security needs are met. A family in which the parent(s) abandons the children is not one in which a sense of belonging is enhanced. However, even families who try to meet these needs are not always successful. They may include family members who just don't know any better or who are so busy providing some of the needs (for example, economic support) that other needs go unmet (for example, love). One observer of families, author Jane Howard, found the following characteristics expressed in effective families:

1. *They have a chief;* that is, there is someone around whom other family members cluster.
2. *They have a switchboard operator;* that is, there is someone who keeps track of what all the others are up to.
3. *They are much to all their members but everything to none;* that is, family members are encouraged to be involved with and have some of their needs met by people outside of the family.
4. *They are hospitable;* that is, they recognize that hosts need guests as much as guests need hosts, and they maintain a surrounding of honorary family members. These "guests" become additional support systems for family members.
5. *They deal squarely with direness;* that is, when trouble comes—and in family life occasional trouble is unavoidable—it is dealt with quickly and openly, and is not allowed to threaten family bonds.
6. *They prize their rituals;* that is, they observe holidays together, grieve at funerals together, and in other ways encourage a sense of continuity and connectedness.
7. *They are affectionate;* that is, family members hug, kiss, and gingerly shake hands. They are quick to demonstrate love and caring for one another.
8. *They have a sense of place;* that is, there is a house or a town or some other place to which they feel connected. Even families who have moved often can feel connected to the place in which they presently find themselves.
9. *They connect with posterity;* that is, family members feel as though something came before them and something will continue when they die to which they are linked.
10. *They honor their elders;* that is, grandparents and other elderly relatives are respected and cared for. Their experience and wisdom—and they themselves—are valued.

We may all be tempted to judge our families against these characteristics of effective families and assign blame wherever we come up short. We would be better advised, however, to *analyze* our families as objectively as possible and

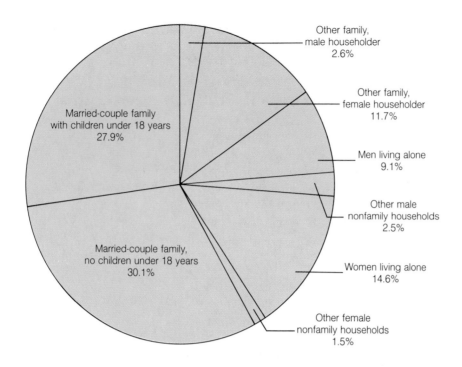

Other family,
male householder
2.6%

Other family,
female householder
11.7%

Men living alone
9.1%

Other male
nonfamily households
2.5%

Women living alone
14.6%

Other female
nonfamily households
1.5%

Married-couple family,
no children under 18 years
30.1%

Married-couple family
with children under 18 years
27.9%

Figure 17.1
Distribution of
households, by type:
March 1985

Source: U.S. Bureau of
Census, Current Population
Reports, Series P-23, No.
150, *Population Profile of the
United States: 1984–85*,
Washington, D.C.: U.S.
Government Printing Office,
1987, p. 20.

identify areas for and means of improvement. Assigning blame is dysfunctional, and it will interfere with improving the family's effectiveness. Where can your family be improved? How can this improvement best be made?

The predominant family style in America is the breadwinning father, homemaking mother, and resident children. Right? Wrong! In fact, only 27.9 percent of American families fit this stereotype (see fig. 17.1).[2] In 1985, 23.4 percent of the United States' children under 18 years of age lived with only one parent.[3] Figure 17.2 depicts the change in the causes of children living with only one parent from 1970 to 1985. As noted in that figure, divorces and never-married parents with children have significantly contributed to the increase in the number of children living with only one parent. Of children living with one parent in 1985, the largest proportion lived with a divorced parent (41.2 percent) followed by similar proportions living with a separated parent (22.5 percent) or a parent who had never been married (25.7 percent).

The Changing
Family

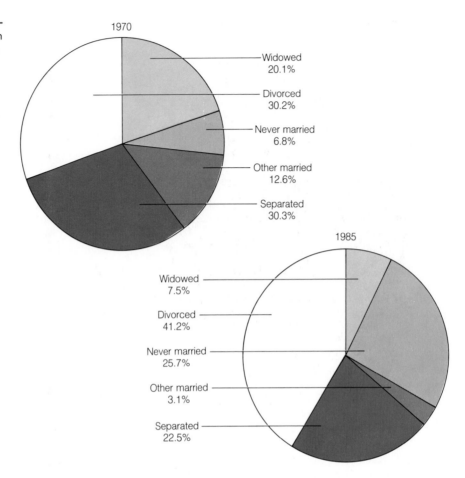

Figure 17.2 Children living with one parent, by marital status of parent

Source: U.S. Bureau of the Census, Current Population Reports, Series P-23, No. 150, *Population Profile of the United States: 1984–85,* Washington, D.C.: U.S. Government Printing Office, 1987, p. 23.

1970

Widowed
20.1%

Divorced
30.2%

Never married
6.8%

Other married
12.6%

Separated
30.3%

1985

Widowed
7.5%

Divorced
41.2%

Never married
25.7%

Other married
3.1%

Separated
22.5%

Marriage

The age at which people are getting married is increasing.[4] More and more people are going to college and preparing for careers and, consequently, postponing marriage. As shown in table 17.1, in 1985 the median age for a bride never married before was 23.0 and for a groom was 24.8. In 1987, the age at first marriage was even higher: 23.6 for brides and 25.8 for grooms.[5] More than ever, people are choosing to postpone marriage even longer, or perhaps not marry at all (see fig. 17.3).

Table 17.1
Median Age of Bride and Groom by Previous Marital Status

| | | Median Age of Bride | | | | | Median Age of Groom | | | |
| | | | Remarriage | | | | | Remarriage | | |
Year	Total	First Marriage	Total	Previously Divorced	Previously Widowed	Total	First Marriage	Total	Previously Divorced	Previously Widowed
1985	25.2	23.0	33.6	32.7	54.4	27.4	24.8	37.0	36.0	62.4
1984	25.0	22.8	33.3	32.5	54.2	27.2	24.6	36.8	35.9	62.4
1983	24.8	22.5	32.9	32.0	54.0	27.0	24.4	36.2	35.3	62.0
1982	24.4	22.3	32.5	31.6	54.1	26.7	24.1	35.7	34.9	61.7
1981	24.1	22.0	32.1	31.2	53.6	26.3	23.9	35.3	34.4	61.0
1980	23.7	21.8	32.0	31.0	53.6	25.9	23.6	35.2	34.0	61.2
1979	23.4	21.6	31.9	30.8	55.2	25.8	23.4	35.3	33.9	61.7
1978	23.2	21.4	31.5	30.5	52.6	25.5	23.2	35.1	33.8	59.7
1977	22.9	21.1	31.4	30.2	53.1	25.2	23.0	34.9	33.6	60.1
1976	22.7	21.0	31.7	30.1	53.0	25.0	22.9	35.1	33.7	60.0
1975	22.4	20.8	32.0	30.2	52.4	24.7	22.7	35.5	33.6	59.4
1974	22.0	20.6	32.1	30.0	51.9	24.2	22.5	35.7	33.6	59.2
1973	21.9	20.6	32.3	30.2	52.1	24.1	22.5	36.3	33.9	59.3
1972	21.7	20.5	32.8	30.3	51.4	23.8	22.4	36.5	34.0	59.1
1971	21.7	20.5	32.9	30.2	51.8	23.7	22.5	36.9	34.1	59.1
1970	21.7	20.6	33.3	30.1	51.2	23.6	22.5	37.5	34.5	58.7
1969	21.6	20.6	33.8	30.4	51.3	23.5	22.4	38.2	34.7	59.0
1968	21.5	20.6	33.8	30.7	50.6	23.6	22.4	38.3	35.1	57.9
1967	21.4	20.5	35.0	31.3	50.0	23.8	22.6	39.1	35.5	57.7
1966	21.5	20.3	35.2	31.4	50.2	23.8	22.6	39.2	35.8	57.9
1965	21.4	20.4	35.5	31.7	50.1	23.6	22.5	39.6	36.0	57.8
1964	21.4	20.4	35.6	31.7	50.3	23.6	22.4	39.7	36.4	58.0
1963	21.3	20.3	35.6	31.8	49.7	23.7	22.5	39.8	36.3	58.0

Source: National Center for Health Statistics, "Advance Report of Final Marriage Statistics, 1982," *Monthly Vital Statistics Report* 37(29 April 1988):13.

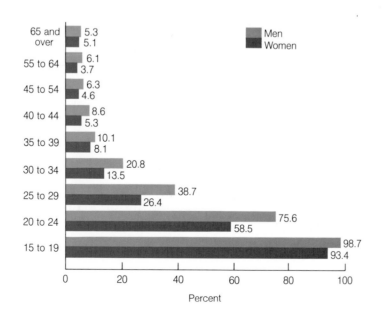

Figure 17.3
Percentage of persons who were never married, by age and sex: 1985

Source: U.S. Bureau of the Census, Current Population Reports, Series P-23, No. 150, *Population Profile of the United States: 1984–85*, Washington, D.C.: U.S. Government Printing Office, 1987, p. 22.

Are You Ready for Marriage?

The following questions are designed to assist you in clarifying your readiness for marriage. Although there are no absolute "right" or "wrong" answers, these questions can help identify some issues for you to focus on as you read this chapter. Check the appropriate blank for each of the following questions.

Yes   *No*

_____ _____ 1. Even though you may accept advice from other people (parents, instructors, friends), do you make important decisions on your own?

_____ _____ 2. Do you have a good working knowledge of the physiology of human sexuality, and do you understand the emotional and interpersonal factors that are involved in sexual adjustment?

_____ _____ 3. Have you had the experience of contributing to or sharing in the financial support of yourself and at least one other person?

_____ _____ 4. Have you and someone with whom you have had an intimate relationship ever worked through disagreements to a definite conclusion that was acceptable to both of you?

_____ _____ 5. Are you usually free of jealousy?

_____ _____ 6. Have you thought carefully about the goals you will strive for in marriage?

_____ _____ 7. Do you find yourself able to give up gracefully something you wanted very much?

_____ _____ 8. Can you postpone something you want for the sake of later enjoyment?

_____ _____ 9. Do you generally feel embarrassed or uneasy about giving or receiving affection?

Are *you* ready for marriage? Complete the "Are You Ready for Marriage" box to help you decide.

_____ _____   10. Are your feelings easily hurt by criticism?

_____ _____   11. In an argument, do you lose your temper easily?

_____ _____   12. Do you frequently feel like rebelling against responsibilities (work, family, school, and so on)?

_____ _____   13. Are you often sarcastic toward others?

_____ _____   14. Do you find yourself strongly emphasizing the more glamorous aspects of marriage, such as its social components?

_____ _____   15. Are you often homesick when you are away from your family?

Scoring and Interpretation

In questions 1 through 8, the more *yes* responses you have, the readier you are for marriage. In questions 9 through 15, the more *no* responses you have, the readier you are for marriage. Each question can help you identify areas that need some attention before you enter into marriage.

- Questions 1, 3, 4, 6, 7, and 8 explore *behaviors* that will affect the success of your marriage.
- Question 2 concerns *knowledge* that will affect the success of your marriage. Knowledge about human sexuality is an important prerequisite to sexual adjustment in marriage.
- Questions 5, 9, 10, 11, 12, 13, 14, and 15 enable you to estimate your *emotional readiness* for marriage. Question 5, for example, explores jealousy, an emotion that has been shown to be destructive to marital stability. If you are a jealous person in general, it may be important for you to seek professional guidance in dealing with issues such as trust and self-esteem before you contemplate marriage.

Source: Questions adapted from L. A. Kirkendall and W. J. Adams, *The Students' Guide to Marriage and Family Life Literature,* 8th ed. (Dubuque, Iowa: Wm. C. Brown Publishers, 1980), p. 157.

Cohabitation

More and more, people are choosing to live with someone of the opposite sex to whom they are not married. Between 1970 and 1980 alone, cohabitation rates tripled, with 1.6 million people living together in this way. By 1985, 2 million people were cohabiting. Cohabiting is prevalent on college campuses but not exclusive to young adults. Many elderly people who are widowed are living together because of the financial benefits—their two separate social security checks may be larger than one check when remarried—or because they feel no need to formalize their union. The separated and divorced are also choosing to cohabit more than in the past.

Divorce

Table 17.2 shows the divorce rate from 1950 through 1986. As can be seen, the divorce rate rose consistently from 1958 to about 1981, when it then dropped to remain relatively constant ever since. In 1985, there were over 2 million people divorced with over 1 million children involved (see table 17.3). It is interesting

Table 17.2
Divorces and Annulments and Rates: United States, 1950 to 1986

Year	Divorces and Annulments	Rate per 1,000	
		Total Population	Married Women 15 Years and Over
1986	1,159,000	4.8	—*
1985	1,190,000	5.0	21.7
1984	1,169,000	5.0	21.5
1983	1,158,000	4.9	21.3
1982	1,170,000	5.0	21.7
1981	1,213,000	5.3	22.6
1980	1,189,000	5.2	22.6
1979	1,181,000	5.3	22.8
1978	1,130,000	5.1	21.9
1977	1,091,000	5.0	21.1
1976	1,083,000	5.0	21.1
1975	1,036,000	4.8	20.3
1974	977,000	4.6	19.3
1973	915,000	4.3	18.2
1972	845,000	4.0	17.0
1971	773,000	3.7	15.8
1970	708,000	3.5	14.9
1969	639,000	3.2	13.4
1968	584,000	2.9	12.5
1967	523,000	2.6	11.2
1966	499,000	2.5	10.9
1965	479,000	2.5	10.6
1964	450,000	2.4	10.0
1963	428,000	2.3	9.6
1962	413,000	2.2	9.4
1961	414,000	2.3	9.6
1960	393,000	2.2	9.2
1959	395,000	2.2	9.3
1958	368,000	2.1	8.9
1957	381,000	2.2	9.2
1956	382,000	2.3	9.4
1955	377,000	2.3	9.3
1954	379,000	2.4	9.5
1953	390,000	2.5	9.9
1952	392,000	2.5	10.1
1951	381,000	2.5	9.9
1950	385,000	2.6	10.3

Sources: National Center for Health Statistics, "Advance Report of Final Divorce Statistics, 1985," *Monthly Vital Statistics Report* 36(7 December 1987):5, and National Center for Health Statistics, "Annual Summary of Births, Marriages, Divorces, and Deaths: United States, 1986," *Monthly Vital Statistics Report* 35(24 August 1987):5.

Note: Data for Alaska included beginning 1959 and for Hawaii, 1960.

*Unavailable

Table 17.3

Estimated Number of Children Involved in Divorces and Annulments, Average Number of Children Per Decree, and Rate Per 1,000 Children Under 18 Years of Age: United States, 1954 to 1985

Year	Estimated Number of Children Involved	Average Number of Children Per Decree	Rate Per 1,000 Children Under 18 Years of Age
1985	1,091,000	0.92	17.3
1984	1,081,000	0.92	17.2
1983	1,091,000	0.94	17.4
1982	1,108,000	0.94	17.6
1981	1,180,000	0.97	18.7
1980	1,174,000	0.98	17.3
1979	1,181,000	1.00	18.4
1978	1,147,000	1.01	17.7
1977	1,095,000	1.00	16.7
1976	1,117,000	1.03	16.9
1975	1,123,000	1.08	16.7
1974	1,099,000	1.12	16.2
1973	1,079,000	1.17	15.7
1972	1,021,000	1.20	14.7
1971	946,000	1.22	13.6
1970	870,000	1.22	12.5
1969	840,000	1.31	11.9
1968	784,000	1.34	11.1
1967	701,000	1.34	9.9
1966	669,000	1.34	9.5
1965	630,000	1.32	8.9
1964	613,000	1.36	8.7
1963	562,000	1.31	8.2
1962	532,000	1.29	7.9
1961	516,000	1.25	7.8
1960	463,000	1.18	7.2
1959	468,000	1.18	7.5
1958	398,000	1.08	6.5
1957	379,000	0.99	6.4
1956	361,000	0.95	6.3
1955	347,000	0.92	6.3
1954	341,000	0.90	6.4

Source: National Center for Health Statistics, "Advance Report of Final Divorce Statistics, 1985," *Monthly Vital Statistics Report* 36(7 December 1987):7.

Table 17.4
A Summary of Demographic Factors Related to Divorce

Factor	Comment
Race	Blacks have a much higher divorce rate than do whites in our society, at all income, educational, and occupational levels
Income	For both races, the higher the income, the lower the divorce rate; however, the black divorce rate does not drop as fast as the white rate as income increases
Educational level	For whites, the lower the educational level, the higher is the divorce rate; the black divorce rate is not so responsive to educational level
Occupational status	For whites, low-status occupations have a much higher divorce rate than high-status, such as managerial or professional groups; occupational status does not affect the rate of black divorce
Age at time of marriage	For both blacks and whites, teenage marriages have a much higher divorce rate than marriage in the twenties (or later)
Family background	For both blacks and whites, individuals whose homes were broken in childhood by divorce or desertion have a higher divorce rate than individuals whose parents remained married
Geographic location	For both blacks and whites, divorce rates by states increase from east to west and from north to south

Source: Lloyd Saxton, *The Individual, Marriage, and the Family,* 4th ed. © 1980 by Wadsworth, Inc. Reprinted by permission of Wadsworth Publishing Company, Belmont, California 94002. Pages 47, 87–88.

to note that the divorce rate varies by geographical area within the United States: in 1985, 3.8 per 1,000 population in the Northeast, 4.5 in the Midwest, 5.6 in the South, and 5.8 in the West.[6] The divorce rate ranged from lows of 2.9 in Connecticut and 3.3 in both Minnesota and North Dakota to highs of 7.2 in Alaska, 7.5 in Oklahoma, and 14.0 in Nevada.[7] Table 17.4 summarizes general demographic factors related to divorce.

Remarriage

With an increasing number of divorces, we would expect an increasing number of remarriages, and the data are consistent with this expectation. Divorced men have the highest rate of remarriage of all marital status groups (divorced women, first-married men and women, and widowed men and women). Divorced men marry at a rate three times that of women in general and at a rate two-thirds greater than divorced women. In addition to the divorced, the widowed are re-marrying as well.

Issue: Is Family Life Worse Than It Used to Be?

A recent Gallup Poll prepared for the White House Conference on Families found 45 percent of Americans think family life has gotten worse during the years 1965 to 1980. Of the 1,592 adults polled, 18 percent said they personally knew of a child-abuse situation, and 18 percent also knew of husband or wife abuse cases. Lastly, 25 percent reported alcohol-related problems had adversely affected their family lives.

Others believed that, although it has certainly changed during the past decade, family life has not worsened. Citing more equal sex roles and chores of family members, the greater opportunity for women to work outside the home, the increased availability of quality child care services, and the positive effect of divorce upon children when the historical alternative has been to grow up with two parents constantly bickering, some people actually perceive the family to have evolved into a more effective unit.

Do you believe the family unit has worsened, or do you believe it has become more responsive to its members' needs? Why did you answer as you did?

Source: Greenberg, Bruess, and Sands, *Sexuality: Insights and Issues* (Wm. C. Brown Company Publishers, 1986).

Single-Parent Families

The United States Census Bureau reports that the number of families maintained by one parent increased by 80 percent from 1970 to 1980. By 1985, 32 percent of all families with children still at home were maintained by one parent. Figure 17.4 illustrates the increase of families headed by women. This increase in single-parent families is a result of increased marital separation, divorce, and out-of-wedlock pregnancies rather than widowhood. Further, in 1984, 59 percent of black families with children at home were maintained by one parent.

Family Stressors

Although the family may not be dying—as some sociologists argue—it certainly is in transition. All the changes in family life previously cited need to be adapted to and are therefore stressful. Some of these stressors are discussed in this section.

The Dual-Career Family

More women who are married and have young children are working outside the home than ever before. We've discussed this in more detail in chapter 16, but its mention here is also necessary. Not only does a woman who works outside the home experience stress about juggling all of her responsibilities, but she is also bothered over what she is missing. As one mother who worked out of economic necessity put it: "Having to deal with a baby-sitter is very painful. All I can see is another woman holding, loving, and caring for my new baby. I am actually paying her to do all the things I wish I could be doing."[8]

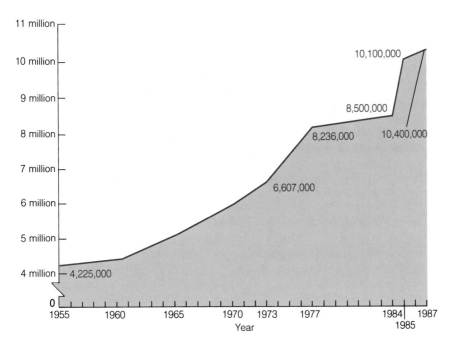

Figure 17.4 Number of families headed by women

Sources: U.S. Bureau of the Census, Current Population Reports, Series P-23, No. 150, *Population Profile of the United States: 1984–85,* Washington, D.C.: U.S. Government Printing Office, 1987, p. 20; and U.S. Bureau of the Census, Current Population Reports, Population Characteristics, Series P-20, No. 417, *Households, Families, Marital Status, and Living Arrangements: March 1987* (Advance Report), Washington, D.C.: U.S. Government Printing Office, 1987, p. 1.

Now enter the husband who must adapt his life to the new family style involving his wife's work. He must assume a larger share of the household and child-rearing responsibilities than before, and these changes are stressful.

Finally in this equation, the child must also adapt to mother's not being around as much. The child must cope with a baby-sitter or day-care staff and learn to be more self-sufficient at an earlier age.

All of this is not to say that women should not or need not work outside the home. A woman who is trained for a career and not pursuing it may experience more stress than that associated with combining mothering, homemaking, and a career. If she feels more stress, the chances are that so will her husband and child. However, that dual-career families are potentially stressful should not be denied.

Financial Concerns

When high inflation is coupled with high unemployment, things cost more, but people have less money to pay for them. The frustration of watching prices go up and income go down can be very stressful for families. Eating habits may have to change because foods previously affordable may no longer be so. Vacations may be postponed and trips to the dentist curtailed. These and other adjustments must be made and add to the usual stressors that families expect to occur.

On the other side of this coin are the families that prosper financially. Maybe Aunt Abigail died and left a large sum of cash to Mom or Dad. Maybe a killing was made in the stock market or some other investment. In any case, newfound wealth is accompanied by its own set of stressors. You now need to protect that money to minimize tax payments. This means tax shelters, real estate deals, money market funds, or some other financial wizardry. The fear of losing the new wealth raises its head, and you must direct attention, time, and energy at preventing such a loss. In addition, you may go out and buy a new car, move into a bigger house in a better neighborhood, buy more fashionable clothing, or arrange for vacations to faraway places instead of visiting relatives nearby. While these may be life-style adaptations you feel good and are excited about, they are adjustments and changes nevertheless. That means they are stressors with the potential to result in illness or disease.

Children

A friend once warned me that children are geometric, rather than arithmetic, stressors. What he meant was that a couple who has a child has added stressors equivalent to two extra adults; a couple with one child who have another have multiplied their stress by some number other than one or two; and a couple with two children . . . Anyone who has ever read any of Erma Bombeck's newspaper columns or books knows what my friend meant. Children are wonderful, but they certainly are stressful. This is understandable since stress involves adjusting to change. Although all of us are changing, children are changing more rapidly, repeatedly, and dramatically than mature adults. Children's bodies are changing, their minds developing, and their social skills and life-space expanding. To expect such change not to be stressful is unrealistic.

Further, when children change, so does the family. They are able to assume more responsibilities, take on more jobs, become more self-sufficient, and hold more firm opinions than when younger. These changes affect other members of the family. For example, when children become old enough to drive the family car, the parents no longer need to make themselves available for car pools. However, they must take on other stressors: "Will Johnny and the car both get home in one piece tonight?" This leads us to those notorious teenage years.

Parents who see their children approaching "teenagehood" sometimes find their knees knocking together, their hearts racing, and their headaches visiting more frequently. The problem is best summed up by the title of a book, which would not have been written or published had there not been a market for it. It's entitled *Living with Teenagers*[9] and is designed to help parents survive the tumult of their children's teens. Teenagers may get involved with drugs, sex, vandalism, shoplifting, automobile accidents, or truancy; they may be impossible to discipline, talk with, or get to see very often; or they may have problems with their teachers, their friends, or their bosses. On the other hand, they may be companions, helpers, and interesting to talk with; they may be brilliant, committed to causes, and willing to persevere to achieve goals; and they may be someone of whom we are very, very proud. Lest we forget the teenagers, these years are stressful for them as well. A sobering piece of evidence of this is the number of attempted suicides by teenagers.

Other years of growing up may be stressful for parents and children too. The parent-child relationship has been described as three-phased: bonding, detachment, and reunion.[10] During the **bonding** years, the child learns love, approval, and acceptance from the family. During the **detachment** years, the child learns independence and relies less on the family. The **reunion** years occur after the child is independent and is secure enough to rebond with the family. Bonding is a preteen phase, detachment a teen phase, and reunion a postteen phase. Each of these phases has its own stressors and its own joys.

A discussion of stress and children must include a discussion of planning for how many children to have. Two topics pertaining to this consideration are discussed below: contraception and abortion and their relationship to family stress. **Family Planning**

When couples decide to control conception to limit the number of children they have, they must decide upon a method. There is no perfect method of birth control. Each has its advantages and disadvantages, and all should be studied before one is chosen. This choice, however, may generate disagreement between the sexual partners and cause distress. Who should be responsible for birth control, the man or the woman? How much inconvenience or interruption are we willing to tolerate in sexual activity? What religious proscriptions should we adhere to? How much risk—both in terms of our health and in terms of the chances of a pregnancy—are we willing to accept?

Once the decision about birth control is made, there is still the possibility of pregnancy. No method except abstinence is 100 percent effective. If unwanted pregnancy does occur, what then? Another child? An abortion? These decisions, too, can be very stressful and more complicated than at first thought. To demonstrate the complexity and stress associated with abortion, complete the accompanying questionnaire.

Abortion Decisions

	Yes	No
1. Should abortions ever be allowed?	___	___
2. If yes, under which circumstances?		
a. If conception is a result of rape	___	___
b. If the pregnancy will be an economic hardship	___	___
c. If the pregnancy is harmful to the woman's physical health	___	___
d. If the pregnancy is unwanted	___	___
e. If the pregnancy is dangerous to the woman's physical health	___	___
f. If the pregnancy is a result of not using contraception	___	___

	Yes	No
g. If the pregnancy is a result of the failure of contraception that was used	___	___
h. If the woman is unmarried	___	___
i. If the woman is a teenager	___	___
j. If the woman is over forty	___	___
3. Should government funds be used for abortions for women who can't afford it?	___	___
4. Should the father's signature be required before an abortion can be performed?	___	___
5. Should the father be held financially responsible for paying for half of the cost for the abortion?	___	___

Mobility

There was a time when the extended family all lived in the same town and visited frequently. When I was growing up, we established a "family circle" that met one Sunday a month. All the aunts, uncles, cousins, and Grandma Mary and Grandpa Barney gathered to talk, play cards, play ball, argue, and eat. We would sometimes pile in the back of my grandfather's pickup truck, sit on empty wooden milk crates, and be off for a day at the beach. We all felt close to one another and were caught up in one another's lives. I knew who my cousin Marcia was dating, and she knew what sports I liked.

How times have changed! My children were born in Buffalo and now live in the Washington, D.C. area. We have no relatives living in either of these places. We make a point of renewing family ties once a year at a Passover Seder rather than once a month as when I was young. My children rarely play with their cousins and don't know much about their relatives' lives. Their grandmother doesn't come over every Friday night for dinner as mine did. She lives 300 miles away. When they have a baby-sitter, it isn't their cousin Larry from next door as it was for me. For them it is a nonrelative from a list of sitters we maintain (support might be a more accurate term).

What's more, families pick up and move so often nowadays that even close friends who might serve as surrogate extended family are left elsewhere. New friendships need to be developed and it takes time for these new relationships to become meaningful.

In addition to the lack of involvement with extended family, mobility has led to other stressors. When you move, you need to find new physicians, dentists, gas stations, shopping malls, libraries, and so forth. Much of your surroundings and habits change—and we know by now that change can be stressful.

Other Stressors

There are many other stressors for which space dictates only a mention. How to discipline children and disagreements between parents regarding this can be stressful. What to do with elderly parents—place them in a nursing home or have

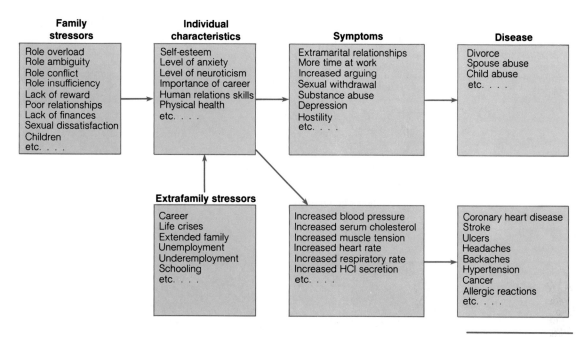

Family stressors	Individual characteristics	Symptoms	Disease
Role overload Role ambiguity Role conflict Role insufficiency Lack of reward Poor relationships Lack of finances Sexual dissatisfaction Children etc. . . .	Self-esteem Level of anxiety Level of neuroticism Importance of career Human relations skills Physical health etc. . . .	Extramarital relationships More time at work Increased arguing Sexual withdrawal Substance abuse Depression Hostility etc. . . .	Divorce Spouse abuse Child abuse etc. . . .

Extrafamily stressors

Career Life crises Extended family Unemployment Underemployment Schooling etc. . . .	Increased blood pressure Increased serum cholesterol Increased muscle tension Increased heart rate Increased respiratory rate Increased HCl secretion etc. . . .	Coronary heart disease Stroke Ulcers Headaches Backaches Hypertension Cancer Allergic reactions etc. . . .

Figure 17.5 Family stress model

them live with you—creates stress for many families. Other families find their sexual lives stressful; for example, how often should we have sexual intercourse, who should initiate it, or which sexual activities should we engage in. Still other families are plagued with child or spouse abuse. Some parents are raising children alone or are in the midst of a divorce. Some parents, usually fathers, may be living apart from their children. I'm sure you can add to this list. Since family life is dynamic, it is always changing—and therefore stressful.

A Model of Family Stress

In order to intervene in family stress, it is necessary to have a clear understanding of the situation. I have developed a model of family stress (see fig. 17.5) to help with this task. People who have applied the model have found it useful to help appreciate the components and manifestations of stress in families they know.

This model is similar to the one on occupational stress presented in chapter 14. It demonstrates that there are stressors occurring within the family, but these stressors are screened through individuals who differ on a number of important variables. It also demonstrates how these individual family members are affected by stressors which occur outside the context of the family but which nonetheless affect how family stressors are perceived and reacted to. The result of the interaction of family stressors and extrafamily stressors upon differing family members may be signs and symptoms of family stress or full-blown family disease. Once this complex of family stress is understood, the interventions described in this chapter can be better tailored to meet each family's needs.

Effective families express love and affection toward each other and help children to do the same.

Interventions

Family stress can be prevented from resulting in illness and disease through employing life-situation interventions, perception interventions, emotional arousal interventions, and physiological arousal interventions.

Life-Situation Interventions

Lack of time is a major stressor in dual-career families. This lack of time prevents some chores from being done, takes time away from other family members, and creates stress when you hurry to complete as much as possible in the little time available. To manage this stress, you can seek the help of other family members or friends. For example, they can do some shopping for you or pick up the kids from soccer practice. You might also hire someone to do some of the less important chores, such as cleaning the house or doing the laundry, to free you to do the more important ones. Your first priority after work hours, whether you are a male or female, should be your family. To maximize your time with the family, you can plan vacations for work holidays and weekends—vacations that will get you all away from friends and chores so you can focus more upon each other. Fishing trips or hiking excursions provide a relaxing setting and an opportunity for conversing with each other. Trips to fancy hotels where the kids attend a day camp and the parents golf all day are not conducive to sharing meaningful family time together.

Marriage is said to be hard work. Maintaining all family relationships can be substituted for the word "marriage" in the previous sentence. In his study of couples married to the same person for over twenty years, David Fenell found successful marriage partners shared a commitment to their mates as demonstrated by the following:

1. Loyalty to spouse
2. Respect for spouse
3. Spouse considered "best friend"
4. Willingness to forgive and to be forgiven
5. Desire to please and support spouse[11]

Perhaps all of us need to spend time and energy developing similar feelings for our families. To do so, though, requires a commitment to organize our lives so as to be together sharing meaningful activities and developing a positive family history. The suggestions in this chapter should help.

For most of the family stressors described in this chapter, improving the communication between members of the family would be helpful. The conflict-resolution and communication sections in chapter 6 will help with this, since conflicts that go unresolved or are ineffectively resolved will interfere with other types of communication.

One of the most important prerequisites of communication, and one that is so obvious it is almost forgotten, is that you need time set aside to communicate. Family members are usually involved in so many activities that they almost never have time to sit and talk and get to know one another. The kids are out playing, or have practice for some team they are on, or are doing schoolwork. The parents are busy with their careers, sports, or friends. To make sure that time will be available for other family members, some families actually schedule it in. Other families set up weekly gripe sessions for any member to complain about anything bothering him or her. Recently, I realized that I wasn't spending enough time with my son and, in particular, understanding what he was doing in school. We now spend fifteen minutes together after dinner on Tuesdays and Thursdays (a time convenient to both of us). During this time, he shows me all of his schoolwork and points out how far he has gone in his textbooks. At other times either my son or daughter will sit on my lap and we'll have a "conversation"—our key word for a discussion of our feelings. We'll discuss what makes us happy, sad, frightened, angry, or any other emotion one of us suggests. Far from being the perfect parent, I cite these examples of our family life because they work for us. Maybe they will work for you and your family.

Regarding stress associated with divorce, the best advice is to get involved with people. Also work at maintaining your sense of self-worth (see chapter 7). One author presents some advice to the divorced parent who does not have custody of the children:[12]

Avoid	*Aim at*
Arguing directly against whatever the other parent has been saying	Listening to what your child has to say, and taking a friendly interest
Trying to pull the other parent down in your child's estimation	Answering questions in a way that expands conversation; i.e., without laying down the law
Trying to persuade your child that your view of everything is the right one	Noticing any problems, where you might be able to help
Reacting defensively at any hint of criticism from child or other parent	Being around, on a dependable, reliable basis
Preaching any particular religious, moral, or social doctrines that you know are contradictory to the home views	Showing that you have your own standards and that, even if these are different from those at home, at least you are consistent
Trying to solve your problems through your child	Enjoying time together, rather than treating it as an opportunity to impress or persuade

This advice will help the formation of a more positive relationship with the children and the ex-spouse, and thereby decrease the stress experienced as a result of the divorce.

Regarding stress about family planning, you might want to talk with a counselor—for example, one at Planned Parenthood—to better understand your options. One of the best sources of information about family planning, which identifies the methods available, their effectiveness, and their advantages and disadvantages, is a book entitled *Contraceptive Technology,* written by Robert Hatcher and published by the Irvington Publishers (551 Fifth Avenue, New York, NY 10017). You might want to write for that book. If you have moral, ethical, or religious concerns about birth control, consult with your clergy. In addition to all of these steps, remember to involve your partner. To be less distressed over these decisions, you need to work together, relying on each other to help sort out all the issues involved.

Regarding the stress of living long distances from your extended family, you can plan vacations visiting them rather than going other places. You can also telephone them regularly. Regular phone calls will allow some time for small talk—important in getting to know each other—since less time between calls will mean there are fewer major issues to discuss. Another means of maintaining your connection with your extended family—less expensive than visiting or telephoning—is exchanging letters with them. Notice I said *letters,* not cards. Birthday or anniversary cards won't serve the same purpose. Your relatives should know that you are making a special effort to communicate with them; then they will understand how important keeping in touch is to you and will be more apt to write back. Letters will better convey this need than will cards.

Many of the perception interventions presented in chapter 7 are applicable to family stress. For example, you can use selective awareness to perceive the changes in your family life as exciting, interesting, and challenging; and remind yourself that in the long run you will all be closer for having experienced these changes together. Viewed in this way, family transitions will be less stressful.

Perception Interventions

You can also "smell the roses"; that is, enjoy your family life as fully as possible. Sometimes I'll be doing some reading, and my daughter will climb onto my lap. My first inclination is to figure out a way to get her off without having her feel rejected so I can continue reading undisturbed, and she will grow up with one less psychological scar. Most of the time, however, I put down what I am reading and try to appreciate Keri on my lap. I stop to recognize that in all too few more years, lap-sitting with her Dad will be a thing of the past—my loss more than hers, I'm sure. With that realization, I want to soak up as much lap-sitting and appreciation from lap-sitting as I can get. The interesting thing, though, is that with this attitude of "smelling the roses," *each* new phase of our relationship will be experienced fully. It may be lap-sitting today and boyfriend problems tomorrow. Because one phase is over, I need not be distressed over its loss if I experienced it to its fullest, since the next phase offers new wonders. Children will cause less stress if we wonder at them—if we watch them grow and marvel at their uniqueness.

The lessons learned earlier about the Type A behavior pattern can be used to manage family stress. If you'll recall, one characteristic of Type A people is that they are concerned more with quantity than quality. They try to do many things, allowing the quality of each to suffer, rather than doing fewer things well. Generalizing this characteristic and relating it to stress caused by too little time to spend with family members, spend the limited time you have qualitatively. Talk with each other rather than watching television together. Go out for dinner rather than to a movie where you can't converse. With elderly family members, try to get them to talk about the past and maybe even tape-record those discussions so they won't be lost to future generations. The elderly, you will find, have so many interesting stories and have experienced a world so different from ours that honoring their past in this manner will not only alleviate some of their stress— they will feel as though they have something worthwhile to offer—but will help us connect to the past from which we sprang. It will give us roots and help us to see that our lives are not just fleeting moments, but rather a link in the chain of humankind.

It has been found that wives do about thirty hours of housework per week while their husbands do about four to six hours of housework per week. For working wives the situation is somewhat improved: they do only 70 percent of the housework compared to 83 percent for full-time domestic engineers (homemakers).[13] One might argue that a fifty-fifty split of the housework between husbands and wives who work outside the home full-time would be the only fair arrangement. However, some experts on family relations suggest that women may have difficulty sharing home and parenting duties because of the fear of losing their identities as women and mothers.[14] If you or someone you know is experiencing these concerns, discuss the quality-of-time versus quantity-of-time issue with them to better help them perceive the need to be willing to share routine household and parenting responsibilities. Only if they realize they are not superwomen and cannot do everything themselves will women who work outside the home free up time to improve their family relationships and decrease the potential for family stress. Men, too, need to perceive their limitations and delegate responsibilities to other family members when they are overburdened. However, as the data above indicate, this need, at least at home, is not as much of a concern for men as it is for women.

Lastly, your perceptions of the control you can exercise over events that affect your life—your locus of control—will influence how you respond to family stressors. If you work to develop internality, you will believe you can do something to experience less stress from your family life. You will therefore try some of the suggestions appearing in this chapter and even seek others. One of the best ways to develop internality is to try controlling some events and analyzing how that attempt fared. Was it successful? If so, why? If not, why not? Experience in actually exercising control over aspects of your life will reinforce your notion that such control is possible. Try some of the suggestions above. Choose one that you think has the best chance of being successful and then move on to some others. You will find that you really can do something to manage family stress better.

Emotional Arousal Interventions	Family stress can be less unhealthy if you regularly practice some relaxation technique. Any of the techniques described in this book will do (see chapters 8, 9, 10, and 11). With family stress as your particular concern here, you might want to engage in relaxation as a family. Perhaps you can schedule a "relaxation time" when everyone in the family meditates. Maybe you can all take a yoga class together. Regular practice of relaxation will help you cope better with normal family transitions as well as unusual and unanticipated family stressors.

Physiological Arousal Interventions	Like other stressors, family stressors increase serum cholesterol, heart rate, and blood pressure and change other body processes (see chapter 2). Exercise can use these stress products in a healthy manner and prevent them from making you ill. Consult chapter 12 to begin an exercise program. One last thought: Why not exercise as a family? You could bike, swim, play tennis, or even jog as a family.

Families both create stress and serve as social support networks to help us manage stress better.

Summary

1. A family is a unique set of intimate relationships.

2. The nuclear family is a married couple and their children. The extended family includes relatives other than spouses and their children.

3. The family satisfies several needs. These include the social control of reproduction and child rearing, economic support, security and safety needs, and the emotional needs of love and a sense of belonging.

4. The effective family has a leader and someone who keeps track of what others are doing. It encourages members to be involved with people outside the family, is hospitable, deals squarely with dire events, prizes its rituals, is affectionate, provides a sense of place, allows for a connection for posterity, and honors its elders.

5. The family has changed in recent years. People are marrying later and more people are choosing to remain single. More people are cohabiting rather than marrying, and a large number of divorces are occurring with over one million children involved each year.

6. Family stressors include financial concerns, dual-career marriages, increased mobility, child rearing, contraception decisions, separation from extended families, and spouse and child abuse.

7. Family stress is a complex of family stressors, individual family members' characteristics, and extrafamily stressors. These can lead to symptoms of family stress or stress-related illness.

8. Effective communication and conflict resolution skills can help manage family stress.

Notes

1. A. Cherlin, "Remarriage as an Incomplete Institution," *American Journal of Sociology* 84 (1978): 634.

2. U.S. Bureau of the Census, *Current Population Reports, Series P-23, No. 150, Population Profile of the United States: 1984–85* (Washington, D.C.: U.S. Government Printing Office, 1987).

3. Ibid.

4. National Center for Health Statistics, "Advance Report for Final Marriage Statistics, 1985," *Monthly Vital Statistics Report* 37(29 April 1988):13.

5. U.S. Bureau of the Census, Current Population Reports, Population Characteristics, Series P-20, No. 417, *Households, Families, Marital Status, and Living Arrangements: March 1987 (Advance Report)* (Washington, D.C.: U.S. Government Printing Office, 1987).

6. National Center for Health Statistics, "Advance Report of Final Divorce Statistics, 1985," *Monthly Vital Statistics Report* 36(7 December 1987):1.

7. National Center for Health Statistics, "Annual Summary of Births, Marriages, Divorces, and Deaths: United States, 1986," *Monthly Vital Statistics Report* 35(24 August 1987):4.

8. Janet DiVittorio Morgan, "I Work Because I Have To," in *The Mothers' Book: Shared Experiences,* ed. Ronnie Friedland and Carol Kort (Boston: Houghton Mifflin, 1981), 96.

9. Jean Rosenbaum and Veryl Rosenbaum, *Living with Teenagers* (New York: Stein & Day, 1980).

10. Ibid., 5.

11. Personal communication from David L. Fenell, University of Colorado at Colorado Springs, 3 November 1987.

12. Peter Rowlands, *Saturday Parent* (New York: Continuum, 1980), 24.

13. Eleanor Grant, "The Housework Gap," *Psychology Today* 22(1988):8.

14. Holly Hall, "A Woman's Place . . ." *Psychology Today* 22(1988):28–29.

18

Stress and the Elderly

Like most of us, I have always taken my parents for granted. They will always be here, and they will be relatively stress-free. After all, while I was growing up they seemed invincible; they were always right, they were always able to raise and support a family, and they always seemed to know who would make the best president. How wrong I was! As I approached adulthood and was looked up to by my children as I looked up to my parents, I came to realize that they did the best they could but were certainly not invincible.

As though to drive this point home with a hammer, my father died this past year. As we hugged and cried together in his hospital room, his vulnerability came through. He was, after all, human; with human fears, insecurities, and foibles. My mother survives and makes the best of a bad situation. She organizes a new life for herself with new activities and a new cohort of friends. This type of change we have come to know as stressful and fraught with the consequences of stress discussed in earlier chapters.

In retrospect, I can see the stressors that my parents endured then and the stressors my mother endures now. However, these are not unique to my family. Old age is a time of life that is replete with changes. There may be retirement, failing health, the death of friends and relatives, and financial insecurity that all create the need for adjustment. These may all be stressful and a threat to our health and happiness.

On the other hand, old age has been described as a "state of mind." You are old when you allow yourself to feel old. This can occur at age thirty for some, at age sixty-five for others, or may never arrive for those who remain "young at heart." It makes us recall our earlier discussion of selective awareness. That is, you can focus on the stressful parts of old age or you can focus upon the pleasing aspects. You can bemoan the inability to play tennis as you once could, or you can be grateful to still be able to play doubles. You can feel sorry for yourself because of a forced retirement, or you can welcome the availability of time to spend with your grandchildren. The focus is up to each and every one of us. It is our choice what we will pay most attention to.

So, my mother remains thankful for the years spent with Dad, and we often laugh at how he would become the life of the party with a crowd around him as he told one of the hundreds of jokes he committed to memory. Certainly we cry during particular moments, but generally we go on with our lives because there is no other choice if we want to be happy and healthy.

This chapter is concerned with showing how one can recognize and manage the stress associated with the later years. We will see that certain stressors can be anticipated and their consequences minimized, while other stressors—those less predictable—can be perceived in ways to decrease their potential for harm. Finally we will recognize that the later years can be just as rewarding as the earlier years if we insist they be that way; and if we apply the stress management skills presented in this book and, in particular, in this chapter.

The Elderly: A Description

In 1900 the number of people in the United States over sixty-five years of age was slightly over 3 million, or 3.9 percent of the population. By 1985 there were over 29 million Americans over sixty-five, or 12 percent of the population. The United States Census Bureau estimates that the percentage of Americans over sixty-five will increase to 13 percent by the year 2000 and to 21 percent by 2030.[1] That estimate translates into 65 million Americans over the age of sixty-five by 2030. Even the population of Americans eighty years and older is increasing—6 million in 1985 and estimated to increase to 17.4 million by 2030.

Test of Knowledge about the Elderly

How much do you know about the elderly? To find out, decide which statements are true and which are false.

    ___ 1. Over 20 percent of Americans over eighty years old live in institutions.
    ___ 2. The majority of the elderly have serious health problems.
    ___ 3. Not having enough money is a problem for the elderly.
    ___ 4. Poor housing is a problem for the elderly.
    ___ 5. Insufficient medical care is a problem for the elderly.
    ___ 6. Loneliness is a problem for the elderly.
    ___ 7. The elderly are not very interested in sex.
    ___ 8. The focus of the elderly on the past is unhealthy.
    ___ 9. Older people are generally not efficient at work and should retire.
    ___ 10. Older workers are absent from the job more often than younger workers.

All of these statements are misconceptions. If you thought these were true, I had an eighty-five-year-old grandmother who would have liked to "punch your lights out."

Contrary to popular belief, only 5 percent of those aged sixty-five or older live in institutions.[2] Most of these people are healthy and active in the community. Other myths about the elderly also exist. For example, 62 percent of Americans polled cited "not enough money to live on" as a problem for the elderly, but only 15 percent of the elderly themselves reported experiencing this problem. Over 40 percent of Americans believed poor housing and insufficient medical care to be problems for the elderly, but only 4 percent of the elderly themselves reported experiencing poor housing, and only 10 percent had problems with medical care.[3] Mental health problems of the elderly are limited to 20 to 25 percent of the older population.[4] In spite of the belief that old age is a lonely time, 53 percent of Americans over age sixty-five (excluding those in institutions) are married and living with their spouses; and an additional 14 percent are living with other relatives.[5] Of the remaining elderly, some of them are living with other people (nonrelatives), although most live alone. In the United States in 1984, there were 17 million noninstitutionalized people aged 70 and older, 11 million of whom lived with another person (7 million with a spouse and 4 million with someone other than a spouse).[6] Regarding sex, in spite of the notion that it doesn't occur in the elderly population, it does. Vaginal lubrication and penile erection may occur later and leave sooner, but study after study finds the elderly still sexually active. Masters and Johnson even reported studying a sexually active ninety-four-year-old male.

Two final myths need discussing. The elderly do often reminisce, but this is not unhealthy. As we shall soon see, one of the needs of the later years is to see ourselves as part of humankind—as being attached to a past and a future. Reminiscing helps with this task. Lastly, elderly workers are not frequently absent, nor should they necessarily retire. Older workers have a 20 percent better absenteeism record than do younger workers.[7] As a matter of fact, older workers have fewer disabling injuries and the frequency of accidents *decreases* with age.

When the elderly were asked to look back on their lives, 80 percent of them expressed satisfaction with it; and 75 percent felt that their lives at present were as interesting as ever.[8]

There are several theories of adult development that attempt to explain stress in the elderly. A discussion of these theories follows.

Adjustment in the Later Years

Erik Erikson—Life Crises

Erik Erikson described life as consisting of eight stages during which crises are encountered. The crisis of late adulthood is acquiring a sense of integrity and fending off a sense of despair. Erikson saw this stage of life as one in which the successful person had some fairly clear understanding of identity, was aware of both successes and failures, and was willing to affirm the life-style he or she lived. Death would, therefore, not seem the ultimate end of life. A person who is unsuccessful with this crisis is likely to be overcome by despair because the time left is so short, death approaches too rapidly, and there is no time to try another route to integrity. Disgust may be used to hide this despair; the person then becomes bitter, depressed, and paranoid.[9]

Robert Havighurst— Developmental Tasks

Robert Havighurst viewed life as a series of developmental tasks that we must master before moving on to the next stage of development.[10] Havighurst defines a developmental task as one that "arises at or about a certain period of the life of the individual, successful achievement of which leads to happiness and success with later tasks, while failure leads to unhappiness in the individual, disapproval by the society, and difficulty with later tasks."[11] Havighurst's final stage, later adulthood, begins at age fifty-five. This stage is characterized by new experiences and new situations to deal with, as are the earlier stages. Havighurst considers that old age is still developmental. The six developmental tasks of the elderly as outlined by Havighurst follow:

1. Adjusting to decreased physical strength and health
2. Adjusting to retirement and reduced income
3. Adjusting to death of spouse
4. Establishing an explicit affiliation with one's age group
5. Meeting social and civic obligations
6. Establishing satisfactory physical living arrangements[12]

Since a major stressor involves adapting to change, one can readily see the implications of stress for old age according to Havighurst's theory.

Positive Change

Lest we forget the good changes (eustress) accompanying old age, let's cite some here. For many of the elderly, their grandchildren become a source of joy. The relationship between grandparents and grandchildren is unique. Free of the responsibility for disciplining the children, grandparents can just play with them and help them learn and have fun.

In many societies, old age has another benefit. The elderly are viewed as the wisest in the society and consulted and honored for their wisdom. Unfortunately in American society this is more often the exception than the rule. However, some companies and some governmental agencies do value the knowledge and experience of their elderly workers and have even been known to ask the advice of some retirees.

Old age also often presents us with free time to pursue interests earlier postponed. For example, Grandma Moses didn't paint until she was quite old. We often hear that people have retired and moved to where they always wanted to live or are doing something (maybe traveling) they always longed to do but never did.

I think you get the picture; that is, some stressors of old age are adaptations that have good results, but they are stressors nevertheless.

Retirement

Retiring from work is one of the most significant events of one's life. How successfully this event is adjusted to has a major effect on the satisfaction and rewards of later life. When we recognize that retirement has far-reaching

implications, we can see its importance. What will retirees think of their self-worth when no longer "productive" at work? Will they miss fellow workers themselves or the idea of people with whom to interact? Can they replace the stimulation of learning new skills? Will they miss the sense of being needed that work provided?

Retirement affects not only retirees but their families as well. Will the retirement benefits be so meager as to force the spouse to make sacrifices along with the retiree? Will more frequent visits be made to family members who live out of town?

Because a growing number of elderly people are choosing not to retire and because our social security system is being taxed by the large increase in the elderly population, the government is encouraging later retirements. When one heard Buckminster Fuller or René Dubos or some other elderly person of tremendous wisdom and ability, one could not help but be supportive of later retirements. In 1978, Congress extended the mandatory retirement age from sixty-five to seventy and removed the age limit completely for federal employees. President Reagan was seventy-three years old when elected for his second term of office, demonstrating that chronological age is not as important as mental and physiological age. Many people will choose to work their whole lives, whereas others will choose to retire to another job or from work completely. This choice allows people to exercise greater control over their lives than when retirement was mandatory at age sixty-five.

Two Views of Retirement

It's Boring

"They gave me a gold watch—a beautiful thing—six month's pay, a new car, and a fabulous pension," Baird explained. "We spent three months traveling, playing golf, fishing, and getting lazy. At first, I thought it was great. You know, for years you look forward to the freedom, the leisure time, the no hassles. But, let me tell you friend, it gets old. After six months I was bored stiff, and my wife, she was getting fed up too. You know, she had her friends and her activities and didn't need me underfoot. Then, I found this job, and it's great. I love it! New people; people from all over and I am able to make their stay a little more pleasant. Don't ever retire friend; if you got a job, stick with it. Retirement is for the birds. Unless you're a lazy bird."

It's Great

"I don't feel any great loss at all. No, no. I taught math and science for thirty-one years, and if I hadn't taken time out to raise two daughters, I would have made it forty. I loved every minute of it, but now it is time to take a rest. After all that time I have earned it, don't you think? Why would I want to go on teaching? I have my retirement, my insurance, and my health. Now I just want to enjoy it."

Adjusting to Retirement

Retirement, whether it's viewed as a positive or negative experience, requires adjustment. Our work is such an important part of our lives for such a long time that self-worth becomes tied to it. When retirement occurs, we may lack other ways to affirm our self-worth and status. Retired workers may see themselves as neither needed nor contributing to some useful endeavor.

In addition, retirement often means an adjustment to a leisure-oriented way of life. No longer required to wake up early, to be at work at a particular time, to limit when and how long lunch will be, and to save leisure-time activities for evenings and weekends, retired people encounter a whole new life-style to which they must adjust. For those not used to having leisure—for example, the workaholics described in chapter 14—this adjustment is a major one. They may lack leisure skills such as conversing well with others, various sports skills, or just being able to enjoy themselves at an activity that is not specifically "productive."

To further complicate retirement, many retirees must adjust to decreased financial resources. With more leisure time and less money available to spend on leisure activities, many retirees feel frustrated.

Also, retirees must sometimes put up with the negative attitudes of others (workers) who may consider them outsiders. For example, one researcher found that health professionals are significantly more negative in their attitudes toward treating older people than they are toward treating younger people.[13] **Ageism,** like sexism and racism, is a negative social reality with which the elderly are faced.

Mixed into this brew of necessary adjustments during retirement are alone-ness—not necessarily "loneliness" but rather living alone after the death of a spouse—and health problems. Those with degenerative diseases such as diabetes, arthritis, or arteriosclerosis may find these conditions worsening as they get older, and more restrictions may be placed on their activity during their retirement years.

Now, the test of your knowledge about the elderly presented earlier showed that many of the problems named were experienced by a minority of the elderly. Although they are in the minority, significant numbers of the aged do experience stressors to which they must adapt upon retirement. Some adapt better than others. When retirees were studied by the National Institute of Mental Health (NIMH), four patterns of adjustment were found:[14]

1. *Maintenance:* the pattern of people who try to satisfy the same needs after retirement as before retirement in the same kind of way. They continue work in one way or another; for example, they take part-time jobs.
2. *Withdrawal:* the pattern of people who consider retirement as a time to relax. They give up many of their former activities and adopt new ones; for example, they take up golf.
3. *Changed activities:* the pattern of people who attempt to satisfy the same needs as before retirement, but by different means; for example, they volunteer to work as aides in hospitals or for charitable organizations.
4. *Changed needs:* the pattern of people who attempt to satisfy a different set of needs than before retirement. They view retirement as a time of relaxation but may continue many of their previous activities. In addition, they may adopt a few new activities.

All in all, NIMH found that over half of the retirees studied felt positively toward their retirement, while a large number had negative feelings.

Caregiving

In spite of large numbers of the elderly being able to care for themselves, there is a significant population of older Americans who do need taking care of. As noted in table 18.1, as a person gets older, the care they need tends to increase. Overall, 10 percent of noninstitutionalized persons sixty-five and older were func-tionally limited in the sense that they received help with one or more personal care activities.[15] Caregivers of the elderly may experience a great deal of stress from the feeling of being captive to the needs of the elderly person for whom they are caring and because of the changes necessitated in their daily family lives. Just who these caregivers are can be seen in figure 18.1.

Elder care, as the issue has sometimes been called, can also result in lost wages of employees who must juggle caregiving and work responsibilities. Tar-diness, absenteeism, and lack of concentration are some of the costs to both workers and the organizations for whom they work when elderly relatives need care.[16]

Table 18.1

Percent of Persons 65 Years of Age and Over Who Have Difficulty Performing Selected Personal Care Activities by Sex and Age: United States, 1984

Sex and Age	Personal Care Activity						
	Bathing	Dressing	Eating	Trans-ferring	Walking	Getting Outside	Using Toilet
Both Sexes				Percent			
65 years and over	9.8	6.2	1.8	8.0	18.7	9.6	4.3
65–74 years	6.4	4.3	1.2	6.1	14.2	5.6	2.6
65–69 years	5.2	3.9	1.2	5.3	12.2	4.9	2.2
70–74 years	7.9	4.8	1.1	7.1	16.6	6.6	3.0
75–84 years	12.3	7.6	2.5	9.2	22.9	12.3	5.4
75–79 years	9.8	6.4	2.1	7.5	19.5	9.9	4.1
80–84 years	16.8	9.7	3.2	12.4	29.0	16.8	7.8
85 years and over	27.9	16.6	4.4	19.3	39.9	31.3	14.1
Male							
65 years and over	7.6	5.8	2.0	5.6	15.5	6.3	3.1
65–74 years	5.7	4.4	1.5	4.8	12.9	4.5	2.4
65–69 years	5.3	4.1	1.7	4.7	11.5	4.3	2.3
70–74 years	6.1	4.9	1.4	5.0	14.9	4.7	2.4
75–84 years	9.2	7.3	2.5	6.0	18.3	7.5	3.6
75–79 years	7.8	6.7	2.3	4.7	15.6	6.3	2.7
80–84 years	12.3	8.5	3.0	8.7	24.2	10.2	5.6
85 years and over	23.1	14.1	4.3	12.7	32.2	21.9	10.0
Female							
65 years and over	11.2	6.5	1.7	9.7	20.9	11.8	5.1
65–74 years	6.9	4.2	0.9	7.0	15.1	6.5	2.7
65–69 years	5.1	3.7	0.9	5.7	12.9	5.3	2.2
70–74 years	9.1	4.8	1.0	8.6	17.8	8.0	3.4
75–84 years	14.2	7.7	2.4	11.2	25.7	15.3	6.5
75–79 years	11.1	6.2	3.3	9.3	22.2	12.3	5.0
80–84 years	19.2	10.2	3.4	14.3	31.4	20.2	9.0
85 years and over	30.1	17.7	4.4	22.2	43.3	35.4	15.9

Source: National Health Interview Survey, National Center for Health Statistics.

Recognizing this cost, some businesses have begun to offer support services for their employees. For example, Southern Bell has published a manual that lists services in the community that can help workers identify assistance in caring for their elderly relatives; Stride Rite Corporation has added an adult-care component to their existing child-care center; and the Potomac Electric Power Company gives workers unpaid leaves to care for both elders and children. We shall soon see that in addition to these societal adjustments recognizing the needs of caregivers, educational programs have been developed to help them be more effective and to be better able to cope with the stress they experience.

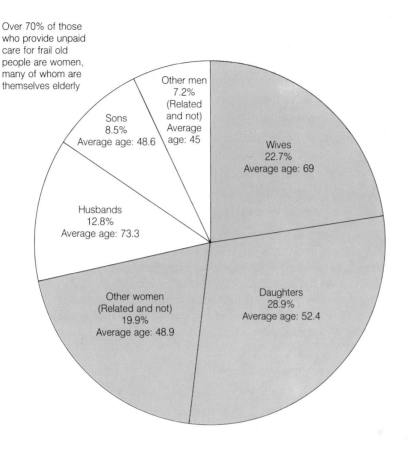

Over 70% of those who provide unpaid care for frail old people are women, many of whom are themselves elderly

Other men 7.2% (Related and not) Average age: 45

Sons 8.5% Average age: 48.6

Husbands 12.8% Average age: 73.3

Wives 22.7% Average age: 69

Other women (Related and not) 19.9% Average age: 48.9

Daughters 28.9% Average age: 52.4

Figure 18.1 Who are the caregivers?

Source: Older Women's League: data from *Exploring the Myths: Caregiving in America*, the Subcommittee on Human Services, Select Committee on Aging, U.S. House of Representatives.

Death and Dying

Before beginning this section, complete the scale measuring attitudes toward death.

Attitudes-Toward-Death Scale

What are your attitudes regarding death? Circle the number to the left of each item below with which you agree.

249 The thought of death is a glorious thought.

247 When I think of death I am most satisfied.

245 Thoughts of death are wonderful thoughts.

243 The thought of death is very pleasant.

241 The thought of death is comforting.

239 I find it fairly easy to think of death.

237 The thought of death isn't so bad.

235 I do not mind thinking of death.

233 I can accept the thought of death.

231 To think of death is common.

229 I don't fear thoughts of death, but I don't like them either.

227 Thinking about death is overvalued by many.

225 Thinking of death is not fundamental to me.

223 I find it difficult to think of death.

221 I regret the thought of death.

219 The thought of death is an awful thought.

217 The thought of death is dreadful.

215 The thought of death is traumatic.

213 I hate the sound of the word death.

211 The thought of death is outrageous.

To determine your attitude toward death, disregard the first digit of the numbers (2), place a decimal point between the remaining two digits, and average all the circled responses. Then place the number 2 back in front of that average and eliminate the decimal point. The average will either be exactly at an attitude statement or between two attitude statements. This represents your attitude toward death. By way of example, if you circled numbers 241, 235, and 215 the computation would look like this:

$4.1 + 3.5 + 1.5 = 9.1$

$9.1 \div 3 = 3.0$ (to the nearest tenth)

Therefore your attitude would fall between the attitude statements 231 and 229 on the above scale, since there is no item numbered 230.

If you discuss the results of this exercise with others, you will find that attitudes toward death vary greatly. No one is right and no one is wrong. Different attitudes just exist.

Death

One of the stressors for all of us, and for the aged in particular, is death. We try to postpone it, and to some extent we can—by not smoking, exercising, watching our diet and our weight, and managing our stress—but a major influence on the age at which we die is our heredity. Born to parents who lived long, our chances of living long are greatly increased. A reporter once asked a 103-year-old man the question, "If you had your life to live over again, would you do anything differently?" "Well," the old man said thoughtfully, "if I knew I was going to live to be 103, I sure would have taken better care of myself."[17]

To learn more about what death means to you and how it influences your life, complete the accompanying death analysis.

A. To learn more about your thoughts and feelings about death, complete the following statements:

1. Death is _____ .

2. I would like to die at _____ .

3. I don't want to live past _____ .

4. I would like to have at my bedside when I die _____
_____ .

5. When I die, I will be proud that when I was living I _____
_____ .

6. My greatest fear about death is _____ .

7. When I die, I'll be glad that when I was living I didn't _____
_____ .

8. If I were to die today, my biggest regret would be _____
_____ .

9. When I die, I will be glad to get away from _____
_____ .

10. When I die, I want people to say _____
_____ .

B. On a separate sheet of paper, list the ten material possessions of yours that you cherish the most.

What do you want done with these (each one) when you die?
How can you assure that these possessions will be handled as you want them to be at your death?
Do you want these possessions given to someone while you're living so you can enjoy their appreciation, or would you prefer to wait until you die?

C. Imagine you are a reporter for your local newspaper and must write your own obituary. What would you like to have written?

_____

_____

_____

_____

_____

D. List four of the people in your life that you love the most. Have you told them that you love them? List four people who have had a tremendous positive influence upon your life. Have you told them that? List ten things you love to do. When is the last time you did them?

E. On a separate sheet of paper write what you have learned from this exercise.

Source: Jerrold S. Greenberg, *Student Centered Health Instruction: A Humanistic Approach,* © 1978. Addison-Wesley, Reading, Mass., pp. 236–38. Reprinted with permission.

Dying

Just as the thought of death is a stressor for the aged, so is dying. Some people may not fear death itself but the dying process; for example, the pain and humility. The significance of dying as a stressor is better understood when it is recognized that 67 percent of the people who die in the United States have chronic degenerative diseases, which usually include a prolonged period of dying. Further, 70 percent of all people die in institutions, where care is often expensive and dehumanizing. When people were asked where they would prefer to die, 63 percent said they'd prefer to die at home, 75 percent did not want to die in a hospital, and 82 percent did not want to die in a nursing home.

Grief

Part of life as an aged person is the death of loved ones. Be they spouses, children, brothers, sisters, or friends, the death of these loved ones results in grief for their loss. The grieving process has been described as a three-stage phenomenon (see table 18.2). The first stage involves shock and disbelief regarding the death and is accompanied by crying and a great deal of distress. The second stage is characterized by a painful longing for and preoccupation with the deceased. There is a loss of appetite, crying, and difficulty in sleeping. The last stage of grief brings with it diminishing sadness and a resumption of normal activities.

Numerous studies have investigated the relationship between grief and subsequent illness and death of those bereaved. For example, in an early investigation Young and colleagues studied 4,486 widowers age fifty-five and older and found a higher than expected mortality rate during the first six months after bereavement.[18] Subsequently, Parkes and colleagues concluded that the disease resulting in increased deaths among widowers was heart disease.[19] The phrase "broken heart" acquired a new and more fatal meaning. A more recent study found several factors associated with this increased death rate among those bereaved. Helsing and his colleagues found that those widows and widowers living alone had higher mortality rates.[20] Helsing concluded that his findings add "further support for the hypothesis that a social support network is effective in ameliorating the effects of a stressful life event such as bereavement."[21] Other researchers support this conclusion.[22] Lastly, a finding has been made that explains the physiological mechanism behind the susceptibility of the bereaved—a finding that at this point should not surprise you. Schleifer and his associates have found a suppression of lymphocyte stimulation—meaning a decrease in the effectiveness of the immunological system—among grieving men.[23] No wonder grief and bereavement, and the stress associated with them, can make people ill and/or kill them.

Interventions

As with other areas, stressors of the later years of one's life need not result in illness or disease. Interventions can occur at the life-situation level, the perception level, the emotional arousal level, or the physiological arousal level of the stress model described in chapter 4.

Table 18.2
Stages of Ordinary Grief

Timetable	Manifestations
Stage 1:	
Begins immediately after death, lasts one to three days	Shock
	Disbelief, denial
	Numbness
	Weeping
	Wailing
	Agitation
Stage 2:	
Peaks between two to four weeks after death; begins to subside after three months, lasts up to one year	Painful longing
	Preoccupation
	Memories
	Mental images of the deceased
	Sense of the deceased being present
	Sadness
	Tearfulness
	Insomnia
	Anorexia
	Loss of interest
	Irritability
	Restlessness
Stage 3:	
Should occur within a year after death	Resolution
	Decreasing episodes of sadness
	Ability to recall the past with pleasure
	Resumption of ordinary activities

Source: Robert B. White and Leroy T. Gathman, "The Syndrome of Ordinary Grief," *American Family Physician* 8(1973):98. © 1973 American Academy of Family Physicians, Kansas City, Missouri. Reprinted with permission.

There are many people nowadays who decide to work until they die. They will not voluntarily retire, and if they are forced to, they'll take another full-time or part-time job. They do this to continue to feel needed and productive, thereby maintaining their sense of self-worth. Others will retire but, rather than consider themselves useless, will use their retirement to do all those exciting and interesting things they were unable to do earlier. They become active in helping others, in periodically using their experience to act as consultants, or in serving their families more directly than they had time to do before their retirement.

If loneliness or aloneness are problems, the elderly can arrange to spend time with their compatriots. They could move to Florida or other areas of the country where there are large populations of elderly citizens. They could move into living facilities that cater to the elderly, or while living at home they could visit places where the elderly congregate. My grandmother—the eighty-five-year-old matriarch of the family—regularly spent her Saturdays with her sister at a shopping

Life-Situation Interventions

mall in Brooklyn window-shopping and conversing with other people her own age. It seemed that this shopping mall was a "hangout"—not for teenagers but for the elderly.

Since the elderly are in the latter stages of their lives, the need to see their lives as having some meaning is important. Time spent with children and grandchildren will help the aged see themselves as connected to life—a connection that will be continued after their death. This connection need not be with people; it might be with organizations. For example, the dean of my college recently retired. He has been very important to the growth of the college and is proud of its national reputation. The college will be a monument, so to speak, to Marv Eyler's talents and efforts and will connect him to life long after he is dead. In fact, I wouldn't be surprised to see the name of the building in which our offices are housed named after him.

All of us could adopt interventions at the life-situation level in our earlier years that will serve us well when we become aged. If you have not yet adopted life-situation interventions, try the following exercise. For each decade of your life list one major goal.

Decade	Goal
0–10	
11–20	
21–30	
31–40	
41–50	
51–60	
61–70	
71–80	
80 +	

Now rank these goals in order of importance. Next, cross out the goals already achieved. If you were to die ten years from now, which goals would not have been accomplished? Of these unaccomplished goals, how many are in the top four of importance?[24]

Can you reestablish your goals so that the important ones are achieved earlier in life? If so, you might relieve the stress associated with unaccomplished goals and the feeling that life is running out. Recognizing that for all of us, regardless of age, death can occur momentarily, we can see that to have at least accomplished our important goals is stress reducing.

You can also prevent stress by arranging your affairs so as to feel organized in the eventuality of death:

1. You should have a will that identifies what should be done with your belongings and estate.
2. There should be funeral and burial instructions (who should officiate, where you want to be buried, how your body should be disposed of, who the pallbearers ought to be).
3. You should leave the names, addresses, and telephone numbers of people to contact (friends, relatives, clergy, banker, attorney, stockbroker, and insurance agent).
4. There should be a record of bank accounts and their numbers, and who is authorized access to those accounts.
5. You should leave a record of the location and contents of any safety deposit boxes.
6. There should be a record of all credit card numbers and billing addresses.
7. Other records that should be left are certificates of deposit, outstanding loans, retirement accounts, profit-sharing plans, past income tax returns, and insurance policy information.

A good reference regarding getting things in order in case of death is entitled "Putting Your House in Order" and is available from the Continental Association of Funeral and Memorial Societies, 2001 S Street NW, Washington, D.C. 20009.

You can also prevent stress by developing a "living will" (see fig. 18.2). In this way you can be assured that your desires regarding medical intervention and the prolonging of your life when all hope for life as we know it is gone, will be stated.

Perhaps you want to donate parts of your body to be used after your death by someone needing them. Figure 18.3 presents a sample donor card that you can carry with you at all times. Then when you die, your organs can be used to save or enhance the life of someone else. In this manner, you will be assured that your life will have some beneficial purpose regardless of what else you might do.

If you need more guidance regarding living wills or organ donation, contact the Older Women's League (OWL) at 1325 G Street NW, Washington, D.C. 20005; (202)783–6686.

In addition to these life-situation interventions, behaviors adopted throughout your life will affect the stress, illness, and disease you experience in your later years. You should be concerned about the following:

1. Eating nutritionally balanced meals
2. Smoking cigarettes
3. Abusing or misusing alcohol and other drugs
4. Managing stress
5. Having significant others in your life to act as a support system
6. Having a positive outlook on life
7. Having periodic medical examinations
8. Living in an urban, suburban, or rural environment (urban dwellers die at younger ages)
9. Being wealthy (annual salary in excess of $50,000) or poor (both extremes create stress)
10. Maintaining a clean and safe physical environment at home
11. Spending your days in useful, meaningful activity
12. Maintaining appropriate body weight
13. Enjoying leisure time
14. Exercising regularly

All of these are within your control, which means the quality of your later adult years is a function of what you do prior to those years.

A LIVING WILL

Figure 18.2 A living will

IMPORTANT

Declarants may wish to add specific statements to the Living Will to be inserted in the space provided for that purpose above the signature. Possible additional provisions are suggested below:

1. a) I appoint _____
to make binding decisions concerning my medical treatment.
OR

   b) I have discussed my views as to life sustaining measures with the following who understand my wishes

   _____,
   _____;
   _____.

2. Measures of artificial life support in the face of impending death that are especially abhorrent to me are:
   a) Electrical or mechanical resuscitation of my heart when it has stopped beating.
   b) Nasogastric tube feedings when I am paralyzed and no longer able to swallow.
   c) Mechanical respiration by machine when my brain can no longer sustain my own breathing.
   d) _____

3. If it does not jeopardize the chance of my recovery to a meaningful and sentient life or impose an undue burden on my family, I would like to live out my last days at home rather than in a hospital.

4. If any of my tissues are sound and would be of value as transplants to help other people, I freely give my permission for such donation.

To make best use of your LIVING WILL

1. Sign and date before two witnesses. (This is to insure that you signed of your own free will and not under any pressure.)

2. If you have a doctor, give him a copy for your medical file and discuss it with him to make sure he is in agreement.

   Give copies to those most likely to be concerned "if the time comes when you can no longer take part in decisions for your own future". Enter their names on bottom line of the Living Will. Keep the original nearby, easily and readily available.

3. Above all discuss your intentions with those closest to you, NOW.

4. It is a good idea to look over your Living Will once a year and redate it and initial the new date to make it clear that your wishes are unchanged.

35th printing
Revised May, 1978

Prepared by

CONCERN FOR DYING

an educational council

Figure 18.2 *(continued)*

To My Family, My Physician, My Lawyer and All Others Whom It May Concern

Death is as much a reality as birth, growth, maturity and old age—it is the one certainty of life. If the time comes when I can no longer take part in decisions for my own future, let this statement stand as an expression of my wishes and directions, while I am still of sound mind.

If at such a time the situation should arise in which there is no reasonable expectation of my recovery from extreme physical or mental disability, I direct that I be allowed to die and not be kept alive by medications, artificial means or "heroic measures". I do, however, ask that medication be mercifully administered to me to alleviate suffering even though this may shorten my remaining life.

This statement is made after careful consideration and is in accordance with my strong convictions and beliefs. I want the wishes and directions here expressed carried out to the extent permitted by law. Insofar as they are not legally enforceable, I hope that those to whom this Will is addressed will regard themselves as morally bound by these provisions.

Signed _____

Date _____

Witness _____

Witness _____

Copies of this request have been given to _____

_____

_____

_____

UNIFORM DONOR CARD

OF_____

Print or type name of donor

In the hope that I may help others, I hereby make this anatomical gift, if medically acceptable, to take effect upon my death. The words and marks below indicate my desires.

I give: (a) _____ any needed organs or parts

        (b) _____ only the following organs or parts

_____

Specify the organ(s) or part(s)

for the purposes of transplantation, therapy, medical research or education;

        (c) _____ my body for anatomical study if needed.

Limitations or
special wishes, if any :_____

- -

Signed by the donor and the following two witnesses in the presence of each other:

_____ _____
Signature of Donor   Date of Birth of Donor

_____ _____
Date Signed   City & State

_____ _____
Witness   Witness

This is a legal document under the Uniform Anatomical Gift Act or similar laws.

For further information consult your physician or

KF Kidney Foundation of Iowa
3615 Douglas Avenue
Des Moines, Iowa 50310

Figure 18.3 Sample donor card

When we recognize we are not immortal, the fact of death can help us live more fully by setting priorities.

Retirement is a good life situation to use when discussing perception interventions. Imagine two different people who retire. One considers retirement a signal of dropping out of life, being unproductive, and having a diminished self-worth. The other views retirement as a reward for years of hard work, as an opportunity to do things time did not permit earlier, or as a chance to help others or spend time helping family members enjoy their lives more. They face the same event but have different perceptions of it.

We can spend our time complaining about aches and pains or be grateful for the degree of mobility and intellectual ability we still have. We can dwell on how fast the years went and on how few remain or consider the remaining years as more than some others have had. We can perceive our aloneness as loneliness or as an opportunity to get to know ourselves better. We can bemoan the little time our families spend with us or be appreciative for the love and time they do give us.

In short, we can dwell on the negative aspects of old age or its positive ones. The choice is ours. Focusing on the negatives will only make them more negative. For example, complaining to our families about the little time they spend with us will make them enjoy that time less. They might then spend even less time with us. Focusing upon death might so concern us that we don't live out our remaining years to the fullest. Paying too much attention to aches and pains might make them more bothersome. If we could focus on something or someone else, perhaps we'd forget about our aches and pains for a while.

An example of how our negative thoughts can make us ill or, on the other hand, positive thoughts can insulate us from stress is that of caregiving. Researchers asking the question "Why do some caregivers maintain high levels of care with little stress, while others all but crumble under the strain?" hypothesize that perception is important to the answer. They believe that people who perceive caring for a loved one in terms of fulfillment rather than sacrifice don't feel burdened but, instead, feel privileged.[25] With this rationale, the Elderly Support Project has developed a program to help caregivers identify and increase the positive aspects of caregiving they get from those for whom they provide care—affection, companionship, and cooperation. Once again, self-awareness comes to the rescue!

As with the life-situation interventions, perception interventions are up to us. We have the ability to intervene in the stress of old age by perceiving the good associated with those years. The choice is ours.

Chapters 8, 9, and 10 describe relaxation techniques that can be used as emotional arousal interventions. These certainly are appropriate for the elderly. In addition to these interventions, many elderly people use prayer to focus outside themselves and achieve an emotional peace. The repetitive nature of some prayers makes them even more particularly suited to emotional arousal intervention.

Another intervention used by the elderly is similar to one used by a younger friend of mine. He has tanks and tanks of tropical fish and spends an endless amount of time watching these fish swim back and forth. He is "into" his fish and "out of" his problems. As he watches them swim, he has forgotten his business problems. He has relaxed. Many of the elderly will do the same, except that the rest of us become their fish. Watching from their windows, they see us going to work, returning from work, arguing with the kids, playing, and doing various other life activities. Unfortunately, too many people view the elderly who engage in this emotional arousal intervention as "nosy." However, they are able to prevent emotional arousal by watching us "fish" in our tanks of life and focusing away from the negative aspects of old age. We'd be better advised to help them clean their windows so they can see better than to complain about their nosiness.

The elderly, like everyone else, can profit from regular exercise. Sometimes, because of particular disabilities or health concerns, the exercise has to be adapted to the individual, but exercise itself need not be eliminated. Recognizing this, some elderly people will play doubles in tennis or handball rather than singles. Some will run a marathon a little slower than when they were younger, but they will complete the twenty-six-mile course just the same. Some will swim fewer miles than when they were imitating Johnny Weissmuller, but they will swim each day just the same. Using the products of stress—the increased muscle tension, serum cholesterol, and blood pressure—is as important for the elderly as for the rest of us, and the psychological benefits of exercise are not exclusive to the young. Even if your whole life has been inactive, you can still begin regular exercise when you are older. However, consult a physician prior to beginning a program. A walking program is a good way to begin if you have been inactive most of your life. Consult chapter 12 for more specific information on exercise. Another good source of advice regarding exercise for the elderly has been prepared by the government and is available upon request.[26]

Well, the choice is yours. If you are elderly, you can manage your stress by intervening at various levels of the stress model presented in this book. If you are younger, you can prepare yourself now with numerous intervention strategies to diminish the harmful effects of stress during your later years.

Summary

1. In 1900 the number of elderly people in the United States over sixty-five years of age was slightly over 3 million, or 3.9 percent of the population. By 1985, there were over 29 million Americans over sixty-five, or 12 percent of the population.

2. Generally, the elderly do not live in institutions, most are healthy, have enough income to live on, live in adequate housing, live with someone else so they are not lonely, and engage in sexual activity.

3. Erik Erikson theorized that the elderly who have developed a clear understanding of who they are do not view death as the ultimate end. However, the elderly who haven't accomplished that task may become bitter and depressed that time is too short to try another route to finding themselves.

Physiological Arousal Interventions

4. Robert Havighurst described six developmental tasks of the elderly as adjustments to decreasing strength and health; retirement and reduced income; and death of a spouse; establishing affiliations with one's age group; meeting social and civic obligations; and establishing satisfactory living arrangements.

5. Old age brings with it the potential for positive change. Grandchildren can become sources of joy. In addition, the free time many elderly people have can be used to pursue interests earlier postponed.

6. Retirement requires adjustment which often is stressful. It can lead one to question his or her self-worth, miss fellow workers, and long for the sense of being needed. Retirement can also be viewed positively and the extra time relished.

7. The National Institute of Mental Health found four patterns of adjustment to retirement: maintenance, withdrawal, changed activities, and changed needs.

8. Caregivers of the elderly help provide for those who have difficulty performing daily chores. Caregivers tend to be women, predominantly daughters and wives of the person for whom they provide care.

9. Elder care has the potential to impact negatively on workers and the organizations for which they work by taking the form of tardiness, absenteeism, and a lack of concentration. Consequently, many businesses are providing elder care (as they do child care) or providing unpaid leaves for employees who must care for elderly relatives.

10. Grief can be described as a three-stage process. Stage one lasts one to three days and involves shock, denial, and disbelief. Stage two peaks two to four weeks after death and can last up to one year. It involves painful longing, mental images of the deceased, loss of appetite, tearfulness, and insomnia. Stage three occurs within a year after the death and involves a sense of resolution, decreasing episodes of sadness, and resumption of ordinary activities.

11. The death of a spouse has been found to cause poor health and even death in the surviving partner. Lack of social support is a contributing factor in these cases. The operative physiological mechanism is suspected of being a suppression of lymphocyte stimulation resulting in a decrease in the effectiveness of the immunological system.

Notes

1. U.S. Bureau of the Census, *Current Population Reports, Series P-23, No. 150, Population Profile of the United States: 1984–85* (Washington, D.C.: U.S. Government Printing Office, 1987), 6.

2. National Center for Health Statistics, "Use of Nursing Homes by the Elderly: Preliminary Data from the 1985 National Nursing Home Survey," *Advance Data,* 14 May 1987, 1.

3. Louis Harris, *Harris Poll* (Washington, D.C.: National Council on the Aging, 1975).

4. A. Simon, "The Neurosis, Personality Disorders, Alcoholism, Drug Use and Misuse, and Crime in the Aged," in *Handbook of Mental Health and Aging,* ed. J. E. Birren and R. B. Sloane (Englewood Cliffs, N.J.: Prentice-Hall, 1980), 653–70.

5. U.S. Bureau of the Census, Current Population Reports, Series P-23, No. 150, *Population Profile of the United States: 1984–85* (Washington, D.C.: U.S. Government Printing Office, 1987), 23.

6. National Center for Health Statistics, "Aging in the Eighties, People Living Alone—Two Years Later," *Advance Data,* 4 April 1988, 1–2.

7. Alex Comfort, *A Good Age* (New York: Crown Publishers, 1976).

8. Harris, *Harris Poll.*

9. Erik H. Erikson, *Childhood and Society* (New York: W. W. Norton, 1963).

10. Robert J. Havighurst, *Developmental Tasks and Education* (New York: David McKay Company, 1972).

11. Ibid., 2.

12. Ibid., 108–13.

13. L. Aiken, *Later Life* (Philadelphia: W. B. Saunders Co., 1978).

14. National Institute of Mental Health, *Retirement: Patterns and Predictions* (Washington, D.C.: National Institute of Mental Health, 1975).

15. National Center for Health Statistics, "Aging in the Eighties: Functional Limitations of Individuals Age 65 Years and Over," *Advance Data,* 10 June 1987, 4.

16. Molly Sinclair, "Coping with Careers and 'Elder Care'," *Washington Post,* 19 July 1987, A1, A6.

17. George B. Dintiman and Jerrold S. Greenberg, *Health Through Discovery* (Reading, Mass.: Addison-Wesley, 1980), 491.

18. M. Young, B. Benjamin, and C. Wallace, "The Mortality of Widowers," *Lancet* 3 (1960):254–56.

19. C. M. Parkes, B. Benjamin, and R. E. Fitzgerald, "Broken Heart: A Statistical Study of Increased Mortality Among Widowers," *British Medical Journal* 1(1969):740–43.

20. Knud J. Helsing, Moyses Szklo, and George W. Comstock, "Factors Associated with Mortality after Widowhood," *American Journal of Public Health* 71(1981):802–9.

21. Ibid., 808.

22. Jaakko Kaprio, Markku Koskenvuo, and Heli Rita, "Mortality after Bereavement: A Prospective Study of 95,647 Widowed Persons," *American Journal of Public Health* 77(1987):283–87.

23. Steven Schleifer et al., "Suppression of Lymphocyte Stimulation Following Bereavement," *JAMA* 250(1983):374–77.

24. Jerrold S. Greenberg, *Student-Centered Health Instruction: A Humanistic Approach* (Reading, Mass.: Addison-Wesley, 1978), 237–38.

25. Cheryl Simon, "A Care Package," *Psychology Today,* April 1988, 44–49.

26. Office of Disease Prevention and Health Promotion, "Exercise for Older Americans," *Healthfinder* (Washington, D.C.: Office of Disease Prevention and Health Promotion National Health Information Center, November 1987).

Epilogue

Someone told me of a person who came home one evening holding the steering wheel of the family car, hair and clothes disheveled and replete with glass from the windshield, and smelling of engine oil, and who, with a faint, halfhearted smile, said to the waiting spouse, "Well, at least you won't have to waste your Fridays at the car wash any longer."

If only we could adopt that attitude toward the future and the stressors it will bring. Alvin Toffler wrote of the nature of the future in his classic book *Future Shock*.[1] Toffler described the rapid and pervasive changes that we will, and do, experience. As we have learned, such changes have the potential to elicit a stress response; that is, they're stressors.

The knowledge of today often becomes the misinformation of tomorrow. For example, most of us were taught and believed that parallel lines never meet. Yet today, physicists tell us that they do meet somewhere in infinity. We learned that eggs and liver were healthy, and we should eat them frequently. Yet, some cardiologists now believe eggs and liver contain too much cholesterol and recommend we limit how much of them we eat. Knowledge is expanding exponentially, with new knowledge often replacing old "knowledge." This situation has led to confusion—what do we believe? It has led to frustration, one example of which is the oft-heard "Everything seems to cause cancer." It has led to stress—how do we manage in a world that has so much scientific knowledge and technology that it could destroy itself pushing several buttons? Well, at least we won't have to waste our Fridays at the car wash.

In Toffler's best-selling *The Third Wave,*[2] he continues describing a changing society, focusing upon the influence of science and technology on our daily lives. I recalled Toffler's description of the effects that new forms of communication and computers would have upon us (for example, we will shop, bank, and work from the desktop computer terminals in our homes) when I read of an experiment that took place during a football game. The Racine Gladiators were playing the Columbus Metros in a semipro football game in July of 1980. The cable TV system televising the game allowed subscribers to communicate through it instantaneously by punching buttons on a hand-held control unit in their homes, and that is exactly what over five thousand viewers did. Prior to each play, the viewers voted on the next play they wanted their hometown Metros to run, out of a choice of five different plays. In ten seconds the responses were tallied and flashed on a screen at the stadium—unseen by the players—and the vote relayed to the quarterback. The Metros lost the game 10–7, but their coach said he probably couldn't have called the plays any better. "The times they are a-changing."

If we are going to survive and flourish in a rapidly changing society, we had better learn how to manage the stress accompanying it. We must adjust our life situations to eliminate unnecessary stressors and to find comfort in rewarding, routine, and stable relationships and activities. We need to strengthen our families, do meaningful and enjoyable work, and organize our leisure time to be fun and re-creating (which is where the word recreation came from). Furthermore, we need to perceive those distressing life-situations that we cannot change as less threatening and disturbing. This includes viewing ourselves as worthwhile beings, believing we can control many events and consequences in our lives, and considering life's tests as challenges and growth experiences rather than plagues to be shunned, avoided, and forgotten.

Added to these recommendations must be the regular practices of relaxation and exercise. Relaxation skills provide us with a "reservoir of relaxation" upon which we can draw when our lives become particularly stressful. These skills will also serve to intervene between life-situations that we perceive to be distressing and subsequent illnesses and diseases by diminishing the physiological arousal caused by stressors.

In the hope that this book has contributed to your ability to manage the stress in your life, I leave you with the following thought. It has meant much to me, and my hope is that it will also have significance for you. Since it is short, you can easily commit it to memory:

I murmured because I had no shoes,
Until I met a man who had no feet.

Persian Proverb

Notes

1. Alvin Toffler, *Future Shock* (New York: Random House, 1970).
2. Alvin Toffler, *The Third Wave* (New York: William Morrow & Co., 1980).

Appendix
Stress Information Resources

Information on stress and stress management is available from the publications and organizations described below. Compiled for the general public and for health professionals who provide information to the public, it is divided into two sections. The first describes organizations and the second describes publications. The publications, all free or low-cost materials written for the lay public, concern general adult and childhood stress. Order publications directly from the sources indicated. Prices include postage and handling and are subject to change.

Emotions Anonymous (EA), P.O. Box 4245, St. Paul, MN 55104, (612)647–9712. Supports local peer support groups open to anyone seeking help for their emotional or living problems. Publishes a magazine, literature on emotional illness, and guidelines for conducting local groups. There are currently about 600 EA groups in the United States, and contact information on local groups is available from the national office.

Organizations

National Institute of Mental Health (NIMH), Public Inquiries Section, Science Communication Branch, Parklawn Bldg., Room 15C-17, 5600 Fishers Lane, Rockville, MD 20857, (301)443–4513. Provides informative publications about stress and stress management, as well as other aspects of mental health. NIMH is the primary source of mental health information in the federal government. Publications are targeted to the lay public as well as to health professionals.

National Mental Health Association (NMHA), Public Information and Education, 1021 Prince St., Alexandria, VA 22314, (703)684–7722. Works to improve public understanding of mental health and mental illness and to assist the mentally ill and their families. A total of 850 state and local chapters provide information services to individuals and community groups, emotional support for families, and assistance to school systems and local governments. Contact information for state and local chapters and a publications catalog are available from the national office.

Publications

Help for Your Troubled Child. 24 pages. Discusses troubled children and ways to identify them, using a fictitious family as an example. Talks about applying for therapeutic help if needed and types of treatment. For sale by Public Affairs Pamphlets, 381 Park Ave. South, New York, NY 10016, (212)683–4331. $1; bulk discounts available.

Helping Children Face Crisis. 24 pages. Analyzes parents' and children's reactions to crisis. Discusses specific examples, such as death in the family, separation and divorce, and starting school, and ways in which parents can help to reduce a child's anxiety surrounding these events. For sale by Public Affairs Pamphlets, 381 Park Ave. South, New York, NY 10016, (212)683–4331. $1; bulk discounts available.

How to Get Unstressed: The Bare Facts. 14 pages. Defines stress; describes how it affects the body. Discusses the difference between good and bad stress and suggests techniques for coping with stress. For sale by the Wisconsin Clearinghouse, University of Wisconsin Hospitals and Clinics, 1954 East Washington Ave., Madison, WI 53704, (608)263–2797. $1; bulk discounts available.

How to Handle Stress: Techniques for Living Well. 28 pages. Defines stress and discusses the stress response, strategies for managing stress, and strategies for living well. The reader can also use this booklet as a workbook to analyze his or her own stress responses. For sale by Public Affairs Pamphlets, 381 Park Ave. South, New York, NY 10016, (212)683–4331. $1; bulk discounts available.

Plain Talk about the Art of Relaxation. 2 pages. Defines relaxation, explains some causes of stress, and suggests ways to relax. Single copy free from the Public Inquiries Section, Science Communication Branch, National Institute of Mental Health, Parklawn Bldg., Room 15C-17, 5600 Fishers Lane, Rockville, MD 20857, (301)443–4513.

Plain Talk about Dealing with the Angry Child. 2 pages. Discusses ways parents can help a child cope with feelings of anger and aggression. Also available in Spanish: *Charla franca: como tratar al nino enojado.* Single copy free from the Consumer Information Center, Dept. M, Pueblo, CO 81009.

Plain Talk about Handling Stress. 2 pages. Defines stress, explaining how our bodies react to stress and how to handle it. Also available in Spanish: *Charla franca: sobre la tension.* Single copy free from the Public Inquiries Section, Science Communication Branch, National Institute of Mental Health, Parklawn Bldg., Room 15C-17, 5600 Fishers Lane, Rockville, MD 20857, (301)443–4513.

Pressures on Children. 28 pages. Describes various inner and outer pressures on children, specifically pressures on preschoolers, school-age children, and early adolescents. Discusses concerns about drugs. Concludes with suggestions on what can be done to alleviate the pressures. For sale by Public Affairs Pamphlets, 381 Park Ave. South, New York, NY 10016, (212)683–4331. $1; bulk discounts available.

Stress. 96 pages. Presents articles by experts, in lay language, on many aspects of this topic, including stress in childhood, adolescence, and aging; stress at home and on the job; and ways to relax. Contact your local Blue Cross/Blue Shield Association.

Stress and Your Health. 4 pages. Defines stress, explains the different types, and suggests ways to avoid physical and mental problems associated with stress. Lists other sources of information. Single copy free with stamped, self-addressed envelope from the Metropolitan Life Insurance Company, Health and Safety Education Division, One Madison Ave., New York, NY 10012, (212)578–2211.

Tensions and How to Master Them. 28 pages. Describes the adverse effect of tensions in our society, the causes of tension and anxiety, and childhood tensions. Describes ways to control and get rid of tensions. For sale by Public Affairs Pamphlets, 381 Park Ave. South, New York, NY 10016, (212)683–4331. $1; bulk discounts available.

Understanding Stress. 20 pages. Discusses the meaning of stress, our bodies' responses to stress, stress as a disease-causing factor, and ways to protect against the effects of stress. For sale by Public Affairs Pamphlets, 381 Park Ave. South, New York, NY 10016, (212)683–4331. $1; bulk discounts available.

What Everyone Should Know about Stress. 15 pages. Focuses on change as one of the main causes of stress; also discusses anxiety and depression. Suggests ways to cope with and relieve these conditions, as well as where to find outside help. For sale by Channing L. Bete Company, 200 State Rd., South Deerfield, MA 01373, (413)665–7611, (800)628–7733. $.69, minimum order of 25; bulk discounts available.

Select Bibliography

Adler, Ronald B. *Confidence in Communication: A Guide to Assertive and Social Skills.* New York: Holt, Rinehart & Winston, 1977.

"Aerobic Instructor Burnout." *Reebok Instructor News* 1(1988):1, 4–5.

Aiken, L. *Later Life.* Philadelphia: W. B. Saunders Co., 1978.

Allen, Roger J. *Human Stress: Its Nature and Control.* Minneapolis: Burgess, 1983.

Allen, Roger J., and David Hyde. *Investigations in Stress Control.* Minneapolis: Burgess, 1980.

Allison, J. "Respiratory Changes during Transcendental Meditation." *Lancet* no. 7651(1970):833–34.

American Academy of Family Physicians. *A Report on Lifestyles/Personal Health Care in Different Occupations.* Kansas City: American Academy of Family Physicians, 1979.

American Cancer Society. *Cancer Facts and Figures—1987.* New York: American Cancer Society, 1987.

American College of Sports Medicine. *Guidelines for Exercise Testing and Prescription.* 3d ed. Philadelphia: Lea and Febiger, 1986.

American Podiatry Association. *Jogging Advice from Your Podiatrist.* Washington, D.C.: American Podiatry Association, n.d.

Anand, B. K., G. S. Chhina, and B. Singh. "Some Aspects of Electroencephalographic Studies in Yogis." *Electroencephalography and Clinical Neurophysiology* 13(1961):452–56.

Anand, B. K., et al. "Studies on Shri Ramananda Yogi during His Stay in an Air-Tight Box." *Indian Journal of Medical Research* 49(1961):82–89.

Anderson, G. E. "College Schedule of Recent Experience." Master's thesis, North Dakota State University, 1972.

Anderson, Jack. "Whistleblower Stress." *Washington Post,* 24 March 1985, C7.

Anderson, J. R., and I. Waldon. "Behavioral and Content Components of the Structured Interview Assessment of the Type A Behavior Pattern in Women." *Journal of Behavioral Medicine* 6(1983):123–34.

Anderson, N. B., P. S. Lawrence, and T. W. Olson. "Within-Subject Analysis of Autogenic Training and Cognitive Coping Training in the Treatment of Tension Headache Pain." *Journal of Behavioral Therapy and Experimental Psychiatry* 12(1981):219–23.

Arafat, I., and W. L. Cotton. "Masturbation Practices of Males and Females." *Journal of Sex Research* 10(1974):293–307.

Bagchi, B. K., and M. A. Wengor. "Electrophysiological Correlates of Some Yogi Exercises." In *Electroencephalography, Clinical Neurophysiology and Epilepsy,* edited by L. van Bagaert and J. Radermecker. First International Congress of Neurological Sciences, vol. 3. London: Pergamon, 1959.

Baker, D. B. "The Study of Stress at Work." *Annual Review of Public Health* 6(1985):367–81.

Barefoot, J. C., W. G. Dahlstrom, and W. B. Williams. "Hostility, CHD Incidence, and Total Mortality: A 25 Year Follow-Up Study of 255 Physicians." *Psychosomatic Medicine* 45(1985):59–64.

Barling, Julian. "Interrole Conflict and Marital Functioning amongst Employed Fathers." *Journal of Occupational Behaviour* 7(1986):1–8.

Becker, Marshall H., and Lawrence W. Green. "A Family Approach to Compliance with Medical Treatment—A Selective Review of the Literature." *International Journal of Health Education* 18(1975):1–11.

Beehr, V. A., and J. E. Newman. "Job Stress, Employee Health, and Organizational Effectiveness: A Facet Analysis, Model, and Literature Review." *Personnel Psychology* 31(1978):665–99.

Belar, Cynthia D., and Joel L. Cohen. "The Use of EMG Feedback and Progressive Relaxation in the Treatment of a Woman with Chronic Back Pain." *Biofeedback and Self-Regulation* 4(1979):345–53.

Belisle, Marc, Ethel Roskies, and Jean-Michel Levesque. "Improving Adherence to Physical Activity." *Health Psychology* 6(1987):159–72.

Benson, Herbert. *The Relaxation Response.* New York: Avon Books, 1975.

Berger, Richard A. *Applied Exercise Physiology.* Philadelphia: Lea and Febiger, 1982.

Berkovec, T. D., and D. C. Fowles. "Controlled Investigation of the Effects of Progressive and Hypnotic Relaxation on Insomnia." *Journal of Abnormal Psychology* 82(1973):153–58.

Berstein, D. A., and B. Given. "Progressive Relaxation: Abbreviated Methods." In *Principles and Practice of Stress Management,* edited by R. Woolfolk and P. Lehrer. New York: Guilford Press, 1984.

Blanchard, Edward, et al. "Three Studies of the Psychologic Changes in Chronic Headache Patients Associated with Biofeedback and Relaxation Therapies." *Psychosomatic Medicine* 48(1986):73–83.

Blanchard, Edward B., and Leonard H. Epstein. *A Biofeedback Primer.* Reading, Mass.: Addison-Wesley, 1978.

Blanchard, Edward B., et al. "Two, Three, and Four Year Follow-Up on the Self-Regulatory Treatment of Chronic Headache." *Journal of Consulting and Clinical Psychology* 55(1987):257–59.

Boller, Jon D., and Raymond P. Flom. "Behavioral Treatment of Persistent Post-traumatic Startle Response." *Journal of Behavior Therapy and Experimental Psychiatry* 12(1981):321–24.

Breeden, S., et al. "EMG Levels as Indicators of Relaxation." Paper presented at the Biofeedback Research Society Meeting, Monterey, Calif., 1975.

Brody, Jane E. "Effects of Beauty Found to Run Surprisingly Deep." *New York Times,* 1 September 1981, C1–C3.

Brosse, Therese. "A Psychophysiological Study of Yoga." *Main Currents in Modern Thought* 4(1946):77–84.

Brouha, Lucien. "The Step Test: A Simple Method of Testing the Physical Fitness of Boys." *Research Quarterly* 14(1943):23.

Brown, Barbara B. "Recognition Aspects of Consciousness through Association with EEG Alpha Activity Represented by a Light Signal." *Psychophysiology* 6(1970):442–52.

———. *Stress and the Art of Biofeedback.* New York: Harper & Row, 1977.

Brown, G. W., M. Bhroclain, and T. Harris. "Social Class and Psychiatric Disturbance among Women in an Urban Population." *Sociology* 9(1975):225–54.

Brownell, K. D., et al. "The Effect of Couples Training and Partner Cooperativeness in the Behavior Treatment of Obesity." *Behavior Research Therapy* 16(1978):323–33.

Bruess, Clint E., and Jerrold S. Greenberg. *Sexuality Education: Theory and Practice.* New York: Macmillan, 1988.

Budzynski, Thomas, Johann Stoyva, and C. Adler. "Feedback-Induced Muscle Relaxation: Application to Tension Headache." *Journal of Behavior Therapy and Experimental Psychiatry* 1(1970):205–11.

Budzynski, Thomas H., et al. "EMG Biofeedback and Tension Headache: A Controlled Outcome Study." *Psychosomatic Medicine* 35(1973):484–96.

Burke, Ronald J. "Beliefs and Fears Underlying Type A Behavior: What Makes Sammy Run So Fast and Aggressively?" *Journal of Human Stress* 10(1984):174–82.

Burks, Nancy, and Barclay Martin. "Everyday Problems and Life Change Events: Ongoing versus Acute Sources of Stress." *Journal of Human Stress* 11(1985):27–35.

Bushnell, D. D., and T. J. Scheff. "The Cathartic Effects of Laughter on Audiences." In *The Study of Humor,* edited by H. Mindesc and J. Turek. Los Angeles: Antioch University, 1979.

Byrd, Robert. "Job-Stress Illness Up, Report Says; More Injury Claims Cite Mental Anxiety." *Washington Post,* 3 October 1986, F2.

Cairns, D., and J. A. Pasino. "Comparison of Verbal Reinforcement and Feedback in the Operant Treatment of Disability Due to Chronic Low Back Pain." *Behavior Therapy* 8(1977):621–30.

Callon, Eleanor W., et al. "The Effect of Muscle Contraction Headache Chronicity on Frontal EMG." *Headache* 26(1986):356–59.

Cannon, Walter B. *The Wisdom of the Body.* New York: W. W. Norton, 1932.

Caplan, G. *Support Systems and Community Mental Health.* New York: Behavioral Publications, 1974.

Caplan, R. D., S. Cobb, and J. R. P. French. "Relationships of Cessation of Smoking with Job Stress, Personality, and Social Support." *Journal of Applied Psychology* 60(1975):211–19.

Carruthers, Malcomb. "Autogenic Training." *Journal of Psychosomatic Research* 23(1979):437–40.

Case, R. B., et al. "Type A Behavior and Survival after Acute Myocardial Infarction." *New England Journal of Medicine* 312(1985):737–41.

Cauthen, N. R., and C. A. Prymak. "Meditation versus Relaxation: An Examination of the Physiological Effects with Transcendental Meditation." *Journal of Consulting and Clinical Psychology* 45(1977):496–97.

Chadwick, J., et al. "Psychological Job Stress and Coronary Heart Disease." NIOSH report under contract no. CDC–99–74–42, National Institute for Occupational Safety and Health, 1979.

Chapman, Stanley L. "A Review and Clinical Perspective on the Use of EMG and Thermal Biofeedback for Chronic Headaches." *Pain* 27(1986):1–43.

Charlesworth, Edward A., and Ronald G. Nathan. *Stress Management: A Comprehensive Guide to Wellness.* Houston, Tex.: Biobehavioral Publishers, 1982.

Chase, Anne. "Police Psychologist: Post Remains Vacant for 9 Months Despite Growing Stress in Department." *Prince George's Journal,* 14 March 1980, A4.

Cherlin, A. "Remarriage as an Incomplete Institution." *American Journal of Sociology* 84(1978):634.

Clark, N., E. Arnold, and E. Foulds. "Serum Urate and Cholesterol Levels in Air Force Academy Cadets." *Aviation and Space Environmental Medicine* 46(1975):1044–48.

Coates, T. J., and C. E. Thoreson. "What to Use Instead of Sleeping Pills." *American Medical Association Journal* 240(1978):2311–12.

Cobb, S., and R. M. Rose. "Hypertension, Peptic Ulcer, and Diabetes in Air Traffic Controllers." *Journal of the American Medical Association* 224(1973):489–92.

Cohen, Sheldon. "Sound Effects on Behavior." *Psychology Today,* October 1981, 38–49.

Collet, L. "MMPI and Headache: A Special Focus on Differential Diagnosis, Prediction of Treatment Outcome and Patient: Treatment Matching." *Pain* 29(1987):267–68.

Collet, L., J. Cottraux, and C. Juenet. "GSR Feedback and Schultz Relaxation in Tension Headaches: A Comparative Study. *Pain* 25(1986):205–13.

Comfort, Alex. *A Good Age.* New York: Crown Publishers, 1976.

Cooper, Kenneth H. *The Aerobics Way: New Data on the World's Most Popular Exercise Program.* New York: M. Evans, 1977.

Coopersmith, Stanley. *The Antecedents of Self-Esteem.* San Francisco: W. H. Freeman, 1967.

Corbett, Ann. "Too Stressed for Sex: The Decline and Fall of Married Love." *Washington Post,* 8 October 1985, B5.

Corbin, Charles B., and Ruth Lindsey. *Concepts of Physical Fitness with Laboratories.* 6th ed. Dubuque, Iowa: Wm. C. Brown, 1988.

Cory, Christopher T. "The Stress-Ridden Inspection Suite and Other Jittery Jobs." *Psychology Today,* January 1979, 13–14.

Cowing, Patricia S. "Reducing Motion Sickness: A Comparison of Autogenic-Feedback Training and an Alternative Cognitive Task." *Aviation, Space, and Environmental Medicine* 53(1982):449–53.

Cox, D. J., A. Freundlich, and R. G. Meyer. "Differential Effectiveness of Electromyographic Feedback, Verbal Relaxation Instructions, and Medication Placebo with Tension Headaches." *Journal of Consulting and Clinical Psychology* 43(1975):892–98.

Crittendon, Ann. "We 'Liberated' Mothers Aren't." *Washington Post,* 5 February 1984, D4.

Curtis, John D., and Richard A. Detert. *How to Relax: A Holistic Approach to Stress Management.* Palo Alto, Calif.: Mayfield, 1981.

Curtis, John D., Richard A. Detert, Jay Schindler, and Kip Zirkel. *Teaching Stress Management and Relaxation Skills: An Instructor's Guide.* La Crosse, Wis.: Coulee Press, 1985.

Danskin, David G., and Mark A. Crow. *Biofeedback: An Introduction and Guide.* Palo Alto, Calif.: Mayfield, 1981.

Davis, Martha, Matthew McKay, and Elizabeth Robbins Eshelman. *The Relaxation and Stress Reduction Workbook.* Richmond, Calif.: New Harbinger Publications, 1980.

Dean, Dwight. "Alienation: Its Meaning and Measurement." *American Sociological Review* 26(1961):753–58.

Deaux, K. *The Behavior of Women and Men.* Monterey, Calif.: Brooks/Cole, 1976.

DeLamater, John, and Patricia MacCorquodale. *Premarital Sexuality: Attitudes, Relationships, Behavior.* Madison: University of Wisconsin Press, 1979.

DeLongis, Anita, et al. "Relationship of Daily Hassles, Uplifts, and Major Life Events to Health Status." *Health Psychology* 1(1982):119–36.

DiCara, L. V., and Neal E. Miller. "Instrumental Learning of Vasomotor Responses by Rats: Learning to Respond Differentially in the Two Ears." *Science* 159(1968):1485.

Dillbeck, M. C. "The Effect of the Transcendental Meditation Technique on Anxiety Levels." *Journal of Clinical Psychology* 33(1977):1076–78.

Dinoff, M., N. C. Rickard, and J. Colwick. "Weight Reduction through Successive Contracts." *American Journal of Orthopsychiatry* 42(1972):110–13.

Dintiman, George B., and Jerrold S. Greenberg. *Health through Discovery.* 3d ed. New York: Random House, 1986.

Dintiman, George B., et al. *Discovering Lifetime Fitness: Concepts of Exercise and Weight Control.* St. Paul: West, 1984.

Dion, Maureen. "A Study of the Effects of Progressive Relaxation Training on Changes in Self-Concepts in Low Self-Concept College Students." *Dissertation Abstracts International* 37(1977):4860.

Dixon, N. F. "Humor: A Cognitive Alternative to Stress?" In *Stress and Anxiety,* edited by I. Sarason and Charles Spielberger. New York: Hemisphere, 1980, 281–89.

Downing, G. *Massage Book.* Berkeley, Calif.: Book Works Publishing Co., 1972. Distributed by Random House, Inc.

Dreyfuss, F., and J. Czaczkes. "Blood Cholesterol and Uric Acid of Healthy Medical Students under Stress of an Examination." *Archives of Internal Medicine* 103(1959):708–11.

Dunbar, Flanders. *Psychosomatic Diagnosis.* New York: Harper, 1943.

Egdahl, R., and D. Walsh. *Mental Wellness Programs for Employees.* New York: Springer-Verlag, 1980.

Eldridge, William, Stanley Blostein, and Virginia Richardson. "A Multi-Dimensional Model for Assessing Factors Associated with Burnout in Human Service Organizations." *Public Personnel Management* 12(1983):315.

Elias, Marilyn. "Type A's: Like Father, Like Son." *USA Today,* 7 August 1985, D1.

Eliot, Robert S. "Are You a Hot Reactor: How Do You React to Stress?" *Shape,* February 1987:66–73, 128–31, 138.

Ellis, Albert, and Robert Harper. *A Guide to Rational Living.* N. Hollywood: Melvin Powers, Wilshire Book Company, 1975.

———. *A New Guide to Rational Living.* Englewood Cliffs, N.J.: Prentice-Hall, 1979.

Elson, B. D., P. Hauri, and D. Cunis. "Physiological Changes in Yogi Meditation." *Psychophysiology* 14(1977):52–57.

Engel, George L. "Studies of Ulcerative Colitis. III. The Nature of the Psychological Processes." *American Journal of Medicine,* August 1955.

Erikson, Erik H. *Childhood and Society.* New York: W. W. Norton, 1963.

Everly, George S., and Daniel A. Girdano. *The Stress Mess Solution: The Causes of Stress on the Job.* Bowie, Md.: Robert J. Brady, 1980.

Eversaul, G. A. "Psycho-physiology Training and the Behavioral Treatment of Premature Ejaculation: Preliminary Findings." *Proceedings of the Biofeedback Research Society,* Denver, Colo., 1975.

Fee, Richard A., and Daniel A. Girdano. "The Relative Effectiveness of Three Techniques to Induce the Trophotropic Response." *Biofeedback and Self-Regulation* 3(1978):145–57.

Feist, Jess, and Linda Brannon. *Health Psychology: An Introduction to Behavior and Health.* Belmont, Calif.: Wadsworth, 1988.

Feldman, Robert H. L. "The Assessment and Enhancement of Health Compliance in the Workplace." In *Occupational Health Promotion: Health Behavior in the Workplace,* edited by George S. Everly and Robert H. L. Feldman. New York: John Wiley & Sons, 1985, 33–46.

Fentress, David W., Bruce J. Masek, James E. Mehegan, and Herbert Benson. "Biofeedback and Relaxation-Response Training in the Treatment of Pediatric Migraine." *Developmental Medicine and Child Neurology* 28(1986):139–46.

Ferguson, P., and J. Gowan. "TM—Some Preliminary Findings." *Journal of Humanistic Psychology* 16(1977):51–60.

Fier, B. "Recession Is Causing Dire Illness." *Moneysworth,* 23 June 1975.

Forman, Jeffrey W., and Dave Myers. *The Personal Stress Reduction Program.* Englewood Cliffs, N.J.: Prentice-Hall, 1987.

Forney, Deanna S., Fran Wallace-Schutzman, and T. Thorn Wiggers. "Burnout among Career Development Professionals: Preliminary Findings and Implications." *Personnel and Guidance Journal* 60(1982):435–39.

Frankenhauser, M., and B. Gardell. "Underload and Overload in Working Life: Outline of a Multidisciplinary Approach." *Journal of Human Stress* 2(1976):35–46.

Frazier, T. W. "Avoidance Conditioning of Heart Rate in Humans." *Psychophysiology* 3(1966):188–202.

French, J. R. P., and R. D. Caplan. "Psychosocial Factors in Coronary Heart Disease." *Industrial Medicine* 39(1970):383–97.

Freudenberger, Herbert J., and Gail North. *Women's Burnout.* New York: Doubleday & Co., 1985.

Friedman, Meyer, and Ray H. Rosenman. "Association of Specific Overt Behavior Pattern with Blood and Cardiovascular Findings: Blood Clotting Time, Incidence of Arcus Senilis, and Clinical Coronary Artery Disease." *Journal of the American Medical Association* 169(1959):1286–96.

———. *Type A Behavior and Your Heart.* Greenwich, Conn.: Fawcett, 1974.

Friedman, Meyer, and Diane Ulmer. *Treating Type A Behavior and Your Heart.* New York: Alfred A. Knopf, 1984.

Friedman, Meyer, A. E. Brown, and Ray Rosenman. "Voice Analysis Test for Detection of Behavior Pattern: Responses of Normal Men and Coronary Patients." *Journal of the American Medical Association* 208(1969): 828–36.

Friedman, Meyer, Ray Rosenman, and V. Carroll. "Changes in the Serum Cholesterol and Blood Clotting Time in Men Subjected to Cycle Variation of Occupational Stress." *Circulation* 17(1958):852–64.

Fuller, George D. *Biofeedback: Methods and Procedures in Clinical Practice.* San Francisco: Biofeedback Press, 1977.

Funk, Steven C., and Kent B. Houston. "A Critical Analysis of the Hardiness Scale's Validity and Utility." *Journal of Personality and Social Psychology* 53(1987):572–78.

Galway, W. Timothy. *The Inner Game of Tennis.* New York: Random House, 1974.

Gerschman, Jack A., et al. "Hypnosis in the Control of Gagging." *Australian Journal of Clinical and Experimental Hypnosis* 9(1981):53–59.

Getchel, Bud. *Physical Fitness: A Way of Life.* New York: John Wiley, 1983.

Gillespie, David F. "Correlates for Active and Passive Types of Burnout." *Journal of Social Service Research* 4(Winter 1980–81):1–16.

Girdano, Daniel A., and George S. Everly. *Controlling Stress and Tension: A Holistic Approach.* Englewood Cliffs, N.J.: Prentice-Hall, 1986.

Glass, David C. "Stress Behavior, Patterns, and Coronary Disease." *American Scientist* 65(1977):177–87.

Goleman, Daniel, and Gary E. Schwartz. "Meditation as an Intervention in Stress Reactivity." *Journal of Consulting and Clinical Psychology* 44(1976):456–66.

Gore, S. "The Effects of Social Support in Moderating the Health Consequences of Unemployment." *Journal of Health and Social Behavior* 19(1978):157–65.

Gorton, B. "Autogenic Training." *American Journal of Clinical Hypnosis* 2(1959):31–41.

Grant, Eleanor. "The Housework Gap." *Psychology Today* 22(1988):8.

Green, Elmer E., A. M. Green, and E. D. Walters. "Voluntary Control of Internal States: Psychological and Physiological." *Journal of Transpersonal Psychology* 2(1970):1–26.

Green, Lawrence W., David M. Levine, and Sigrid Deeds. "Clinical Trials of Health Education for Hypertensive Outpatients: Design and Baseline Data." *Preventive Medicine* 4(1975):417–25.

Green, Tim. "My Favorite Routine: Chair Aerobics." *Shape,* June 1986, 150–53.

Greenberg, Jerrold S. "The Masturbatory Behavior of College Students." *Psychology in the Schools* 9(1972):427–32.

———. *Student-Centered Health Instruction: A Humanistic Approach.* Reading, Mass.: Addison-Wesley, 1978.

———. "A Study of Stressors in the College Student Population." *Health Education* 12(1981):8–12.

———. "A Study of the Effects of Stress on the Health of College Students: Implications for School Health Education." *Health Education* 15(1984):11–15.

Greenberg, Jerrold S., and David Pargman. *Physical Fitness: A Wellness Approach.* Englewood Cliffs, N.J.: Prentice-Hall, 1986.

———. *Physical Fitness: A Wellness Approach.* 2d ed. Englewood Cliffs, N.J.: Prentice-Hall, 1989.

Greenberg, Jerrold S., Clint E. Bruess, and Doris Sands. *Sexuality: Insights and Issues.* Dubuque, Iowa: Wm. C. Brown, 1986.

Greenberg, Jerrold S., Clint E. Bruess, Kathleen Mullen, and Doris Sands. *Sexuality: Insights and Issues.* 2d ed. Dubuque, Iowa: Wm. C. Brown, 1989.

Greene, W. A. "Operant Conditioning of the GSR Using Partial Reinforcement." *Psychological Reports* 19(1976):571–78.

Greenwood, James W. "Management Stressors." *NIOSH Proceeding: Reducing Occupational Stress.* Cincinnati, Ohio: National Institute for Occupational Safety and Health, April 1978, 41.

Griest, J. H., et al. "Running as Treatment for Depression." *Comparative Psychiatry* 20(1979):41–54.

Guitar, B. "Reduction of Stuttering Frequency Using Analogue Electromyographic Feedback." *Journal of Speech and Hearing Research* 18(1975):672–85.

Hall, Holly. "A Woman's Place . . ." *Psychology Today* 22(1988):28–29.

Harris, Louis. *Harris Poll.* Washington, D.C.: National Council on the Aging, 1975.

Hartzmark, Gini. "Teeth." *Ms.,* May 1985, 106–8.

Havighurst, Robert J. *Developmental Tasks and Education.* New York: David McKay Company, 1972.

Haynes, S. G., and M. Feinleib. "Women at Work and Coronary Heart Disease: Prospective Findings from the Framingham Heart Study." *American Journal of Public Health* 70(1980):133–41.

Haynes, Suzanne G., M. Feinleib, and W. B. Kannel. "The Relationship of Psychosocial Factors to Coronary Heart Disease in the Framingham Study III. Eight Year Incidence of Coronary Heart Disease." *American Journal of Epidemiology* 3(1980):37–58.

Haynes, S. G., et al. "Electromyographic Biofeedback and Relaxation Instructions in the Treatment of Muscle Contraction Headaches." *Behavior Therapy* 6(1975):672–78.

Heide, E. J., and T. D. Borkovec. "Relaxation-Induced Anxiety: Mechanisms and Theoretical Implications." *Behaviour Research and Therapy* 22(1984):1–12.

Helsing, Knud J., Moyses Szklo, and George W. Comstock. "Factors Associated with Mortality after Widowhood." *American Journal of Public Health* 71(1981):802–9.

Henig, Robin Marantz. "The Jaw Out of Joint." *Washington Post, Health,* 9 February 1988, 16.

Hill, C., Z. Rubin, and L. Peplau. "Breakups before Marriage: The End of 103 Affairs." In *Divorce and Separation,* edited by G. Levinger and O. Moles. New York: Basic Books, 1979.

Hjelle, L. A. "Transcendental Meditation and Psychological Health." *Perceptual and Motor Skills* 39(1974):623–28.

Holahan, C. K., C. J. Holohan, and S. S. Belk. "Adjustment in Aging: The Roles of Life Stress, Hassles, and Self-Efficacy." *Health Psychology* 3(1984):315–28.

Holmes, David S. "Meditation and Somatic Arousal Reduction: A Review of the Experimental Evidence." *American Psychologist* 39(1984):1–10.

Holmes, Thomas H., and Richard H. Rahe. "The Social Readjustment Rating Scale." *Journal of Psychosomatic Research* 11(1967):213–18.

Holmes, T. S., and Thomas H. Holmes. "Short-Term Intrusions into the Life-Style Routine." *Journal of Psychosomatic Research* 14(1970):121–32.

Hovell, Melbourne F., Beverly Calhoun, and John P. Elder. "Modification of Students' Snacking: Comparison of Behavioral Teaching Methods." *Health Education* 19(1988):26–37.

Howard, John H., David A. Cunningham, and Peter A. Rechnitzer. "Personality (Hardiness) as a Moderator of Job Stress and Coronary Risk in Type A Individuals: A Longitudinal Study." *Journal of Behavioral Medicine* 9(1986):229–44.

"How to Prevent Back Trouble." *U.S. News & World Report,* 14 April 1975, 45–48.

Hull, Jay G., Ronald R. Van-Treuren, and Suzanne Virnelli. "Hardiness and Health: A Critique and Alternative Approach." *Journal of Personality and Social Psychology* 53(1987):518–30.

Hunt, Morton. *Sexual Behavior in the 1970s.* Chicago: Playboy Press, 1974.

Hurrell, J. J., and M. J. Colligan. "Psychological Job Stress." In *Environmental and Occupational Medicine,* edited by W. N. Rom. Boston: Little, Brown, 1982, 425–30.

Hurrell, Joseph. "An Overview of Organizational Stress and Health." In *Stress Management in Work Settings,* edited by Lawrence R. Murphy and Theodore F. Schoenborn. Washington, D.C.: National Institute for Occupational Safety and Health, 1987, 31–45.

Hypertension Update. Chicago: Abbott Laboratories, 1976.

—— I ——

Ivancevich, John M., Michael T. Matteson, and Edward P. Richards III. "Who's Liable for Stress on the Job?" *Harvard Business Review,* March-April 1985, 66.

Iyengar, B. K. S. *Light on Yoga.* New York: Schocken Books, 1965.

—— J ——

Jackson, S., and R. Schuler. "A Meta-Analysis and Conceptual Critique of Research on Role Ambiguity and Role Conflict in Work Settings." *Organizational Behavior and Human Decision* 36(1985):16–28.

Jacobson, Edmund. *Progressive Relaxation.* 2d ed. Chicago: University of Chicago Press, 1938.

——. *You Must Relax.* New York: McGraw-Hill Book Co., 1970.

Jenkens, C. D. "Recent Evidence Supporting Psychologic and Social Risk Factors for Coronary Disease." *New England Journal of Medicine* 294(1976):987–1038.

Jennings, Charles, and Mark J. Tager. "Good Health Is Good Business." *Medical Self-Care,* Summer 1981, 14.

Jones, John W. "A Measure of Staff Burnout among Health Professionals." Paper presented at the annual meeting of the American Psychological Association, Montreal, September 1980.

Jones, M. A., and J. Emmanuel. "Stages and Recovery Steps of Teacher Burnout." *Education Digest* 45(1981):9–11.

—— K ——

Kamiya, J. "Conscious Control of Brain Waves." *Psychology Today* 1(1978):57–60.

Kanner, A. D., et al. "Comparison of Two Modes of Stress Management: Daily Hassles and Uplifts versus Major Life Events." *Journal of Behavioral Medicine* 4(1981):1–39.

Kaprio, Jaakko, Markku Koskenvuo, and Heli Rita. "Mortality after Bereavement: A Prospective Study of 95,647 Widowed Persons." *American Journal of Public Health* 77(1987):283–87.

Karasek, R. A., J. Schwartz, and T. Theorell. *Job Characteristics, Occupation, and Coronary Heart Disease.* Final report on contract no. R–01–0H00906. Cincinnati, Ohio: National Institute for Occupational Safety and Health, 1982.

Kasamatsu, A., and T. Hirai. "Studies of EEG's of Expert Zen Meditators." *Folia Psychiatrica Neurologica Japonica* 28(1966):315.

Kasl, Stanislav V., and Sidney Cobb. "Health Behavior, Illness Behavior, and Sick-Role Behavior." *Archives of Environmental Health* 12(1966):246–66.

Katz, Jane. "The W. E. T. Workout: A Swimmer's Guide to Water Exercise Techniques." *Shape,* June 1986, 82–88+.

Keefe, J. F., R. S. Surwit, and R. N. Pilon. "Biofeedback, Autogenic Training, and Progressive Relaxation in the Treatment of Raynaud's Disease: A Comparative Study." *Journal of Applied Behavior Analysis* 13(1980): 3–11.

Kelly, Colleen. *Assertion Training: A Facilitator's Guide.* LaJolla, Calif.: University Associates, 1979.

Kiesling, Stephen. "Loosen Your Hips: Walkshaping." *American Health,* October 1986, 62–67.

Kimmel, H. D. "Instrumental Conditioning of Autonomically Mediated Behavior." *Psychological Bulletin* 67(1967):337–45.

Kimmel, H. D., and F. A. Hill. "Operant Conditioning of the GSR." *Psychological Reports* 7(1960):555–62.

Kittleson, Mark J., and Becky Hageman-Righey. "Wellness and Behavior Contracting." *Health Education* 19(1988):8–11.

Kobasa, Suzanne C. "Stressful Life Events, Personality, and Health: An Inquiry into Hardiness." *Journal of Personality and Social Psychology* 37(1979):1–11.

Kobasa, Suzanne C., Salvatore R. Maddi, and Mark C. Puccetti. "Personality and Exercise as Buffers in the Stress-Illness Relationship." *Journal of Behavioral Medicine* 5(1982):391–404.

Kobasa, Suzanne C., Salvatore R. Maddi, and Marc A. Zola. "Type A and Hardiness." *Journal of Behavioral Medicine* 6(1983):41–51.

Kobasa, Suzanne C., et al. "Effectiveness of Hardiness, Exercise, and Social Support as Resources against Illness." *Journal of Psychosomatic Research* 29(1985):525–33.

Kondo, C., A. Canter, and J. Knott. "Relaxation Training as a Method of Reducing Anxiety Associated with Depression." Paper presented at the Biofeedback Research Society Meeting, Monterey, Calif., 1975.

Koop, C. Everett. *Understanding AIDS: A Message from the Surgeon General.* Washington, D.C.: Department of Health and Human Services, 1988.

Kriyananda. *Yoga Postures for Self-Awareness.* San Francisco: Ananda Publications, 1967.

Kukla, Kenneth J. "The Effects of Progressive Relaxation Training upon Athletic Performance during Stress." *Dissertation Abstracts International* 37(1977):6392.

Labott, Susan M., and Randall B. Martin. "The Stress-Moderating Effects of Weeping and Humor." *Journal of Human Stress* 13(1987):159–64.

Lacroix, J. Michael, Melissa A. Clarke, J. Carson Bock, and Neville C. Doxey. "Physiological Changes after Biofeedback and Relaxation Training for Multiple-Pain Tension-Headache Patients." *Perceptual and Motor Skills* 63(1986):139–53.

Lamont, Linda S., and Mary T. Reynolds. "Developing an Individualized Program for Physical Fitness." *Occupational Health Nursing* 28(1980):16–19.

Lamott, Kenneth. *Escape from Stress: How to Stop Killing Yourself.* New York: G. P. Putnam, 1974.

Lazarus, Richard S. *Psychological Stress and the Coping Process*. New York: McGraw-Hill Book Co., 1966.

———. "Puzzles in the Study of Daily Hassles." *Journal of Behavioral Medicine* 7(1984):375–89.

Lazarus, Richard S., and A. DeLongis. "Psychological Stress and Coping in Aging." *American Psychologist* 38(1983):245–54.

Lazarus, Richard S., and Susan Folkman. *Stress, Appraisal, and Coping*. New York: Springer, 1984.

Lear, Martha Weinman. "How Many Choices Do Women Really Have?" *Woman's Day,* 11 November 1986, 109–11, 180–83.

Lehrer, P. M., and R. L. Woolfolk. "Are Stress Reduction Techniques Interchangeable, or Do They Have Specific Effect?: A Review of the Comparative Empirical Literature." In *Principles and Practice of Stress Management,* edited by R. L. Woolfolk and P. M. Lehrer. New York: Guilford, 1984.

LeShan, Lawrence. "An Emotional Life-History Pattern Associated with Neoplastic Disease." *Annals of the New York Academy of Sciences,* 1966.

LeShan, Lawrence, and R. E. Worthington. "Some Recurrent Life-History Patterns Observed in Patients with Malignant Disease." *Journal of Nervous and Mental Disorders* 124(1956):460–65.

Levine, A. *When Dreams and Heroes Died*. San Francisco: Jossey-Bass, 1983.

Lindemann, Erich. "Symptomatology and Management of Acute Grief." In *Stress and Coping: An Anthology,* edited by Alan Monet and Richard S. Lazarus. New York: Columbia University Press, 1977.

Linden, W. "Practicing of Meditation by School Children and Their Levels of Field Independence-Dependence, Text Anxiety, and Reading Achievement." *Journal of Consulting and Clinical Psychology* 41(1973):139–43.

Linton, Steven J. "Behavioral Remediation of Chronic Pain: A Status Report." *Pain* 24(1986):125–41.

Litt, Mark D. "Mediating Factors in Non-Medical Treatment for Migraine Headache: Toward an Interactional Model." *Journal of Psychosomatic Research* 30(1986):505–19.

Long, Nicholas J., and Jody Long. *Conflict and Comfort in College*. Belmont, Calif.: Wadsworth, 1970.

Lundberg, V., T. Theorell, and E. Lind. "Life Changes and Myocardial Infarction: Individual Differences in Life-Change Scaling." *Journal of Psychosomatic Research* 19(1975):27–32.

Luthe, Wolfgang. "Method, Research and Application of Autogenic Training." *American Journal of Clinical Hypnosis* 5(1962):17–23.

———, ed. *Autogenic Training*. New York: Grune & Stratton, 1965.

———, ed. *Autogenic Therapy*. Vols. 1–6. New York: Grune & Stratton, 1969.

Machlowitz, Marilyn. *Workaholics: Living with Them, Working with Them.* Reading, Mass.: Addison-Wesley, 1980.

Mac Kinnon, Catherine. *Sexual Harassment of Working Women.* New Haven, Conn.: Yale University Press, 1979.

McLean, Alan A. *Work Stress.* Reading, Mass.: Addison-Wesley, 1979.

McLeroy, K. R., Lawrence W. Green, K. D. Mullen, and V. Foshee. "Assessing the Health Effects of Health Promotion in Worksites: A Review of the Stress Program Evaluations." *Health Education Quarterly* 11(1984):379–401.

McNeil, Kevin, et al. "Measurement of Psychological Hardiness in Older Adults." *Canadian Journal on Aging* 5(1986):43–48.

McQuade, Walter, and Ann Aikman. *Stress.* New York: Bantam Books, 1974.

Maddi, Salvatore R. "Personality as a Resource in Stress Resistance: The Hardy Type." Paper presented in the symposium on "Personality Moderators of Stressful Life Events" at the annual meeting of the American Psychological Association, Montreal, September 1980.

Mahoney, M. J., and C. E. Thoresen. *Self-Control: Power to the Person.* Monterey, Calif.: Brooks/Cole, 1974.

Maier, Steven F., and Mark Laudenslager. "Stress and Health: Exploring the Links." *Psychology Today,* August 1985, 44–49.

Makara, G., M. Palkovits, and J. Szentagothal. "The Endocrine Hypothalamus and the Hormonal Response to Stress." In *Selye's Guide to Stress Research,* edited by Hans Seyle. New York: Van Nostrand Reinhold, 1980.

Malec, J., and C. N. Sipprelle. "Physiological and Subjective Effects of Zen Meditation and Demand Characteristics." *Journal of Consulting and Clinical Psychology* 45(1977):339–40.

Mann, R. A. "The Behavior-Therapeutic Use of Contingency Contracting to Control an Adult-Behavior Problem: Weight Control." *Journal of Applied Behavioral Analysis* 5(1972):99–109.

Manuso, J. S. J. "Stress Management in the Workplace." In *Health Promotion in the Workplace,* edited by M. P. O'Donnell and T. Ainsworth. New York: John Wiley & Sons, 1984, 362–90.

Margolis, B. L., W. H. Kroes, and R. P. Quinn. "Job Stress: An Unlisted Occupational Hazard." *Journal of Occupational Medicine* 16(1974): 654–61.

Martin, R. A., and H. M. Lefcourt. "Sense of Humor as a Moderator of the Relationship between Stressors and Mood." *Journal of Personal and Social Psychology* 45(1973):1313–24.

Mason, James W. "A Historical View of the Stress Field." *Journal of Human Stress* 1(1975):22–36.

Massage Therapy Journal. Available from the American Massage Therapy Association, P.O. Box 1270, Kingsport, TN 37662.

Masuda, M., et al. "Life Events and Prisoners." *Archives of General Psychiatry* 35(1978):197–203.

Matthews, Karen A. "Psychological Perspective on Type A Behavior Pattern." *Psychological Bulletin* 91(1982):293–323.

Matthews, Karen A., and Suzanne G. Haynes. "Reviews and Commentary: Type A Behavior Pattern and Coronary Disease Risk. Update and Critical Evaluation." *American Journal of Epidemiology* 123(1986):923–60.

Merit System Protection Board report on sexual harassment in the workplace given before the Subcommittee on Investigations, Committee on the Post Office and Civil Service, U.S. House of Representatives, September 1980.

Mikevic, P. "Anxiety, Depression and Exercise." *Quest* 33(1982):140–53.

Miller, Neal E. "Learning of Visceral and Glandular Response." *Science* 163(1969):434–45.

———. "RX: Biofeedback." *Psychology Today,* February 1985, 54–59.

Mitchell, K. R., and D. M. Mitchell. "Migraine: An Exploratory Treatment Application of Programmed Behavior Therapy Techniques." *Journal of Psychosomatic Research* 15(1971):137–57.

Monat, Alan, and Richard S. Lazarus, eds. *Stress and Coping: An Anthology.* New York: Columbia University Press, 1985.

Moos, R. H., and George F. Solomon. "Psychologic Comparisons between Women with Rheumatoid Arthritis and Their Nonarthritic Sisters." *Psychosomatic Medicine* 2(1965):150.

Morgan, Janet DiVittorio. "I Work Because I Have To." In *The Mothers' Book: Shared Experiences,* edited by Ronnie Friedland and Carol Kort. Boston: Houghton Mifflin, 1981, 96.

Moskowitz, Daniel B. "Workers' Compensation Awards for Job Stress on the Rise." *Washington Post, Business,* 14 October 1985, 39.

Moss, G. E. *Illness, Immunity and Social Interaction.* New York: John Wiley & Sons, 1973.

Naranjo, C., and R. E. Ornstein. *On the Psychology of Meditation.* New York: Viking, 1971.

National Center for Health Statistics. "Advance Report for Final Marriage Statistics, 1985." *Monthly Vital Statistics Report* 37 (29 April 1988).

———. "Advance Report of Final Divorce Statistics, 1985." *Monthly Vital Statistics Report* 36 (7 December 1987).

———. "Aging in the Eighties: Functional Limitations of Individuals Age 65 Years and Over." *Advance Data,* 10 June 1987.

———. "Aging in the Eighties, People Living Alone—Two Years Later." *Advance Data,* 4 April 1988.

———. "Annual Summary of Births, Marriages, Divorces, and Deaths: United States, 1986." *Monthly Vital Statistics Report* 35(24 August 1987).

———. "Blood Pressure Levels and Hypertension in Persons Ages 6–74 Years: United States, 1976–80." *Advance Data,* 8 October 1982.

———. "Use of Nursing Homes by the Elderly: Preliminary Data from the 1985 National Nursing Home Survey." *Advance Data,* 14 May 1987.

National Institute of Mental Health. *Retirement: Patterns and Predictions.* Washington, D.C.: National Institute of Mental Health, 1975.

Noland, Melody P., and Robert H. L. Feldman. "An Empirical Investigation of Exercise Behavior in Adult Women." *Health Education* 16(1985): 29–33.

Nowak, Kenneth M. "Type A, Hardiness, and Psychological Distress." *Journal of Behavioral Medicine* 9(1986):537–48.

Nuckolls, K., J. Cassel, and B. Kaplan. "Psychosocial Assets, Life Crises, and the Prognosis of Pregnancy." *American Journal of Epidemiology* 95(1972):431–41.

"Nutrients and Stress." *Medical Self-Care,* Summer 1985, 18.

O'Brien, F., and K. Sothers. "The UW-SP Stress Management Program." *Health Values* 8(1984):35–40.

"Of Rats and Men." *Psychology Today,* July 1985, 21.

Office of Disease Prevention and Health Promotion. "Exercise for Older Americans." *Healthfinder.* Washington, D.C.: Office of Disease Prevention and Health Promotion National Health Information Center, November 1987.

"On the Pulse." *Washington Post,* 6 February 1985, 5.

Orme-Johnson, David W. "Autonomic Stability and Transcendental Meditation." *Psychosomatic Medicine* 35(1973):341–49.

Ornstein, Robert, and David Sobel. *The Healing Brain: A New Perspective on the Brain and Health.* New York: Simon & Schuster, 1987.

Osipow, Samuel H., and Arnold R. Spokane. "Occupational Environment Scales." Unpublished Scales, University of Maryland, 1980.

Otis, Leon, et al. "Voluntary Control of Tension Headaches." Paper presented at the Biofeedback Research Society Meeting, Colorado Springs, Colo., 1974.

Ouchi, Wm. *Theory Z.* Reading, Mass.: Addison-Wesley, 1981.

Pargman, David. *Stress and Motor Performance: Understanding and Coping.* Ithaca, N.Y.: Mouvement Publications, 1986.

Parkes, C. M., B. Benjamin, and R. E. Fitzgerald. "Broken Heart: A Statistical Study of Increased Mortality among Widowers." *British Medical Journal* 1(1969):740–43.

Patlak, Marjie. "Eating to Avoid Cancer Gets More Complicated." *Washington Post, Health,* 2 April 1986, 16–17.

Patrick, Pamela K. S. *Health Care Worker Burnout: What It Is, What to Do About It.* Chicago: Blue Cross Association, Inquiry Books, 1981.

Pelletier, Kenneth R. *Mind as Healer, Mind as Slayer.* New York: Dell Publishing Co., 1977.

———. *Healthy People in Unhealthy Places: Stress and Fitness at Work.* New York: Delacorte Press/Seymour Lawrence, 1984.

Peters, Ruanne K., Herbert Benson, and John M. Peters. "Daily Relaxation Response Breaks in a Working Population: II. Effects on Blood Pressure." *American Journal of Public Health* 67(1977):954–59.

Pollock, Susan E. "Human Response to Chronic Illness: Physiologic and Psychosocial Adaptation." *Nursing Research* 35(1986):90–95.

Pond, Jim. "Survey Shows Studying Freshmen's Top Worry." *The Diamondback,* 15 April 1985, 1, 3.

President's Council on Physical Fitness and Sports. *An Introduction to Running: One Step at a Time.* Washington, D.C.: President's Council on Physical Fitness and Sports, 1980.

———. *Aqua Dynamics.* Washington, D.C.: President's Council on Physical Fitness and Sports, 1981.

———. *Building a Healthier Company.* Washington, D.C.: President's Council on Physical Fitness and Sports, n.d.

"Putting the Heart in Cardiac Care." *Psychology Today,* April 1986, 18.

Rabkin, S., and F. Matthewson. "Chronobiology of Cardiac Sudden Death in Men." *Journal of the American Medical Association* 244(1980):1357–58.

Raskin, M., G. Johnson, and J. Rondestvedt. "Chronic Anxiety Treated by Feedback-Induced Muscle Relaxation." *Archives of General Psychiatry* 23(1973):263–67.

Rathus, Spencer A. "A 30-Item Schedule for Assessing Assertive Behavior." *Behavior Therapy* 4(1973):398–406.

Rice, Phillip L. *Stress and Health: Principles and Practice for Coping and Wellness.* Monterey, Calif.: Brooks/Cole, 1987.

Rich, Spencer. "Study Details Income Lost in Giving Birth." *Washington Post,* 15 March 1988, A21.

Richburg, Keith B. "College Students' Average Age Rises." *Washington Post,* 14 August 1985, A4.

Riddle, Patricia, and Geraldine A. Johnson. "Sexual Harassment: What Role Should Educators Play?" *Health Education* 14(1983):20–23.

Riley, V. "Mouse Mammary Tumors: Alternation of Incidence as Apparent Function of Stress." *Science* 189(1975):465–67.

Robinson, Vera M. "Humor in Nursing." In *Behavioral Concepts and Nursing Intervention,* 2d ed., edited by C. Carlson and B. Blackwell. Philadelphia: Lippincott, 1978.

———. "Humor and Health." In *Handbook of Humor Research,* edited by Paul E. Mcghee and Jeffrey H. Goldstein. New York: Springer-Verlag, 1983.

Rodin, J., and J. Slochower. "Externality in the Obese: Effects of Environmental Responsiveness on Weight." *Journal of Personality and Social Psychology* 33(1976):338–44.

Roman, J. A. "Cardiorespiratory Functioning in Flight." *Aerospace Medicine* 34(1963):322–37.

Rosato, Frank D. *Fitness and Wellness: The Physical Connection.* St. Paul, Minn.: West, 1986.

Rosch, Paul J., and Kenneth R. Pelletier. "Designing Worksite Stress
  Management Programs." In *Stress Management in Work Settings,* edited
  by Lawrence R. Murphy and Theodore F. Schoenborn. Washington, D.C.:
  National Institute for Occupational Safety and Health, 1987, 69–91.
Rosenbaum, Jean. "Aerobics without Injury." *Medical Self-Care,* Fall 1984,
  30–33.
Rosenbaum, Jean, and Veryl Rosenbaum. *Living with Teenagers.* New York:
  Stein & Day, 1980.
Rosenman, Ray H., Richard Brand, and C. David Jenkins. "Coronary Heart
  Disease in the Western Collaborative Group Study: Final Follow-Up
  Experience of 8½ Years." *Journal of the American Medical Association*
  223(1975):872–77.
Rosenman, Ray H., Meyer Friedman, and Reuban Strauss. "A Predictive
  Study of Coronary Heart Disease: The Western Collaborative Group
  Study." *Journal of the American Medical Association* 189(1964):15–22.
Rotter, Julian B. "Generalized Expectancies for Internal vs. External Control
  of Reinforcement." *Psychological Monographs* 80(1966):whole no. 609.
Rowland, K. F., and B. A. Sokol. "A Review of Research Examining the
  Coronary-Prone Behavior Pattern." *Journal of Human Stress* 3(1977):
  26–33.
Rowlands, Peter. *Saturday Parent.* New York: Continuum, 1980.
Rubin, R. T. "Biochemical and Endocrine Responses to Severe Psychological
  Stress." In *Life Stress and Illness,* edited by E. K. E. Gunderson and
  Richard H. Rahe. Springfield, Ill.: Charles C. Thomas, 1974.
Rubin, R. T., E. Gunderson, and R. J. Arthur. "Prior Life Change and Illness
  Onset in an Attack Carrier's Crew." *Archives of Environmental Health*
  19(1969):753–57.
Russek, Henry I., and Linda G. Russek. "Is Emotional Stress an Etiological
  Factor in Coronary Heart Disease?" *Psychosomatics* 17(1976):63.

Sadker, Myra, and David Sadker. "Sexism in the Schools of the '80s."
  Psychology Today, March 1985, 54–57.
Safran, Claire. "What Men Do to Women on the Job: A Shocking Look at
  Sexual Harassment." *Redbook,* November 1976, 149, 217–24.
Salameh, Waleed Anthony. "Humor in Psychotherapy: Past Outlooks, Present
  Status, and Future Frontiers." In *Handbook of Humor Research,* edited
  by Paul E. Mcghee and Jeffrey H. Goldstein. New York: Springer-Verlag,
  1983, 75–108.
Sands, Steven. "The Use of Humor in Psychotherapy." *Psychoanalytic Review*
  71(1984):458.
Sargent, J. D., E. E. Green, and E. D. Walters. "Preliminary Report on the
  Use of Autogenic Feedback Techniques in the Treatment of Migraine and
  Tension Headaches." *Psychosomatic Medicine* 35(1973):129–35.

Sargent, Joseph, et al. "Results of a Controlled, Experimental, Outcome Study of Nondrug Treatments for the Control of Migraine Headaches." *Journal of Behavioral Medicine* 9(1986):291–323.

Schleifer, Steven, et al. "Suppression of Lymphocyte Stimulation following Bereavement." *JAMA* 250(1983):374–77.

Schmied, Lori A., and Kathleen A. Lawler. "Hardiness, Type A Behavior, and the Stress-Illness Relation in Working Women." *Journal of Personality and Social Psychology* 51(1985):1218–23.

Schultz, Johannes. *Das Autogene Training.* Stuttgart, Germany: Geerg-Thieme Verlag, 1953.

Schultz, Johannes, and Wolfgang Luthe. *Autogenic Training: A Psychophysiologic Approach to Psychotherapy.* New York: Grune & Stratton, 1959.

Schwinn, Beth. "Burned in Pursuit of the Burn." *Washington Post, Health,* 14 August 1986, 12.

Seeman, M., and J. W. Evans. "Alienation and Learning in a Hospital Setting." *American Sociological Reviews* 27(1962):772–83.

Selye, Hans. *The Stress of Life.* New York: McGraw-Hill Book Co., 1956.
———. *Stress without Distress.* New York: J. B. Lippincott, 1974.

Shapiro, D. H., and D. Giber. "Meditation and Psychotherapeutic Effects." *Archives of General Psychiatry* 35(1978):294–302.

Shapiro, Shoshana, and Paul M. Lehrer. "Psychophysiological Effects of Autogenic Training and Progressive Relaxation." *Biofeedback and Self-Regulation* 5(1980):249–55.

Shearn, D. W. "Operant Conditioning of Heart Rate." *Science* 137(1962): 530–31.

Sheikh, A. A. *Imagery: Current Theory, Research, and Application.* New York: Wiley, 1983.
———. *Imagination and Healing.* Farmingdale, N.Y.: Baywood Publishing Company, 1984.

Shekelle, R. B., J. A. Schoenberger, and J. Stamler. "Correlates of the JAS Type A Behavior Pattern Score." *Journal of Chronic Diseases* 29(1976):381–94.

Shekelle, R. B., et al. "Hostility, Risk of Coronary Heart Disease and Mortality." *Psychosomatic Medicine* 45(1983):109–14.
———. "The MRFIT Behavior Pattern Study II. Type A Behavior and Incidence of Coronary Heart Disease." *American Journal of Epidemiology* 122(1985):559–70.

Shostak, Arthur B. *Blue-Collar Stress.* Reading, Mass.: Addison-Wesley, 1980.

Silver, B. V. "Temperature Biofeedback and Relaxation Training in the Treatment of Migraine Headaches." *Biofeedback and Self-Regulation* 4(1979):359–66.

Simeons, A. T. W. *Man's Presumptuous Brain: An Evolutionary Interpretation of Psychosomatic Disease.* New York: E. P. Dutton, 1961.

Simon, A. "The Neurosis, Personality Disorders, Alcoholism, Drug Use and Misuse, and Crime in the Aged." In *Handbook of Mental Health and Aging,* edited by J. E. Birren and R. B. Sloane. Englewood Cliffs, N.J.: Prentice-Hall, 1980, 653–70.

Simon, Cheryl. "A Care Package." *Psychology Today,* April 1988, 44–49.

Simonton, Carl O., and Stephanie Matthews-Simonton. "Belief Systems and Management of the Emotional Aspects of Malignancy." *Journal of Transpersonal Psychology* 7(1975):29–48.

Sinclair, Molly. "Coping with Careers and 'Elder Care'." *Washington Post,* 19 July 1987, A1, A6.

Singer, Jefferson A., Michael S. Neale, and Gary E. Schwartz. "The Nuts and Bolts of Assessing Occupational Stress: A Collaborative Effort with Labor." In *Stress Management in Work Settings,* edited by Lawrence R. Murphy and Theodore F. Schoenborn. Washington, D.C.: National Institute for Occupational Safety and Health, 1987, 3–29.

"Sleeping with the Boss." *Forum,* December 1979, 7.

Smith, H. P. R. "Heart Rate of Pilots Flying Aircraft on Scheduled Airline Routes." *Aerospace Medicine* 38(1967):1117–19.

Smith, Jonathan C. *Relaxation Dynamics: Nine World Approaches to Self-Relaxation.* Champaign, Ill.: Research Press, 1985.

———. *Meditation: A Senseless Guide to a Timeless Discipline.* Champaign, Ill.: Research Press, 1986.

———. "Meditation, Biofeedback, and the Relaxation Controversy: A Cognitive-Behavioral Perspective." *American Psychologist* 41(1986):1007–9.

Somers, P., and J. Clementson-Mohr. "Sexual Extortion in the Workplace." *The Personnel Administrator,* April 1979, 23–28.

Sorenson, Jacki. *Aerobic Dancing.* New York: Rawson, Wade, 1979.

Sparacino, Jack. "The Type A Behavior Pattern: A Critical Assessment." *Journal of Human Stress* 5(1979):37–51.

Squires, Sally. "When You're Smiling, the Whole Immune System Smiles with You." *Washington Post,* 9 January 1985, 16.

———. "The Power of Positive Imagery: Visions to Boost Immunity." *American Health,* July 1987, 56–61.

Stellman, Jeanne, and Mary Sue Henifen. *Office Work Can Be Dangerous to Your Health.* New York: Pantheon, 1983.

Stone, Arthur A., et al. "Evidence That Secretory IgA Antibody is Associated with Daily Mood." *Jounal of Personality and Social Psychology* 52(1987):988–93.

Stone, William J. *Adult Fitness Programs: Planning, Designing, Managing, and Improving Fitness Programs.* Glenview, Ill.: Scott, Foresman and Company, 1987.

Straits, B. C., and L. Secherst. "Further Support of Some Findings about Characteristics of Smokers and Nonsmokers." *Journal of Consulting Psychology* 27(1963):282.

Swell, Lila. *Success: You Can Make It Happen.* New York: Simon & Schuster, 1976.

Szekely, Barbara. "Nonpharmacological Treatment of Menstrual Headache: Relaxation-Biofeedback Behavior Therapy and Person-Centered Insight Therapy." *Headache* 26(1986):86–92.

Tasner, Mary. "TMJ." *Medical Self-Care,* November-December 1986, 47–50.

Taub, Edward. "Self-Regulation of Human Tissue Temperature." In *Biofeedback: Theory and Practice,* edited by Gary E. Schwartz and J. Beatty. New York: Academic Press, 1977.

Taylor, Shelly E. *Health Psychology.* New York: Random House, 1986.

Theorell, T., and T. Akerstedt. "Day and Night Work: Changes in Cholesterol, Uric Acid, Glucose, and Potassium in Serum and in Circadian Patterns of Urinary Catecholamine Excretion—A Longitudinal Cross-Over Study of Railroad Repairmen." *Acta Medicine Scandinavia* 200(1976):47–53.

Theorell, T., and B. Floderus-Myrhed. "Workload and Myocardial Infarction—A Prospective Psychosocial Analysis." *International Journal of Epidemiology* 6(1977):17–21.

Theorell, T., and R. Rahe. "Life-Change Events, Ballistocardiography and Coronary Death." *Journal of Human Stress* 1(1975):18–24.

Thomas, D., and K. A. Abbas. "Comparison of Transcendental Meditation and Progressive Relaxation in Reducing Anxiety." *British Medical Journal* no. 6154(1978):1749.

Tobias, Maxine, and Mary Stewart. *Stretch and Relax: A Day by Day Workout and Relaxation Program.* Tucson, Ariz.: The Body Press, 1975.

Toffler, Alvin. *Future Shock.* New York: Random House, 1970.

———. *The Third Wave.* New York: William Morrow & Co., 1980.

Tom, G., and M. Rucker. "Fat, Full, and Happy: Effects of Food Deprivation, External Cues, and Obesity on Preference Ratings, Consumption, and Buying Intentions." *Journal of Personality and Social Psychology* 32(1975):761–66.

Tucker, Larry A., Galen E. Cole, and Glenn M. Friedman. "Stress and Serum Cholesterol: A Study of 7,000 Adult Males." *Health Values* 11(1987): 34–39.

Turk, D. C., Donald H. Meichenbaum, and W. H. Berman. "Application of Biofeedback for the Regulation of Pain: A Critical Review." *Psychological Bulletin* 86(1979):1322–38.

U.S. Bureau of the Census. *Current Population Reports, Population Characteristics, Series P-20, No. 417. Households, Families, Marital Status, and Living Arrangements: March 1987. Advance Report.* Washington, D.C.: U.S. Government Printing Office, 1987.

———. *Current Population Reports, Series P-20, No. 419. Household and Family Characteristics: March 1986.* Washington, D.C.: U.S. Government Printing Office, 1987.

———. *Current Population Reports, Series P-23, No. 150. Population Profile of the United States: 1984–85.* Washington, D.C.: U.S. Government Printing Office, 1987.

———. *Current Population Reports, Series P-70, No. 10. Male-Female Differences in Work Experience, Occupations, and Earnings: 1984.* Washington, D.C.: U.S. Government Printing Office, 1987.

van Doornen, L., and K. Orlebeke. "Stress, Personality and Serum Cholesterol Level." *Journal of Human Stress* 8(1982):24–29.

Wallace, Robert Keith. "Physiological Effects of Transcendental Meditation." *Science* 167(1970):1751–54.

Wallace, Robert Keith, and Herbert Benson. "The Physiology of Meditation." *Scientific American* 226(1972):84–90.

Walsh, Sharon Warren. "Confronting Sexual Harassment at Work." *Washington Post, Business,* 21 July 1986, 16–17.

Walster, Elaine, and G. William Walster. *A New Look at Love.* Reading, Mass.: Addison-Wesley, 1978.

Wanning, Esther, and Michael Castleman. "Healing Your Aching Back." *Medical Self-Care,* Fall 1984, 26–29.

Weiman, Clinton G. "A Study of the Occupational Stressor and the Incidence of Disease/Risk." *Journal of Occupational Medicine* 19(1977):119–22.

———. "A Study of the Occupational Stressor and the Incidence of Disease/Risk." *NIOSH Proceeding: Reducing Occupational Stress.* Cincinnati, Ohio: National Institute for Occupational Safety and Health, April 1978, 55.

Weldon, Gail. "The ABC's of Aerobics Injuries." *Shape,* September 1986, 86–90+.

White, Louise M. "Attention Type A's! You May Be 'Talking Yourself Into' Coronary Heart Disease." *The University of Maryland Graduate School Chronicle* 19(1985):6–7.

Wolf, Stewart. *The Stomach*. Oxford: Oxford University Press, 1965.

Wolf, Stewart, and Harold G. Wolff. *Headaches: Their Nature and Treatment*. Boston: Little, 1953.

Wolff, Harold G. *Stress and Disease*. Springfield, Illinois: Charles C. Thomas, 1953.

Wolpe, Joseph. *The Practice of Behavior Therapy*. 2d ed. New York: Pergamon, 1973.

Women on Words & Images. *Dick and Jane as Victims*. Princeton, N.J.: Women on Words & Images, 1975.

Women's Bureau. *Facts on Women Workers*. Washington, D.C.: U.S. Department of Labor, 1984.

"Women's Health: More Sniffles in Splitsville." *American Health,* July/August 1986, 96, 98.

Young, M., B. Benjamin, and C. Wallace. "The Mortality of Widowers." *Lancet* 3(1960):254–56.

Zaichkowsky, L. D., and R. Kamen. "Biofeedback and Meditation: Effects on Muscle Tension and Locus of Control." *Perceptual and Motor Skills* 46(1978):955–58.

Zarski, J. J. "Hassles and Health: A Replication." *Health Psychology* 3(1984):243–51.

Zimbardo, Philip G. *Shyness: What It Is and What to Do about It*. Reading, Mass.: Addison-Wesley, 1977.

Zimmerman, Tansella, "Preparation Courses for Childbirth in Primipara: A Comparison." *Journal of Psychosomatic Research* 23(1979):227–33.

Credits

Line Art and Text

Chapter 1

Figure 1.2: From Weiman, Clinton G., "A Study of Occupational Stressors and the Incidence of Disease/Risk" in *Journal of Occupational Medicine, 19,* 1977, 119, 122. © 1977 American Occupational Medical Association, Chicago, Illinois. Reprinted by permission. **Page 5:** Figure 3. "The three phases of the general adaptation syndrome" (p. 39) in *Stress Without Distress* by Hans Selye (J. B. Lippincott Company). Copyright © 1974 by Hans Selye, M.D. Reprinted by permission of Harper & Row, Publishers.

Chapter 2

Figure 2.1: From Hole, John W., Jr., *Human Anatomy and Physiology, 2d ed.* © 1978, 1981 Wm. C. Brown Publishers, Dubuque, Iowa. All Rights Reserved. Reprinted by permission. **Figures 2.4, 2.5, 2.6, 2.7, and 2.11:** From Hole, John W., Jr., *Human Anatomy and Physiology,* 3d ed. © 1978, 1981, 1984 Wm. C. Brown Publishers, Dubuque, Iowa. All Rights Reserved. Reprinted by permission. **Figure 2.8:** From Hole, John W., Jr., *Human Anatomy and Physiology,* © 1978 Wm. C. Brown Publishers, Dubuque, Iowa. All Rights Reserved. Reprinted by permission. **Figures 2.9 and 2.10:** From Van De Graaff, Kent M., *Human Anatomy Laboratory Textbook, 2d ed.* © 1981, 1984 Wm. C. Brown Publishers, Dubuque, Iowa. All Rights Reserved. Reprinted by permission.

Chapter 5

Figure 5.2 and Page 85: From Dintiman, George B. and Jerrold S. Greenberg, *Health Through Discovery, 2d ed.* © 1983 Random House, Inc., New York. Reprinted by permission. **Pages 87–88:** From Anderson, G. E., "College Schedule of Recent Experience." Unpublished Master's Thesis, 1972. Reprinted by permission of the Department of Education, North Dakota State University. **Pages 88–89:** Reprinted with permission from Holmes, Thomas H. and Richard H. Rahe, "The Social Readjustment Rating Scale," *Journal of Psychosomatic Research, 11:* 213–218, 1967. © 1967. Pergamon Press, Ltd.

Chapter 6

Page 97: From Dintiman, George B. and Jerrold S. Greenberg, *Health Through Discovery, 2d ed.* © 1983 Random House, Inc., New York. Reprinted by permission. **Pages 98–100:** From Rathus, Spencer A., "A 30-Item Schedule for Assessing Assertive Behavior" in *Behavior Therapy 4,* 398–406, 1973. © 1973 Academic Press, Orlando, Florida. Reprinted by permission. **Pages 102–103:** From Sharon A. Bower and Gordon Bower, *Asserting Yourself: A Practical Guide for Positive Change* © 1976, Addison-Wesley Publishing Company, Inc., Reading, Massachusetts. Pg. 126 (list). Reprinted with permission. **Pages 103–104:** From Swell, Lila, *Educating for Success: Workbook.* © 1972 Dr. Lila Swell. Reprinted by permission. **Pages 116–117:** From Dean, Dwight G., "Alienation: Its Meaning and Measurement" in *American Sociological Review, 26,* 1961, pp. 753, 758. © 1961 American Sociological Association, Washington, D.C. Reprinted by permission. **Pages 105–107:** Reprinted with permission of Macmillan Publishing Company from *Sex Education: Theory and Practice,* 2nd edition, by Clint E. Bruess and Jerrold S. Greenberg. Copyright © 1987 by Macmillan Publishing Company.

Chapter 7

Pages 127–128, 131–132: From *Type A Behavior and Your Heart,* by Meyer Friedman and Ray Rosenman. Copyright © 1974 by Meyer Friedman. Reprinted by permission of Alfred A. Knopf, Inc. **Page 132:** Reproduced by special permission of the publisher, Consulting Psychologists Press, Inc., Palo Alto, CA from *The Self Esteem Inventory, School Form* by Stanley Coopersmith, Ph.D. Copyright 1975. Further reproduction is prohibited without the publisher's consent. **Pages 139–140:** From Taylor, Janet A., "A Personality Scale of Manifest Anxiety" in *Journal of Abnormal and Social Psychology,* 48, pp. 285–290. © 1953 American Psychological Association, Washington, D.C. Reprinted by permission. **Pages 133–134:** From *Sex Education, Theory and Practice* by Clint E. Bruess and Jerrold S. Greenberg. © 1981 by Wadsworth, Inc. Reprinted by permission of Wadsworth Publishing Company, Belmont, California.

Chapter 10

Pages 186–190: Reprinted with permission from *Managing Stress Before it Manages You,* by Jenny Steinmetz, et al. Palo Alto, CA. Bull Publishing Company, 1980, pp. 20–27.

Chapter 11

Page 196: From *Stress and the Art of Biofeedback* by Barbara B. Brown. Copyright © 1977 by Barbara B. Brown. Reprinted by permission of Bantam Books, Inc. All Rights Reserved.

Chapter 12

Page 210: From George B. Dintiman and Jerrold S. Greenberg, *Health Through Discovery.* © 1983 Random House, Inc., New York. Reprinted by permission. **Page 216:** Committee on Exercise and Physical Fitness, "Evaluation for Exercise Participation," *Journal of the American Medical Association* 219:900–901, 1972. Copyright 1972, American Medical Association. **Page 218:** American College of Sports Medicine, *Guidelines for Exercise Testing and Prescription.* Philadelphia: Lea & Febiger, 1986, pp. 2 and 7. **Page 219:** From Jerrold S. Greenberg and David Pargman, *Physical Fitness: A Wellness Approach.* © 1986, pp. 43, 272–273. Reprinted by permission of Prentice-Hall, Englewood Cliffs, N.J.

Chapter 13

Figure 13.2: Adapted with permission from Melody P. Noland, "The Efficacy of a New Model to Explain Leisure Exercise Behavior" (Ph.D. Dissertation, University of Maryland, 1981). **Pages 257–258:** From Wallston, Kenneth, A., Barbara S. Wallston and Robert DeVellis "Development of the Multidimensional Health Locus of Control (MHLC) Scales" in *Health Education Monographs, 6,* 1978:160–70. © 1978 Society for Public Health Education, San Francisco, CA. Reprinted by permission.

Chapter 14

Figure 14.1 and Pages 274–275: From Weiman, Clinton G., "A Study of the Occupational Stressor and the Incidence of Disease/Risk" in *Journal of Occupational Medicine, 19,* pp. 119–122, 1977. © 1977 American Occupational Medicine Association, Chicago, Illinois. Reprinted by permission. **Figure 14.2:** Source: From Cary L. Cooper and Judi Marshall, "Occupational Sources of Stress: A Review of the Literature Relating to Coronary Heart Disease and Mental Ill Health" *NIOSH Proceedings of Occupational Stress Conference.* (Cincinnati, Ohio: National Institute of Occupational Safety and Health, March, 1978), p. 9. **Figure 14.3:** Reprinted, by permission of the publisher, from "Organizational Stress and Individual Strain" by John R. P. French and Robert D. Caplan, *The Failure of Success,* Alfred J. Marrow, Ed., p. 52. © 1972 AMACOM, a division of American Management Association, New York. All rights reserved. **Figure 14.4:** From Plunkett, W. Richard, *Supervision: The Direction of People at Work.* © 1979 Wm. C. Brown Publishers, Dubuque, Iowa. All Rights Reserved. Reprinted by permission. **Figure 14.5:** Data (for diagram) based on Hierarchy of Needs in "A Theory of Human Motivation" in *Motivation and Personality, 2nd Edition* by Abraham H. Maslow. Copyright © 1970 by Abraham H. Maslow. Reprinted by permission of Harper & Row, Publishers, Inc. **Pages 281–282:** From Alan A. McLean, *Work Stress.* © 1979, Addison-Wesley Publishing Company, Inc., Reading, Massachusetts. pgs. 49–53 (adapted material). Reprinted with permission. **Pages 284–288:** From Machlowitz, Marilyn, *Workaholics: Living With Them, Working With Them.* © 1980 Addison, Wesley Publishing Co., Reading, MA. Reprinted with permission of Marilyn Machlowitz. **Pages 288–289:** From Pamela K. S. Patrick, *Health Care Worker Burnout: What it is, What to do About It.* © 1981 Blue Cross Association, Chicago, Illinois. Reprinted by permission. **Pages 288–289:** From Ferguson, Tom, "Contented Workaholics" reprinted from *Medical SelfCare Magazine,* Point Reyes, California. **Page 291:** "Burn-out Quiz" from *Burn-Out* by Herbert J. Freudenberger, Ph.D. and Geraldine Richelson. Copyright 1980 by Herbert J. Freudenberger, Ph.D. and Geraldine Richelson. Reprinted by permission of Doubleday & Company, Inc.

Chapter 15

Pages 304–305: From *The Colours of Love* by John Alan Lee, New Press, 1973. Reprinted by permission of the author and New Press, Toronto, Canada. **Pages 314–315:** From Philip G. Zimbardo, *Shyness.* © 1977 Addison-Wesley Publishing Company, Inc., Reading Massachusetts. Pgs. 12, 158–160 (list). Reprinted with permission.

Chapter 16

Figure 16.7: Courtesy Alliance Against Sexual Coercion, Cambridge, Massachusetts. **Page 330:** From *The Individual, Marriage, and the Family,* 4th edition, by Lloyd Saxton. © 1980 by Wadsworth, Inc. Used by permission of Wadsworth Publishing Company, Belmont, CA 94002. Pp. 47, 87, 88. **Pages 328–329:** From Jourard, Sidney, *The Transparent Self.* © 1971 Van Nostrand Reinhold Co., Inc., New York. **Page 338:** Source: *The 9to5 National Survey of Women and Stress* (Cleveland, Ohio: 9to5, National Association of Working Women, 1983).

Chapter 17

Page 350: From Jane Howard, *Families.* Copyright © 1978 by Jane Howard. Reprinted by permission of Simon & Schuster, Inc., New York. **Page 363:** From George B. Dintiman and Jerrold S. Greenberg, *Health Through Discovery.* © 1983 Random House, Inc., New York. Reprinted by permission.

Chapter 18

Figure 18.2: Reprinted with permission of Concern for Dying, 250 West 57th St., New York, NY 10107. Copies available upon request. **Figure 18.3:** Courtesy of the National Kidney Foundation of Iowa. **Pages 381–382:** Source: Dale V. Hardt, "Development of an Investigatory Instrument to Measure Attitudes Toward Death" in *The Journal of School Health,* 45, 1975, pp. 96–99. © 1975 American School Health Association, Kent, Ohio. Reprinted by permission.

Illustrators

Figures: 1.1, 2.7, 2.8, 2.10, 3.3, 9.1, 9.2, 9.3, 10.1, 12.2, 12.3, 12.4, 12.5, 12.6, 12.7, 12.11, 12.12, 12.13, 12.14, 12.15, 12.16, 12.17, 12.18, 12.19, 12.20, 12.21, 14.4, 16.1, 16.2, 16.3, 16.4, 16.5, 17.1, 17.2, 17.3, 18.1: Rolin Graphics.

Photographs

Chapter 1

Pages 9 and 10: *The Diamondback,* University of Maryland, College Park, MD.

Chapter 2

Page 18: From "The Illustrations from the Works of Andreas Vesalius of Brussels," Dover Publications, Inc.

Chapter 3

Page 48: *The Diamondback,* University of Maryland, College Park, MD; **Page 51:** Stanford Weinstein.

Chapter 4

Page 64: Library of Congress Collection; **Page 71:** *The Diamondback,* University of Maryland, College Park, MD.

Chapter 5

Page 91: *The Diamondback,* University of Maryland, College Park, MD.

Chapter 6

Page 118: *The Diamondback,* University of Maryland, College Park, MD.

Chapter 7

Pages 122 and 144: *The Diamondback,* University of Maryland, College Park, MD; **Page 125:** NASA; **Page 130:** James Shaffer.

Chapter 10

Page 183: *The Diamondback,* University of Maryland, College Park, MD.

Chapter 11

Page 197: Courtesy of The Cyborg Corporation; **Page 201:** *The Diamondback,* University of Maryland, College Park, MD.

Chapter 12

Pages 211, 214, and 215: *The Diamondback,* University of Maryland, College Park, MD.

Chapter 13

Page 262: Alan Carey/The Image Works, Inc.; **Page 264:** *The Diamondback,* University of Maryland, College Park, MD.

Chapter 14

Page 289: *The Diamondback,* University of Maryland, College Park, MD.

Chapter 15

Pages 300 and 313: *The Diamondback,* University of Maryland, College Park, MD.

Chapter 16

Page 329: *The Diamondback,* University of Maryland, College Park, MD.

Chapter 17

Page 371: *The Diamondback,* University of Maryland, College Park, MD.

Chapter 18

Page 386: James Shaffer; **Page 391:** *The Diamondback,* University of Maryland, College Park, MD.

Index